גלגול

GILGUL

ESSAYS ON TRANSFORMATION, REVOLUTION AND PERMANENCE IN THE HISTORY OF RELIGIONS

STUDIES
IN THE HISTORY OF RELIGIONS

(SUPPLEMENTS TO *NUMEN*)

EDITED BY

M. HEERMA VAN VOSS • E. J. SHARPE • R. J. Z. WERBLOWSKY

L

גלגול

GILGUL

ESSAYS ON TRANSFORMATION, REVOLUTION
AND PERMANENCE IN THE HISTORY OF RELIGIONS

גלגול
GILGUL

ESSAYS ON TRANSFORMATION, REVOLUTION AND PERMANENCE IN THE HISTORY OF RELIGIONS

DEDICATED TO R. J. ZWI WERBLOWSKY

EDITED BY

S. SHAKED • D. SHULMAN • G.G. STROUMSA

E.J. BRILL
LEIDEN • NEW YORK • KØBENHAVN • KÖLN
1987

ISSN 0029-5973
ISBN 90 04 08509 2

PRINTED IN THE NETHERLANDS BY E. J. BRILL

Table of Contents

Foreword VII

Bibliography of R.J. Zwi Werblowsky 1

Uri ALMAGOR, The structuration of meaning in a "primitive religion" 11

Eileen BARKER, A short history, but many changes: A new religious movement 35

Ugo BIANCHI, Dualism in religious ethnology 45

Carsten COLPE, Das deutsche Wort "Judenchristen" und ihm entsprechende historische Sachverhalte 50

Jacques DUCHESNE-GUILLEMIN, Agnus Dei 69

David FLUSSER, Paul's Jewish-Christian opponents in the Didache 71

Jan C. HEESTERMAN, Self-sacrifice in Vedic ritual 91

Steven KAPLAN, Te'ezāza Sanbat: A Beta Israel work reconsidered 107

Joseph M. KITAGAWA, Religious visions of the end of the world 125

Nahum MEGGED, A social and religious revolution among the Mayan tribes as suggested by mythology 138

Wendy D. O'FLAHERTY, The good and evil shepherd 169

Michael PYE, This-worldly benefits in Shin Buddhism 192

Kurt RUDOLPH, The history of religions (*Religionswissenschaft*) and the religious situation in Eastern Europe: Some comments 203

Annemarie SCHIMMEL, Some remarks about Muslim names in Indo-Pakistan 217

Anna SEIDEL, *Post-mortem* immortality — or: the Taoist resurrection of the body 223

Shaul SHAKED, First Man, First King. Notes on Semitic-Iranian syncretism and Iranian mythological transformations 238

Eric J. SHARPE, The secularization of the history of religions ... 257

David SHULMAN, The anthropology of the Avatar in Kampaṉ's Irāmāvatāram ... 270

Ninian SMART, The importance of diasporas ... 288

Michael E. STONE, The parabolic use of natural order in Judaism of the Second Temple age ... 298

Gedaliahu G. STROUMSA, Myth into metaphor: The case of Prometheus ... 309

M. HEERMA VAN VOSS, Der einzelne Stern ... 324

FOREWORD

This humble collection of essays dealing with various aspects of the general theme of גלגול, Transformation, *Umwandlung*, Metamorphosis in the History of Religions, is presented with deference and affection to the master in this field, R. J. Zwi Werblowsky. The doctrine of *gilgul*, or metempsychosis, central to the anthropology of the Kabbala, has been studied by Werblowsky, who has pointed out its probable Manichaean origins, referring to Augustine, who speaks of *revolutions* (see Werblowsky, *Joseph Karo, Lawyer and mystic*, 234-236). This standard kabbalistic term, we feel, may thus be an appropriate symbol for Werblowsky's own *Beruf*.

Werblowsky has brought a unique style and flair to the study of religious phenomena, and his contribution has also been a unique one — not by virtue of having created a new theory or method, but rather in his remarkable ability to make full and skilful use of all the available approaches and disciplines so as to create from them as rounded and complete a discussion of religious problems as is possible within our culture and discipline. Werblowsky is a true *viator*, whose virtuosity comes into expression in his free and easy travelling within and across the borders of the major humanistic sciences, which for this purpose also include the social sciences. This gift is manifest in the fact that he feels equally at home almost everywhere in time and space in human history. He has discussed and written about Judaism throughout its recorded existence, but especially the mystical tradition within that religion; Christian thought and theology; Buddhism and Chinese religion; Japanese religions, especially the modern religious movements; and the so-called "primitive" religions. Not a dry-as-dust scholar, Werblowsky is a man of insatiable curiosity and lust for knowledge and understanding. His articles and books do not constitute knowledge systematized and codified; they are a series of enquiries, sometimes playful, sometimes polemical and even pugnacious, aimed at making their author and his readers aware of problems, issues and controversies, and always expressing the confession of faith of a scholar and a humanist.

Werblowsky has also been a man of action, and his merit lies in things done not less than in words spoken and written. In 1956 he established, with David Flusser, the Department of Comparative Religion at the Hebrew University in Jerusalem, and may be said to have created the discipline and awareness of this independent field of research in Israel. His contribution to the organization of the study of the human sciences in Jerusalem was recognized when he was elected, in 1965, to serve as Dean of the Faculty of Humanities. He has been active internationally, and some of the highlights of his career in this field have been the period in which he served as Secretary General of the International Association for the History of Religions (1975-1985) as well as vice-president of the International Council for Philosophy and Humanistic Studies of UNESCO. There must be few places in the universe, and very few institutions of higher learning worthy of their name, which he has not visited and where he has not been asked to deliver lectures.

Werblowsky has also been actively concerned, and greatly involved, with the effort to enhance tolerance and mutual understanding among religious groups and communities. As part of this concern he created the Israeli Interfaith Association, at the head of which he still stands. Upon his voluntary part-time retirement from teaching at the Hebrew University some of his former pupils, colleagues and friends, have come together in order to present him with this *anthos* in token of gratitude and friendship. Because of severe limitations of space only relatively few could be invited to participate. Of Israeli scholars, only those who teach in the Department of Comparative Religion have been included, and no more than a handful of colleagues and friends from other countries.

Sadly, Mircea Eliade, who was about to send us an article, passed away before he could fulfil his promise.

All of Werblowsky's many admirers are sure to join us in wishing him many fruitful years of further contribution to *Religionswissenschaft* and to human wisdom and understanding.

The editors wish to thank M. Heerma van Voss and E. J. Brill, for willingly accepting, without Werblowsky's knowledge, this volume in the series *Supplements to Numen*. They also wish to thank Mrs. Judy Goldberg for her remarkably fast and accurate processing of the typescripts. Finally, they would like to acknowledge the generous help received from the President of the Hebrew University and the Research Fund of the Faculty of Humanities at the Hebrew University towards defraying the costs of printing.

Bibliography of
R. J. Zwi Werblowsky

Books

1. *Lucifer and Prometheus: A Study of Milton's Satan*, with a Foreword by C.G. Jung (London: Routledge & Kegan Paul, 1952).
2. *Joseph Karo: Lawyer and Mystic* (Oxford: Oxford University Press, 1962). Revised paperback edition: (Philadelphia: Jewish Publication Society of America, 1977).
3. R.J.Z. Werblowsky and M. van Praag, *Antisemitisme, antizionisme* (Bussum: W. de Haan, 1969).
4. *Beyond Tradition and Modernity: Changing Religions in a Changing World* (Jordan Lectures in Comparative Religion 11; London: Athlone, 1976). Italian version: *Oltre la tradizione e la modernità: religioni in trasformazione in un mondo che cambia* (Brescia: Morcelliana, 1978).

Books Edited and Translated

5. J. L. Palache, *Semantic Notes on the Hebrew Lexicon*, ed. and translated by R.J.Z. Werblowsky (Leiden: Brill, 1959).
6. *The Encyclopedia of the Jewish Religion*, ed. by R.J.Z. Werblowsky and G. Wigoder (Jerusalem: Massadah, and Holt Rinehart & Winston, New York, 1966).
7. *Studies in Mysticism and Religion, presented to G. G. Scholem*, ed. by E.E. Urbach, R.J.Z. Werblowsky and C. Wirszubski (Jerusalem: Magnes Press, 1967).
8. *Types of Redemption*, Contributions to the Theme of the Study-Conference held at Jerusalem, 14th to 19th July, 1968, ed. by C.J. Bleeker and R.J.Z. Werblowsky (Supplements to *Numen* 18; Leiden: E.J. Brill, 1970).
9. *The Jerusalem Colloquium on Religion, Peoplehood, Nation and*

Land, ed. by R.J.Z. Werblowsky and M.H. Tanenbaum (Jerusalem: H. S. Truman Research Institute, 1972).

10. G. Scholem, *Sabbatai Ṣevi, the Mystical Messiah, 1626-1676*, translated by R.J.Z. Werblowsky (Bollingen Series 93; Princeton: Princeton University Press, 1973.

Articles and Pamphlets

11. "Psychology and Religion" (Broadcast Talk, B.B.C. Third Programme), *The Listener* xlix no. 1260 (April 23rd, 1953), 677-87.
12. "God and the Unconscious" (Broadcast Talk, B.B.C. Third Programme), *The Listener* xlix no. 1262 (May 7th, 1953), 758-75.
13. "Hanouca et Noël: Note phénoménologique sur les rapports du mythe et de l'histoire," *Revue de l'Histoire des Religions* 145 (1954), 30-68.
14. "The Male God and the God of Males," *Hibbert Journal* 53 (1955), 334-342.
15. "De Amsterdamse Opperrabbijn Aylion," *Nieuw Israelitisch Weekblad* vol. 87, no. 1 (16.9.1955), 3-5.
16. "Milton and the Conjectura Cabbalistica," *Journal of the Warburg and Courtauld Institutes* 18 (1955), 90-113.
17. "A Note on the Text of *Seder Eliyahu*," *Journal of Jewish Studies* 6 (1955), 201-211.
18. "Stealing the Word," *Vetus Testamentum* 6 (1956), 105-106.
19. "Some Psychological Aspects of the Kabbalah," *Harvest* 3 (1956), 77-96.
20. "Kabbalistische Buchstabenmystik und der Traum: des Josef b. Abraham Gikatilas Exkurs über Herkunft und Bedeutung der Traume," *Zeitschrift für Religions- und Geistesgeschichte* 8 (1956), 164-169.
21. "On the Baptismal Rite according to St. Hippolytus," in: K. Aland and F. L. Cross, eds., *Studia Patristica* I, vol. II (Texte und Untersuchungen; Berlin: Akademie, 1957), 93-105.
22. "Revelation, Natural Theology and Comparative Religion," *Hibbert Journal* 55 (1957), 278-284.
23. "Observations on the Renewal of the Dialogue between the Church and Israel," *Hibbert Journal* 52 (1958), 273-282.
24. "Crises of Messianism," *Judaism* 7 (1958), 106-120.
25. "Original Monotheism and Primitive Monotheism" (in Hebrew), *Iyyun: A Hebrew Philosophical Quarterly* (1958), 152-162.
26. "On the Maggid of Joseph Karo" (in Hebrew), *G. Scholem Ju-*

bilee Volume, 1958, 184-195.

27. "Das Gewissen in jüdischer Sicht," in: *Das Gewissen* (Studien aus dem C. G. Jung-Institut), Zurich, vol. 7 (1958), 89-117.
28. [Review of: Y. Kaufmann, *Toledoth ha-Emunah ha-Yisra'elith]*, *Tarbiz* 28 (1959), 409-417.
29. "The Comparative Study of Religions," *Judaism* 8 (1959), 352-360.
30. "On the Role of Comparative Religion in Promoting Mutual Understanding," *Hibbert Journal* (October 1959), 30-35.
31. "Philo and the *Zohar*," *Journal of Jewish Studies* 10 (1959), 25-44, 112-135.
32. "Judaism, or the Religion of Israel," in: R.C. Zaehner, ed., *The Concise Encyclopaedia of Living Faiths*, (London: Hutchinson (1959), 23-50.
33. "Analytical Psychology and the History of Religions. Review of: S. Hurwitz, *Die Gestalt des sterbenden Messias*" (in Hebrew), *Kiryat Sefer* 35 (1960), 186-196.
34. "Messianism in Primitive Societies" (Broadcast Talk, B.B.C. Third Programme), *The Listener* lxiv no. 1647 (October 20th, 1960), 684-86.
35. "Biblical Criticism as a Religious Problem" (in Hebrew), *Molad* 18 (May 1960), 162-68.
36. "On Hugo Bergmann's *Hogim U-Ma'aminim*," (in Hebrew), *Iyyun* 11 (1960), 152-61.
37. [Review of: B. Blumenkranz, ed., *Gisleberti Crispini Disputatio Christiani cum Iudaei]* , *Journal of Jewish Studies* 29 (1960), 77-96. Hebrew version: *Tarbiz* 30 1961, 292-298.
38. [Review of: M. Benayahu, "Hayyim Joseph David Azulay"], *Molad* 155 (May 1961), 262-266.
39. "Mystical and Magical Contemplations," *History of Religions* 1 (1961), 9-36.
40. "Prayers and Devotional Compositions by Solomon Alkabets" (in Hebrew), *Sefunoth* (1962), pp. 137-82.
41. [Review of: F.S. Drower, *The Secret Adam. A Study of Nasoraean Gnosis*], *Journal of Semitic Studies* 8 (1963), 129-133.
42. [Review of: Jose Ma. Millas Vallicrosa, ed., *El "Liber Predicationis contra Judeos" de Ramon Lull*], *Tarbiz* 32 (1963), 207-211.
43. "Führe uns Mutter: Analyse eines indianischen Rituals," *Eranos Jahrbuch* 31 (1962), Zurich, 1963, 171-197.
44. [Review of: Z. Ankori, *Karaites in Byzantium]*, *Journal of Semitic Studies* 8 (1963), 264-268.

45. "On the notions of 'East' and 'West'," *Transactions of the Institute of Japanese Culture and Classics* 13 (1963), 149-156.
46. "Religion in the Twentieth Century" (in Hebrew), in: Y. Klausner and S. Bloch, eds., *Sefer Toledoth ha-meah ha-'esrim* (Tel Aviv: Yizreel, 1963), vol. 3, 218-238.
47. "Religions in Japan," *Contemporary Religions in Japan* 4 (1963), 189-202.
48. "Pilgrimage Liturgies at the Tomb of Nabi Samuel" (in Hebrew), *Sefunoth* 8 (1964), 237-253.
49. "Faith, Hope and Trust: A Study in the Concept of *Bittaḥon*," *Papers of the Institute of Jewish Studies*, (London, 1964), 95-139.
50. [Review of: I. Tishby, *Mishnath ha-Zohar*], *Tarbiz* 34 (1965), 192-209.
51. "On the Mystical Rejection of Mystical Illuminations. A Note on the Non-Cognitive Mysticism of St. John of the Cross," *Religious Studies* 1 (1965-66), 177-184. Hebrew version: *Iyyun* 14 [1964], 205-212.
52. [Review of: V. Lanternari, *The Religion of the Oppressed: A Study of Modern Messianic Cults*], *Review of Religion* 45 (1965), 67-68.
53. "A New Heaven and a New Earth: Considering Primitive Messianism," *History of Religions* 5 (1965), 164-172.
54. "The New Religions of Japan" (review article), *Journal for the Scientific Study of Religion* 5 (1966), 299-304.
55. "Shinto and Zen" (reviews), *Journal for the Scientific Study of Religion* 6 (1965), 120-123.
56. "Buber and his Thought" (in Hebrew), *Devarim 'al M. Buber* (Jerusalem: Magnes Press, 1966), 17-21.
57. [Review of: *Studien aus dem C.G. Jung Institut*], *Erasmus*, (1966), pp. 390-395.
58. "Israel et Eretz Israel," *Les Temps Modernes* 253 bis (1967), 371-393.
59. "The Rebuilding of the Temple and the Renewal of Sacrifice in the Light of Rabbinic Judaism," *Jerusalem Post Week-End Magazine*, August 25th, 1967, 8-11.
60. *Commitment and Indifference: Some Reflections on Expansionism, Exclusiveness and Co-existence*, The Robert Waley Cohen Memorial Lecture 1967 (London, 1967).
61. "Some Observations on Recent Studies of Zen," in: E.E. Urbach, R.J.Z. Werblowsky and C. Wirszubski, eds., *Studies in Mysticism and Religion presented to G.G. Scholem* (Jerusalem:

Magnes Press, 1967), 317-335.

62. "Prolegomenon," in: A. Marmorstein, *Studies in Rabbinic Theology* [reprint] (New York: Ktav Publ. House, 1968), pp. V-XVIII.
63. "The Heavenly and the Terrestrial Jerusalem," *Jerusalem through the Ages* (in Hebrew), (Jerusalem: Israel Historical Society, 1968), 172-178.
64. "Messianism in Jewish History," *Journal of World History*, 9 (1968), 30-45.
65. [Review of: D.J. Silver, *Maimonidean Criticism and the Maimonidean Controversy 1180-1240*], *Orientalistische Literaturzeitung* 63 (1968), 46-49.
66. "The Place of the University in Israeli Society," *The University and Social Welfare* (Jerusalem: Magnes Press, 1969), 161-171.
67. "Satan in the Old Testament," *Journal of Jewish Studies* 20 (1969), 91-96. (Also printed in *Journal for the Scientific Study of Religion* 8 (1969), 169-172.)
68. "Universal Religion and Universalist Religion," *International Journal for the Philosophy of Religion* 2 (1971), 1-3.
69. "Judaism," in: C.J. Bleeker and G. Widengren, eds., *Historia Religionum, Handbook for the History of Religions* II (Leiden: Brill, 1971), 1-48.
70. [Review of: A.J. Arberry, ed., *Religion in the Middle East, Three Religions in Conflict*, I], *Jewish Journal of Sociology* 13 (1971), 95-101.
71. "Bernard of Clairvaux, the Order of the Templars and the Relationship to the Holy Land" (in Hebrew), *Eretz-Israel*, 10 [*Festschrift Zalman Shazar*] (1971), 743-745.
72. "Ape and Essence," *Ex Orbe Religionum: Studia Geo Widengren*, II (Supplements to Numen, 22; Leiden: Brill, 1972), 318-329.
73. "Religion, Peace and Human Rights: Between the Crossfires," *Religion for Peace: Proceedings of the Kyoto Conference on Religion and Peace*, 1970 (Bombay, 1973), 95-110. (Reprinted in *Ariel* 33-34 [1973], 43-60).
74. "Religion and Peoplehood," in: R.J.Z. Werblowsky and M.H. Tanenbaum, eds. *The Jerusalem Colloquium on Religion, Peoplehood, Nation and Land* (Jerusalem: H.S. Truman Research Institute, 1972), 11-17.
75. "Mysticism and Messianism: The Case of Hassidism," *Man and His Salvation: Essays in Memory of S.G.F. Brandon* (Manchester: Manchester University Press, 1973), 305-314.

76. "On Carl Jung," (in Hebrew) *Molad* 5 (1973), 634-637.
77. "Structure and Archetype," *The Journal of the Ancient Near Eastern Society of Columbia University* 5 (1973) [*Theodore Gaster Festschrift*], 435-442.
78. "Tora als Gnade," *Kairos* 15 (1973) [*Festschrift Endre von Ivanka*], 156-163.
79. "Jewish-Christian Relations, with particular reference to the Contribution of the State of Israel." *Christian News from Israel* 24 (1973), 116-121.
80. "Le Prophétisme dans le Judaisme contemporain," *Lumière et Vie* 115 (1974), 40-48.
81. "The Authority of Religion," *Mélanges d'Histoire des Religions offerts à Henri-Charles Puech* (Paris: Presses Universitaires de France, 1974), 625-629.
82. "Jerusalem, Holy City of Three Religions" *Jaarbericht Ex Oriente Lux* 23 (1973-1974), 423-439.
83. *Zionism, Israel and the Palestinians* (Jerusalem: Israel Universities Study-Group for Middle Eastern Affairs, 1975).
84. "A Life Worth Living: Virtues and the Good Life in the Jewish Tradition," *The Center Magazine* 8 (1974), 25-35.
85. "Zen" (interview), *The Center Magazine* 8, n. 2 (1975), 61-70.
86. "Exposé," *Solitude d'Israël* (Paris: Presses Universitaires de France, 1975), 165-171.
87. "Le Shabbat d'Israël: Symbole Religieux et Réalité sociale," in *Le Shabbat dans la conscience Juive* (Paris: Presses Universitaires de France, 1975), 93-100.
88. "On Studying Comparative Religion: Some Naive Reflections of a Simple-minded Non Philosopher," *Religious Studies* 11 (1975), 145-156.
89. "A Note on Purification and Proselyte Baptism," *Christianity, Judaism and Other Greco-Roman Cults: Studies for Morton Smith at Sixty*, 3 (*Studies in Judaism in Late Antiquity*, 12; Leiden: Brill, 1975), 200-205.
90. "Paulus in jüdischen Sicht," *Paulus — Apostat oder Apostel? jüdische und christliche Antworten* (Regensburg: F. Pustet Verlag, 1977), 135-146.
91. Introduction to: *In Praise of the New Knighthood*, in: *The Works of Bernard of Clairvaux VII, Treatises III*, (Kalamazoo: Cistercian Publications, 1977), 115-123.
92. "Religious Values," *The Search for Absolute Values: Harmony among the Sciences* (New York: International Cultural Foundation, 1977), I, 77-83.

93. "Greek Wisdom and Proficiency in Greek," *Paganisme, Judaïsme, Christianisme, Mélanges Marcel Simon* (Paris; E. de Boccard, 1978), 55-60.
94. Preface to: Y. Malachi, *American Fundamentalism and Israel* (Jerusalem: Hebrew University, 1978), V-X.
95. "Salvation in Judaism," *Tantur Year-Book*, 1976-1977 (Jerusalem: Ecumenical Institute for Advanced Theological Studies, 1978), 51-58.
96. "Modernism and Modernisation in Buddhism," *The Search for Absolute Values in a Changing World* (ICUS, 1978), 121-131.
97. "The Japanese and the Jews" (Review Article), *Jewish Journal of Sociology* 20 (1978), 75-81.
98. Postscript to: "The Japanese and the Jews," *Jewish Journal of Sociology* 21 (1979), 95-96.
99. "Die verbotene Meditation," *Munen Muso, ungegenständliche Meditation* (Mainz: Mattias Grunewald, 1978), 237-242.
100. "Die Krise der liberalen Theologie," in: R. von Thadden, ed., *Die Krise des Liberalismus zwischen den Weltkriegen* (Göttingen: Vandenhoeck & Ruprecht, 1978), 147-154.
101. "Mystics and Zen Masters," *Cistercian Studies* 4 (1978), 318-321.
102. "O Felix Culpa: A Cabbalistic Version," in: S. Stein and R. Loewe, eds., *Studies in Jewish Religious and Intellectual History Presented to Alexander Altmann* (Univ. of Alabama Press, 1979), 355-362.
103. "Histories of Religion," *Numen* 26 (1979), 250-255.
104. "Krisenbewusstsein und Zukunft," in: O. Schatz, ed. *Hoffnung in der Überlebenkrise*? (Salzburg: Styria, 1980), 128-144. French version: "Conscience de crise et religion," *Diogène* 113 (1981), 63-80. Spanish version: "Conciencia de la crisis y el futuro," *Diogene* 113-114 (1981), 59-73.
105. "Society, Polity and Religion" [Review of: J.L. Kraemer, I. Alon, eds., *Religion and Government in the World of Islam*], *Israel Oriental Studies* 10 (1980), 233-245.
106. [Review of: T. Jacobsen, *The Treasures of Darkness: A History of Mesopotamian Religion*], *Israel Exploration Journal* 30 (1980), 240-241.
107. "Religions New and not so New" (Review article), *Numen* 27 (1980), 155-166.
108. "Confucius and Christ" (Review article), *Numen* 27 (1980), 173-178.
109. "Myth, Ritual and Syncretism: A Japanese Example," *Perenni-*

tas, Studi in onore di Angelo Brelich (Rome: Ateneo, 1980), 635-643.

110. "Is there a 'Phenomenology of Religion' in the Study of Religions?" *Studi e materiali di storia delle religioni* 7 (1981), 55-60. (Polish version: Czy istnieje fenomenologia religii? *Evhemer* 116 [1980], 17-22).

111. "Broad-Minded Narrow-Mindedness," *Christian Jewish Relations* 14 (1981), 36-39.

112. "Polemics" (Review article), *Numen* 28 (1981), 86-87.

113. "Religions New and Not so New: Fragments of an Agenda", in: E. Barker, ed., *New Religious Movements: A Perspective for Understanding Society* (Studies in Religion and Society, 3; Toronto; E. Mellen, 1982), 32-46.

114. "What's in a Name? The Sephardim: The Origin of their Name and their Liturgical Customs," *American Jewish History* 72 (1982), 165-171.

115. "Das nachbiblische jüdische Messiasverständnis," in: *Jesus, Messias? Heilserwartung bei Juden und Christen* (Regensburg: F. Pustet, 1982), 69-88.

116. "The Humanities and the Notion of 'Health,' " *Mobius* 2 (1982), 39-43.

117. [Review of: C. Caldarola, *Christianity: the Japanese Way*], (in Hebrew), *Hamizrah Hehadash* 30 (1983), 265-266.

118. "Denial and Religion," in: S. Breznitz, ed., *The Denial of Stress* (New York: International Universities Press, 1983), 213-221.

119. "Das Chinabild von Leibniz bis de Groot," *China Report* (Vienna) 71 (1983), 15-20.

120. "What is the specificity of the Relationships between Orthodox and Secularists in Israel?" (in Hebrew), *Haomnam kasheh lihyoth Israeli*? (Jerusalem: Van Leer, 1983), 201-212.

121. " 'Das Land' in den Religionen," in: G. Strecker, ed., *Das Land Israel in biblischen Zeit* (Gottingen: Vandenhoeck & Ruprecht, 1983), 1-6.

122. "On Religion and Human Rights with Reference to the Jewish Tradition," *Comprendre* 47-48 (1981-1983), 175-183.

123. Introduction to: *Messianism and Eschatology* (in Hebrew), (Jerusalem: Z. Shazar Center, 1984), 21-24.

124. "Gedenkrede auf Gerschom Scholem (1897-1982)," *Berliner Theologische Zeitschrift* 1 (1984), 97-106.

125. *In nostra tempore*, in: H.P. Duerr, ed., *Die Mitte der Welt: Aufsätze zu Mircea Eliade* (Frankfurt am Main: Suhrkamp, 1984), 128-137.

126. R.J.Z. Werblowsky and I. Klutstein-Rojtman, "Leibniz: *De cultu confucii civili*. Introduction, édition du texte et traduction," *Studia Leibnitiana* 16 (1984), 93-101.
127. "Judentum," *Neues Handbuch theologischen Grundbegriffe* (Munich: Kasel, 1984), 264-272.
128. "Gott als das Nichts im 'Sohar'," in: W. Strolz, ed., *Sein und Nichts in der abendländischen Mystik* (Freiburg, Basel, Wien: Herder, 1984), 73-81.
129. "Tolerance as a Value" (in Hebrew), *Studies in Adult Education* (Jerusalem: M. Buber Center, 1984), 176-187.
130. "L'étude des religions et son influence sur la religion: note sur la dialectique de la tradition, de la modernité et des relations interculturelles," in: *Douze cas d'interaction culturelle* (Conseil International de la Philosophie et des Sciences Humaines; UNESCO, 1984), 153-165.
131. "Iudaica Mystica et non Mystica," *Numen* 31 (1984), 148-151.
132. "Commerce with the Supernaturals" (Review article), *Numen* 31 (1984), 129-135.
133. "What's in a Name: Reflections on God, Gods, and the Divine," *Japanese Journal of Religious Studies* 12 (1985), 3-16.
134. "Fernöstliche Weisheit und christlicher Glaube," in: *Fernöstliche Weisheit und christlicher Glaube, Festgabe fur H. Dumoulin, S.J.* (Mainz: Matthias-Grunewald, 1985), 260-267.
135. "Religion and Culture" (in Hebrew), in J. Dan and J. Hacker, eds., *Studies in Jewish Mysticism, Philosophy and Ethical Literature Presented to Isaiah Tishby on his 75th Birthday* (Jerusalem, 1985), 721-728.

Articles in Encylcopedias (selection)

Encyclopedia Hebraica

Demonology and Demonism
Anthropomorphism
Revelations
Religion
Jesuits
Lutheranism
Logos

Encyclopaedia Britannica (14th edition)

Animal Worship
Flagellation (non Christian)
Funerary Rites and Customs
Judaism
Messiah
Miracle
Prophet
Priests and Priesthood
Soul
Syncretism

Encyclopaedia Britannica (15th edition)

Hero Worhsip
Miracle
Messiah and Messianic Movements

Encyclopaedia Judaica

Consulting Editor and Divisional Editor (Judaism); also contributed numerous articles.

THE STRUCTURATION OF MEANING IN A "PRIMITIVE RELIGION"

Uri Almagor, Jerusalem

Introduction

When one reads a monograph on a "primitive religion," especially in Africa, it is not always clear whether cultural symbols and various manifestations of ritual and non-ritual practices which are attributed to a particular society are specifically religious in nature, or represent some generalized parameters of the social order, or life itself. The tendency to include a wide range of non-religious issues in a religious framework derives, perhaps, from the attitude of many anthropologists who regard the religious sphere not only as being interwoven with other spheres, especially in a tribal society where the delineation of boundaries of institutional spheres is difficult, but also, and mainly, as a system which provides meaning to these spheres. This is expressed, for example, in Geertz's well-known article claiming that the religious beliefs of a people represent "their most comprehensive ideas of order" (1966:3). Yet, in spite of the fascination with the detailed classification and rich data of their belief and ritual systems, one cannot avoid the feeling that often such a coherent and a systematic picture of religious classifications is no more than a mapping out of the various spheres of spirits, divinities, symbols, rituals and their functions, all of which are presented to us as if they were God's "revealed law," or were always there. At most, these classifications are seen as a result of a process. The Durkheimian legacy of "collective representation" which asserted that religion is common to all members of society, transmitted from one generation to the next and imposed on individuals from an external source, both pre-existing them and surviving them (Lévy-Bruhl 1910:1; Horton 1973:251) gave rise, perhaps, to the notion that the interpretation of primitive religion is a matter of mere translation (Evans-Pritchard 1962; Lienhardt 1961). Little attention, however, is paid to the activities of individuals who give meaning to various phenomena and events and to the process itself through which these classifications are articulated or changed. This paper, then, focuses on two interrelated issues: the cultural categories from which meaning is derived and the process through which meaning is explicated, conveyed from one individual to another and eventually changed.

The notion of meaning has two features. One alludes to the construction of taxonomies, to the logic of basic notions, or to their origin. This feature of meaning is not my concern here. Rather, I shall concentrate on two facets of the second feature of meaning which refers, first, to a given cultural frame of reference which contains various categories through which any event, experience, or phenomenon can be explained and valued; and second, to the cognitive way through which a certain event or experience is connected and selectively applied to some of these categories. In other words, in spite of the relatively honmogeneous experiences which people in a tribal society undergo and the symbols of shared meaning, the people apply subjective interpretations to their experiences. There is no objective meaning which lies in an event or in an experience itself. Rather, the events and experiences which are meaningful to an individual are those which he grasps reflectively (or as Shutz noted: "The meaning is the way in which Ego regards its experience..." [1967:69]), and these inevitably derive from the subjective way in which he selectively uses his cultural repertoire. Here the questions that come to the fore are: How widespread is religious knowledge in society? How far can an anthropologist go in generalizing and attributing meaning to an event or phenomenon as if all members of society share its meaning? Indeed, we investigate religious phenomena and accord them meaning, but sometimes we are in doubt whether some phenomena are really as meaningful to all the members in society as they are made out to be. Furthermore, the meaning which anthropologists attribute to events and practices, as well as the coherent and systematic picture of beliefs which they construct, are often based on bits and pieces of information which are expressed by the people themselves in inconsistent and vague forms of thought.[1] In other words, when we speak of meaning, besides the obvious question of "meaning for whom?," we should also ask ourselves, how are the participants engaged in defining and interpreting various phenomena and events, or how is meaning negotiated?

In discussing the process through which meaning is explicated and changed, I find Giddens' notion of structuration a suitable concept for the analysis of meaning. Structuration, as defined by Giddens, is: "... the ways in which (the social system), via the application of generative rules and resources, and in the context of unintended outcomes, is produced and reproduced in interaction" (1979:66). Though Giddens' structuration is a theory which is concerned with all types of social processes and modes of reproduction, and refers to the general conditions governing the continuity or transformation of structures, its advantage for the present analysis lies in the concept of duality of structure, as both the medium and the outcome of the practices that constitute social systems. Thus Giddens states: "The theory of structuration ... rejects any differentiation of synchrony and diachrony, or statics and dynamics. The identification of structure with constraints is also rejected: Structure is both enabling and constraining, and it is one of the specific tasks of social theory to study the conditions in the organization of social systems that govern the interconnections between the two" (1979:69-70). Indeed, the purpose of this paper is to illustrate that giving meaning is an ongoing process which is carried out by human agents who memorize, imagine, apply and mobilize their experiences and knowledge through interaction. Through this process they point out that not only is there no clear and simple relation between various categories, or rules of causation, and events and phenomena in the world as culture dictates, but also that the meaning which is ascribed to an event or a

---

1 This subject was recently raised by Kessing (1985) who asks bluntly: "Have we ethnographers acted as theologians to create nonexistent theologies?" (1985:201). He notes that "ordinarily few, if any, informants articulate to us coherent and global accounts of their belief systems and ritual meaning" (1985:202). The problem is not only one of overinterpretation, but also, and even worse, a danger that the anthropologist may construct a coherent picture of religion which is based on bits and pieces of information that have been collected from only a limited number of selected informants.

ascribed to an event or a phenomenon is explicated through human praxis. In other words, the interaction between human agents and the imagined interpretations they give to explain the world often transcends the cultural categories and the principles or rules of cause and effect, and in that these human agents are engaged, perhaps unintentionally, in a process which goes beyond the accepted and "frozen" relationships between the various cultural categories and religious classifications.[2]

In discussing the process of structuration of meaning, I intend to limit myself in this paper to one type of religious orientation, that which is known as primitive, primordial monotheism and is often referred to as the notion of High God. The material from which the ideas in this paper were developed are based on data I collected in field work among the semi-pastoral Dassanetch of Southwest Ethiopia. In this necessarily schematic paper, I shall present some data in support of my arguments, but postpone the full exposition of my own material for another occasion. I shall, however, refer in passing, to other works on African tribal religions, but mainly to Wagner's important and lucid work (1972) on the "innovation of meaning in Daribi religion" — pointing out some similarities in the material and assuming that some of the suggestions that this paper offers could be applied to analyze the structuration of meaning in other societies with similar acephalous social structure and religious orientation.

Deus Otiosus of the Dassanetch

The need to reassess our approach and method of analyzing the subject of meaning in the so called "primitive religion" leads me to the distinction made by Bultmann between *Weltanschauung* and belief. Bultmann states that: "A *Weltanschauung* stands in sharpest contrast to belief in God ...(belief) will find God in time-lessness, ... interpreting everything in the world on the basis of one principle ... His transcendence is that of someone always having power over the

---

[2] For a recent evaluation of Giddens' work and its relevance for anthropological analysis, see Karp (1986).

temporal and the eternal ... power which creates and sets limits to our life ... about the meaning of it all ... it is a question of my understanding my life and my destinies on the basis of a general conception of the world — always as an instance of the general rule ... It is the effort to find security in generalizations.'' (1955:8-9). Though Bultmann is referring to a secular world view, the question can equally be applied to ''primitive'' religious systems: what kind of a coherent picture of religion is presented to us? Is it really a religious world-view, or something different, perhaps a world order or universe? This is not merely a matter of a semantics, but is a more fundamental issue in the sociology of knowledge, concerning different approaches to the meanings imputed to various phenomena in the world and to the ways people conceptualize their religious notions, not necessarily only those in rituals, but also those in their day-to-day activities.

The Dassanetch do not attribute meaning to the different manifestations in nature and society as evolving from one will or source, nor are the bits and pieces of different realities considered to be connected to form one picture that can be seen from one point of view. Thus, it is justified to refer to their religious orientation as a *Weltanschauung* rather than as a belief system. For the Dassanetch, deity is what is known as a nonmythological High-God, of the ''originator'' (*Urheber*) type which is associated with the sky, but is inactive (*deus otiosus*) and enjoys no worship (Werblowsky 1958). In other words, God (*waq*) ordained the world by giving mortal man gifts (cattle and children), so that society could be continued, and he also introduced the events in nature in the form of a self-regulating system of alternations. Apart from the first creation, there is almost no intervention by God to direct the life of man and the world continues without Him being there. Though God is the source of all being and meaning, He is removed from the world. God is not concerned with human daily matters, and people live their lives without being aware of God's actions or messages. Notions such as ''fear of God,'' ''love of God,'' or praying to or appeasing Him, are not part of their affairs. The situation is similar to what Silberbauer has noted for the G/wi Bushmen: ''(God) ... created the context in which man lives, but did not ordain precisely the manner of his living.'' (1981:121).

The Dassanetch conceive of God as something beyond man's comprehension and references to God are usually made on three different occasions. First, when there is something which disturbs the social order, such as combining two contradictory elements, or doing something which may cause inconvenience to others. In such instances the Dassanetch may say, "God does not like it" (Almagor 1983:60), accentuating either the proper order of things or an obvious human error, rather than implying God's wish or will, since He remains, as noted, indifferent and remote. Second, references to God are made when something unusual occurs. For example, if someone is generous he may be referred to as: "He is God' " or one may remark upon a certain bird which makes a special noise or whose feathers are colorful by saying that "This bird is God." This expression is similar to the comment in our society, "It's divine!," a statement that has no religious connotations. Third, and more relevant to our subject, is the statement, "God knows." Here the reference is to something which people cannot explain adequately. Such a reference usually concludes a discussion by ascribing the nature or appearance of a certain phenomenon to the sphere of ultimate causation, and acknowledges an inability to offer an explanation with the existing conceptual tools.

I mention all these to note, first, that references to God should not be taken literally when one tries to explicate their meaning, for in such statements words and objects have no objective meaning in themselves. Their meaning is determined by their social and cultural context. Second, such references to God are usually spelled out when people are unable to grasp the complexity of certain phenomena.

The Manipulation of Cultural Categories

The Dassanetch cultural repertoire contains a variety and variability of institutionalized relationships between categories which usually appear in dual forms, and can be divided into three basic groups. The first such group of dual forms exemplifies the complementarity of categories. It includes categories such as men and cattle, male and female, young and elders, sky and earth, right and left, east and west, and so forth. Complementarity here refers to Dassanetch notions that one part of a pair cannot exist without the other, or that one part inevitably alludes the other. The second group relates to alternation, and includes such categories as sun and moon, fertility and decline, rain and dryness and alternations in the generation-set system. The notion here is that there is a regular movement in a kind of pendulum, from one element to the other. The third group refers to the opposition of elements such as red and black, head and tail, fish and cattle, life and death, humans and spirits, and the like. The fact that in each category two elements are placed together may be misleading, for here the idea is that they cannot be matched.''[3]

The distinct division into three basic groups of categories that match, rotate and clash respectively, does not exclude various combinations of relationships between different dual categories or parts of various pairs. Such affiliations inevitably lead to four consequential clusters. First, there is the correlation between some categories which belong either to the same group (such as sun and moon and man and woman) or to different groups (such as sun and moon, and East and West). Here one set of categories can represent the other. Second, there is a partial correlation, when one part of a dual category is seen as almost identical or can stand for one part in another category. For example, dryness partially correlates with sun, female with fertility. Here one can also include one part which stands in a positive relationship, to speak, to its complementary part, such as man and cattle, and yet that same part (e.g. cattle) may be paired in what seems a ''negative'' relationship (e.g. with fish) (Almagor, forthcoming). The third cluster of dual forms depends upon connotation., Here one category connotes another, and in a sense both are seen as equivalents. For exmaple, the connotation of right and left is male and female, or the latter pair may connote sun and moon. The fourth cluster contains single and unrelated parts from different categories, such as fertility, cattle, moon, sky, rain, and so forth. These parts are placed in one cluster without their counterparts, because sometimes they are singled out as the main religious themes in certain rituals and ceremonies, and in one way or another are associated with God.

All told, it should be noted, that the division into binary categories only provides an institutionalized cultural reservoir from which specific meaning is extracted. For the dual categories are not static, and each dual pair is not seen as resting within itself. Each pair is potentially open to be substituted and reshuffled in new

---

[3] For more details on this third group see Almagor (1983).

combinations. Most of the binary categories and some of their parts are regarded as distinct units which may crosscut each other and combine in different ways. These combinations or clashes can be discovered in various phenomena through human experience. Several points should be made here.

Though it seems that the general principle that stands behind each pair, which may characterize either the distinct qualities of one part in the pair of its relationship to its counterpart, permeates meaning, in actuality such a division into binary categories tells us little. At most, it offers a glance into the cosmological view and cultural repertoire. The crux of the matter is how the principles which stand behind dual categories, or parts of categories, are connected to each other and thus give meaning to the events and experiences of day-to-day life. Ordinarily, most of the events and the experiences that people undergo in their routine activities are, and can be, explicated in terms of causes from the known combinations of the above categories and elements. In other words, meaning is ascribed to an event when the principle which stands behind or characterizes it is connected to other events and principles. Thus the event is placed in a certain known and institutionalized relationship.

The principles on which dual categories are based may have been God-given in the primordial past, but at present God does not direct or control them. Their manifestations in daily life have no religious connotation. Both the categories and the principles are seen as existing in the world and appearing and reappearing in regular or irregular forms, but it is up to man to find out by himself, through a process of trial and error, their possible combinations and workings. Obviously, the number of permutations which are based on different parts, principles and categories, that can be combined, is legion. No individual can be aware of all of them or store up such an amount of knowledge. There are, however, some basic or central wisdoms that almost everyone possesses and is aware of, relating to matters such as the cosmological cycles, fertility and decline, man and cattle, life and death, right and left and so forth, including the taboos that are connected with these phenomena. The Dassanetch state that no one knows all the possible combinations of these principles and categories, and hence no person or social unit has a monopoly on such knowledge: knowledge is unequally dispersed among all members of society, though the Dassanetch are aware that some people are more experienced and knowledgeable than others. Let us turn to see a case of divination, which will exemplify the crosscutting and the possible combination and re-combination of categories.

Dassanetch seek the services of diviners, usually when a misfortune occurs, in order to investigate its causes. Perhaps the word diviner is a misnomer, for there is nothing which concerns divine knowledge or authority in this role or actions. Basically, the diviner is a wise man, with a lifetime of experience, who manipulates the same categories which are known to many people. There is no secret knowledge of mysterious forces which the diviner knows about and the client does not. The diviner helps the client to comprehend his problem in an open dialogue. He tries through technical means (throwing sandals or looking at the entrails of a goat) to trace sets of relationships between elements in order to arrive at the causes of a mysterious event. Divination differs from other forms of interpretation in that the anwers the diviner pursues are oriented towards a particular question that someone in urgent need has formulated. It should be noted, however, that throwing sandals or looking at the entrails of small stock are practiced by laymen in leisurely social meetings (see Fig. 1), not to solve individual grievances, but as a means of understanding a problem, or predicting an event, which does not necessarily concern them personally.

The case of divination which I shall elaborate below took place in the settlement of Nyamumery, when a group of three half-brothers approached Yasya, an elderly diviner, to consult him about the causes of the death of several head of cattle in recent months. The young men stated the problem and their suspicion that it must be one of their affines, whose "heart was angry," who had caused it, since it involved the death of cattle, though at different places and times, belonging to one household herd. I am not concerned here with the information the diviner had about the squabbles and enmities among people, the norms of affinal relationships, the affiliation of affines to age-categories[4] or the interaction between the diviner and his clients. These are not immediately relevant here. I shall concentrate on the technique and symbols of divination and the interpretation the diviner gave.

---

[4] For more details see Almagor (1978).

Figure 1. Looking at the entrails of a goat.

The design of Dassanetch sandals provides four basic categories. First is the category of man and cattle. The leather circle at the center on the upper part of the sandals is equated with the rounded kraal and thus with livestock, while the rest of the upper part of the sandal, especially that covering the toes, signifies man. Second, the right and the left sandals respectively represent the category of man and woman. Third, the contrast between life and death is reflected in the difference between the upper and lower parts of the sandal. Fourth, the front and rear parts of the sandals provide an additional indicator of a person's social standing, i.e. seniority or juniority, in identifying people.''[5]

During the repetitious throwing of sandals, the diviner interprets signs through the position of his sandals, and also conducts a dialogue with his clients. Each time the sandals fall in a certain position (see Fig. 2) he gives his interpetation to the specific position of sandals and answers questions, or defends his statements by showing how and why he reached his conclusion. It should be noted that there is no one verdict at which the diviner arrives, for each position of the sandals provides a different interpretation. Yet, the diviner sometimes pursues a specific line, and tries to convince the clients that most of the positions of the sandals point to the direction where the causes of the misfortune are to be found, and thus offers a solution; he deliberately ignores the positions which do not confirm his judgment. Furthermore, the position of the sandals, through their repositioning as the diviner throws them, may bring to the fore some other categories such as the directions of East and West, moon and sun, or even other parts of categories which are not expressed in the design of the sandals such as rain or fish.''[6]

---

[5] Similar divination by throwing sandals is practiced among the Turkana, to determine the initiate's son's position, or the relative seniority between two age mates. See Gulliver (1958:910).

[6] These last categories are often determined by the direction to which the sandals point. If the front part of the sandals point to the direction of Lake Turkana, the diviner may include fishermen in his analysis of the situation. If one sandal stands on its side, he may refer to the skies and thus to rain.

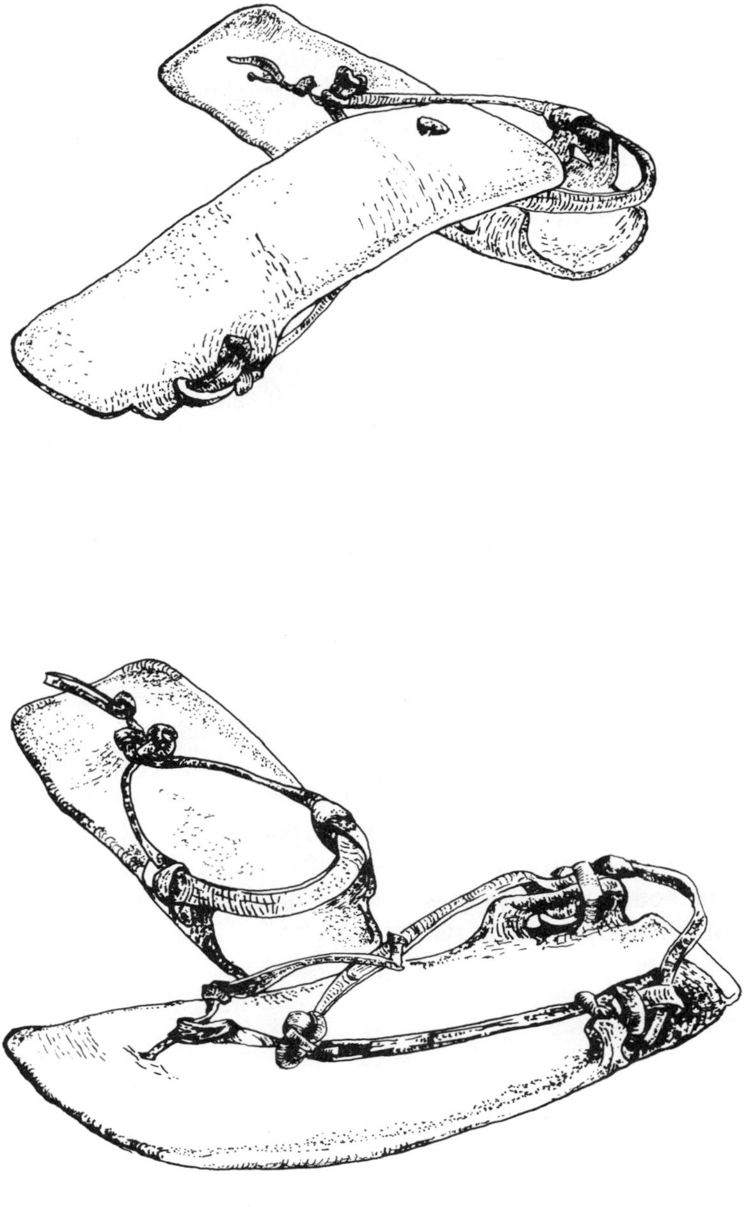

Figure 2. Two positions of sandals in divination.

The diviner informed his clients that a certain person, indeed an affine in the above case, whose "heart was angry," was the source of the death of their cattle. What the diviner did was merely to indicate the logic of association of categories and their parts. It had nothing to do with God, who punishes the wrongdoer but with a legitimate claim to injustice that, in Dassanetch views, almost automatically activates "forces" that lead to an event, especially a misfortune. In practical terms, here one category was leading to the other in a sequence of events — woman as the source for a dispute (bridewealth); unfulfilled claim; wrath of a man of high social standing; death to cattle. The solution the diviner suggested was to use, in fact, the same sequence in reverse: the slaughter of a beast to appease a particular man of a high social standing, then the satisfaction of his claim by transferring bridewealth, thus removing his wrath and eliminating the source for the cattle's death.

All in all, the explication of the causes of certain events in such a form of divination is made through the crosscutting of some categories that are expressed in the technical position of the sandals. Thus, the combination of elements from different categories is compatible with the institutionalized relations between categories, as presented above, and represent everyday standards of reasoning. This whole complex of categories, their parts, and relationships embodies a range of linked concepts that makes a particular cultural domain meaningful and is what Wagner calls an ideology (1972:7:170). Wagner's distinction here between two dimensions of meaning is useful. One dimension, the one which I have mentioned above, is the collective dimension of culture, the conceptual core of society. It includes narratives as well as the meaning which the people ascribe to their collective rituals. Here meaning is derived from a *Weltanschauung*, a common-sense knowledge which is a consensus about the relationshisp between the complementarity or opposition of categories, and their being consistent with, crosscutting, or overlapping one another. The other dimension of meaning relates to the level of individuals, who "deviate" from the rules of the common collective ideology, which they transcend by a different kind of associations, metaphorization and impersonations: here meaning is attributed to events and phenomena in a process which Wagner refers to as innovation, and I call structuration. Let us turn to this latter kind of meaning.

The Structuration of Meaning

Gellner rightly noted that anthropologists are only too willing to describe how individuals manipulate each other according to some rules of a game, but are reluctant to consider the possible manipulation of concepts. He asks, "Why should concepts not be similarly open to manipulation? Why should it not be a part of their use that the ambiguity of words, the logically illicit transformation of one concept into another is exploited to the full by the users of what seems to be 'one' concept?" (1970:42). In fact, conceptual shifts or manipulation of concepts are common in many societies. Most monographs on primitive religions contain the seeds of such elaboration.[7] But since ethnographies belong to agenre of their own and "... the categories of ethnographic recording are also socially constructed" (Karp 1986:132), there is little in the monographs on primitive religions which sees the participants' subjective and interpretive definitions not in a static "native model" of accomplished facts, but as a continuous process which modifies the meanings through interpretations. In this section I wish to concentrate on conceptual shifts and manipulation of categories which differ from what was referred to above as the crosscutting of categories in the collective ideology and the accepted common sense knowledge. The questions that come to the fore are: First, in what way do such conceptual shifts differ from what was noted above? Do we have here a different dimension in the constructon of meaning? Secondly, if, as Wagner notes, there exists a dialectical relation between the ideological aspects of culture and the activities of individuals who apply subjective interpretation and create new meaning, then how can this dialectical relation be explicated? In this section I shall focus on the first question and attempt to answer the second at the conclusion.

The reality of everyday life is often taken for granted, and people do not try to make sense or make order of every event or situation they encounter. But when someone has experienced something which is unusual and cannot be explained, when an unexpected event

[7] Pocock, for example, analyses the way the Dinka solve their problems: "through the use of synthetic categories which contain and transcend the opposition." (1974:77).

occurs, or a disturbance to social life of to cosmic rhythm takes place, it is assumed that the combination of principles behind that event is unknown and should be discovered. Then, conceptual shifts are made, and those configurations of elements and categories which are suggested in order to fathom the nature of the phenomenon or its causes go beyond the accepted concepts of identity, and duality noted above. Such a process of "deviation" has two interwoven spheres. One concerns the conceptual sphere and the other the social one, and although theoretically they could be dealt with as separate themes, I suggest that, for analytical purposes, they should be handled together.

The most common and effective way of communication is the informal meeting in the evening, when a small group of people sit and discuss various subjects in a congenial setting. In a pastoral society like the Dassanetch, where the movement of households and camps takes place frequently, and huts are small and temporary, the life of individuals, apart from intimate relationships, is conducted in the open arena of the settlements. The public and semi-public occasions of eating, chatting, telling stories, dancing, exchanging information and gossip fill a central role in the lives of people. Here in this form of meeting, a vast range of subjects are discussed. People describe their experiences, things they saw or heard, tell old and known stories, and also ask questions which bother them, either about daily matters which concern survival and weather, or on cosmological and philosophical matters.

I am unable to enter into details here about the social context, the number and identity of participants, or the subjects which are discussed at these evening meetings. I shall only note briefly that social networks, bond partnerships, and the unit in the age system to which an individual belongs determine to a large extent the kind of meetings he will be engaged in. The content of the discussions at these meetings differs from one social context to another. The meetings are not held on a basis of households or camp discussions, nor are there common and invariable subjects which most people discuss. Other than a few central themes about which there is a consensus, there are no accepted notions or answers that will always be given when a certain problematic issue is raised.

The Dassanetch seek to give interpetations of causal relationship to various phenomena which they encounter. Most of the subjects they discuss are mundane and potentially repetitive, but whether they succeed in clarifying issues according to shared presuppositions, or fail to do so and have to move from one level of relationships between components and principles to another, they are engaged in a process of constructing meaning. Every interpretation incorporates some prior understanding, and every idea or experience that someone reports or puts forward reinforces previous, similar, or slightly similar experiences in other situations that others have shared. Often, ideas or explanations may not be consistent with previous knowledge that a participant holds. Then he may ask provocatively, *ateii*?, i.e. "how come?," pointing out the absurdity of the explanation and therby giving rise to further discussions, during which the interpretation may be clarified or modified. Seemingly contradictory notions or inconsistent knowledge need not imply that both are meaningless. One of the most frequent expressions in such a clarification is *hela srat le*, which literally translates into "It is its law (or nature)." There are, of course, degrees of clarity: not eveyrthing that is said in such an informal meeting is clear. Some ideas are expressed obliquely, while others are presented as loose concepts that do not seem to be integrated into other categories. Often a discussion ends in a deadlock and not unexpectedly participants may declare, "God knows." However, the main point to note is that, in these conversations, people use their images, alternative metaphorical links, comparisons, paradoxes, proverbs, and examples — all the possible conceptual tools they possess — to arrive at meaning.

Though the Dassanetch do not possess an all-embracing logical picture which is to be referred to as the sphere of religion, nor a coherent core of belief and perception, this does not mean that they live in a cognitive anarchy. Rather, they regard the divergent parts of the world as somehow related to one another, and in this search for causal relationships they often encounter areas of obscurity, or forces of mystery which they cannot explain. Also, one should take into consideration that the social context and the number and identity of the participants in a discussion may give rise to a "show" which can be generalized and exaggerated, but most of all superficial in its performance, and that people may draw cosmological conclusions from one simple case of daily matters. Furthermore, in this process one cannot say whether old knowledge is abandoned, or whether new meaning is added to old and accepted assumptions, in a way which deepens and enriches them. One can only assume that, in this process, subjective impressions and thoughts are conveyed from one individual to another. Finding causal relationships between various phenomena and interpreting experiences bring to the conscious mind some meaningful notions that enlighten a shared existence at the deepest level. It is usually a long process, the results of which can only be tested after many years. Finally, the innovative aspect of this process is not the ability to test empirically the meanings that are ascribed to various phenomena, but the ability to extend these meanings to additional contexts and situations through questioning or explaining other or similar relationships between different categories. In other words it is a distribution not only of personal experiences, but also of notions and meanings which one has learned or heard. This is done through the interaction of individuals who belong to different networks expressed in different social contexts. I have observed a discussion in one settlement on the subject of weak lightning and the lack of rain. A discussion was followed in which it was argued that the cause for the lack of rain was the rain that had fallen during the last *dimi* ceremony (of 1969), at which time it had been considered a bad omen and a disturbance of the cosmological cycle caused by a fisherman's daughter.[8] One passive participant in that meeting was actively engaged in another discussion, in another settlement, which took place five months later. In the latter meeting he imposed a notion that he had heard in the first discussion regarding the reversibility of events. For the argument in the first discussion was that *dimi* blesses the girls for their future fertility. Fertility, which is associated with rain (and menstruation), should follow the blessing and not precede it. He applied this notion to a totally different subject, a dispute regarding the affinal relations of one of the elders. He suggested that the cause of the dispute derived from the fact that the parents of the third wife (of an elder who was accused of not giving bridewealth to the young brothers of his wife) had been visited, many years ago, by the brothers of the elder at the betrothal negotiation, when the bride had not yet had her first menstruation. His argument was that the visit which is known as *kurum size* ("visit with a container of milk") was intended to bless the girl (Almagor

[8] For more details on this particular example see Almagor (forthcoming).

1978:163), but since she had not yet menstruated it was not good, for milk had nothing to be matched with (Almagor 1983:63) — hence all the continuous affinal disputes. His interpretation was challenged as not true or relevant. Nevertheless, he was trying to transfer seemingly unrelated notions from one social context to another, an activity which Wagner calls "metaphorization." However, one cannot say that he constructed the relationship with no cultural basis for there are concepts of identity here, though they operate in different realities and carry different principles: nevertheless, in this case, the relationships between the issues existed solely in his own imagination.

Dassanetch, like Daribi individuals, extend the concepts and categories beyond their defined areas of signification, but pace Wagner's argument that it is mainly charismatic persons who "...have learned how to invoke and compel that 'new' meaning" (1972:171), I am arguing that the individual as an actor establishes that displacement and innovation of meaning mainly in the social context of an informal public meeting and through interaction with others.[9] This is also the context in which new meaning, formed out of loose concepts, is placed in a dialectical relation with the common ideological aspects of the culture and has a chance to be incorporated into them. Also, this is the context where the process of structuration takes place, for it is a meeting ground for the expression of interpretative dilemmas of different persons who ascribe order to the realities in which they live. The setting of the informal social meeting is not a barrier to new formulations; at the same time, loose concepts and intuitive reasoning that are expressed in these meetings do not contradict or negate the existing components of the common ideology and shared cultural categories. The very components and categories of the "given" ideology serve as means of arriving at slightly different answers to explain the world.

Let us draw these threads together. The concept of a High and an indifferent God, to whom no prayers, worship, sacrifice, or acts of celebration are addressed in routine social meetings, encourages a

[9] A similar practice exists among the Ndembu, as Turner noted: "Associated with this process of revealing the unknown, invisible, or the hidden is the process of making public what is private or making social what is personal" (1967:50).

social and conceptual milieu in which the phenomena of the world can be explained through critical reflection. In these meetings, people express perceived relationships between categories, but also ascribe a theoretical objectivization to their experiences, manipulating various elements and principles in order to interpret their relevant concepts. People retrieve their own similar experiences from the past and reformulate the relationship between elements in order to understand their own experiences in the light of new data presented by others. Such expositions of experiences and suggestions regarding the causes of events stimulate a discussion and make a certain impact on the listeners and participants. Such an impact is, in the long run, independent of the reactions of affirmation or dismissal by other participants who may think that a certain explanation deviates from the cultural common sense. Lienhardt uses the notion of "experience" as a key to Dinka religion. But one wonders how the Dinka conceptualize their various realities if, as he puts it, past experiences are not mediated by what we call "mind" (1961:149). The Dassanetch, on the other hand, remember, store and expose their experiences in a slow process of trial and error, through which they cast doubts upon the relationship between categories when the causes which explain a certain event or phenomenon are called into question.

Conclusion

In discussing the understanding of a primitive religion, Eliade noted that "Only a competent hermeneutical work, carried out on the ensemble of the archaic religious expressions, will be able to grasp and interpret the specific dimensions of this type of (religious) creativity." (1967:502). But the concept of hermeneutics can be expanded to include Heidegger's notion of *Auslegung*, which means an informal kind of interpretation that accompanies every act of understanding. In other words, the dialectical relations mentioned above between the "given" and common ideology of shared cultural categories and the explication of new meanings is, in fact, a dialectical process that moves between explaining and understanding, or, to use Weber's terms, between *Erklärung* and *Verstehen*. Without repeating the details, let me briefly summarize how it works.

As noted, the process of interpretation is based on principles or rules which derive from a cultural frame of reference forming the various categories that define the Dassanetch world. Any interpretation, as Mehan and Wood noted, "has its independent meaning. It is an activity and stands apart from the stillness that preceded it. Simultaneously, however, it is dependent upon the stillness that provided it with the understanding upon which the activity arose." (1975:366). Therefore, any act of explanation demands initial knowledge, but the principles used to express the relationship between several different events and phenomena are, simultaneously, tools both for explaining phenomena and explanatory objects which formulate the phenomena. In other words, the principles, or rather their relationships, are interpretations which arise from some previous understanding. The relationship between interpretation and understanding is a dialectical one. One emanates from the other or one serves as a source for the other. In this dialectical process there are several points that should be stressed.

First, even if an interpretation has failed and has not been accepted, the very fact that people have listened to it and thought of it as a possible explanation of phenomena, in terms of "as," or "similar to," or "if," accommodates a potentiality for new meaning. This new meaning may be added to, or replace, an accepted meaning for a certain object or event of another time and place, when the invocation of other principles applies. Second, in this dialectical process, where past interpretation is incorporated into an understanding which itself induces new questions and explanations, not every interpretation is clear and leads to understanding. Nevertheless, obscurities in some manipulation of principles and relationships in explaining a certain phenomenon do not necessarily imply that the very attempt to establish such a relationship is meaningless. Furthermore, the process of explanation and understanding does not necessarily mean that the experiences of some are verified through the experiences of others. Some notions are abstract and concern loose concepts or symbols of the cosmic order and, perhaps, are never repeated in the same manner. However, they may provide elements for thought for the reinterpretation of other observable phenomena and events. In other words, certain queries may not receive proper interpretation, but the insight acquired in one situation may be transferred to another and lead to new attitudes and views.

When we say that informal social meetings provide the setting in which experiences are expressed, we should bear in mind that the same issues which are expressed in terms of experience, such as fertility of humans and cattle, the cosmic order, matters of taboo, or those of the rhythm in nature, are also the issues which are the *raison d'être* for which the sacred ceremonies are performed. Here there is a division between the sacred and the routine sides of the same issue. Such a duality enables a better understanding of the actions of God that concern the social and the natural orders. Ritual performances are aimed at controlling experiences, or bringing about or securing results, while in interpretations there are apparently no limits or constraints that derive from a commitment to ceremonial procedures. Rituals are another side, or a more institutionalized part, of the cultural categories which provide the framework for understanding the world. Rituals are a different language, with different rules, but they touch upon the same themes which also exist in other cultural categories. Though Giddens noted that structuration is concerned with all types of social processes and modes of reproduction, it seems to me that the process of structuration is clearly at work in these informal social meetings. The opportunity for discussing such subjects in a context which is not structurally rigid and loaded with many taboos enables a theoretical understanding of concepts which affect their routine lives. These are not left as sacred, loose concepts beyond man's comprehension, but are open for discussions and explanations on another level and in another context.

An interesting and important question that comes to the fore is why, as a result of the on-going process of structuration or innovation of meaning, there is not a breakthrough from a holistic or a closed system of meanings to another view of the world — or to use Weber's nomenclature, to a greater "rationalization" of the world view? The answer, I think, lies in the pre-Galilean activity which Tylor sees as existing in primitive religions — " ... a close connection between a certain view of the universe as meaningful order and a conception of the close link between understanding and attunement" (1982:96). In other words, the structuration of meaning in a primitive religion is not an open and a loose activity that enables a detachment or a separation between understanding events and phenomena in the world and becoming attuned to them. The imputation of meaning is a process that arises from shared cultural categories, or rather from the relationship between principles which derive from these categories, that are selectively manipulated and applied to various phenomena and situations. These activities of manipulation lead poeple to reformulate the categories and the relationships between various events and phenomena to ascribe order, causes or patterns to these realities, as they are perceived and described.

Finally, we often think of primitive religion as a given system of meaning, as if its principles, symbols, and elements are connected in a definite and institutionalized relationship guaranteed by tradition, institutions, or sacralized customs. We often think that people who profess a religion have no need to give new interpretations or new meanings to their perceived ideas. But if the so-called primitive religion is seen as a network of categories, symbols, principles, and practices, all of which have different kinds of relationships between them which are expressed in everyday reality, then these networks of relationships raise questions of meaning and, at the same time, provide possible answers. Such a view opens up religion to an inquiry about the applicability and scope of every one of these elements.

I am aware that, in some societies, the social conditions and religious concepts are more favorable for opening up channels for such queries and reinterpretations than in other societies. However, I feel that in most tribal societies there exists potentially a multiplicity of situations and social nuclei where the meanings which are given to the connection of general principles with various phenomena and events are different from those which are considered to be the formally accepted ones. Thus, a possibility for structurating new meanings and a potentiality for incorporating these new explanations into the common cultural ideology exists. The time I spent in the field was not sufficient to observe changes in the Dassanetch conception of their world. Furthermore, with lack of records from the past, it will be almost impossible to point out the areas in which changes in their cultural categories took place due to the process of structurating meanings. Nevertheless, I have indicated the potentiality that is entailed in this on-going process. A study which takes into consideration the dialectical relations between the given cultural repertoire and the ways people define, interpret, and give meaning through interaction to the events and phenomena in the world, could shed light on a subject which has been neglected in the study of primitive religions.

References

Almagor, U. 1978, *Pastoral Partners*, Manchester: Manchester University Press.

Almagor, U. 1983, "Colours that Match and Clash: The Explication of Meaning in a Pastoral Society," in *Res — Anthropology and Aesthetics*, No. 5, 49-73.

Almagor, U. (forthcoming), "The Cycle and Stagnation of Smells: Pastoralists-Fishermen Relationships in an East African Society," in *Res — Anthropology and Aesthetics*, No. 14.

Bultmann, R. 1955, *Essays. Philosophical and Theological*, London: SCM Press Ltd.

Eliade, M. 1967, "On Understanding Primitive Religions," in G. Muller and W. Zeller (eds.), *Glaube, Geist, Geschichte, Festschrift für Ernst Benz*. Leiden: E. J. Brill, 498-505.

Evans-Pritchard, E. E. 1962, *Social Anthropology and Other Essays*, Oxford: Oxford University Press.

Geertz, C. 1966, "Religion as a Cultural System," in M. Banton (ed.), *Anthropological Approaches to the Study of Religion*, ASA Monographs, London: Tavistock, 1-46.

Gellner, E. 1970, "Concepts and Society," in B. Wilson (ed.), *Rationality*, Oxford: Basil Blackwell, 18-49.

Giddens, A. 1979, *Central Problems in Social Theory*, Berkeley: University of California Press.

Gulliver, P.H. 1958, "The Turkana Age Organization" in *American Anthropologist*, Vol. 60, 900-922.

Horton, R. 1973, "Lévy-Bruhl, Durkheim and the Scientific Revolution," in R. Horton and R. Finnegan (eds.), *Modes of Thought*, London: Faber and Faber, 249-305.

Karp, I. 1986, "Agency and Social Theory: A Review of Anthony Giddens," in *American Ethnologist*, Vol. 13, 131-137.

Keesing, R.M. 1985, "Conventional Metaphors and Anthropological Metaphysics: The Problematic of Cultural Translation," in *Journal of Anthropological Research*, Vol. 41, 201-218.

Lévy-Bruhl, L. 1910, *Les fonctions mentales dans les sociétés inférieures*, Paris: Alcan.

Lienhardt, G. 1961, *Divinity and Experience: The Religion of the Dinka*, Oxford: Oxford University Press.

Mehan, H. & H. Wood, 1975, "An Image of Man for Ethnomethodology," *Philosophy of the Social Sciences*, Vol. 5, 365-376.

Pocock, D. 1974, "Nuer Religion - A Supplementary View," in *Journal of the Anthropological Society of Oxford*, Vol. 5, 69-79.

Schutz, A. 1967, *The Phenomenology of the Social World*. Translated by G. Walsh and F. Lehnert, Evanston, Illinois: Northwestern University Press.

Silberbauer, G.B. 1981, *Hunter and Habitat in the Central Kalahari Desert*, Cambridge: Cambridge University Press.

Tylor, C. 1982, "Rationality," in M. Hollis and S. Lukes (eds.), *Rationality and Relativism*, Cambridge, Massachusetts: The MIT Press, 87-105.

Turner, V. 1967, "Ritual Symbolism, Morality, and Social Structure among the Ndembu," in V. Turner, *The Forest of Symbols*, Ithaca: Cornell University Press, 48-58.

Wagner, R. 1972, *Habu: The Innovation of Meaning in Daribi Religion*, Chicago: The University of Chicago Press.

Werblowsky, R. J. Z. 1958, "Monotheism Original or Primitive" (Hebrew), in *Iyyun*, Vol. 9, 152-162.

A SHORT HISTORY, BUT MANY CHANGES: A NEW RELIGIOUS MOVEMENT

Eileen Barker, London

The sociologist of religion does not usually have as great an opportunity as the historian to study transitions and transformaions - unless s/he is relying on the work of others. Religions do, of course, undergo some changes during the course of most studies, but the new religious movements would seem to be a particularly fruitful object of study for those who are interested in observing transformations and transitions in a particular religion over a relatively short period of time. In this paper, I discuss some of the changes that have occurred during the course of a single decade (1975-1985) with respect to one particular new religion: the Unification Church.

The Holy Spirit Association for the Unification of World Christianity (HSA-UWC) was formally inaugurated in Seoul in 1954. Its founder was Sun Myung Moon, a Korean, who reports having been told by Jesus, in 1936 (when he was sixteen years old), that God had chosen him to play a special role in the restoration of the Kingdom of Heaven on earth. We are told that during the next nine years Moon received several revelations as the result of intense study and prayer, and spiritual communication with God and a number of reli ious leaders, such as Buddha and Moses. During the 1960s, mis ionaries attempted to spread the movement in Japan and the West, but they did not meet with any great success. In the early 1970s, however, Moon moved to the United States, where he spoke at a series of mass rallies, lavishly entertained dignitaries from various walks of life, and publicly supported Nixon's continuing Presidency during the Watergate Affair.[1] By the end of 1974, the Unification

[1] A general overview of the movement's history and its beliefs (and further references) can be found in Eileen Barker, *The Making of a Moonie: Choice or*

Church was being written about in the media more than any other of the new religions that had emerged since the Second World War.[2] Public attention focussed not only on the movement's theological deviation from conventional Christianity,[3] and its strongly anti-communist stance (with allegations of connections with the Korean CIA),[4] but also on such attention-catching practices as the mass weddings that Moon conducted. The movement was, moreover, accused of using decep ion in its fund-raising activities, of using brainwashing in its recruitment methods, and of breaking up families.

But, while millions of people knew of the existence of Moon and the 'Moonies' (and that they were 'a bad thing'), few had any detailed knowledge about the movement's practices or beliefs. This was partly because the members had very little contact with non-members — except in the pursuit of new members and/or financial resources. I first met the Unification Church in 1974, but it was not until the end of 1976 that I was able to obtain permission officially to carry out my research; although John Lofland had conducted his classic study in the early 1960s,[5] the leaders had become highly suspicious of anyone who was interested in observing (rather than joining) the movement. By the mid-1980s, however, literally thousands of academics throughout the world had attended a Unification-sponsored conference; many of them have now written of their experiences and/or are applying for, and receiving, permission to carry out research into various aspects of the movement.

Brainwashing?, Oxford: Blackwell 1984, chs. 2 & 3.

2 Barend B. van Driel and James T. Richardson, "Print Media and New Religious Movements: A Longitudinal Study," unpublished paper presented at the Western Social Science Association annual meeting, Reno, Nevada, 1986,. Table I.

3 The basic teachings of the Unification Church are to be found in Hyo Won Eu, *Divine Principle*, Washington, DC: HSA-UWC, 1973.

4 Donald Fraser (Chairman), *Investigation of Korean-American Relations: Report of the Subcommittee on International Relations of the Committee on International Relations, US House of Representatives*, Washington DC: US Government Printing Office, 31 October 1978. See also *Our Response to the Report of October 31, 1978, on the Investigation of Korean-American Relations Regarding Reverend Sun Myung Moon and Members of the Unification Church*, New York: HSA-UWC 1979.

5 John Lofland, *Doomsday Cult: A Study of Conversion, Proselytization, and Maintenance of Faith*, Enlarged Edition, New York: Irvington, 1977.

Within the space of these ten years, one of the most telling differences that the student of the Unification Church might remark upon is its definition of membership. When I began my study, one of the main problems that I faced was obtaining a membership list; but once I had managed to do this, I had no problem in knowing who was a member. Almost everyone who was associated with the movement and accepted its beliefs lived in a Unification centre and had given up outside employment or study. From the point of view of the movement itself, the world was very much divided into 'them' and 'us,' with a generally prevailing attitude that 'those who are not with us (on the side of God) are against us (on the side of Satan).'

The Unification Church has always had a high turn-over rate (the majority of members leave, of their own free will, within two years of joining). In the mid-1970s, leaving the movement was a decisive step, which was usually the result of a soul-searching and lonely decision. Remaining members would consider that those who had left had abandoned God for Satan; they might expect some dire consequence to befall their erstwhile brother or sister; and they would be unlikely to continue any contact with the leaver.

By the mid-1970s, the British Moonies were quite prepared to allow me access to their membership files, but the apparently simple exercise of head-counting has become fraught with new kinds of difficulty. Now, one hears of any number of categories of membership - there are Centre members, Core members, Home Church members, CARP (student) members, Associate members, A-members, B-members, C-members; sometimes a distinction is made between members of the Unification Church and Unificationists; and it is not unusual to hear people referred to as fringe members - or even as 'friends of the Church' or 'sympathisers.' These categories attempt to draw distinctions between levels of understanding and/or acceptance of the Unification theology, whether or not a person lives in a centre with other members, and the amount of time that he or she spends on Unification missions rather than working for him or herself in the 'outside world.'

In other words, instead of conversion, commitment and involvement necessarily going together, these have become independent, distinguishable variables. Details about the various combinations need not concern us here; the point to be made is that the sharp boundary between 'them' and 'us' has become exceedingly fuzzy; and the fuzziness of this boundary becomes even more evident when one considers apostasy. Nowadays, it is almost possible to talk of people drifting out of the movement, after, perhaps, discussing their plans with other members - or ex-members. The members themselves frequently are unable to distinguish those who are still 'in' from those who are now 'out'; they may be unsure whether someone who is not living in a Unification centre and is working in an outside job would still consider him or herself to be a member; the person in question might also be unsure - s/he may be ambivalent about some of the movement's practices, but remain more or less convinced that Unification ideals are worthy of respect. And hard-core, centre-members may, without being overly fearful of recriminations from their leaders, remain on quite good terms with those who have clearly left. Gone are the days of absolute black and white distinctions. Grey has crept into the Unification movement - for a number of reasons.

Space does not permit a general discussion of such sociological 'types' as church, sect and denomination, but those who are familiar with the literature will recognise the fact that the Unification Church was, in the mid-1970s displaying many of the characteristics that sociologists have traditionally classified as sectarian,[6] and that many of the changes which have occurred since that time are commonly found as part of the process referred to as denominalisation.[7] Similarly, those who are familiar with the writings of Mary Douglas will recognise a gradual movement away from what she would call a strong 'group' situation to one in which the members define themselves and are controlled by reference to individual, rather than group, criteria, and in which previously impermeable boundaries are questioned, renegotiated and crossed.[8]

These are by no means straightforward, or even inevitable processes, however. What has emerged and will, no doubt, continue to be evident, are numerous tensions betweeen the group and the

---

[6] See Bryan Wilson *Religious Sects: a sociological study*, London: Weidenfeld and Nicolson, 1970, for an excellent classifica ion of types of sects.

[7] David Martin, "The Denomination," *British Journal of Sociology*, Vol. III, No.1, March 1962, characterizes the differences between a sect and a denomination.

[8] See *inter alia* Mary Douglas, *Natural Symbols: Exploration in cosmology*, London: Barrie & Rockcliff, 1970.

individual and between denominationalising and sectarian tendencies: in the theology, there are tensions between literal and liberal interpretations of the beliefs; there are tensions between the inward and outward-looking standards; there are tensions between wanting to preserve pristine purity and to make the beliefs and practices more acceptable to a wider audience. This last tension, for example, has become evident in CAUSA (the political branch of Unificationism), when the movement is torn between the desire to unite all anti-communists in a single common cause, and yet risks losing many of its allies when it espouses ''Godism'' as the unifying ideology. A further, ironic twist of fate becomes evident when Unificationists attempt to unite all religious people against secular humanism, especially in cases where the first Amendment to the United States' Constitution is deemed to be under threat, and then find that once they start teaching the *Divine Principle* they risk losing their religious allies - and it is frequently the secular humanists who are most staunchly left defending their (the Unificationists') rights under the First Amendment.

One of the most obvious ways in which a new religious movement is likely to differ from a well-established religion is in its demographic composition. Although the age distribution of the well-established religion may contain the occasional 'bulge,' it is likely to exhibit a fairly normal spread of members of all ages. The new religion, on the other hand, may have a very limited age distribution during its early years. Furthermore, within a few years, this distribution is almost bound to change quite radically so that a different distribution, with different characteristics, emerges.

Most of those who have joined the Unification Church in the West have been single and aged between 18 and 30, the mean age of joining being 23 years of age. Although the average age of the membership does not rise by as much as one year for each calendar year (on account of the high turn-over), many of the Western Moonies, particularly those who have been in the movement for some times and are in relatively important and/or responsible positions, are now in their mid-thirties - and married.[9] There are still relatively few Western members who have reached their half-

[9] Most of the top leadership is older and Korean (or, less frequently, Japanese).

century, but, at the other end of the spectrum, there is a growing number of children - and a second-generation membership (consisting of 'bornintos') tends to have attitudes towards its religion that are of a different genre from those of first-generation converts (the 'born-agains'). Moreover, converts who are part of a first generation of members (rather than converts to a well-established religion) have something of the pioneer spirit, which is rarely recaptured by subsequent generations, who, unlike the first generation, will be fed on stories (that soon become myths) about the early disciples and martyrs who endured persecution in their struggle for the faith.

Although as yet relatively unburdened by the financial and other needs of the elderly, the movement has, during the past decade, increasingly had to face to the demands of supporting non-productive children who need food, clothing, and all manner of expensive paraphernalia, and who remove their mothers, for a minimum of weeks, but sometimes for months, from active mission. This has given rise to tensions that go far beyond those of mere economic resources, touching upon some of the most fundamental aspects of the movement's belief system.

One of the key tenets of Unification theology is that Adam and Eve were created in order that they should be blessed in a God-centred marriage in which their children would be brought up in a loving, God-centred environment, enjoying a close and loving relationship with each of their parents. It is believed that Moon, by marrying his present wife in 1960, laid the foundation upon which the ideal family unit could be established. In 1975, Moon married 1800 couples. He had conducted mass weddings before that time, but this was the first occasion on which a large proportion of the members from the West were involved. Once the members have agreed to accept the partner that Moon has chosen for them (they can refuse), the couples take part in an important ritual, known as the Holy Wine Ceremony, during which it is believed that the participants' satanic lineage (inherited since the original Fall of Adam and Eve) is changed into a heavenly one.[10] It is also believed that the children born of the union will be born without original sin, although, like Adam and Eve, they can fall.

---

[10] *The Blessing Quarterly*, Vol. 3, No. 1, 1980, p. 12.

These beliefs are still held by most of the members, but there has been a noticeable change in the *way* that they are held and the expectations that the members have of both their marriage and their children. By the mid-1980s (after several thousand more couples had been married, and a significant proportion of these marriages had been dissolved) the belief that marriages arranged by Moon, are bound to succeed has become increasingly questioned. Furthermore, a growing suspicion that not all the 'blessed' children (including some of Moon's own offspring) are quite as unusal in their behaviour as was once anticipated has led several members to modify their general expectations about several of the more miraculous and Utopian-sounding claims of the theology.

Furthermore, while many of the early members joined with the expectation that they would play their part in establishing the Kingdom of Heaven on earth by setting up one of the ideal family units, time has shown that if the movement wants to save the *whole* world (rather than to establish a separate ideal community), it has to mobilise all the forces it can, and this has involved asking husbands to leave their wives and mothers to leave their children while they are sent out on missions, possibly thousands of miles away from each other. This has led a number of young parents to revolt against the leadership, sometimes leaving the movement altogether in order to establish the close-knit nuclear family that they still believe ought to be the foundation of a good (if not the best) society. While they may have been the sort of people who were willing, even eager, to lead sacrificial lives in their early twenties, renouncing the material advantages with which most of them had been brought up, they are also likely to be the sort of people who are unwilling to sacrifice their children in the pursuit of a goal that, for a number of reasons, they are less likely to believe is immediately around the corner.

Millennial movements that have prophesied a definite date for radical change have, throughout history, had to renegotiate dates and/or reinterpret their understanding of just what it is that is expected. The Unification Church is no exception. During its early days in America, many of the members believed that a great and sudden transformation would take place before 1967.[11] By the mid-

[11] See Lofland, *op. cit.*, pp. 25-8.

1970s, immanent transformations were still expected, but the exact form that these would take was not very clear, and by the mid-1980s many of the Kingdom-builders were considerably more sanguine about the changes that they could expect to witness within their life-time. One member, who had joined the movement in 1970, told me in the early 1980s:

> When I first joined, I thought that if I stuck around long enough I would be there among the chosen when God waved his magic wand. Now I realize that if anyone is going to build the Kingdom of Heaven on earth it's got to be people like me.

Despite the fact that it is popularly believed that those who join the Unification Church must be rather weak people who drift into the movement, Moonies are usually idealistic 'doers' who have been unable to find a way of making their impact in creating a better world.[12] It is not infrequent for them to be quite ambitious. In the early days of a messianic, millenarian movement, with the expectation of a New Age around the corner, there are many new and exciting things to do. So long as the movement is visibly growing and new missions are being introduced, there is enough mobility, variety and urgency for the ambitious to feel that they are achieving something. As the years pass, however, the members become less inclined to accept demands for constant change and a sacrificial life that no longer seem unambiguously to promote either social improvement or personal advancement.

By definition, a movement in which the leader enjoys a charismatic authority is bound neither by tradition nor by rational, circumscribed rules. Even while the charismatic leader is still alive, a maturing membership is liable to begin looking for some sort of order and predictability. Some Unificationists have responded to the passing years by starting up their own businesses or embarking upon a career that offers relatively reliable chances of promotion, and affords security for their children's future. At the same time, one can observe a certain degree of bureaucratisation taking place within the organisation, and, even more interestingly, the concpet of a Unification 'Tradition' is of growing importance within the movement.[13] Many rituals that were once regarded as esoteric gnoses are

---

[12] See Barker, *op. cit.*, chs. 8 & 9.

[13] See, for example, the 3 volumes entitled *The Way of Tradition*, New York:

now in printed form for (almost) anyone to see,[14] although certain rites (such as the 3-day ceremony during which the marriages are consummated) are still kept secret, even from most of the unmarried members.

Of course, it can be expected that there will be even more sweeping changes with the further aging of the membership, and the death of Moon (who is now in his late sixties). The current wave of new religions is already providng researchers with some interesting comparative material that is directly related to tensions arising out of the death of the founder.[15] And already one can observe considerable rivalry between various second-level 'fiefdoms' within the Unification Church, headed mainly (although not exclusively) by early, Korean members. A recent development that would have been unthinkable, even in the early 1980s, is the circulation of two 'underground' papers within the movement. These appear monthly and contain articles, news-items and letters that are sceptical of some of the beliefs, and highly critical of many of the practices of the movement, the Korean leadership (although rarely Moon himself) being singled out for some especially sharp questioning. Without Moon's physical presence as the undisputed leader, it is not difficult to envisage the emergence of a number of warring factions and schisms. The routinisation of charisma has been well-documented in many instances, but it is probable that there will be numerous tensions and competing claims to the succession before a bureaucratised organisation becomes more fully institutionalised.

In this paper, I have made no attempt to document all the changes that have occurred within the Unification Church during the past decade. What I offer is merely a single, illustrative contribution to the sort of comparative analysis that might be undertaken by a polymath of the stature of Zwi Werblowsky. It has, for example, been suggested that insofar as a new religion starts with an atypical demographic composition that changes to another (still atypical) composition within the life-cycle of a single generation, the

---

HSA-UWC, 1980 and innumerable articles in the in-house glossy monthly, *Today's World*. See also note 15.

[14] *The Tradition*, Book One, New York: HSA-UWC, 1985.

[15] See, for example, E. Burke Rochford *Hare Krishna in America*, New Brunswick, NJ: Rutgers University Press, 1985.

movement will exhibit changing characteristics that differ significantly from those of a religion in which each age-cohort is automatically replaced by a younger one. And, insofar as the founder of a new religion claims (charismatic) authority that is not based on appeals to either tradition or rational/legal rules, the power-structure will be predictably unpredictable, but may, within a short period (possibly during the leader's lifetime) move toward a less erratic style, and (possibly after the leader's death) give rise to power struggles and schism. And, insofar as quasi-empirical claims are made by a belief system that has not previously been put to the test of time, significant reinterpretations of the Truth may be witnessed within a relatively short period.

Of course, not all the new religions experience the changes that have been discussed; and, of course, demographic disturbances, schisms, and reinterpretations of belief systems occur in well-established religions. What I do suggest, however, is that a religion with a short history may be expected to undergo transformations and transitions that can, in both intensity and content, differ from those that occur in the more established religions.

DUALISM IN RELIGIOUS ETHNOLOGY*

Ugo Bianchi, Rome

Dualism in religious ethnology is a theme particularly fit for a methodological discussion in the study of religion. Treating it from the comparative research point of view means to make a sharp distinction between phenomenological (typological) and historical (idiographic) approaches - a third possibility being a typological-historical approach, on the basis of a comparative-historical inquiry into phenomena of diffusion or, alternatively, parallel developments.

In other terms: Is religious dualism — at least religious dualism in the illiterate cultures — a general category or structure beyond the specificity of historical problems (such as diffusion, cultural exchange, stimulus diffusion, acculturation), or, on the contrary, are some limited historical processes of this kind to be traced within more or less restricted cultural areas, suitable to rigorous historical research (all the more so as the ambitious cultural-historical project about *Kulturkreise* is *démodé* in present times)? Or are we, as a third hypothesis, to trust in 'historical typology,' the aim of which, as the name indicates, is to trace analogies between *genomena* (whether interconnected or not) in geographical areas far removed from each other (e.g., the insurgence of polytheisms and related, archaic 'high cultures' in regions as remote from each other as the Near East, Eastern Asia and Central America)?

---

* Contributing to a *Festschrift* in honour of a scholar deeply interested in the epistemological problems within the history of religions and anthropology gives me the opportunity to develop some reflections on comparative-historical study I have had the privilege to discuss with him on many occasions in the past.

Such examples (to which the classical one of feudalism in medieval Europe, Iran and Japan can be added) should suffice to establish the truth, that comparison, in order to be effective, need not choose between being either idiographic-historical or typological. The two approaches may interact and the boundary between them may change in the course of research. So e.g., as far as religious dualism is concerned, the study of some figures of ''demiurges' in the marginal sects of Iraq, Turkey, etc. raises the question of their affinity — typological but, at the same time, not devoid of possible historical contiguity — with other demiurgic characters on two sides: the gnosticisms of Antiquity and the surviving inner-Asian folklore of today. Similar questions arise in connection with the dualistic traditions characteristic of the Balkan and East-European cultural areas and with the apocryphal literature which was particularly alive there. Now, it would be unfair to object programmatically to comparative research in those fields, since the drawing of a borderline between the different possibilities (diffusion, convergence etc.) in these different cases is precisely *the* problem. Suffice it here to mention the testimony of an anthropologist particularly interested in historical research — E.E. Evans-Pritchard. He criticizes the 'general distaste' of British functionalist anthropologists for the historical method, observing that ''the historical character of the social anthropological studies should be assured by the fact that today the social anthropologists also aim at the study of communities that, though being minor in entity and simple in structure, form part of big historical ties...''[1] He rightly asks whether social anthropology is to be considered some kind of historical science. In fact, it renders its objects sociologically intelligible, discovering ''the structural patterns of a society,'' which are then compared with others in order ''to construct a typology of forms and to determine their essential features and the reasons of their variations.'' All this should be said without forgetting that Evans-Pritchard's ideas about the 'general' and the 'particular,' as well as his acceptance of the notion of 'ideal type' as a category connected with 'general abstractions'[2] are not

---

1 *Social Anthropology: Past and Present* (Marett Lectures 1950), in ''Man'' 1950; reprinted as Chapter One of *Essays in Social Anthropology*, London 1962, p. 23f.

2 *Ibid.*, p. 48.

necessarily identical with what we advocate in comparative-historical research and historical typology.

Some brief considerations concerning 'dualism in religious ethnology' must start from a description, say, a definition of dualism, based on previous research. "Dualistic are those doctrines, myths and world-views which posit the dichotomy of the principles (be these conceived as coeternal or not) that account for what exists or is conceived to exist in the world."[3] It would be hard to deny that the figure of a demiurge, who is a kind of 'second creator,' acting both as collaborator and opponent of the 'basic creator' (we mean a demiurge or 'second creator' who is particularly connected with the critical aspects of human existence, such as the Coyote in most North-American cultural areas, the Raven or Crow in Eastern Siberia, North-Western America and Australia, the *Vulpes Pallida* among the Bambaras of Mali, the Rabbit or Spider or *Mantis religiosa* in other African cultures) is important for understanding some essential aspects of such a person as a Prometheus-Epimetheus, as regards his figure, function, and *modus operandi*; or of the angel-demiurge of Yazidi and Mandaean mythologies, or the ambivalent Seth of Old Egypt, or the Antagonist of a number of cosmogonies in East European and Central Asian folklore, let alone the cosomogonies and anthropogonies of gnostic sects, including the Bogomils. These constitute a long series of *récits* to which peculiar mythological episodes brought into being by the Zurvanite currents of Zoroastrianism or attested in Manichean literature may be added. To be sure, comparison does not mean identification. To take only one example, the specificity of gnostic dualism as illustrated by Hans Jonas — where the notion of an inferior demiurge is crucial — is beyond doubt, even from a *religionsgeschichtlich* point of view.

In previous studies on dualism I tried to sketch a systematic typology of it - systematic not in the sense of making abstract generalization or of placing different logical 'possibilities' of dualism in contrast with each other, but in the sense of setting up a taxonomy constantly in touch with historical concreteness. So we can distinguish: 1) radical vs. mild (or monarchian) dualism; 2) dialectical vs. eschatological dualism; 3) pro-cosmic vs. anti-cosmic dualism.

[3] See p. 50 of the *Selected Essays* quoted in n. 4.

These opposing positions may be useful for a comparative analysis of the different forms of dualism characteristic for such 'high' religions or systems as Zoroastrianism, Manicheism, Gnosticism, Orphism, Platonism, the dualism of the medieval heresies in Europe etc. They are however not always applicable to the dualism of illiterate culture. This is not because 'savage thought' is less systematic than the 'cultivated' one (to be persuaded of this suffice it to consider the the lineage systems, or the complexities of illiterate cosomologies, as those studied by M. Griaule and G. Dieterlen, or by Werner Müller). The inborn ambiguity, or rather the well-integrated complexity of an inferior demiurge in relation to the destiny of mankind (as we find it in a series of illiterate cultures) is important here, as well as the prevalence, in quite a lot of these cultures, of protology (the description of primordial times) over history (the history of the concerned tribe) and eschatology.

Let us consider the (relative) primordiality of the role of a demiurgical trickster in the Californian and East-Siberian mythologies. These myths are not expressed as a systematic alternative between the notion of a 'coeternity' of the two characters (the Supreme Being and the Coyote, or the Raven) and the notion of the Coyote coming later into being. The oscillation between a Coyote who is there from the beginning, in the same boat as the Creator, and one who is a newcomer, during an absence of the Creator, need not be based on 'primitivity'; it may rather represent a typically dualistic intuition of the Coyote as an elusive actually a coalescence) of contingency and fatality, which is eminently suitable for the figure of a demiurgic trickster. The same holds true with the figure of another demiurge trickster, the Raven of the Paleo-Siberians. According to a Chukchee myth, the Creator has 'forgotten' to create Raven, but the latter nevertheless comes to life during the night, from a garment of the Creator — a splendid expression of their ambivalent relationship to each other. He cannot come into existence independently of the Creator, but at the same time his emergence is in a sense 'autogenous'; he has not existed before because he had been forgotten. It must also be noted that the adjective 'Big,' given sometimes to the Raven or the Coyote (sometimes in connection with his genetic autonomy, which is either partial or problematic as with the Coyote in a myth of the Crow Indians), bears a grandiose, nearly 'metaphysical,' connotation of the personage, notwithstanding the very dubious ethical quality of his performance and the attitude of the narrators and the audiences of many 'trickster stories,' which is not quite proper and respectful.

In conclusion, the integrated ambivalence, or rather (in order to avoid this somewhat discredited term) the integrated personality of this hero which occurs in a number of illiterate (as well as literate) cosmogonies, is one of the most striking forms of dualistic thought. This integration is not meant merely in the sense that this paradoxical figure may be viewed as a Janus *bifrons*, or a generic manifestation of polarity, still less as a syncretistic coalescence of disparate figures, or a degraded god, or a simple rival of the Creator. It is rather an element in a cosmogony which is not the serene *fiat* of a Creator, an element of crisis inscribed in a kind of pre-human prologue on earth or in the primordial waters, which lies at the very beginning of creation. *Mutatis mutandis*, this crisis has something in common with the one that occurs in primordial times according to Orphic, Gnostic or Indian oneness/multiplicity speculation. These are monistic speculations when considered from one point of view, but they are also thoroughly dualistic (as they contain the concept of an innate crisis or a fatal split in the primordial) when viewed from a different point of view[4].

---

[4] For a description and a discussion of the documentary materials mentioned in this article, see Ugo Bianchi, *Il dualismo religioso. Saggio storico ed etnologico*, 2nd Edition, Rome, Ed. Ateneo, 1983 (with bibliography). See also the articles reprinted in my *Selected Essays on Gnosticism, Dualism and Mysteriosophy*, Leiden 1978) (Supplements to Numen XXXVIII), pp. 65-156, with the article "Edschou, le *trickster* divin yoruba," in *Paideuma* 24 (1978) (studi in onore di V.L. Grottanelli), pp. 121-129.

DAS DEUTSCHE WORT "JUDENCHRISTEN" UND IHM ENTSPRECHENDE HISTORISCHE SACHVERHALTE

Carsten Colpe, Berlin

i

Unter den "Transformationen" in der Religionsgeschichte ist diejenige, die vom Judentum zum Christentum geführt hat, vielleicht immer noch der historische schwierigste Fall, obwohl ihr mehr Untersuchungen als anderen Transformationen gewidmet worden sein dürften. Der Begriff "Judenchristentum" drückt oft nicht mehr als die Schwierigkeit dieses Tatbestandes aus. Damit dieser Begriff noch mehr leiste, bemüht man sich neuerdings, ihn schärfer zu fassen, wie es sich überhaupt auch in einer auf der Theorieebene so rückständigen Wissenschaft wie der von den Religionen einzubürgern beginnt, zu definieren, wovon man reden will. Wo dies beim Judenchristentum geschieht, pflegt man Einzelheiten zusammenzutragen oder auszugrenzen, die noch oder nicht dazugehören könnten, um sodann zu einer Begriffsbestimmung fortzuschreiten, die richtiger sein soll als solche, die bis dahin vorgenommen wurden. Dieses Verfahren ist nur halb richtig, denn es lässt ausser Acht, dass die Darstellung ein historisches Objekt nicht einfach ausdrückt, sondern ihrerseits dieses auch erst konstituiert, dass als zwischen beiden ein dialektisches Verhältnis besteht. Um dieses aufzuzeigen, muss man sich einmal mit der Sprache beschäftigen, in der man darstellt. Dabei geht man am sichersten, wenn man sich seine Muttersprache vornimmt. Das ist zugleich ein legitimes Alibi für den *homo unius linguae*, Zwi Werblowsky, den Vielsprachigen, zu ehren, ohne dem Verdacht des Chauvinismus zu verfallen.

Diejenigen Forscher, welche den Begriff "Judenchristentum" einfach am Gegenstand korrigieren, verhalten sich wie Naturwissenschaftler angesichts des mikrophysikalischen Bereichs, welche meinen, man könne unter Absehen von der Tatsache, dass ihre Methoden in diesen eingreifen, Beobachtungs - oder Protokollsätze formulieren. Man kann dieses Verfahren mittels Herstellung einer Analogie zu dem dialektischen Verhältnis, das hier auch in den Naturwissenschaften besteht, korrigieren und wird schon dann zu anderen Ergebnissen kommen. In den historischen Wissenschaften kommt aber als Komplikation noch hinzu, dass sie es oft auch mit Terminologien zu tun haben, in denen sich der Gegenstand gleichsam selbst definiert. Will man ihn als Forscher definieren, als ihm eine Fremddefinition zuteil werden lassen, darf man die Terminologie nicht einfach übersetzen, indem man in den Wörterbüchern nachschlägt. Denn die Bedeutungen, die dort angegeben werden, mussen oft, erzwungen durch die der Gattung Wörterbuch gesetzten Grenzen, die Dialektik ausser Betracht lassen, die in der Semantik, d.h. dem Verhaltnis zwischen einem Begriff und "seiner" Sache, beschlossen liegt. Um dieser Schwierigkeit Herr zu werden, hat Rudolf Carnap die Unterscheidung zwischen Objekt- und Metasprache eingeführt. Sie sei hier einmal erprobt. Der Objektsprache entsprechen die Sprachen der Quellen, als Hebräisch, Griechisch und Lateinisch; statt Metasprache kann man auch Wissenschaftssprache sagen — es ist in diesem Falle die deutsche. Auch mit diesem Versuch wird man Zwi Werblowsky gerecht, der unter den Religionshistorikern einer der wenigen ist, der auf wissenschaftstheoretische Probleme achtet.

ii

Auch das deutsche Wort "Judenchristen" gehört zur Wissenschaftssprache. Auf den ersten Blick mag es ganz verständlich aussehen. Bei näherem Hinsehen aber enthält es mehrere Probleme. Man kann für es in den Quellensprachen gewisse Anhaltspunkte in bestimmten Wörtern oder Wortverbindungen finden, doch gibt es von diesen aus keine Ableitungen in Form einer "Ubersetzung". Das Wort "Judenchristen" ist mehrdeutig. Die Semantik des Adjektivs "judenchristlich" liegt teilweise anders als die des Substantivs, weshalb für dessen Gebrauch keine analogen Regeln gelten. Eine historisch-semasiologische Untersuchung des wissenschaftlichen

Sprachgebrauchs fehlt. Von Fall zu Fall ist es aber schon heute manchmal möglich, dem Zusammenhang, in welchem das Wort "Judenchristen(tum)" begegnet, die mitgemeinte Bedeutung zu entnehmen. Das substantivische Kompositum kann dreifach verstanden werden: einmal als *Kasuskomposition*, in der das erste Glied dekliniert wird wie in "Landesfürst", "Griechenland", "Ältesten-amt" oder "Gottessohn". Bei "Judenchristen" kann hier das erste Glied in der (kollektiven) Einzahl oder Mehrzahl gedacht werden ("des" oder "der" Juden), wobei das deklinierte Glied in diesem Falle ein genitivus partitivus wäre. "Judenchristen" bedeutet dann etwa "die Christen aus" oder "unter den Juden" im Griechischen entspräche dem sachlich *hoi ek tēs peritomēs (pistoi)* "die (Gläubigen) aus der Beschneidung" (= die aus der Judenschaft gekommen sind) (Act. 10, 45; 11,2; Gal. 2, 12 u.ö.); sodann als *Determinativkompositum*, in welchem das erste Glied undekliniert ist und das zweite inhaltlich näher bestimmt wie in "Tagelöhner", "Randprovinz", "Opferaltar" oder "Menschensohn". Hier wäre bei der fraglichen Bezeichnung an "judenähnliche" oder "judaisierende" Christen zu denken; im Griechischen kann man anknüpfen an solche *Ioudaioi*, welche getauft und als Christen sind, aber bestimmte jüdische Bräuche und Ansichten ungerechtfertigter Weise wieder übernehmen (ganz selten so genannt: wohl nur Gal. 2, 13 <sinngleich mit *Ioudaizontes* Gal. 2, 14> und vielleicht Act. 21, 20); endlich als *Additionswort* oder Dvandva, in welchem die Bedeutungen sachlich gleichgeordneter (und im ersten Glied in der Stammform belassener, im zweiten Glied deklinierter) Substantive summiert werden oder in ein Sowohl-als-auch-Verhältnis zueinander treten wie in "Räubernomaden", "Grenzfluss", "Almosen-(ab)gabe" oder "Gottmensch". Judenchristen wären dann Personen, die sowohl Juden als auch Christen sind. Im Griechischen gibt es dafür keine eindeutige Entsprechung, doch sind solche Personen mit den "aus der Pharisäerpartei zum Glauben Gekommenen" (Act. 5, 15) gemeint, die auch als solche auf der Beschneidung bestehen, in diesem Falle als wohl Pharisäer bleiben; wo man so interpretierte, hat man sie als "christliche Pharisäer" wiedergegeben.

Der Sinn der Bezeichnung. Von den drei Kompositumsarten haben die beiden ersten miteinander, die dritte mit ihnen nur mit Einschränkung gemeinsam, was für die meisten Komposita grundsätzlich gilt: das zweite Glied ist das Grundwort, welches die Hauptbedeutung trägt. Welcher Bedeutung und damit welcher

Kompositionsart man beim Gebrauch des Wortes "Judenchristen" den Vorzug geben soll, ist bisher nicht vereinbart worden. Dies wäre schon nötig, wenn man auch nur eine Kompositionsart beibehalten will; es wären dann die jeweils beiden anderen in freie Formen zu zerlegen.

Unterschiede in den Wissenschaftssprachen haben oft Verwirrung geschaffen. Für den internationalen wissenschaftlichen Dialog ist es besonders wichtig festzusstellen, dass es eine den germanischen Sprachen gemeinsame Kompositumsbildung solcher Art gibt (im Niederländischen, Dänischen und Schwedischen liegen die Dinge wie im Deutschen), während andere Wissenschaftssprachen dazu nur Teiläquivalente bieten. In den romanischen und den slawischen Sprachen bedient man sich gern eines Substantivs für "Christen(tum)" und eines Adjektivs für "jüdisch" ("israelitisch", "hebräisch"), welches attributiv in verschiedenem Sinn und leicht zur Verdeutlichung paraphrasierbar dazugestellt wird. Kommt es doch einmal zu einer Zusammensetzung wie in französisch (und entsprechend italienisch) Judéo-Christianisme, so bleibt sie auf den Fall des Determinativkompositums beschränkt. Im Englischen scheint es sich einzubürgern, mit dem Determinativkompositum "Judaeo-Christianity" einen theologischen Sinnzusammenhang zu bezeichnen, während die auf derselben semantischen Ebene liegende Attributivbildung "Jewish Christianity" einem im einzelnen noch näher zu bestimmenden sozialen Tatbestand vorbehalten bleibt.

Zum Gegenbegriff des "Heiden(christen)tums" gelten parallele Erwägungen, doch muss das Verständnis als Kasuskomposition vorwiegen, während die Möglichkeit, das Wort als Additionswort zu verstehen — "sowohl Heiden als auch Christen" —, aus sachlichen Grunden ganz wegfällt (auch hier liegen für das Adjektiv, "heidenchristlich", die Dinge teilweise anders).

Der häufig geübte Brauch, Judenchristentum im Gegensatz zu Heidenchristentum zu definieren, trägt nicht viel aus, weil in das letztere mit dem Heidenbegriff auch noch ein grober Anachronismus hineingekommen ist. Das deutsche Wort "der Heide" ist entweder eine Lehn*übersetzung* von *paganus*, welche, vielleicht in Anlehnung an das in die gotische Bibelübersetzung als *haithi*, *haithns*, *haithno* entlehnte **hethnos*, aber in erster Linie auf der Basis eines anderen, verbreiteteren gemeingermanischen Wortstammes in solchen deutschen Volksstämmen geschaffen worden sein muss, die nähere Beruhrung mit christlichen Römern und über diese Kenntnis bestimmter lateinischer

Kirchenväter hatten, oder es ist indirekt — über das Gotische — ein Lehn*wort* aus dem Griechischen (eben aus **hethnos*). Im ersten Falle bedeutet es "der vom unbebauten Lande, aus der Ödnis, der Heide" Stammende. Im zweiten Falle bedeutet es wie *ethn(ik)os* "der einem ausländischen Volk Zugehörige", wobei der Ausländer in apostolischer Zeit nach damaliger Selbstdefinition als Nichtjude, nach unserer Definition sowohl als Nichtjude als auch als Nichtjudenchrist, in nachapostolischer Zeit nach damaliger wie nach heutiger Definition als Nichtchrist (aber noch mit Ausnahme des Juden) zu verstehen ist. Die Lehn*übersetzung* würde sinngemäss die Bëdeutung nachbilden, welche *paganus* im christlichen Latein seit dem Anfang des 4. Jahrhunderts bekam: "der aus dem nichtchristlichen Landgau, dem *pagus* Stammende, der Bauerliche" im Unterschied zum inzwischen christlich-urban gewordenen *civis Romanus*. Es nimmt nicht wunder, dass die i.J. 398 begonnene Vulgata dieses Wort oder eine seiner Ableitungen überhaupt nicht verwendet, sondern *gentilis/gent(il)es* sagt. Über dessen spätlateinishce Angleichung an *paganus/pagani* wäre das Wort "Heide(n)", wenn man es als Lehn*wort* versteht, zu derselben Bedeutung gekommen wie die etwaige Lehn*übersetzung*. So oder so ist es als Direktübersetzung für das biblische *gentilis/gent(il)es* wie auch für das dahinterstehende griech. *ethnos/ethnē* und das diesem zugrundeliegende hebr. *goj/gojim* denkbar ungeeignet. Nur die Adjektive "heidnisch" und "heidenchristlich" sind für bestimmte zusammenfassende Charakterisierungen wissenschaftssprachlich vertretbar.

Zum Teilbegriff des "Juden" bleibt man auf eine Definition ohne Gegenbegriff angewiesen. Aber ein inhaltliches Verständnis des "Judenchristentums" wird ausser durch die Kompositionsart der Bezeichnung auch vom Inhalt ihres ersten, das zweite näher bestimmenden Gliedes her erschwert. Denn wie eindeutig die Definition des Juden unter jüdischem Gesichtspunkt auch möglich sein mag, unter dem Aspekt, eine bestimmte Beziehung zum Christen in sie aufzunehmen, ist sie es nicht. Metasprachlich muss man in solchen Beziehungen den ethnischen, sprachlichen, culturellen und religiösen Aspekt des Jüdischen unterscheiden; diese Aspekte können zusammenfallen, müssen es aber nicht, und der eine oder andere oder sogar mehrere Aspekte können fehlen. Nach christlich-objektsprachlichem Zeugnis kann jemand Christ geworden sein, dessen früherer Status als Angehöriger des *'am JHWH/laos theou* ("Volk Gottes") wie des *goj qadoš/ethnos hagion* ("heiliges Volk"), als ein *ger/proselytos*

("Fremder" im Sinne von "Gast"/"Hinzugekommener") oder wie als *tošab/paroikos* ("Beisasse"), ja sogar als *jare šamajim/ phoboumenos ton theon* ("Gottesfürchtiger") vom neuen Standpunkt aus als jüdisch bezeichnet werden kann, während es sich vom jüdisch-objektsprachlichen Standpunkt aus beim Proselyten um keinen vollen Juden, beim Gottesfürchtigen nur um einen Halbproselyten, beim Beisassen um einen Nichtjuden handelt.

Sowohl objekt- als auch metasprachlich sind die Bezeichnungen der Diaspora- bzw. Galuthangehörigen und der Samaritaner gerechtfertigt. Während aber jeder der beiden von uns Heutigen vor seiner christlichen Taufe als Sondertypus eines Juden angesehen werden kann, war der erstere für den bodenständigen palästinischen Zeitgenossen je nach dem Grade seiner "Ethnisierung" ein Halb-, Drittel- oder Vierteljude (Klausner 372), der letztere gar ein Ungläubiger oder Fremdbürtiger (*allogenēs*). Nach anachronistischer, d.h. die Distanz zwischen Quellen- und Wissenschaftssprache nicht beachtender Übersetzung wäre der Paroikos wie der Samaritaner ein "Heide", nach zeitgenössisch möglicher Definition der letztere ein "Fremdstämmiger" (*allophylos*).

iii

Bedeutungen in der Forschungsgeschichte lassen sich in Ansätzen ausmachen, wenn sie auch noch nicht präzise unterschieden werden. Die Forschungsgeschichte bietet nur spärliche Entfaltungen der möglichen Beziehungen, in denen Christen zu den verschiedenen Formen des Judentums gestanden haben; zumeist überdeckt sie sie durch Begriffe, in denen jeweils mehrere Aspekte solcher Beziehungen gemischt auftreten. Faktisch meint man: einmal *Christen jüdischer Herkunft*, die für sich an der *Beobachtung des Gesetzes* festhalten, in Auseinandersetzung mit Paulus aber dasselbe von gebürtigen Nichtjuden nicht vollständig verlangen — es gab es immer wieder extreme Vertreter, die es doch taten —, und die in der Grosskirche verblieben. Ohne eine besondere Partei zu sein, hielten sie an der ursprünglich nur als Gottesbundzeichen interpretierten Männerbeschneidung auch als an einem Merkmal nationaler Identität fest und übten so auf die Gemeinden, die aus Diasporajuden hervorgegangen wären, aber auch auf solche, die sich aus Nichtjuden neu bildeten, einen gewissen Einfluss aus. Das früheste Dokument dafür ist das Aposteldekret (Act. 15, 23-29), das von Nichtjuden die Einhaltung eines jüdischen Minimalkodexes (ohne Beschneidung) verlangt. Als Judenchristen in diesem Sinne sind wohl die *Jewish Christians*, *Nazarene Jews*; oder *Messiah-Men* in sachlichem Unterschied von, aber in realer Symbiose mit den *Gentiles* (engl.) bzw. *Gentile Christians* nach der Interpretation von Thomas Morgan (Bd.1, S. 377-380; Bd. 2, Appendix S. 25; Bd. 3, S. 188-190) zu verstehen; aber auch das, was John Toland (bes. Kap. 9-14) "Jewish Christianity" nennt — neben "Gentile" und "Mahometan Christianity"! —, kommt dem nahe. Deutsch würde "Judenchristentum" in diesem Sinne am ehesten eine Kasuskomposition mit Tendenz zum Determinativkompositum sein; sodann *Christen gleich welcher Herkunft, welche jüdisch weiterdenken*, auch eigene Pseudepigraphen zur hebräischen oder zur griechischen Bibel und ausser einigen Schriften, die später Bestandteil des neutestamentlichen Kanons sein werden, auch solche verfassen, die im Verhältnis zu diesem später als Apokryphen gelten. Die Beschneidung spielte keine Rolle. Jüdisch-theologisch weitergedacht wird z.B., wenn von Gott als von "dem Namen" die Rede ist, wenn die Auferstehung Jesu mit seiner Himmelfahrt gleichgesetzt wird, wenn Engel eine grosse Rolle spielen, wenn die Schriftauslegung den Methoden von Targum und Midrasch verpflichtet bleibt, wenn Überlieferungsformen wie Halachah und Haggadah wiederauftauchen, wenn die Apokalyptik strukturell unverändert weitergeführt wird. Dergleichen klingt schon bei W.M.L. de Wette an, wenn er "judenchristliche" von "alexandrinischen" oder "hellenistischen" und von "paulinischen" Schriften nach ihrem Inhalt unterschied. In der Gegenwart ist diese Sicht breit von J. Daniélou ausgearbeitet worden, der auch Beziehungen in der Beobachtung des liturgischen Jahres, der Gottesdienstordnung und der Alltagsnormen einbezog. Begrifflich ist "Judenchristentum" in diesem Sinne am ehesten als Determinativkompositum zu verstehen; endlich *Christen jüdischer Herkunft, die als solche eine eigene Partei bildeten*, in der sich bildenden Grosskirche nicht aufgingen und statt dessen ein besonderes Gruppenschicksal erlitten. Beschneidung war selbstverständlich. Schon der früheste Kirchenhistoriker, Hegesippos (um 180), vertritt die Sicht der katholischen Kirche, wenn er sie *haireseis* nennt (bei Eus., h.e. 3. 32. 6), die von den jüdischen *haireseis* herkommen (bei Eus., h.e. 4, 22, 4f), und sie dadurch von anderen "Judenchristen" unterscheidet. In Ansätzen findet sich die Hervorhebung dieser Richtung schon bei J.S.

Semler (bes. Bd. 4, Vorrede), wenn er von einer Partei von Christen spricht, welche zu der Diozese von Palästina, der Diözese des Jacobus, Petrus, Judas gehören und an die Christen aus der Diözese des Paulus keine Briefe schreiben. Weiter ausgeführt wird diese Sicht von der jüngeren Tübinger Schule, vor allem ihren Begründer F. Chr. Baur, der diese Partei u.a. an Hand der Pseudoklementinen bis nach Rom weiterverfolgte und ihr Kirchenverständnis in der Organisation der katholischen Kirche wiedererkannte. In der Gegenwart ist diese Gruppierung vor allem von H.J. Schoeps weiter bestimmt worden, indem er namentlich die Ebioniten des Ostjordanlandes und Syriens als dazugehörig aufwies. Doch ist damit über eine historische Kontinuität zwischen der "Urgemeinde" einerseits, den Pseudoklementinen oder den Ebioniten andererseits in Wirklichkeit nichts gesagt. Die Sachbezeichnung "Judenchristentum" tendiert hier vom Determinativkompositum stark zum Additionswort hin: in manchen Fällen oder in mancher Hinsicht ist es tatsächlich berechtigt, von Gläubigen zu sprechen, die sowohl Juden als auch Christen wären.

Es ist zu beachten, dass die vorgenommene Unterscheidung eine idealtypische ist, welche einer klareren historischen Erkenntnis dienen soll, dass aber in der historischen Realität diese Typen an allerlei Stellen und auf vielerlei Weise ineinander übergehen. Insbesondere lassen sich manche Schriften nicht eindeutig einem bestimmten Typus ausschliesslich zuordnen; die Pseudoklementinen z.B. dürften dem zweiten wie dem dritten, Forderungen wie die im Aposteldekret niedergelegten dem ersten wie dem dritten, die Didache dem ersten wie dem zweiten Typus zugehören. Es ist jedoch wichtig, Rückschlüsse aus altkirchlicher Überlieferung, welche hier für historische Rekonstruktionen zwingend gefordert sind, unter weitestmoglicher Berücksichtigung der idealtypischen Unterscheidung vorzunehmen, damit man zu einem moglichst differenzierten Bild der gemeinde-, glaubens- und theologiesoziologischen Verhältnisse gelangt (was nicht heissen soll, dass die Zeugnisse für Glauben und Theologie in jedem Falle den Blick auf Gemeindeverhältnisse freigeben).

Von der idealtypischen Unterscheidung nicht mitbetroffen ist der allgemeinste Sinn von "Judenchristentum": den Tatbestand, dass das Christentum schlechthin im Judentum wurzelt, mit ihm die hebräische Bibel teilt und mit ihm eine gemeinsame, wenn auch meist verfehlte Geschichte hat, pflegt man überhaupt nicht in ein Wort zu fassen. Hatte jene Ideologie, welche diese Grundgegebenheit leugnete und damit das

Christentum von jüdischen "Schlacken" oder "Einflüssen" befreien wollte, sich durchgesetzt, dann wäre das Christentum seiner Identität verlustig gegangen. Sieht man von dieser allgemeinen Bedeutung ab, in welcher bis heute und in alle Zukunft jeder Christ ein Judenchrist ist, dann spielen in der Forschung nur die vorstehend erörterten historischen Verständnisse von "Judenchristentum" eine Rolle, denen sich die analysierten Kompositumsformen des Wortes teilweise oder überschneidend, aber nicht prazise identifizierend zuordnen lassen.

iv

Über diese allgemeineren Charakterisierungen hinaus sei nun noch eine speziellere Anwendung der wissenschaftssprachlichen Erwägungen auf den zentralen Trägerkreis des transformatorischen Prozesses versucht, der sich durch die stichworte "Jerusalemer Gemeinde, Hellenisten, Stephanus-Kreis, früheste Missionare" vorläufig bezeichnen lässt. Da wir noch nicht sicher sein wollen, ob es sich wirklich um eine "christliche Urgemeinde" gehandelt hat, setzen wir sie in Anführungszeichen.

Zu Anfang wird eine Entwicklung sichtbar, die anfangs durch den Namen des Petrus, am Ende durch die des Jesusbruders Jakobus, wieder des Petrus und des Zebedäussohnes Johannes repräsentiert wird. Den Übergang leitet der Streit ein, der in der Ermordung des Stephanus gipfelte (Act. 7, 57). Als er stattfand, konnte noch niemand wissen, dass er zu einem Nebeneinander zweier recht verschiedener Kirchenverständnisse führen würde. Dieser Streit war weder eine "Christenverfolgung" seitens der Juden noch ein "Zwist innerhalb der jungen christlichen Gemeinde"; denn mit beidem wäre gesagt, dass sich die "Urgemeinde" als eigenständige Gruppe ausserhalb der Synagogalgemeinde verstanden hätte. Dies war jedoch nicht der Fall.

Entscheidend war offenbar die *Stellung zum Tempel.* Die in Qumran gefundene Tempelrolle, welche nicht die Opposition der Essener, sondern die Ideale der gesamten jüdischen Priesterschaft reflektiert, lässt eindringlich erkennen, wie sich von aussen, vom Lande aus, über zwei Wegzonen rings um die Stadt durch die Stadt selbst und auf den Berg in den äusseren Hof, die Bereiche für kultfähige Männer, für Priester und für die kultischen Dienste bis ins Allerheiligste als dem Sitz der Gottesgegenwart die Heiligkeit konzentrisch verdichtet. Auf

Verletzung einzelner Grade von Heiligkeit — die im Text mit Reinheit gleichgesetzt wird — bezieht die Darstellung der Tempelrolle, die von innen nach aussen geht, auch bestimmte Sanktionen. Das sind z.B. die Todesstrafe für Bestechlichkeit (53, 13-18), für aufrührerisches Verhalten eines Sohnes (64, 2-6; Steinigung), für Verrat des Volkes an ein fremdes Volk Kapitalverbrechen, Verfluchung Israels (64, 7-11: ans Holz Hängen). Jede Art von Rechtsbeugung verunreinigte, an Intensität abnehmend, den Tempel, die Stadt und das Land. Der direkte Angriff auf den Tempel lag wohl ausserhalb aller Vorstellungen; jedenfalls wird darüber nichts gesagt.

Folglich musste ein solcher Angriff erst recht den Tod zur Folge haben, und konnte man ihm umso sicherer entgehen, je weiter man sich vom Allerheiligsten entfernte. Irrtümliche Anerkennung eines Messias war offenbar kein gleich gewichtiger Strafgrund - das zeigt noch das Davonkommen Rabbi Akibas, der einhundert Jahre später den Bar Kochba als Messias begrüsste -, es sei denn, der Betreffende, ob er nun Messias war oder nicht, hätte sich gerade durch Verletzung oder Verleugnung der Tempelheiligkeit hervorgetan. Das aber war bei Jesus der Fall gewesen: die Weissagung, der Tempel werde verschwinden und einem neuen Platz machen (Mk. 14, 58), lässt sich weder aus jüdischen Traditionen noch aus dem Urchristentum ableiten, sondern war seine eigene, mit der er zugleich eine in der Landbevölkerung verwurzelte Opposition gegen den Tempel aufgegriffen hatte. Die "Hebräer" in der "Urgemeinde" brachten durch ihre Haltung zum Ausdruck, dass sie mit der Auferweckung Jesu seine Tempelkritik nicht wieder in Gültigkeit gesetzt sahen, während seine Anerkennung der Torah als uneingeschränkt aufgenommen wurde. Die Stephanusleute unter den Hellenisten hingegen — nicht die letzteren insgesamt, denn die Mitglieder der vier landsmannschaftlich organisierten Synagogen, die mit Stephanus gestritten hatten (Act. 6,9), wären auch Hellenisten — nahmen offenbar wie er den zweiten Teil der Weissagung Jesu positiv auf, wenn auch spiritualisiert: nicht der Tempel sollte wiedererrichtet werden, sondern die Torah des Mose sollte bestehen bleiben, aber natürlich sinngemäss verändert (Act. 6, 14). Das war eigentlich etwas noch Schlimmeres gewesen, als Jesus gesagt hatte, und die Reaktion, welche priesterliche Heiligkeitsideale wieder durchsetzen sollte, nimmt nicht wunder. Sie war aber unter den Augen der Römer wohl nur in einer ganz bestimmten Konstellation möglich und konnte sich so gegen die Anhänger des Stephanus nicht wiederholen.

Kaiser Tiberius (14-37) hatte etwa seit dem Jahre 18 der späteren christlichen Zeitrechnung zwölf Jahre lang die Vollmacht, die Prokuratoren von Judäa zu bestätigen bzw. zu ernennen, an den Gardepräfekten Sejanus delegiert, der zu derselben Klasse — den *equites* — gehörte wie diese. Der Prokurator Valerius Gratus (15-26) schwenkte nach Bestellung des Sejanus ganz auf dessen Programm rigoroser Durchsetzung römischer Souveränität ein, und sein Nachfolger, Sejans besonderer Günstling Pontius Pilatus (26-36), setzte diese Politik fort. Beide fanden in Kaiphas, dem Schwiegersohn des Hannas, einen Hohenpriester, welcher Loyalität gegen Rom mit Repräsentation der Juden zu vereinigen wusste. Aber als die Parther wieder einmal Ansprüche auf das alte Seleukidenreich erhoben, zu welchem für sie immer noch Palästina mit Judäa gehörte, fiel den Juden ihre Rolle als geborene Bundesgenossen der Römer gegen deren östliche Erbfeinde wieder zu. Tiberius hatte den Judenhasser Sejanus im Jahre 31 fallen lassen und beauftragte, fünf Jahre später, seinen Legaten in Syrien, Vitellius (35-38), den Pilatus, der nun ohne Protektion amtierte, auch formell abzusetzen. Mit ihm musste Kaiphas gehen. Zum Nachfolger des ersteren bestimmte Vitellius seinen Schützling Marcellus, und dieser ernannte als neuen Hohenpriester Jonathan, einen Sohn des Hannas. Marcellus wurde vom Kaiser nicht bestätigt und amtierte nur ein Jahr lang, sodass Jonathan — er muss in Act. 7, 1 mit dem Hohenpriester gemeint sein, der sich am Streit mit Stephanus beteiligt - der eigentliche Machthaber im Lande wurde. Er konnte die Steinigung des Stephanus geschehen lassen, ohne mit einem Eingreifen der Römer rechnen zu müssen.

Diese Konstellation, sie war wohl im Jahre 36, wiederholte sich nicht. Danach, unter dem wieder kaiserlich bestellten Prokurator Marullus (37-41), dem von diesem ernannten Hohenpriester Theophilos (einem Bruder des Jonathan), dem Legaten Publius Petronius (39-42) und dem Kaiser Caligula (37-41), blieb der Tempelpartei nur die Moglichkeit, die Tempelopponenten und Gesetzeskritiker unter den Hellenisten aus der Stadt hinauszudrängen, ins Land hinein, wo die Heiligkeit abnahm (Act. 8). Die Vertriebenen werden ihrerseits im Lande genügend Leute angetroffen haben, welche mit ihrer Haltung und dem daraus folgenden Geschick solidarisch wären. Fortan ist die Geschichte der "Urgemeinde" in zwei Lokalitäten gleichzeitig zu verfolgen, in Jerusalem und ausserhalb davon. Wenn man in faktischer Ausbreitung den Willen Gottes walten sieht, dann darf man das, was jetzt beginnt, Mission nennen, d.h. Erfüllung eines göttlichen Sendungsauftrages. Aber um Entsendung durch eine Institution oder Korporation von menschen handelt es sich nicht.

Die Tatsache, dass gerade *vertriebene Hellenisten als Missionare* tätig wurden, wirft mehrere wichtige Fragen auf. Warum mussten sie erst vertrieben werden, um die "Frohbotschaft", die doch wohl von vornherein für alle Menschen bestimmt war, "weiterzusagen"? Machten sie aus der Not eine Tugend? Zeigt sich auch darin ein Unterschied zu den anderen Hellenisten- und zu allen Hebräergruppen, dass sie dazu überhaupt theologisch imstande wären (sie hatten ja auch, wenn sie schon vertrieben wurden, schweigend zugrunde gehen konnen, wie es Essener in solchen Fällen taten vrgl. Jos. bell. 2,143; 1QS7-9 passim)? Und: Bedeutete die Mission den entscheidenden Bruch mit der Endzeiterwartung? Hätte — umgekehrt — nicht Zweifel am oder Verzweiflung über das Nichtkommen des Endes gerade den Verzicht auf jegliche missionarische Aktivität zur Folge haben müssen?

Hier kommen sozialpsychologische Faktoren ins Spiel, die auch bei der Untersuchung neuer und neuester messianischer und millenaristischer Bewegungen erkennbar geworden sind. Sie dürfen als Erklärungskategorien auf die Verhältnisse von damals bis zum Tode des Paulus angewandt werden, weil letztere ja erst durch Analyse der Vorgänge von heute in ein Muster gebracht werden konnten; dieses Muster hat also nicht, wie es mit anderen für nachchristliche Bewegungen bestimmend gewordenen, traditional bekannt gebliebenen Faktoren (in Texten ablesbare Apokalyptik, Messianologie, Gemeinschaftsorganisation, Binnenmoral) der Fall ist, die Rollen in heutigen Gruppen geprägt und ihre Erfahrungen nicht vorstrukturiert. Wie sieht das Muster aus? Ein Ereignis, das man erwartet und das für die Welt entscheidend werden soll, tritt nicht ein. Die Ideen, Überzeugungen und Handlungen, mit denen sich die Gruppe auf das erwartete Ende eingestellt hat, und die statt dessen bestehen bleibenden Verhältnisse oder unerwartet eintretenden Ereignisse "tönen verworren" oder "unharmonisch" mit dem Erwarteten, stimmen mit diesem nicht mehr überein, werden im Verhältnis zu diesem "dissonant". Diese Dissonanz wird nicht dumpf empfunden, sodass irrationale Ausbrüche folgen müssten, sondern sie wird klar erkannt. Die kognitive Dissonanz, die so entsteht, wird nicht ertragen und muss beseitigt werden. Dies kann auf zweierlei Weise geschehen: ist der soziale Rückhalt für die Individuen innerhalb der Gruppe stark genug, bleibt die Existenz der

Gruppe wichtiger als die Erfullung der Prophezeiung. Unterschreitet der soziale Rückhalt aber ein bestimmtes Minimum, dann muss die unerträglich werdende kognitive Dissonanz vermindert werden. Das kann nur in dem Masse geschehen, wie Aussenstehende, Spottende, Ungläubige davon überzeugt werden, dass die Gruppe recht hat.

In dieser Lage wären die vertriebenen Hellenisten. In Jerusalem selbst wären sie eine Minderheit innerhalb einer Minderheit, ihre theologische Position war problematisch, die Vertreibung schwächte ihren sozialen Rück- und Zusammenhalt noch weiter. Die kognitive Dissonanz, in die sie Jerusalem gerieten, bestand zwischen den eschatologischen Erwartungen, die sie in Jerusalem gehegt hatten, und der Tatsache, dass sie sich nun gerade dort wiederfanden, wo sie das Ende nicht gemeint hatten erwarten zu dürfen, und wo es nun auch tatsächlich nicht stattfand. Die Vertriebenen konnten sich dann nicht gezwungen sehen, die Eschatologie aufzugeben - eben mit Enteschatologisierung wird heute oft erklärt, warum die Kirche überhaupt begann, Mission zu treiben -, sondern im Gegenteil: um Recht zu behalten, mussten sie die Eschatologie gerade aufrecht erhalten. Das war in ihrer damaligen Situation sogar einfacher, als es für heutige Millenaristen ist: während die am Tempel verbleibenden Hebräer und die in Jerusalem verbleibenden Hellenisten, in welcher durch den Heiligen Geist modifizierten Weise auch immer, den Tag des Herrn am richtigen Ort erwarteten, konnten die Stephanusleute ihre Vertreibung als Zeichen auffassen, den Völkern zu sagen, dass nunmehr auch für sie der Zeitpunkt gekommen sei, sich zum Zion aufzumachen. Das ist eine Hypothese auf Grund historischer Indizien. Sie wird durch den Text der Apostelgeschichte, die schon missionschristlich darstellt, natürlich nicht bestätigt, aber auch nicht widerlegt.

Es ist bemerkenswert, dass die Mission in Samaria begann (Act. 8, 4-13). Die Samaritaner waren Juden nicht vom Tempel, sondern von der Torah her, und es galt, gegen jahrhundertelange jerusalemer Missachtung diesen Tatbestand eschatologisch wiederherzustellen. Nach der Darstellung der Apostelgeschichte, bei der es nicht wichtig ist, ob sie die historisch genaue Reihenfolge bietet, wurden dann Lydda, Joppe (9, 31-43), Phönizien, Cypern (!) und Antiochien erreicht (11, 19); binnenländische Stationen sind u.a. aus dem Markusevangelium zu erschliessen, vor allem in Galiläa (so auch Act. 9. 31). Bei den Juden, an welche die Missionare sich bewusst hielten (Act. 11. 19; Mk. 7. 2), kann es sich auch um hellenistische Juden gehandelt haben. Dies würde jedoch nicht bedeuten, dass das hellenistische Judentum den Jerusalemern eine Ausbreitungsideologie, die Möglichkeit uneschatologischer Predigt und die Lockerung der Bindungen an den Tempel vermittelt hätte. Wo Juden eine solche Haltung, die gesellschaftlich in Kosmopolitismus überging und theologisch zu einer theistischen Doktrin einschliesslich Morallehre führte, eingenommen haben sollten, wäre sie durch die Predigt der vertriebenen Hellenisten aus Jerusalem wieder rückgängig gemacht worden. Dass in den Heimruf zum Zion dann auch Nichtjuden, zunächst also: die Griechen unter den Völkern, einbezogen wurden, war selbstverständlich, zumal es, zwischen beiden vermittelnd, die "Gottesfürchtigen" gab. Eben dies aber geschah nun in Antiochien und, wohl ungefähr gleichzeitig, auch in Galiläa, wobei es im ersteren Falle wieder nicht wichtig ist, ob die Reihenfolge von den Juden zu den Völker faktisch eingehalten wurde (Act. 11. 28, eine Bruchstelle, scheint auf das Gegenteil zu weisen), oder ob Lukas es nach diesem Schema darstellt. Denn Alltagsläufe und grosse Theologie wirkten hier zusammen: man konnte es keinem Griechen verwehren, zuzuhören, und als äusserer Kreis der zum Zion Gerufenen wurden die Völker erwartet. Der Ruf galt ihnen mit derselben Dringlichkeit. Noch Paulus wusste sich davon getrieben.

Während dieser Vorgänge allerdings müssen ursprüngliche Glaubensinhalte, die untereinander wie mit der Eschatologie zusammenhingen, ihre Gestalt geändert haben. Nicht etwa hat das Ausbleiben der Parusie die Entwicklung einer nichteschatologischen Missionstheologie erzwungen, nach der dann gehandelt wurde. Vielmehr hat die normative Kraft des Faktischen aus dem eschatologischen Ruf zum zentralen Ort des Heils die Verbreitung einer Botschaft von dort nach draussen werden lassen. Wahrscheinlich erklärt sich so besser als durch jede andere Theorie die enorme soziale Kraft der Mission. Es wäre eine Bestätigung der Regel, dass Ziele, die sich erst im Verlauf eines Prozesses entwickeln, der dann auf sie zusteuert, nachhaltiger erreicht werden als solche, die geplant und beschlossen sind und wegen ihrer Konstruiertheit nie so voll realisiert werden können, wie es beabsichtigt war.

Die vertriebenen Hellenisten folgten also mit ihren Antritt zur Mission derselben eschatologischen Motivation wie die bleibenden Hellenisten und die Hebräer mit ihrem Festhalten am Tempel in Jerusalem. Für beide Gruppen stellt sich nun präziser als früher die Frage, wie man sie nennen soll, und was sie demgemäss "waren": die christliche

"Urgemeinde", von der ein Teil den Weg ins Römerreich und damit zur weltweiten Ausbreitung einleitete, während der andere im Orient im historischen Abseits versank; oder "Judenchristen" im unter II an dritter Stelle definierten Sinne; oder einfach Juden.

V

Die Fragestellung darf freilich nicht so angesetzt werden, als biete sie den Rahmen des Allgemeinen, innerhalb dessen die Verifikation am Gegenstand dann zum Besonderen führen würde. Das sähe so aus: Man fragt nach Christen und erhält die Spezifikation "Urchristen"; man fragt nach Juden und erhält als Antwort "eine Gruppe unter vielen, wegen des Initiationsrituals, der exegetischen Methode, der Tempelkritik, der Torah-Verschärfung, der Radikalität der Naherwartung" (die Nennung dieser Stichworte bedeutet keine Zustimmung zu allen damit verbundenen Thesen) "und manch anderem am ehesten mit den Qumranessenern vergleichbar"; man fragt nach Judenchristen und erhält als Spezifikation eine Definition im oben (II) an die dritte Stelle gesetzten Sinne (Additionswort, "sowohl Juden als auch Christen"). Bei solchen Fragestellungen würde das subjektiv-dezisionistische Moment der Begriffsbildung seine im Gegenstandsbereich liegenden Bestimmungsgründe überdecken. Vorweg entschieden werden darf nur, ob man im Interesse historischer Erkenntnis oder gegenwartsgerichteten Verstehens fragen will. Im ersten Fall kann man noch unterscheiden zwischen dem Gegenstand als einer in sich definiten Grösse und demselben als weiterreichenden Faktor in einer Geschichte oder Vorgeschichte von irgendetwas, im zweiten Fall zwischen der Hermeneutik gegenwärtiger historischer Grössen und gegenwärtiger Selbst- oder Existenzerhellung (welch letztere heute durch Aufstellung von Handlungsnormen ersetzt werden sollte, die auf historische Zusammenhänge verweisen).

Soweit es in diese herangebrachten Formalkategorien passt, aber nicht weiter, darf sich dann auch das inhaltliche Ausmass der dem Gegenstandsbereich zu entnehmenden Elemente erstrecken. Dann ergibt sich etwa: die Fragestellung nach dem Gegenstand als einer in sich definiten Grösse, also ohne Berücksichtigung etwaigen Weiterwirkens ergibt als Begriff für den unter IV untersuchten Fall eine Judenschaft, deren eine Gruppe dem Tempelkult ihrer Zeit distanziert gegenübersteht, aber gleichwohl das endzeitliche Heil auf dem Zion erwartet, während die andere gerade im Tempelkult die Repräsentation dieses Heiles sieht. Beide Gruppen sind durch eine Taufe zur Anhängerschaft des hingerichteten Juden Jesus zusammengeschlossen, doch scheint die Gruppe, die sich zum Tempel loyal verhielt, die "Hebräer", also sich solidarischer mit denjenigen — ungetauften — Juden gefühlt zu haben, denen sie durch Mose und den Tempel, als mit den "Hellenisten" und Stephanusleuten, denen sie durch Jesus verbunden wären. — Fragt man nach etwas, in dessen Vorgeschichte diese Gruppen eine Rolle gespielt haben könnten, so gibt es einmal das nicht mehr jüdische Christentum, das Paulus weiterführen wird; sofern der Bekehrung des Cornelius durch Petrus in Cäsarea am Meer (Act. 19, 1) vorgearbeitet worden ist, muss das von seiten der Stephanusleute geschehen sein (8, 40 Philippus in Cäsarea), aber diese selbst wären damit noch keine potentiellen "Heiden"-Christen. Es gibt zum andern die Ebioniten im Ostjordanland und ähnliche Gruppen in der syrisch-arabischen Steppe bis in die islamische Zeit hinein; sofern hier Kontinuität zu den getauften "Hebräern" und zu den "Hellenisten" besteht, die zu Beginn des jüdischen Krieges von Jerusalem nach Pella auswanderten, sowie zu den dreissig Jahre früher geflohenen Hellenisten, von denen einige aus Samaria und Galiläa hinzugekommen sein mögen, kann man alle (ehemaligen) Jerusalemer von heute aus als Judenchristen im dritten Sinne (siehe unter II: Additionswort, sowohl Juden als auch Christen) bezeichnen. — Das gegenwartsgerichtete, hermeneutisch angesetzte Verstehen hat als historische, evtl. bis in die Gegenwart reichende Gegenstände, auf welche zugleich Handlungsnormen verweisen können (nicht: durch welche Handlungsnormen begründet werden), weil sie erinnernswert sind und den Aufbau geschichtlicher Verläufe aus Handlungen demonstrieren, wohl die folgenden Grössen: aus dem Zusammenhang der Kontinuität ein Judentum, einerlei ob in Jerusalem oder in der Diaspora, welches auch für die Völkerwallfahrt zum Zion auf den Tempel verzichten kann, und ein solches, für welches der Tempel unverzichtbar ist; aus den Zusammenhängen mit Diskontinuität neuerdings ein nichtjüdisches fundamentalistisches US-Amerikanisches Christentum, welches notfalls gewaltsam den Wiederaufbau des Tempels anstrebt, damit der Gang der apokalyptischen Ereignisse anheben kann, welche im Sieg der Guten über die Bösen bei Harmageddon gipfeln werden.

Es gibt kein "Judenchristentum" im dritten Sinne mehr, auf das heutige Handlungsnormen verweisen könnten. (Gäbe es dies noch, dann würde es zu dem — nicht mehr unter die hier gestellten Fragen fallenden — Judentum gehören, das nicht nur auf den Tempel, sondern auch auf den Zion verzichten kann.) Ob es ein Judenchristentum im zweiten Sinne gibt (Determinativkompositum), ist von Fall zu Fall Interpetationssache. Sicher gibt es, wie seit Beginn der Neuzeit überhaupt, ein Judenchristentum im ersten Sinne (Kasuskomposition). Die beiden letztgenannten Grössen sind andere als die, welche unter IV untersucht wurde, und deshalb wird nach Handlungsnormen, welche darauf verweisen könnten, hier nicht gefragt. Soviel aber dürfte sich ergeben: das Kompositum, das in allen germanischen Sprachen aus den Wörtern für "Juden" und "Christen" gebildet wird, trägt so gut wie garnichts zur Klarheit bei, die sich der jüdisch-christliche Dialog über die Dinge verschaffen will; mit seiner Tendenz zu falscher Harmonisierung und damit Verundeutlichung zwingt dies Kompositum auch dort zu Analysen, die mit seiner Beibehaltung umständlicher geraten als ohne. Man sollte sich deshalb überlegen, in der historischen Wissenschaft wie im Versöhnungsdialog auf das Wort "Judenchristentum" bis auf weiteres zu verzichten. Vielleicht lässt es sich irgendwann eineindeutig wiederverwenden, oder es fällt den Beteiligten eine Terminologie ein, die genau so genau ist wie eine Analyse, nur kürzer.

Literatur

Baur, Ferdinand Christian: "Die Christuspartei in der korinthischen Gemeinde, der Gegensatz des petrinischen und paulinischen Christentums in der Alten Kirche, der Apostel Petrus in Rom", in: *Tübinger Zeitschrift für Theologie* 1831, H.4, S.61-206 (ND: K. Scholder <Hsg.>, F.Chr.B.: Ausgewählte Werke in Einzelausgaben, Bd.1, Stuttgart-Bad Cannstatt 1963, S.1-146).

Bubner, Rüdiger: *Geschichtsprozesse und Handlungsnormen*, Frankfurt/M., 1984.

Carnap, Rudolf: *Introduction to Semantics and Formalization of Logic*, Berkeley (Los Angeles) 1959.

Carnap, Rudolf: *Foundations of Logic and Mathematics*, Chicago (1939), 1967 (deutsch von W. Hoering: *Grundlagen der Logik und Mathematik*, München 1973).

Colpe, Carsten: "Die Ausbildung des Heidenbegriffs von Israel zur Apologetik und das Zweideutigwerden des Christentums", in: R. Faber - R. Schlesier (Hsg.), *Die Restauration der Götter. Antike Religion und Neo-Paganismus*, Würzburg 1986, S.61-87.

Colpe, Carsten: "Die älteste judenchristliche Gemeinde", in: J. Becker (Hsg.), *Die Anfänge des Christentums*, Stuttgart 1986, S.59-79.

Colpe, Carsten: "Die Mhagrāyē — Hinweise auf ein arabisches Judenchristentum?", in *Internationale Kirchliche Zeitschrift* 4/1986 (Festgabe B.Spuler).
Conzelmann, Hans: *Die Apostelgeschichte*, Tübingen, 1963.
Daniélou, Jean: *Théologie du Judéo-Christianisme*, Paris 1958; engl. *The Theology of Jewish Christianity*, transl. by John Baker, London-Chicago 1964 (seit Ders.: *Gospel Message and Hellenistic Culture*, London-Philadelphia 1973 soll dieser Titel verstanden werden als "Judaeo-Christianity").
Festinger, Leon - H.W. Riecken - S. Schachter, *When Prophecy Fails. A Social and Psychological Study of a Modern Group That Predicted the Destruction of the World*, New York 1956.
Festinger, Leon: *Theorie der kognitiven Dissonanz*, Bern-Stuttgart-Wien 1978.
Gager, John G.: "The End of Time and the Rise of Community", in: Ders., *Kingdom and Community*, Englewood Cliffs/N.J., 1975, S. 19-49, 57-64.
Holl, Karl: "Der Kirchenbegriff des Paulus in seinem Verhältnis zu dem der Urgemeinde", *Sitzungsberichte der Berliner Akademie der Wissenschaften* 1921, S.920-947 (ND: Ders.: *Gesammelte Aufsätze zur Kirchengeschichte* Bd.2, Tübingen 1928, S.44-67; K.H. Rengstorf <Hsg.>, *Das Paulusbild in der neueren deutschen Forschung*, Darmstadt 1964, S. 144-178).
Klausner, Joseph: *Von Jesus zu Paulus*, aus dem Hebr. übers. von Fr. Theiberger, Jerusalem 1950 (ND Konigstein/Ts. 1980).
Lüdemann, Gerd: "The Successors of Pre-70 Jerusalem Christianity: A Critical Evaluation of the Pella-Tradition", in: E.P. Sanders (Hsg.), *The Shaping of Christianity in the Second and Third Centuries* (= Jewish and Christian Self-Definition I), Philadelphia 1980, S.161-173.
Maier, Johann: *Die Tempelrolle vom Toten Meer*, Munchen 1978.
Morgan, Thomas: *The Moral Philosopher in a Dialogue between Philalethes a Christian Deist and Theophanes a Christian Jew*, 2. Aufl.London 1738; vol. II: *Being a Farther Vindication of Moral Truth and Reason* ..., by Philalethes, London 1739; vol-.III: *Superstition and Tyranny Inconsistent with Theocracy*, by Philalethes, London 1740. (Nachdruck Bd. 1-3 hsg. von G. Gawlick, Stuttgart-Bad Cannstatt 1969).
Pines, Shlomo: *The Jewish Christians of the Early Centuries of Christianity According to a New Source*, Jerusalem 1966.
—: *An Arabic Version of the Testimonium Flavianum and its Implications*, Jerusalem 1971.
Schiffman, Lawrence H.: "At the Crossroads: Tannaitic Perspectives on the Jewish-Christian Schism", in: E.P. Sanders - A.I. Baumgarten - A. Mendelson (Hsgg.), *Aspects of Judaism in the Graeco-Roman Period* (= Jewish and Christian Self-Definition II), Philadelphia 1981, S.115-156.
Schoeps, Hans Joachim: *Theologie und Geschichte des Judenchristentums*, Tübingen 1949.
Semler, Johann Salomo: *Abhandlung von freier Untersuchung des Canon*, 4 Bde, Halle 1771/76; Nachdruck Bd. 1, S.1-128 hsg. von H. Scheible, Gütersloh, 2.Aufl. 1980.
Strecker, Georg: *Das Judenchristentum in den Pseudoklementinen*, Berlin 1958.
Theissen, Gerd: "Die Tempelweissagung Jesu", in ders., *Studien zur Soziologie des Urchristentums*, Tübingen 1979, S.742-759.
Toland, John: *Nazarenus: or Jewish, Gentile and Mahometan Christianity*, London 1718; französisch: *Le Nazaréen, ou Le Christianisme des Juifs, des Gentils et des*

Mahometans, London 1777.
de Wette, Wilhelm Martin Leberecht: *Lehrbuch der historisch-kritischen Einleitung in die kanonischen Bücher des Neuen Testaments*, Berlin 1826; G. verm. u. verb. Aufl. von H. Messner and G. Lünemann, Berlin 1860.

AGNUS DEI

Jacques Duchesne-Guillemin, Liège

Τοῦτό μού ἐστιν τὸ σῶμα (1Cor. 11:24); Τοῦτό ἐστιν τὸ σῶμα μου (Matth. 26:27; Luke 22:19); Τοῦτο γάρ ἐστιν τὸ αἷμα μου (Matth. 26:28). These phrases, pronounced once at Passover in Jerusalem, may serve to vindicate the dogma of the Real Presence; grammatically, they are nominal sentences expressing equation of aubject and a predicate. The presence or absence of a copula is irrelevant. In the Russian version we find *eto jest' telo moe, eto jest' krov' moja*. This is archaic, for in modern usage the copula is absent, and replaced in writing by a dash.

Such equations, with no copula, are the daily bread in the Vedic commentaries. For example, the *Bṛhadāraṇyaka* begins thus: *Uṣā vā aśvasya medhyasya śiraḥ, sūryaś cakṣuḥ, vātaḥ prāṇaḥ, ...saṃvatsaram ātmā* "Truely, dawn is the head of the sacrificial horse, the sun the eye, the wind the breath, ...the year its essence". Already in the *Śatapathabrāhmaṇa* Prajāpati is identified with the sacrifice and with the year, and in the *Atharvaveda* "the abstractions Kāla, 'time', and Rohita, 'the ruddy one', probably the sun as the more concrete expression of time, are identified with Prajāpati" (A.B. Keith, *The Religion and Philosophy of the Vedas and Upanishads*, 1925, p. 444). The Brāhamaṇa literature may almost be said to consist of a vast system of such equations; it has even been possible plausibly to etymologize the word *upaniṣad* as the act of bringing together, in sets of correspondences, notions pertaining to the ritual, to the physical reality and to the divine world.

In Chinese speculation, according to the *Hong-fan* (Great Rule) of the *Chou-king* (Book of Annals), "les cinq éléments fournissent, correspondant aux quatre points cardinaux plus le centre, une ordonnance dans l'espace. Le Bois est l'est et le printemps; le Feu, le sud et l'été, etc." (Guillaume Dunstheimer, "La Chine depuis les Han", in *Histoire des Religions*, Pléiade, III, 1976, p. 391).

In Muslim mysticism, Jelāl-eddīn-e Rūmī uses nominal sentences with the copula to identify Allāh with a cypress: *To sarv-ī ravān-ī* (Rubai 1988). In J.-Chr. Bürgel's fine translation: "Ach, du bist ein Zypressenbaum"; or, the world-soul with a sea and himself with a single drop: *To daryāy-ī va man yak qatre, ay jān* (Ghazal 684). In a more profane sense, such identifications abound in poetry:

Mon âme est un paysage choisi
Où vont chantant masques et bergamasques (P. Verlaine)

The identification may even be expressed by a mere jusxtaposition. Thus in Yasna 9:26: *frā tē mazdå barāt pauruuanīm aiβiiåŋhanem stehrpaēpsaŋhem mainiiu.tāštem vaŋuhīm daēnąm māzdaiiasnīm* "To Thee brought Mazdā the ...[1] girdle, adorned with stars, wrought by spirits, the good Mazdaean Religion". The sacred girdle, be it identified or not with the Milky Way, is equated with the Good Religion.

Finally, as I have recalled in *Acta Orientalia* 30, 1966, p. 47, in connexion with my explanation of the Pahlavi and Persian word *gosfand* "sheep", literally "sacred ox", the sacrificial ox among the Nuer is replaced by a cucumber, which they, for the circumstance, call an ox. More generally in Black Africa, identification may express ritual substitution. According to Dominique Zahan, "Religion de l'Afrique noire," in *Histoire des Religions*, Pléiade, III, 1976, p.601: "On arrive ainsi, on passant par la chèvre et le poulet, à remplacer un boeuf par un pincée de cendres prises dans le foyer domestique. Mais, dans la pensée des officiants, les cendres 'sont' le boeuf".

Similarly, in Paul, Matthew, and Luke, quoted above, the bread and the wine *are* the body and the blood of Jesus, who himself is the Paschal Lamb.

---

[1] I leave aside, as obscure, the epithet *pauruuanīm*, despite the temptation to connect it with *paoiriiaēinī*, the name of the Pleiades (a connexion already surmised by Haug but declared unconvincing by Bartholomae, s.u.), implying, perhaps, the identification of the sacred girdle with the Milky Way. (On the name of the Pleiades, add to the references in Anton Scherer, *Gestirnnamen bei den indogermanischen Völkern*, 1953, . 142 sq., A. Van Windekens, *Le Muséon*, 61, 1948, pp. 103-106, who would emend our text into *pauruua-uuanīm*.)

PAUL'S JEWISH-CHRISTIAN OPPONENTS IN THE DIDACHE

David Flusser, Jerusalem

The aim of the present paper is not to clarify the various facets of enmity between so called "Jewish Christianity" and Paul. The real purpose of our study is to show that *Didache* 6:2-3, reflects the position of the majority in the Mother Church towards the Gentile Christian believers while Paul's attitude was more unusual and therefore revolutionary. Both positions represent two genuine interpretations of the necessary obligations of Gentile God-fearers. We believe that both factions based their claims upon the Apostolic Decree. Paul's view became victorious, but even so it is not without interest to learn what was the opposite view with the help of *Didache* 6:2-3, a position which was held, among others, by the apostle Peter. The text of *Didache* 6:2-3, it will be recalled, runs as follows: "If you can bear the whole yoke of the Lord (i.e. of the Law), you will be perfect; but if you cannot, do what you can. Concerning the food, bear what you will be able to bear. But be sure to refrain completely from meat which has been sanctified before idols, for it represents the worship of dead gods."

The Apostolic Decree is quoted three times in the Acts of the Apostles (15:20, 28-29 and 21:25). Already from the beginning of modern scholarship, the question was asked concerning the actual point of contact between the Apostolic Decree and the so called Noachic precepts in Judaism, because both contain a list of religious and moral obligations for non-Jews. The Noachic precepts were thus a Jewish non-Christian parallel to the Apostolic Decree, which was issued by a community of Jews believing in Jesus in order to lay upon the Gentile no greater burden than that which is necessary. The first step towards the solution of the problem was taken by the German scholar Adolf Resch already in 1905.[1] He rightly recognized the eminent value of the so called Western text of the Apostolic Decree. In contrast to the common text, where Gentiles are obliged to abstain from what has been sacrificed to idols, from blood, from what is strangled and from unchastity, in the Western text the prohibition to eat what is strangled is missing. Resch also succeeded in showing that for the most important of the Church Fathers only the three prohibitions — not including the one concerning that which is strangled — formed the text of the Apostolic Decree and that these three prohibitions were originally identical with the three capital sins in early patristic literature, namely idolatry, bloodshed and fornication. He also rightly argued that Paul in reality fulfilled the obligations of the original text and meaning of the Apostolic Decree.

It is not our task here to treat fully the problems of the text and the historical development of the Apostolic decision. This we have already done in another study.[2] Here we only have to mention the fact that the three capital sins, idolatry, bloodshed and fornication, are often mentioned in rabbinic literature and that, according to a decision from the beginning of the second century C.E., a Jew must choose death rather than let himself be coerced to transgress one of these three prohibitions. Some decades later, at the end of the second century C.E., perpetrators of these sins were excluded from the church and their penitence was not accepted. Here the main point which pertains to the present study is that idolatry, bloodshed and fornication are also three of the extant seven Noachic precepts. As has been demonstrated by Resch, the prohibition of the same three crimes formed the original content of the Apostolic Decree. The whole list of seven Jewish Noachic precepts is attested only from the mid-second century C.E. If so, it is more than probable that in the Apostolic Age the official Jewish position was to require the Nocachites, the God-fearing Gentiles, to abstain from idolatry,

[1] G. Resch, "Das Aposteldekret nach seiner ausserkanonischen Textgestalt Untersucht," *Texte und Intersuchungen*, NF, Bd. 3, Leipzig, 1905, pp. 1-179.

[2] David Flusser and Shmuel Safrai, "Das Aposteldekret und die Noachitischen Gebote," *Wer Tora vermehrt mehrt Leben: Festgabe für Heinz Kremers zum 60. Geburtstag*, Neukirchen, Vluyn, 1986, s. 173-192.

bloodshed and fornication. Hence quite naturally this same rule was accepted by the Apostolic Church. I hope to show here that even if the basic rule was then accepted by the church, new problems arose in the interpretation of the Apostolic Decree. The two divergent approaches concerning the application and interpretation of the famous decree are represented by the Petrine and Pauline parties. Moreover one discovers some strong indications that the same problem — albeit probably not in such an earnest and clear formulation — also existed among Jews in the politics pertaining to God-fearing Gentiles.

Does *Didache* 6:2-3 express a 'conservative' Jewish interpretation of the Noachic laws[3] or does the passage represent an analogous Christian position concerning the Apostolic Decree? I think that the function of our passage in the context of the *Didache* dispels all doubts about the Christian origin of *Didache* 6:2-3. The passage clearly reflects the Jewish-Christian understanding of the obligations of Gentile Christians towards Judaism, a position which was utterly unacceptable for Paul.

Almost as soon as the text of the *Didache*[4] was published in 1882 from a Greek manuscript, it was recognized that the first six chapters of the work are actually a Jewish treatise christianized by the author of the *Didache*; from chapter seven on, the book is of Christian provenance. It was only as a consequence of the discovery of the Dead Sea Scrolls that it was recognized that the Jewish treatise contained in the first six chapters of the *Didache* is indeed extant in an old Latin translation.[5] Its real title was *De doctrina Apostolorum*, but today it is commonly referred to as *The Two Ways*. This Jewish

---

[3] This is the opinion of A. Stuiber in his excellent study "Das ganze Joch des Herrn (*Didache* 6,2-3)", in *Studia Patristica*, vol. IV part II, *TUGAL*, Berlin, 1961, pp. 323-329.

[4] The most recent editions of the *Didache* are Klaus Wengst, *Didache (Apostellehre): Schriften des Urchristentums*, II, Darmstadt, 1984, pp. 3-100; Willy Rordorf et André Tuilier, La doctrine des Douze Apotres *(Didaché), SC*, 248, Paris, 1978. A pioneering book about the Jewish roots of the *Didache* was the treatise of Prof. Dr. G. Klein, *Der älteste christliche Katechismus und die jüdische Propaganda-Literatur*, Berlin, 1909.

[5] J.P. Audet, "Affinités littéraires et doctrinales du Manuel de Discipline," *Revue biblique*, 59, 1952, pp. 217-238.

tractate — and not the Christian *Didache* — was used by the author of the apocryphal Epistle of Barnabas of the first half of the second century C.E. All this can lead only to one conclusion: the Jewish treatise *The Two Ways*[6] was already considered to be a manual of Christian ethics in the first decades of Christianity and often it was even viewed as the teaching of the Apostles. Whether the Didachist was aware of the original provenance of his source is not possible to determine with absolute precision. However it would seem that he was convinced that *The Two Ways* was a Christian work, and even one of "apostolic" authority because he did not permit himself to change the wording of his source very much. It is reasonable to believe that the *Didache* was written before the end of the first century C.E. *The Two Ways* was written earlier; there are indications that this Jewish treatise was known to Philo of Alexandria.[7]

The Jewish tractate ended originally with an admonition. Although the Didachist (6:1) abbreviated it, the text is more complete in the Latin version of the Jewish source (*Doctrina* 6:1-6). Nonetheless it is difficult to reconstruct the precise original wording of the admonition.[8] Even so, it is evident that the Latin translation of the ending reflects the original content of the conclusion of *The Two Ways*: "Beware lest anyone cause you to abandon this teaching, otherwise you will be taught apart from the (true) instruction. If you do these things daily with deliberation,[9] you will be near to the living God. But if you fail to do them, you will be far from the truth. Store up all these things in your soul and you will not be beguiled from your hope."

This concluding admonition fits admirably well the ethical imperative and the dualistic vein of the Jewish *Two Ways*, and is an appropriate conclusion of the work. Neither in the Latin *Doctrina* nor in the paraphrastic Epistle of Barnabas was any other new precept added. Here the *Didache* differs. After the abbreviated form of

---

[6] About the treatise *The Two Ways* see also my study, "The Two Ways," in: D. Flusser, *Jewish Sources in Early Christianity*, Tel Aviv: Sifriat Poalim, 1979, pp. 235-252 (in Hebrew).

[7] See the preceding note.

[8] The last sentence of the Latin *Doctrina* (6:6) is surely ahristian medieval addition. It seems to me that *Doctrina* (6:5b) is a later addition too.

[9] Was this written under the influence of the famous versen Joshua 1:8?

the original conclusion and before the Christian "Manual of Discipline" that follows, in *Didache* 6:2-3 an addition to *The Two Ways* was inserted.

As has already been noted, the passage was absent from the original tractate of *The Two Ways*, but the appendix already existed in the copy of the treatise used by the Didachist. Theoretically the passage under question could have been a Jewish addition to the Jewish tractate,[10] but this is highly improbable. We hope to show further that, although *Didache* 6:2-3 was not composed by the Didachist, it was a Christian work, written by a man whose Christian *Weltanschauung* differed from the approach of the Didachist. On the other hand, the addition differs also from the preceding Jewish text. While *The Two Ways* is an inner-Jewish ethical treatise, only *Didache* 6:2-3 is addressed to Gentile believers.

Though *The Two Ways* is of Jewish origin, it was regarded as apostolic instruction not only by the Didachist,[11] but also by the *Doctrina Apostolorum*. If the apostolic ascription appears from the text's very beginnings in all the witnesses without any exceptions, it follows that from the first decades of Christianity, *The Two Ways* was considered a product of the Apostolic Mother Church. As such, the tractate began to be read also by Gentile believers in Christ, and thus it is no wonder that an appendix was added, reflecting the spirit of the majority of the Jewish Mother Church which sought to stipulate the obligations of Gentile Christian believers.

At this stage the tractate reached the Didachist. For him *Didache* 6:2-3 belonged to the *Vorlage* and was an authentic apostolic teaching that carried all the authority of his source. Did he notice that the passage was a child of a spirit different from his own? Even if he had some suspicions, the authority of his *Vorlage* dissipated them. One passage begins with the words: "If you can bear the whole yoke of the Lord, you will be perfect..." The "yoke of the Lord" means here the "yoke of the Law," but as we will see later, the term "the yoke

---

10 This is the opinion of A. Stuiber. See above note 3.

11 I even venture that the supposed Apostolic origin of the *Two Ways* was the main impulse for the Didachist to compose his own book. He believed that the treatise is an apostolic message to the Gentiles. The *Two Ways* became for him a starting point for his *Didache*. About the titles of the work see Rordorf and Tuilier, note 4 above, pp. 13-17.

of the Lord'' is also Jewish and has the same meaning. The Didachist could understand the expression as describing common Christian duties.

But did the Didachist fully understand the passage? Certainly he did not need it when he adopted it from his source. For some of us, the tendency of the whole passage is clear enough, but for many who do not possess historical imagination — or knowledge — it will be easy to miss the central point of *Didache* 6:2-3. At least after the rediscovery of the *Didache* not a few modern scholars were misled.[12] They believed that the passage taught a Christian ascetic attitude concerning both food and sexual life: those who completely renounce sex are perfect. In this field, as also in ascetic dietetics, the Christian believer has to try as far as possible to reach the ideal exigencies. If such a distorted exegesis could arise in modern scholarship, why was the Didachist obliged to understand his *Vorlage* better, even if its approach was more or less foreign to the Didachist, as it was surely foreign to such cognate contemporary Christian circles in which the three Pastoral Epistles were composed? The Didachist understood and accepted the general line of argument presented in the passage: try to reach the highest possible standard of Christian obligations! ''If you can bear the whole yoke of the Lord, you will be perfect; but if you cannot, do what you can!''[13] A kind of contrast *really* does exist between the original exigencies embedded in our passage and the later regulations of the Gentile Christian Churches to which the *Didache* was addressed. Nevertheless, this difference was not felt by the Didachist himself. So he could incorporate *Didache* 6:2-3 into his treatise and at the same time admonish the Churches not to let their fasts fall on the same day as the hypocrites, who fast on Monday and Thursday, ''Rather you should fast on Wednesday and Friday'' (*Didache* 8:1). He also instructs them, ''Nor should you pray as the hypocrites, but pray the Lord's prayer thrice daily'' (*Didache* 8:2-3). Nor does he refer to the Sabbath, but rather to the celebration of the Lord's Day, i.e. Sunday.

---

[12] See A. Stuiber above, note 3, pp. 325-326, and Wengst (above, note 4) pp. 95-96, notes 52-53.

[13] Naturally also he abhors the meat connected with idolatry.

In order to proceed further in our investigation, we must make a few remarks concerning some philological questions. Our passage speaks about the bearing of the whole yoke of the Lord (or of the Law). It is evident that this terminology alludes to the atmosphere of the so called Apostolic Decree. According to Acts 15:10 it was Peter who said in this connection: "Now therefore why do you make trial of God by putting a yoke upon the neck of the disciples which neither our fathers nor we have been able to bear?" And according to Acts 15:28 in the letter which announced the decisions of the Apostolic Church it was written: "For it has seemed good to the Holy Spirit and to us to lay upon you no greater burden than these necessary things," namely, the restrictions of the Apostolic Decree. And it was already recognized that a similar terminology appears also in the message to the church of Thyatira in Rev. 2:24-25. "I do not lay upon you any other burden; only hold fast what you have, until I come." According to *Didache* 6:2-3 those who are able to bear the whole yoke are perfect, but if anyone is not able to reach perfection, it does not matter: he shall bear what he is able to bear. This implies that those who are unable to fulfill all the commandments are somehow imperfect. I do not know any other good parallel for the use of the term 'perfect,' but perhaps the closest text is Math. 19:21. I will try to explain the strange attitude of our passage later.[14]

As we have seen, although it was recognized that the intended audience of *Didache* 6:2-3 was the believing Gentiles, the relevance of this unique text to this complex problem has not, as far as I know, been fully appreciated until now. The proposal contained in *Didache* 6:2-3 is one of the possible solutions to the question regarding the status of believing Gentiles, a problem which was then common to both Judaism and Christianity. The proposed solution is astonishing, but it makes good sense in the context of various trends within

---

14 It is an ironical paradox that the only parallel that contradicts the approach is the Pauline Romans 14:1-15:5. According to Paul, the weak in faith is a believer who is bound by religious and ritual restrictions. "I know and am persuaded in the Lord Jesus that nothing is unclean in itself; but it is unclean for anyone who thinks it unclean" (Romans 15:14). And Paul says (Romans 15:1); "We who are strong ought to bear with the failings of the weak and not to please ourselves." In both cases, in Romans and in *Didache* 6:2-3, the weak or the less perfect has to be fully respected.

Judaism and the early Christian Church. Although the situation was already known in its broad outlines, *Didache* 6:2-3 throws light upon it, and thus the passage becomes a substantial help for understanding both Judaism and primitive Christianity.

It is surely not our task to describe the strong attraction of the Jewish faith among the Gentiles. "The masses have long since shown a keen desire to adopt our religious observances and there is not one city, Greek or barbarian, not a single nation to which our custom of abstaining from work on the seventh day had not spread, and where the fasts and the lighting of lamps and many of our prohibitions in the matter of food are not observed" (Josephus, *Against Apion* 2:282-3; cf. ibid. 2, 123). Many Gentiles were fascinated not only by the theological spirituality and the ethical values of Judaism, but also by its 'ceremonial law'. We know from the sources that levels of observing the Jewish way of life as embraced by Gentiles varied from one person to another; it seems that the Gentile God-fearers were more and more eager to accept and follow further Jewish obligations as they proceeded in learning.[15] Since it was impossible in practice, and from the Jewish point of view even undesirable, for all the God-fearing Gentiles to become full proselytes, the Gentile 'Judaizers' had to decide, how great a burden they desired to assume. In their decisions they necessarily depended upon the advice and the instructions of their Jewish friends.

In this connection the story of the gradual progress of the royal family of Adiabene towards full proselytism (Josephus, *Ant.* 20: 17 ff.) is instructive, but at the same time clearly atypical. The obstacles to becoming full proselytes were far more restrictive for persons of a high social position such as sovereigns of a state than for other Gentiles who were not exposed to public censure. One should moreover not forget that the story is narrated by Josephus from the standpoint of his Gentile readers.

In the process of the full proselytization of the royal house of Adiabene at least two Jews were involved. The first was a certain Jewish merchant, named Ananias: "He taught them to worship God after the manner of the Jewish tradition" (*Ant.* 20:34), and it happened, moreover, that the Queen, Helena, "had likewise been

[15] See Juvenal, *Sat.* 14:96-106.1

instructed by another Jew and had been brought over to their laws'' (ibid 35). Finally Izates came to the conclusion, "that he would not be genuinely a Jew unless he was circumcised and therefore he was ready to act accordingly'' (ibid, 38). Then Ananias tried to dissuade the king from this last step. "The king could, he said, worship God even without being circumcised if he had fully decided to be a devoted adherent of Judaism, for it was this that counted more than circumcision'' (ibid 41). The final decision to complete the process of proselytism was caused by "another Jew, named Eleazar, who came from Galilee and who had the reputation of being extremely strict when it came to the ancestral laws'' (ibid. 43). The Greek wording that describes Eleazar's Jewish way of life shows that he was a Pharisee.[16] In Greek sources the technical term *akribeia* serves as a definition of Pharisaic piety: The Pharisees "are believed to interpret the laws with strictness'' *met' akribeias*, Josephus, *War* 2, 162). According to Acts 22:3 Paul was brought up in Jerusalem at the feet of Gamaliel the Pharisee (see Acts 5:34), "according to the strict manner of the law of our fathers'' (*kata akribeian tou patroou nomou*). And in Acts 26:5 Paul says that he has lived as a Pharisee, "according to the strictest (*akribestate*) party of our religion.''[17] But even if this Eleazar was a Pharisee, this does not mean that his approach represented the opinion of the majority within rabbinic Judaism.

In reality it should be well known already that in general, ancient Judaism neither wished nor required that all the Gentile God-fearers should become full proselytes. On the other hand, the Jews had no choice but to try and find, for the sake of the Gentiles, a formula which would establish the minimum of obligations indispensable for the Gentiles to be saved together with the Jews who were required to observe the whole Law. Today the obligations for the Gentiles are the so called seven Noachic precepts and we have shown elsewhere[18] that these seven obligations are the result of a long

---

[16] See Josephus, *Ant.* 20:43 about Eleazar: *panu peri ta partia dokon akribes einai*. See also note 21 below.

[17] From this small list follows that those who opposed the execution of James, Jesus' brother, were the Pharisees. Even if this designation does not appear explicitly in *Ant.* 20:201, they are described there as those who were thought "to be strict in connection of the laws'' (*peri ton nomon akribeis*).

[18] See above, note 2.

development. We also tried to show that in the earliest stage of development, these seven Noachic precepts originally consisted of only three commandments, the same ones as contained in the better reading of the Apostolic Decree.

Today the Jewish code strictly forbids a non-Jew to observe any Jewish commandment, no mattter how minor. A Gentile has to live only according to the Noachic prescriptions and nothing more is required, unless he decides to "become a Jew." Only after passing all the prescribed ceremonies of proselytism and becoming legally Jewish, does he have to observe the whole Law. What happened in later Judaism is a historical paradox: medieval Judaism finally reached a solution not dissimilar to that which Paul more or less endeavored to enforce in Gentile Christian communities, i.e. Gentiles were not permitted to observe the Jewish commandments, but if they became Jews, then they were obliged to observe the whole law of Moses. In both cases, a similar approach led to similar results. Both Paul and the medieval Rabbis wanted to separate the Jews from non-Jews and the most dangerous obstacle in the way of achieving this aim was when Gentiles began to fulfil, even partially, the Jewish law. Such a constellation makes a complete separation of Jews from Gentiles and *vice versa* quite impracticable. Thus Gentile 'Judaizers' became non desirable for both sides. The question is how far the medieval Jewish separatist solution was stimulated by the ecclesiastical politics of the Church which punished Judaizers and stirctly prohibited all proselytism. Gentile Judaizers and possible proselytes were then a menacing danger for the very existence of the Jewish communities. Thus we cannot completely exclude the possibility that the parallelism between the Church and the Synagogue in their wish to achieve complete mutual separatism also had a hidden, hideous dimension.

Before returning to *Didache* 6:2-3, we have to make the following remark, though with some hesitation. According to Acts 16:4 Paul and Silas, "as they went on their way through the cities, they delivered to them for observance the decisions which had been reached by the apostles and elders who were in Jerusalem," i.e. the Apostolic Decree. I do not see any serious cause which would force us to reject this 'harmonizing' information as non-historical, especially as we believe that the Apostolic Decree contained only the prohibitions against what was sacrificed to idols, bloodshed and unchastity. Another question is how deeply Paul was interested in imposing upon the churches the rule that the Jews believing in Jesus Christ should be forbidden to transgress the Law of Moses that they had been bound to fulfil before becoming Christians. I am aware of the present tendency of many outstanding Christian New Testament scholars to view Paul as a sincerely observant Jew who never doubted that it was the eternal will of God that all Jews, including naturally those saved by Christ, remain under the holy yoke of the Jewish Law. Personally I am not sure that Paul's mind was so simple and undialectical, but fortunately for me Paul's position about the Law is not the object of our present inquiry. In any case, in the extant epistles Paul never says in so many words that there is anything that can release a Jew from his observation of the Law and its works. On the other hand, we also never find an explicit statement by Paul to the contrary, namely that the belief in Christ for the Jew is incompatible with his life according to the ancestral laws. This became the official opinion of the Church only later, some hundred years after Paul's execution. What we read in 1 Corinthians 7:17-24 is: "Only let every one lead the life which the Lord has assigned to him, and in which God has called him. This is my rule in all the churches. Was any one at the time of his call already circumcised? Let him not seek to remove the marks of circumcision. Was anyone at the time of his call uncircumcised? Let him not seek circumcision... Every one should remain in the state in which he was called. Were you a slave when called? Never mind... So, brethren, in whatever state each was called, there let him remain with God." Happily enough it is not our task to decide how great is the theological weight of this passage. In any case, one is at least obliged to recognize from the passage that Paul accepted and delivered to the Churches the rule that Christians from Jewish stock should practise what they did before their call and also that the Gentiles should live as they did before becoming Christians. Thus we are apparently not wrong when we assume that Paul actually enacted the Apostolic Decree with its implications both for the Gentiles and for the Jews, and we have already seen that this was also the regulation of Judaism concerning the Gentile God-fearers.

The Apostolic Decree was evidently no more than a confirmation and reinforcement of the Noachic prescriptions as they were then commonly understood. But this did not unequivocally solve the whole 'Gentile question.' Are these prescriptions the minimum obligations of the Gentiles or are they indeed the maximum rules for the God-fearers, as Paul and later the medieval rabbinism decided? In a famous Jewish homily[19] from the second century C.E., we read that a Gentile who does the (Mosaic) Law[20] is considered to be in the same category as the Jewish High Priest himself. It is not written that God's ordinances and statutes are destined for the priests, Levites and Israelites; it is rather said: "You shall keep my statutes and my ordinances which the man (*adam*) shall do" (Lev. 18:5). In 2 Sam. 7:19, the Law is not given only for the priests, Levites and Israelites, but rather, "This is the Law for man (*adam*)." Moreover, the prophet Isaiah does not say that God's gates are open for the priests, Levites and Israelites, but he says: "Open the gates that the righteous nation (Hebrew: *goy*, the Gentile) which keeps faith may enter in" (Isaiah 26:2). So we see that even a Gentile who practices the (Mosaic) Law is considered to be like the High Priest.

The author of our homily believes that in principle, the Mosaic Law is destined to be observed by all mankind. Therefore he considers a Gentile who 'does the Law' as having great merit, and it is undoubtedly not a proselyte who is meant. Thus there is no doubt that the circles to which the tradent belonged saw in the Noachic

---

[19] *Sifra* to Leviticus 18:5 (*Ahare Moth*, Chapter 13, Codex Assem ani ed. by L. Finkelstein, New York 1936, pp. 373-4); the same text appears in *Midrash Hagadol* to Leviticus, ed. A. Steinsaltz, Jerusalem, p. 518. It is clear that the tradent is Rabbi Jeremiah. W. Bacher, *Die Agada der Tannaiten*, vol. 2, Strassburg, 1890, p. 31 and note 2, where he cites other parallels, Baba Qama 38a, Sanh. 59a were the tradent is Rabbi Meir. This shows that the saying of a comparatively unknown sage, Rabbi Jeremiah (see the materials collected by Bacher) was cited in the name of Rabbi Meir.

[20] About the Jewish expression, "to do the Law" see S. Abramson, *Leshonenu*, Jerusalem, 1954, pp. 61-65. The expression occurs already in Ben Sira 19:20 and in I Macc. 2:67, 13:48, and in the DDS in 1QpHab 7:11; 8:1; 12:4-5 and 4 Qp Ps 2:15, 23 and cf. Dam. Doc. 16:8. For the expression "the works of the Law" in the DSS see E. Qimron and J. Strugnell, "An Unpublished Halachic Letter from Qumran" *Biblical Archaeology Today*, Israel Exploration Society, 1985, pp. 401 and 406, note 5. In the *Testaments of the Twelve Patriarchs* "the works of the Law" appear in T. Dan 6:9 and the expression "to do the Law" occurs in T. Gad 3:2 and T. Joseph 11:1. In the New Testament "to do the Law" occurs in Joh in 7:19, Rom. 2:12, 14, 25 and Gal. 5:3. The "works of the Law" are Pauline. As to the Rabbinic literature see also the preceding note and *Abot de-Rabbi Nathan*, ed. S. Schechter, p. 124, *Deut. Rabba, Zot Haberakha* 11 and the *Targum* to Isa. 1:27.

precepts no more than an indispensable prerequisite, a minimal obligation for the pious Gentiles. According to the spirit of the saying, a God-fearing Gentile is to be praised if he fulfils many commandments of the Mosaic Law. On the other hand, according to Paul and to later medieval Jewish legislation, a believing Gentile should not accept upon himself more obligations than the Noachic precepts. Did such a Jewish view exist already in Paul's day at least as a recommended suggestion? Until now I have not found any decisive Jewish text which would explicitly confirm this approach, but this position fits admirably well the divergent tendencies within Judaism of antiquity.

This 'dialectical' unity in Judaism is often inaccurately described as its universalism and particularism. It was an expression of the genuine Jewish universalistic tendency which regarded the Law as destined for all of mankind and thus came to hold the opinion that it is preferable for a pious Gentile to accept upon himself the Jewish obligations. It is superfluous to repeat here that Judaism was not and is not a missionary religion;[21] however, as it also has a universal message, Judaism in antiquity mostly welcomed proselytes, but logically this approach was not without some ambivalence. The open mindedness of the school of Hillel towards proselytes, and the reserve shown by the school of Shammai against them are well known.[22] No wonder that the prominent disciple of the school of Shamai, Rabbi Eleazar ben Hyrcanos thought that proselytes tended to possess a bad character.[23] Moreover, if sometimes one had to be careful even of full proselytes, how could one ever trust the God-fearing Gentiles? Rabbi Shimeon ben Yochai was pessimistic.[24] When Pharaoh decided to pursue the children of Israel, he "took six

---

21 The Pharisees in Mt. 23:15 seem to be an exception or the saying has to be understood in the vein of the story of the gradual conversion of the kings of Adiabene. We already assumed that Eleazar from Galilee was a Pharisee (see note 16 above). Jesus' saying possibly alludes to such Pharisees who "traverse sea and land" in order to convert the Gentile God-fearers to full proselytes.

22 See e.g. b. Shabbat 31a and W. Bacher, *Die Agada der Tannaiten* vol. 1, Strassburg, 1903, p. 4 and pp. 8-9.

23 See *ibid.*, pp. 106-107, and about the original evil nature of proselytes, see also Tractate *Gerim* 4:2.

24 See the *Mechilta de-Rabbi Ishmael* to Ex. 14:7, ed. S. Horovitz and J.A. Rabin, Jerusalem, 1970, p. 87.

hundred chosen chariots'' (Ex. 14:7) but where did he get the beasts to pull the chariots? The beasts of the Egyptians and those of Pharaoh had already died during the ten plagues, and the cattle of the children of Israel remained with them (see Ex. 10:26). To whom did they belong? The cattle belonged to the God-fearing Gentiles among the servants of Pharaoh. Their cattle was spared, since they had heeded the warning of Moses. We learn this fact from another biblical verse: ''He who *feared the word of the Lord* among the servants of Pharaoh, made his slaves and his cattle flee into the houses'' (Ex. 9:20). So Pharaoh used these beasts which belonged to the God-fearers among his servants against the children of Israel. We thus learn that the God-fearing Gentiles constitute a snare for Israel.[25]

Rabbi Eleazar ben Hyrcanos thought that a proselyte did not cease to be attracted by his pagan past. In addition, Rabbi Shimeon ben Yochai believed the God-fearing Gentiles possessed an unstable and weak character and that they presented a danger for the Jewish people because one could not be sure that when Israel was persecuted they would not join their Gentile compatriots. The exaggerated suspicions of the two Jewish sages resulted from the basic ambivalent theological and psychological structure of Judaism which we have already mentioned. As to the God-fearing Gentiles, it is easy to imagine that besides those who welcomed their zeal for Jewish commandments, there were also many Jews in whose hearts the multitude of ''half-Jews'' evoked an uneasy feeling. Do these Gentiles observe parts of the Mosaic Law because they understand the Jewish call, or perhaps they perform Jewish customs as an act of superstition? Where is the line separating proselytes from God-fearing Gentiles? All who have experienced modern parallels to these ancient Gentile ''Judaizers'' will surely understand the ambivalent feelings concerning practising Gentiles: on the one hand, the high appreciation of a Gentile who ''does the Law''[26] — and on the other, the negative attitude of Rabbi Shimeon ben Yochai against the God-fearing Gentiles.[27] In such a state of affairs, it is plausible to imagine

[25] The translation of the last sentence is according to the text in the edition of Horovitz and Rabin.

[26] See above, note 19.

[27] See above, note 24. Rabbi Jeremiah and Rabbi Shimeon ben Yochai were contemporaries (second half of the second century C.E.).

that already in antiquity there existed among the Jews a tendency to recommend that Gentiles restrict themselves in their observance only to those prescriptions which are indispensable, namely the Noachic precepts. It is not too far-fetched even to suppose that Paul's warning to the Gentiles as reagards the observance of the Law was not merely a consequence of his conversion. It is possible that the point of departure for this component of his theology lies in Paul's "Pharisaic" past. But as we have already stated, the restriction calling on the Gentiles not to observe more than the Noachic precepts is not explicitly attested in ancient Jewish sources. Nevertheless, the view that the believing and already practising Gentiles should be permitted to perform specifically Jewish commandments is also unattested in ancient Judaism.

Shall we therefore accept the view that *Didache* 6:2-3 is a purely Jewish passage in which an anonymous Jewish maximalist appeals to the God-fearing Gentiles to observe the Mosaic Law as far as they can? This seems to me to be almost impossible. Already at first glance one has the impression that, if the passage is purely Jewish, its content is a very clumsy proposal. However, if the passage is Christian, then it is a directive addressed to the Gentile Christians and inspired by the position of the right wing of the Mother Church and in that case, *Didache* 6:2-3 makes good sense. There are two reasons why the passage is Christian and not purely Jewish. The first is decisive, namely the setting of the passage in the midst of the development of the *Didache* from the Jewish *Two Ways* towards our actual *Didache*. The second reason why *Didache* 6:2-3 has to be considered as a Christian work is that although the question of the Believing Gentiles was also a Jewish problem, it really became an urgent matter in the primitive Church, whose future and very nature depended upon the manner in which this decisive issue would be resolved.

Let us first requote the passage itself. "If you can bear the whole yoke of the Lord (i.e. of the Law),[28] you will be perfect; but if you

---

[28] The whole yoke of the Lord was probably original. In the tractate *Gerim* 1:2 there is a *varia lectio*: "if he (the future proselyte) says, 'I am not worthy to place my neck under the yoke of Him Who spoke and the world came into being, blessed by He' they receive him forthwith, and if not, he is dismissed and goes his way." See *The Minor Tractates of the Talmud*, A. Cohen, The Soncino Press, London, 1971, vol. 2, p. 603, note 5. The passage quoted above is also pertinent to Acts

cannot, do what you can. Concerning the food, bear what you will be able to bear. But be sure to refrain completely from meat which has been sanctified before idols, for it represents the worship of dead gods.'' The views expressed in the passage are indeed possible within the framework of ancient Judaism, but it is extremely difficult to imagine that a Jew, or a Jewish authority of the period, would address God-fearing Gentiles and beg them to be perfect and to observe the whole Jewish Law, or at least to observe as much as they can and recommend that their food should be as kosher as possible. I admit that the passage remains somehow grotesque even if it is Christian, but as a Christian composition it becomes far less strange and incredible. Both Jews and Christians are sure that Gentiles will be saved under certain conditions, but as soon as Gentiles accepted the faith in Jesus Christ, the question of their unity with the Christian Jews in one Church was no more essentially identical with the original Jewish religious view about the pious Gentiles. Christians believe that the Messiah has already come and that his expiatory death saves all who believe in him and in this central point there is no difference between Jews believing in Christ and Gentiles. Moreover Christ unites the Jews who believe in him with Christian Gentiles and removes the Christian Jews from the rest of Jewry.

It is necessary to state these truisms in order to understand that a fast and unequivocal solution of the problem of the Christian Gentiles for the Church became from its very beginnings unavoidable. There were two possible kinds of solutions for the Gentile problem in the Church, and both were proposed. The points of departure were naturally the Noachic precepts, for which the Gentiles are held responsible. The first solution was obvious. In order to strenghten the ties of Gentile Christianity with the Jews believing in Christ who were ''all zealous of the Law'' (Acts 21:20), it was desirable for the Gentile Christian believers to observe all the Mosaic Law as far as they were able to do so. In this manner the difference between the Jewish believers and their Gentile brethren would be minimized. We have already seen that this solution was based upon Jewish patterns. The other solution was evidently dictated by the suspicion that if Gentile Christians ''did the Law'', the common bond with the non-

---

15:10, where the expression 'putting a yoke upon the neck' of Gentiles appears.

Christian Jews would be so great that there would be a danger that Gentile Christians would finally become Jewish (non-Christian) proselytes. Therefore Gentile Christians should not be required to observe the special Jewish prescriptions.[29] Although no explicit Jewish parallel from antiquity is available to authenticate this approach, this Pauline solution fits certain tendencies in Judaism. This has become evident, among other things, from the fact noted above, that Paul's position conforms to the later Jewish legislation concerning Gentiles.

Anyone reading Paul even once knows that he always warns Gentiles not to observe Jewish commandments. During the period, some God-fearing Gentiles evidently underwent circumcision without becoming full proselytes, because they thought that circumcision was only one important component of the Jewish way of life. To those who would adhere to this approach Paul answered, "I testify again to every man who receives circumcision that he is bound to keep the whole law" (Gal. 5:3).[30] Here Paul repeats the current Jewish position. However one cannot be sure that at the time some of the Jewish doctors did not think that for the Gentiles, as for Jews, circumcision was only one of the obligations of the Law. Therefore circumcision would not bind the Gentiles to keep the whole Mosaic Law. If such a view ever existed, it expressed the position of those who thought that Gentile God-fearers were permitted and even encouraged to live at least partially in the same manner as Jews. Such a demand was probably adopted by the majority of the Jewish

---

29 For all the questions of the Law in the Church see the personal opinion of Justin Martyr, *Dialogue*, chapter 47. The whole chapter is very instructive. He says (97:21) that the 'good' observant Jewish Christians observe the portions of the law of Moses which may now be observed (cf. possibly expression in Rom. 14:1-7 and 1 Cor. 8:9). He opposes such Jewish Christians who compel Gentile Christians to live according to the Law of Moses (*ibid.* 47:3; the whole passage is evidently also influenced by Gal. 2:11-14). Naturally Justin denies the salvation of those who believed in Christ, began to observe the Mosaic Law and finally abandoned their belief in Christ (*ibid.* 47:4). The last category shows that there were really gentile Christians who "did the Law" and for whom the Christian faith was only an intermediary stage. This happened to the famous proselyte Aquila.

30 The whole passage of Gal. 5:1-6 shows that Paul does not merely repeat a current Jewish opinion but that Gal. 5:3 is also a part of Paul's Christological approach to the Law.

Mother Church, because it evidently seemed to its members that it was the easiest solution to the urgent problem of the Gentile Christians. If they observed the Jewish commandments as far as possible, the ties between the Jewish and Gentile members of the Church would be strengthened. Such 'Church-politics' did not contradict the so called Apostolic Decree, as it agreed with the Jewish viewpoint concerning the Noachic precepts.

Our considerations are based upon the general situation in the Apostolic Church. All its members accepted the authority of the Apostolic Decree but its application depended on two possible interpretations of the indispensable obligations of Gentile believers. The question was whether these obligations constituted a minimum or a maximum. Now we should understand Paul's vehement opposition to such Gentiles who wanted to take upon themselves a heavier Jewish burden. On the other hand, the approach of the faction to which Peter belonged no longer looks as absurd as it often used to do. They adhered to another interpretation of the Apostolic Decree, identical with the Jewish view that the "doing of the Law" by a Gentile is meritorious. Those who tried to persuade Gentile Christians to live more or less like the Jews wanted to reach a high goal, namely the creation of a single Church, composed of both Jews and Gentiles.

Now we can understand the incident which happened in Antioch (Gal. 2:11-14).[31] "For before a certain man[32] came from James, he (Peter) ate with the Gentiles; but when he came he drew back and separated himself, fearing the circumcision party... I said to Cephas (Peter) before them all, 'If you, though a Jew, live like a Gentile and not like a Jew, how can you compel the Gentiles to live like Jews?' " Paul did not blame Peter because he had never before, "eaten anything that is common or unclean" (Acts 10:14) but because he now makes concessions to the Gentiles and at the same time he compels them to live like Jews. We have tried to explain what it meant for Peter and the faction to which he belonged to "compel" the Gentiles

[31] The latest study about this incident is T. Holtz, "Der antiochenische Zwischenfall (Galater 2:11-14)." *New Testament Studies* vol. 32, 1986, pp. 321-343.

[32] "A certain man" and "he came" is the original wording. This can be deduced from Martini's edition.

to live according to the manner of the Jews. Peter and his faction tried to persuade the Gentile Christians not to become full proselytes but to do some "works of the law" (see Gal. 3:1-5). The argumentation of this faction of the Jewish Mother Church was approximately as follows: "If you (i.e. Gentile Christians) can bear the whole yoke of the Lord, you will be perfect; but if you cannot, do what you can. Concerning the food, bear what you will be able to bear. But be sure to refrain completely from meat which has been sanctified before idols for it represents the worship of dead gods" (*Didache* 6:2-3). Incidentally, one of the points that prove that the passage is indeed Christian is the reference to "what has been sacrificed to idols" which is mentioned in the Apostolic Decree (see also 1 Cor. chapter 8 and 10:25-29 and Rev. 2:14, 20).[33]

We are sure that *Didache* 6:2-3 is of Christian and not Jewish origin. It is a precious document from the first years of Christianity. The passage fits the meager and incomplete information about the tendencies and aims of the group in the Apostolic Church which Paul opposed, and thus it enlarges and supplements our knowledge about this trend which was once named the "Petrine" faction. I believe that with the help of our passage one can learn also something about Paul, since it casts light upon the tendencies against which Paul was constrained to fight. If, however, some doubts remain about the Christian origin of *Didache* 6:2-3, it is the position of this passage within the final arrangement of the *Didache* which unequivocally decides the question.

We should like at this stage to repeat the main points of this argument: (1) *Didache* 6:2-3 is addressed to Gentiles while the preceding tractate *The Two Ways* is an inner-Jewish ethical treatise. (2) *Didache* 6:2-3 did not belong to the Jewish treatise, as it can be seen i.a. from the old Latin translation of this Jewish source, where this addition is still absent. (3) Already in the first decades of Christianity *The Two Ways* was considered to be a product of the Apostolic Mother Church. The apostolic ascription of the Jewish source appears in all witnesses without exception. (4) Under such circumstances it is plausible that at the end of the treatise an appendix

[33] See also K. Wengst, op. c. above note 3, p. 96, note 53 and G. Resch, op. c. above, note 1. See also Justin Martyr, *Dialogue* 34:8-35:2.

was added which regulated the obligations of the Gentile believers in the spirit of the majority of the Apostolic Mother Church. (5) The tractate together with the addition reached the Didachist who also believed in the apostolic origin of his *Vorlage*. He interpolated his source and adjoined it, from chapter 7 on, to his own Christian "Manual of Discipline." (6) The Didachist was a Gentile Christian similar to the author(s) of the Pastoral Epistles and his pastoral work concerns Gentile Christian Churches. On the other hand, the author of *Didache* 6:2-3 is a Christian Jew. *Didache* 6:2-3 is a child of a different spirit from the following Christian "Manual of Discipline." But as the Didachist believed that both *The Two Ways* and the addition are a product of the Apostolic Church, he did not pay attention to the different tendencies represented in *Didache* 6:2-3. (7) The progressive development of the text of the *Didache* shows that *Didache* 6:2-3 was written in a period between the Jewish *Two Ways* and the Gentile Christian treatise of the Didachist. Also in this respect, *Didache* 6:2-3 is not a Jewish but a Christian composition.

We have come to the end of our journey, which has led us through the birth pangs which finally produced the "historical" Christian church. There is no doubt that the plan of Paul's opponents was well meant, but in reality it was impractical. How could such a Gentile Christian Church have survived in the long run when it contained a membership of Gentile Christians on various levels of Jewish perfection? Paul was capable of imposing his solution upon the Church. But even the best human decision is potentially dangerous and tends to lead to strange consequences if no strong will exists to avoid the impending evil. So Paul's reasonable arrangement succeeded more or less in keeping Gentile Christians from observing the Jewish way of life. Later on, however, not only were Gentiles who observed the smallest Jewish commandment cruelly punished, but also Jews who became Christians were forbidden by the Christian Church to to live according to the Law of Moses.

SELF-SACRIFICE IN VEDIC RITUAL

J. C. Heesterman, Leiden

i

The Vedic ritual texts abound in statements equating the sacrificer with the sacrificial victim and, generally, with substances offered in the fire. Thus, in a discussion exalting the daily milk offering (*agnihotra*) as the cosmic sacrifice, the sacrificer is said to be the *paśu*, the victim.[1] Likewise, he is equated to the baked grain or rice cake (*puroḍāśa*), the main offering in the vegetal sacrifice (*iṣṭi*) as well as an integral part of the animal and soma sacrifices.[2] Even the otherwise unremarkable ghee libation called *āghāra* that opens the series of preliminary offerings can be identified with the sacrificer.[3] Generally, when fasting in preparation for sacrifice, the sacrificer becomes himself the oblational substance.[4]

Self-sacrifice, then, is a commonplace notion in the ritualistic discussions of the Brāhmaṇa texts. The sacrificer's prototype is Prajāpati, the Lord of Creatures, who is both sacrificer and victim. Holding both ends together in his person, Prajāpati is himself the sacrifice, as the texts never tire of stating. Although stereotyped into a colourless cliché, the Prajāpati-sacrifice identification harks back to the celebrated Puruṣa hymn (Ṛgveda 10.90). By immolating the *puruṣa*, the primordial being, the gods break up the unchecked

---

1 Taittirīya-Brāhmaṇa 2.1.5.2; cf. ib. 2.2.8.2; Aitareya- Brāhmaṇa 2.11.5: "The sacrificer is by inner connection (*nidānena*) the animal victim (*paśu*).

2 Taittirīya-Brāhmaṇa 3.2.8.9; 3.3.8.7; Kauṣītaki-Brāhmaṇa 13.5; Jaiminīya-Brāhmaṇa 3.115 (W. Caland, *Auswahl*, nr. 184).

3 Maitrāyaṇī-Saṃhitā 1.4.12:61.5; Śatapatha-Brāhmaṇa 1.6.1.20.

4 Śatapatha-Brāhmaṇa 11.1.8.4; Maitrāyaṇī-Saṃhitā 3.4.7:53.18.

expansiveness of his vitality and turn it into the articulated order of life and universe. Life and order must be won out of their opposites, sacrificial death and destruction. Fittingly, this paradox is expressed in the enigmatically involute phrases that conclude the hymn: "With sacrifice the gods sacrificed sacrifice, these were the first ordinances".[5] The riddle is the more critical since the *puruṣa* is not just a mythic figure. The word simply means "man." The enigmatic phrase is the riddle of man's life and death.

Sacrifice, then, is not an act of worship, but the mystery of the cosmogonic act. Hence it is performed by the gods and, when man performs sacrifice, the sacrificer and his officiants are equated with gods.[6] The essential point is not who — god or man — performs the sacrifice, but the involute enigma of sacrifice sacrificed with sacrifice. The phrase implies that sacrificer and victim are amalgamated into a single identity, namely "sacrifice." Only then can one imagine sacrifice being sacrificed with sacrifice. In this way Prajāpati, being himself sacrifice, can at the same time be both sacrificer and victim. "One is the sacrifice, the sacrifice is Prajāpati."[7] On the other hand, a definite act, such as sacrifice — the prototypical act (*karman*) — requires a definite actor. In that case, a separate, external sacrificer is indispensable — a function that usually falls to a group, such as "the gods" or "the seers" (*ṛṣi*), so as to blur responsibility for the actual immolation. The perspective then shifts to Prajāpati, giving himself up to the gods' sacrificial act to share the fate of the *puruṣa* with whom he is identified.[8] "Prajāpati gave himself to the gods in the form of sacrifice."[9] The mystery of

---

5 Ṛgveda-Saṃhitā 10.90.6; also 1.164.50.

6 At the "election" of the officiants (*pravara*) these equations are made explicit, see W. Caland - V. Henry, *L'Agniṣṭoma, Description complète de la forme normale du sacrifice de soma dans le culte védique*, 2 vols., Paris 1906-7, pp. 5-6, 166, 186-188; Āpastamba-Śrautasūtra 10.1.13-14; 11.19.5-9.

7 Jaiminīya-Brāhmaṇa 2.70 (*Auswahl*, nr. 128). This phrase concludes the ritualistic myth of the sacrificial contest of Prajāpati and his antagonist, Death. Through the "vision" of the equivalences between his own and his antagonist's ritual, Prajāpati defeats Death and integrates his sacrifice into the one and only sacrifice that is Prajāpati himself. The passage can be seen as programmatic for the ritualists' "reform" of sacrifice (cf. J.C. Heesterman, *The Inner Conflict of Tradition*, Chicago 1985, pp. 32-34).

8 E.g. Śatapatha-Brāhmaṇa 6.1.1.9; 7.4.1.15.

the cosmogonic act of sacrifice, then, comes down to the unresolved tension between the monistic view of self-sacrifice and the dualistic view of sacrifice by a separate agency. The two perspectives do not exclude each other. They keep shifting, fusing and going apart again in each single context.[10] How does ritualist thought give effect to this double perspective in the sacrificial ritual?

ii

There are, to be sure, indications of self-sacrifice pure and simple. Thus, there is the curious *Dārṣadvata Ayana*, the course along the river Dṛṣadvatī.[11] After a year, during which the prospective sacrificer should guard the cows of his Brahmin master,[12] he installs his own domestic fire; after another year of domestic offerings, he should set up the fires for the "solemn" (*śrauta*) ritual and start out along the river Dṛṣadvatī, each day moving the place of sacrifice, till he reaches a place called Triplakṣa, the Three Fig Trees, near the Yamunā River. There he descends for the "final bath" (*avabhṛtha*) and "disappears from (the sight of) men."[13]

While the end of the Dṛṣadvatī course suggests sacrificial suicide by drowning, there are also indications of suicide by fire. The successive days of the *sattra* are equated with the participants' self-sacrifice through fire: setting fire to themselves, cooking themselves,

---

9 Pañcaviṃśa-Brāhmaṇa 7.2.1.

10 It is tempting to see the use of the medial forms of the verb *yaj* for the sacrifice — e.g. *yajamāna*, the technical term for "sacrificer" — as against the active forms used for the priests (specifically the *hotṛ*) as indicative of the ambivalent tension of self-sacrifice and sacrifice by another agent.

11 Pañcaviṃśa-Brāhmaṇa 25.13.1-4; Āpastamba-Śrautasūtra 23.13. 11-15.

12 Guarding the master's cows during transhumance seems to have been a typical duty of the *brahmacārin*, the Veda pupil, see e.g. the case of Satyakāma Jābāla, Chāndogya-Upaniṣad 4.4.5.

13 The sūtra authors are uncertain about the otherwise fairly obvious interpretation (which apparently they want to avoid). The "disappearance from (the sight of) man" is taken either as renouncing the world (*pravrajiṣyat*) or as separation from one's community in order to fare better (migration and settling elsewhere); cf. Lāṭyāyana-Śrautasūtra 10.19.11-15; Jaiminīya-Brāhmaṇa 2.300 speaks of "going to heaven."

cutting off the sacrificial portions and spending themselves as gifts (*dakṣiṇā*) with the aim of "speedily attaining heaven."[14] Although there obviously is no question of actual death by fire, the equation seems to be the reflection or reminiscence of sacrificial suicide by fire — a practice ruled out or superseded by Vedic ritual, but known to have been occasionally, though uncanonically, followed by Buddhist monks.[15] Moreover, the wish "speedily to attain heaven" strongly suggests, if not the reality, at least the notion of self-sacrifice. In a similar figurative vein the sacrificer of the *Agniṣṭut*, the Praise of the Fire, is said to enter the fire — a fire that is, of course, no more daunting than a liturgy entirely addressed to Agni.[16] In this case, the figurative entering into the fire is meant as a purification from blame or redemption from failure, in the way that gold is purified by fire,[17] the liturgical fire being then quenched by equally liturgical means. But the notion of entering the fire is nonetheless suggestive of a reality different from the one countenanced by the ritual. We do, however, find a sacrifice, not very different from the *Agniṣṭut*,[18] which is indeed explicitly meant to bring about the death of the sacrificer who wishes: "May I go to yonder world without suffering from any disease."[19] Although the sacrificer's death is to be brought about by a liturgical peculiarity in the execution of the chants, the position of the sacrificer lying down on the place of sacrifice between his fires with his head to the south and completely covered over strongly suggests the cremation ritual, which is, generally speaking, the sacrificer's last sacrifice.[20] Though this sacrifice, called *Sarvasvāra*, is not itself a cremation, the cremation is fittingly made part of this sacrifice. The ritualists do, however, realize that the ritual may well fail to fulfil the sacrificer's death wish. Interestingly,

---

14 Taittirīya-Saṃhitā 7.4.9. Cf. A. Hillebrandt, "Der freiwillige Feuertod in Indien und die Somaweihe," *Sitzungsber. der Königl. Bayerischen-Akademie der Wiss., Phil.-Hist. Klasse*, München 1917.

15 Cf. J. Filliozat, "La mort volontaire par le feu et la tradition bouddhique indienne," *Journal asiatique* 251 (1963), pp. 21-51.

16 Pañcaviṃśa-Brāhmaṇa 17.5.7.

17 *Ibid.* 17.6.4; Jaiminīya-Brāhmaṇa 2.136.

18 Like the second *agniṣṭut*, the chants of this soma sacrifice — the *Sarvasvārastoma* — are throughout nine-versed.

19 Pañcaviṃśa-Brāhmaṇa 17.12.1; Jaiminīya-Brāhmaṇa 2.167.

20 Pañcaviṃśa-Brāhmaṇa 17.12.5; Āpastamba-Śrautasūtra 22.7.25-26.

it is recommended that he should then seek death by starvation[21] — a practice known from the Jains.

Now these instances of sacrificial suicide by drowning, fire or starvation do indeed suggest that the notion of self-sacrifice may have had a base in reality, at least originally. They are, however, marginal, concerned as they are with self-immolation as an aim in itself. As such they can not tell us much about the essential ambivalence of sacrifice, which, as we saw, hinges on the interplay of self-sacrifice and sacrifice by an outside agent. At best they can be seen as indicative of a latent and, in fact, self-defeating possibility that would only be capable of realization in unusually critical situations. In any event the ritual of sacrifice is not meant to intensify crisis to a self-defeating climax, but, on the contrary, to defuse and normalize such situations.

iii

If we want to get nearer to the realities originally underlying the notion of self-sacrifice that pervades ritualist thought, we shall have to look elsewhere. It then appears that this notion comes out clearest where the texts are dealing not with sacrifice proper, but with the preliminary phases, especially the *dīkṣā*, the consecration of the sacrificer for the soma sacrifice. "He who consecrates himself, seizes himself (as the victim) for Agni and Soma."[22] The *dīkṣita*, the consecrated, as the texts agree, is himself the victim. As such he is no longer his own man, but, bound by the vow of sacrifice, he is in an unborn or death-like state. Therefore, as the same texts point out, one should not eat his food or accept his gifts. Doing so would mean to take over the impurity of death from the *dīkṣita* or, even more drastically, to "eat a man ('s corpse)."[23] The question is how the ritual should deal with this critical situation without having it run to its suicidal end. The easy answer is, of course, substitution. The

21 Lāṭyāyana-Śrautasūtra 8.8.40.

22 Maitrāyaṇī-Saṃhitā 3.7.8:87.12; similarly Kāṭhaka-Saṃhitā 24.7:97.13; Taittirīya-Saṃhitā 6.1.11.6; Śatapatha-Brāhmaṇa 3.3.4.21; Aitareya-Brāhmaṇa 2.3.9; Kauṣītaki-Brāhmaṇa 10.3.

23 Kāṭhaka-Saṃhitā 24.7:97.16.

sacrificer redeems himself, "buys himself free," by substituting another victim. In fact, sacrifice, in general, is a redemption, a buying free (*niṣkrayaṇa*) of oneself.[24] In the same way Prajāpati is said to have given himself up for sacrifice in the form of his likeness (*pratimā*), namely sacrifice. "The sacrifice is Prajāpati, for he emitted it as a likeness of himself."[25]

However, the matter is not so simple as it looks. How is the *dīkṣita* to find those willing to partake of his food and to accept his gifts as his guests at the sacrifice? For, as we saw, this would mean taking over the burden of the *dīkṣita*'s death-like state. The ritual texts[26] discuss the quandary at some length and it is in this context that the equation of the sacrificer with the victim is the most frequent. The point at issue is the sacrifice of a he-goat on the eve of the actual soma sacrifice. By means of this sacrifice the *dīkṣita* "buys himself free" from Agni and Soma so as to enable himself to act as a munificent host and patron at the soma feast that will take place on the next day. But here the problem comes to a head: should one or should one not take part in this sacrifice and partake of the sacrificial viands? In fact, there is no way round it. The ritual, like any show, must go on. As one text consistently argues, if one would refuse to take part in *this* sacrifice, *all* sacrifice would become impossible, for, as already mentioned, all sacrifice is after all a *niṣkrayaṇa*, a "buying free."[27]

iv

The ritualistic discussion on the *agnīṣomīya* he-goat brings out a significant point for our understanding of the original background. That point is the fundamental difference between the *dīkṣita* on the one hand, whose food and gifts are unacceptable and who therefore is not yet qualified to act as a sacrificer, and, on the other hand, the munificent host and sacrificer, presiding over the sacrificial feast.

---

24 Kauṣītaki-Brāhmaṇa 10.3.

25 Śatapatha-Brāhmaṇa 11.1.8.3.

26 See passages mentioned n. 22.

27 See n. 24.

The *śrauta* system of ritual has fused the two roles into the single person of the consecrated sacrificer. The ritual, therefore, is not and, as a matter of principle, can not be clear about the exact point where the transition from one role to the other is effected. Various solutions are given: the *vaisarjana* or "setting free" libations immediately preceding the sacrifice of the *agnīṣomīya* he-goat, the offering of the he-goat's omentum in the fire, the completion of the he-goat sacrifice, or even later, during the ensuing soma sacrifice proper, when the *dakṣiṇās*, the gifts, are distributed, or still later, at the final bath (*avabhṛtha*). Although the ritual system blurred the distinction, it still clearly shows the awareness that the state of *dīkṣā* had to be terminated at some point, to give way to the full status of a sacrificial patron.

Who, then, is the *dīkṣita*? What was the tangible reality of his death-like or embryonic status, what the background of the interdict imposed on him? To make a long story short, the *dīkṣita* was, originally, a consecrated warrior, directly descending from the notorious *vrātya* deprecated by the Vedic ritualists.[28] He is debarred from sacrifice simply because he lacks the goods that are to be spent in sacrifice. As an aggressive warrior vowed to death — either his own or his opponents, — he must obtain by force and wit the goods that will in the end — if he survives the hazards of the warrior's life — enable him to set himself up as a munificent patron and sacrificer. To that end he must, not unlike a knight errant in search of prizes and patronage, visit or force his way into the sacrificial festivals organized by a well-to-do settled magnate, to compete for the lavish prizes set out as *dakṣiṇās*. For being conventional, the competition was no less bloody. The place of sacrifice was a battle field, where one had to stake one's life. This is what is behind the recurrent motif of the "head of the sacrifice." Originally it was the severed head of the victim that kept haunting the ritualists' imagination, especially after they had proscribed immolation by beheading. More specifically, the "head of the sacrifice" refers to the warrior "fallen in battle," whose head is to be buried under the prestigious brick-built altar that only the ultimately successful soma sacrificing magnate can afford.[29]

---

28 Cf. J. C. Heesterman, "Vrātya and Sacrifice," *Indo-Iranian Journal* 6 (1962), pp. 1-37, esp. 11-15.

29 Cf. J. C. Heesterman, *Inner Conflict*, pp. 45-58 ("The Case of the Severed Head").

In this context mention should also be made of another offshoot of the *vrātya* phenomenon, namely the *sattra*, the so-called sacrificial soma pressing "session," lasting from twelve days to several years. Now the *vrātyas* are known to have operated as sworn bands under a *sthapati*. This feature is perpetuated by the *sattra*. Its participants form a single group, the *sattrins*, led by a *gṛhapati*, the "master of the house." In contrast to the normal soma sacrifice, with a single *dīkṣita* and sacrificer assisted by non-*dīkṣita* priests, the *sattrins*, in the classical system of ritual, are all both *dīkṣita* and priest.[30] For our purpose the interesting point is their destitute and rather desperate state.[31] They are said to be "pressed by hunger"[32] and so, having nothing to offer but their lives, they are *ātmadakṣiṇā*, offering themselves as *dakṣiṇā* gifts. This would seem to be the reason for their banding together as consecrated warriors, bent on booty. Thus we learn that "in a year when the *sattra* fails, people do not suffer from hunger, for (the *sattrins*) do not take away their strength and sustenance."[33] The *sattrins*' pious and peaceful activity of pressing, offering and drinking soma, turns out originally to have been a yearly raiding expedition, like those of the notorious *vrātyas*.

30 Cf. J. C. Heesterman, "Vrātya," p. 34. On the *sattra* see now also H. Falk, "Zum Ursprung der Sattra-Opfer," *Zs. der Deutschen Morgenl. Ges., Supplement VI* (Vorträge Orientalistentag Tübingen, 1983), Stuttgart 1985, pp. 275-81. Falk erroneously supposes that I changed my view of the origin of the *sattra* (and of the single sacrificer and śrauta-rituals as well) in the *vrātya* phenomenon ("Vrātya," *loc. cit.*) to a totally different one, namely that the *sattra* would have been devised to spare the Brahmins the embarrassment of having to accept the sacrificer's *dakṣiṇās* ("Brahmin, Ritual and Renouncer," *Wiener Zeitschrift für die Kunde des Morgenlandes* 8, 1964, p. 21). The second passage, however, does not in any way refer to the origin of the *sattra*. It merely mentions the *sattra* as an obvious example of a sacrifice without *dakṣiṇā* to illustrate the relatively late doctrine that the best sacrifice is the one that carries no *dakṣiṇās*.

31 Cf. H. Falk, *op. cit.*, p. 279.

32 Taittirīya-Saṃhitā 7.4.11.2.

33 *Ibid.* 7.5.9.1.

v

The interdict of the *dīkṣita* still bears the imprint of the *vrātya*, the consecrated desperado warrior, awesome as well as deprecated. Being vowed to death and having nothing to offer but himself, he was originally the archetypal victim who, in the sacrificial battle for the goods of life, was called upon literally to put his head on the line. By dint of force and wit he hoped to win through so that he might become himself a liberally spending sacrificer; but he knew that, as likely as not, he might fail and meet his death on the sacrificial battle field. Here, it would seem, we chance upon the reality behind the ritualist notion of self-sacrifice. It is the sacrifice of the consecrated warrior who has lost out in the contest for the goods of life and has to pay for it with his own life.

In this respect, the instances suggesting sacrificial suicide seem to be significant. Although the motivation of the *Sarvasvāra* soma sacrifice is said to be the wish for instant death on the place of sacrifice and not through any illness, the name of the initiator of this sacrifice, Śunaskarṇa, "Dog's ear," should make us pause. It is reminiscent of other such names containing the word "dog," notably that of Śunaḥśepa, "Dog's tail," the sacrificial victim who, by dint of verbal skill in reciting the verses "seen" by him, freed himself and won back his already forfeited life.[34] Of Śunaskarṇa we learn that, notwithstanding a blameless and pious life, he failed to attain success. It was this failure that made him seek death in sacrifice.[35] A similar motivation seems to be behind the *Agniṣṭut* soma sacrifices. The reasons given for performing this sacrifice have invariably to do with failure: the failure to remove ill repute — typically the ill-repute similar to that of Indra, the warrior god, for having slain Viśvarūpa;[36] the failure, though fully qualified by one's learning, to attain Brahmanic lustre; being devoid of cattle, though worthy of such wealth; or, significantly, having failed in sacrifice.[37] Although the *Agniṣṭuts* are meant to remedy these failures and impediments by

---

34 For the Śunaḥśepa story see Aitareya Brāhmaṇa 7.13-18; Śāṅkhāyana-Śrautasūtra 15.17.27.

35 Baudhāyana-Śrautasūtra 18.48:405.18ff.

36 Pañcaviṃśa-Brāhmaṇa 17.5.1-3.

purification and without having recourse to the ultimate remedy — the classical ritual being failsafe does not countenance any such lethal consequence — the notion of figuratively entering the fire is nonetheless highly suggestive. In this sense the case of the *sattrins*, whom we know to be "pressed by hunger," and who figuratively give themselves up to the sacrificial fire, speaks for itself. In the case of the *Dārṣadvata Ayana* there is no mention of any failure or defect. In fact, no special motivation is given, but one hardly imagines that the final step of "disappearing from (the sight of) men" at the concluding bath would be taken without pressing reasons. Even if this disappearance would mean no more than separation from one's community, this can not be taken as a sign of comfortable circumstances.

It would seem, then, that the notion of self-sacrifice does not refer to the substantial, fully qualified sacrificer, but to the poor aspirant warrior who must still qualify by putting his life at stake in the quest for the goods of life. In this way, by dividing the roles of victim and sacrificer over two parties, the essential ambivalence of sacrifice and self-sacrifice can be ritually enacted. Nevertheless, the ambivalence is not definitively resolved. It keeps making itself felt in another form. Even when losing his life, the warrior may still win fame, as was the case of the down-and-out Sthūra who, slain on the place of sacrifice, was miraculously seen by one of his *sattrin* followers to enter the heavenly world. His ultimate glory even reflected on his followers who are said to have previously been a despicable lot.[38] Conversely, winning through and obtaining ample *dakṣiṇās* is no guarantee for ultimate success, for with the *dakṣiṇās* one has to take over the impurity and ill-fortune of the donor. The substantial sacrificer and the consecrated warrior are tied together in an unending cycle in which the roles are constantly reversed, the *dīkṣita* becoming a sacrificer to redeem himself, and the sacrificer reverting again to the warrior's state to remake his fortune.

---

37 *Ibid.* 17.6.3; 7.1; 8.1; Jaiminīya-Brāhmaṇa 2.136-7 (*Auswahl* nr. 140).

38 JB.2.299 (*Auswah*, nr. 156); cf. J. C. Heesterman, *Inner Conflict*, p. 85f.

vi

Although the classical *śrauta* system has fused the opposite roles of *dīkṣita* and sacrificer, the course of the ritual still preserves the distinction as well as the ambivalence and reversibility of the two positions. We have noticed already that, at some point during the ritual, the transition from one state to the other is made. The fact that, as we saw, various points of transition are indicated seems to translate the intractable ambivalence. But its irresolvable nature comes out clearest in the complex of rites concerned with the solemn reception of "King Soma — in the form of the bundle containing the soma stalks that later on will be pressed to deliver the soma beverage — and the following animal sacrifice to Agni and Soma, the fire and the cultic beverage, who together form the base of sacrifice.

After the purchase of the soma stalk — in itself a curious rite preserving distinctly agonistic features[39] — the *dīkṣita* goes with the soma in a solemn procession to the sacrificer's place, where the amply fuelled sacrificial fire is already burning. The procession appears to be meant as a conquering progress. "With King Soma they go on conquering," and when "King Soma" arrives at the sacrificer's place he takes possession of it.[40] At this point the fusion of the *dīkṣita* and sacrificer temporarily breaks down. The consecrated warrior, arriving with his conquering king, confronts the sacrificer and master of the house. The critical nature of the confrontation is clearly marked by the ritual. The master of the house must wait upon the arriving conqueror. Incidentally, one school of ritual understandably tries to ease the awkwardness of the situation by having one of the priests stand in for the host.[41] The interesting point, however, is that the host awaits the arrival standing outside his abode, keeping a he-goat with him. This he-goat, which later is to be immolated for Agni and Soma, is expressly called *vārtraghna*, related to the slaying of the monster Vṛtra, who retained Agni and Soma within himself.[42] By slaying Vṛtra, the warrior god Indra

[39] J. C. Heesterman, "Somakuh und Danaergabe," *Zs. der Deutschen Morgenl. Ges. Supplement viii* (Vorträge Orientalistentag, Würzburg, 1985, forthcoming).

[40] Maitrāyaṇī-Saṃhitā 3.9.1:112.4-8.

[41] Śatapatha-Brāhmaṇa 3.3.4.21.

[42] Maitrāyaṇī-saṃhitā 3.7.8:37.17; Kāṭhaka-Saṃhitā 24.7:97.19; Taittirīya-

released the two basic forces of sacrifice.

The presence of the he-goat clearly shows the critical, even inimical, nature of the encounter between *dīkṣita* and sacrificer, the one arriving with the conquering "King Soma," the other in possession of the sacrificial fire. In fact, the *dīkṣita* embodies Soma (as the sacrificer is identical with his fire). When he receives the soma at the time of the purchase, he presses the bundle of stalks on his right thigh, saying: "Enter Indra's right thigh, willing into the willing, tender into the tender."[43] Identifying with the warrior god, Indra, the *dīkṣita* integrates the soma into himself. This shows that the *dīkṣita*, as we already saw, stands for the sacrificial victim, for, when the soma is later on pressed, it is simply and crudely said to be "killed." But this is not all. By integrating Soma into himself he becomes equal to the archetypal enemy, Vṛtra.[44] When we further realize that Soma being held within Vṛtra is identified with the monster that is to be slain,[45] the full ambivalence comes forcefully to the fore. For the *dīkṣita* who has integrated Soma is both Vṛtra and Indra who slays him. The ambivalence is worked out, not in terms of a direct self-sacrifice — the consecrated warrior immolating himself, which would end the matter once and for all and would leave the sacrificer nowhere — but by reversal of the positions. Thus Indra on the point of delivering the *coup de grâce* is implored by Vṛtra: "Do not hurl (thy weapon) at me; thou art now what I (was before),"[46] for Agni and Soma, the goods of life, are now with Indra. In this way, by turning round the positions, the circulation of the goods of life — from concentration to dispersal to renewed concentration — is kept in motion.

Saṃhitā 6.1.11.6.

43 Āpastamba Śrautasūtra 10.27.3.

44 The identification with Vṛtra is made explicit when the sacrificer is warned not to gasp for breath while fasting in preparation for the sacrifice: it was in that way that Agni and Soma escaped from Vṛtra (Taittirīya-Saṃhitā 2.5.2.4; Āpastamba-Śrautasūtra 4.3.12).

45 Same passages as n. 42.

46 Śatapatha-Brāhmaṇa 1.6.3.17.

vii

Let us now return to the actual ritual. How does it deal with the inextricable ambivalence and cyclical reversibility that comes to a head at the reception of "King Soma?" Since it has fused the two roles of consecrated warrior and host-sacrificer, it can only, as we saw, temporarily and somewhat awkwardly split the two by interposing the *vārtraghna* he-goat, which has, in fact, nothing to do with the occasion and is sacrificed only later, outside the context of the reception. Nothing is done with or to it. It is simply there to mark the confrontation.

The confrontation does, however, not result in mere spoliation of the sacrificer's house and people, but in a bond between "King Soma' and the people of the house. When "King Soma" has established his lordship over the house, its people become his *ápivrata*, his bondsmen,[47] the two parties being united by a common vow. Or, put differently, at the time of the confrontation "Agni (the fire in the sacrificer's abode) and Soma (the soma stalks brought by the *dīkṣita*) unite; both aim at the sacrificer or at his cattle; because the he-goat is kept there, they aim at it (and not at the sacrificer and his cattle)."[48] The *vārtraghna* animal, then, not only marks the risks of the encounter of the two parties, but at the same time deftly restores their ritualistically contrived fusion.

The bond between the two parties — originally a bond characterized by ambivalence, but redesigned as a monolithic unity by the ritualists who no longer recognize the duality[49] — lasts throughout the next phase, the procession with the now united Agni and Soma (that is: the fire and the soma stalks) to the place of sacrifice (the *mahāvedi*). This procession is again characterized as a conquering

47 Maitrāyaṇī-Saṃhitā 3.9.1:112.6. This may well reflect actual practice, insofar as subjected landholders are usually confirmed in their rights and so become tantamount to "co-sharers" in the realm of their new overlord.

48 Maitrāyaṇī-Saṃhitā 3.7.8:87.8; Kāṭhaka-Saṃhitā 24.7:97.12; Taittirīya-Saṃhitā 6.1.11.6; Śatapatha-Brāhmaṇa 3.3.4.21.

49 The original ambivalence is illustrated by Indra plundering his own people, the Maruts, with the permission of "King Soma — an operation said to be perfectly normal (Pañcaviṃśa-Brāhmaṇa 21.1.1; Jaiminīya-Brāhmaṇa 2.249, *Auswahl*, nr. 149).

expedition or, in simple terms, a razzia. The accompanying formulas are replete with unnamed enemies and unspecified booty.[50] Indeed the procession — or rather the raiding part — is now truly Vṛtra-like, since, like Vṛtra, it incorporates both Agni and Soma. The ambivalence we already noticed makes itself felt again. Here the *vārtraghna* animal victim finally comes into its own. When the party has arrived on the place of sacrifice, the fire has been installed on its hearth and the soma is deposited in its shed, the he-goat is sacrificed for Agni and Soma. We already noticed the problem connected with this sacrifice: the victim is the substitute for the *dīkṣita*, who buys himself free from Agni and Soma, and consequently its meat cannot be eaten by the participants in the sacrifice, on pain of taking over the *dīkṣita*'s death and impurity.

We are now in a position to view the problem in a wider perspective. The *dīkṣita*, having come into the hazardous possession of Agni and Soma,[51] is now Vṛtra. Like Indra, he is now what Vṛtra was before.[52] And so, like Vṛtra, he must be slain to set Agni and Soma free again. Hence the he-goat is called *vārtraghna*. Its immolation is the slaying of Vṛtra.

Once again, the familiar problem of self-sacrifice, this time in stark and awesome profile, confronts us. There is, however, one essential difference. The *dīkṣita* is no longer the down-and-out warrior who has only himself to offer. He has successfully managed to obtain, by force and wit, the goods of life. He is now in possession of Agni and Soma. This enables him to circumvent Vṛtra's fate. To that end he "exteriorizes" Agni and Soma. By churning the fire, which he has kept within himself during the preceding period (technically: during the *avāntara-dīkṣā*), and by depositing it on the sacrificial hearth, he puts a distance between himself and the fire. Equally he distances himself from Soma by depositing the bundle with the soma stalks in its shed, on the place of sacrifice. Or, as the relevant mantra has it, "There you, O Soma, have gone, a god towards the gods; here go I, a man towards men."[53] Ritually the "exteriorization" is

[50] See W. Caland-V. Henry, *L'Agniṣṭoma*, pp. 110-12.

[51] Or the other way around: being seized by Agni and Soma, as the texts usually put it.

[52] See above, n. 46.

[53] Āpastamba-Śrautasūtra 11.18.1; cf. Taittirīya-Saṃhitā 6.3.2.4.

marked by the *vaisarjana* ("release") libations, which at the same time terminate the bond between the conquering "King Soma" and his sworn bondsmen.

In this way the ritualists also solved the problem involved in the *agnīṣomīya* animal sacrifice, namely by having it preceded by the *vaisarjana*, the "release." The *agnīṣomīya* sacrifice still is a "Vṛtra-slaying" with all the connotations we have seen, as in fact all sacrifice is. However, the ritualists managed to resolve the ambivalence of sacrifice and self-sacrifice by dissociating the sacrificer from the substance of his sacrifice.

There is no need anymore for the sacrificer to offer himself up for sacrifice as the consecrated warrior must, nor for the participants "to eat a man('s corpse)." The sacrificer is now a substantial host and magnate, fully qualified to entertain his guests at the soma festival on the next day.

viii

What emerges from the ritual and from ritualist speculation is that self-sacrifice as such is invalid. At best, it is the destitute warrior's solution to failure. Sacrifice, on the other hand, cannot be valid by immolating just any victim that presents itself. The person, animal, or substance that is immolated must be that part of the sacrificer that defines him as such, namely the goods of life he has acquired by risking his own life. These goods — call them Agni and Soma — he has by right incorporated in himself. Hence the importance of the bond between the consecrated warrior and the sacrificer. Without this bond uniting the sacrificer and his victim, sacrifice would be as invalid as self-sacrifice is *per se*.

This, it would seem, is at the root of the essential ambivalence of sacrifice and self-sacrifice, which is worked out in the tangled relationship between the sacrificer and his victim. It does, however, mean that the world of sacrifice is permanently and, as a matter of principle, insecure and unstable. The world of the ancient consecrated warrior that made sacrifice its dynamic center was intrinsically doomed to break down.

The definitive break-down was, however, achieved by the ancient Indian ritualists. They replaced the uncertainty, ambivalence and reversibility of sacrifice with the certainty of the strict and unremitting order of ritual. The sacrificial contest for the goods of life has once for all been decided. There is no contest anymore, nor are there any contestants.[54] Therefore the consecrated warrior and the substantial sacrificer had to be fused into a single monolithic entity, the consecrated sacrificer. "The sacrifice is one, Prajāpati is the sacrifice."

[54] Cf. J. C. Heesterman, *Inner Conflict*, pp. 85f, 95ff.; *idem*, "The Ritualists' Problem," in S. D. Joshi (ed.), *Amṛtadhārā* (R. N. Dandekar Fel. Vol.), Poona, 1984, pp. 167-179.

TE'EZĀZA SANBAT: A BETA ISRAEL WORK RECONSIDERED

Steven Kaplan, Jerusalem

Introduction

Ethiopia, which stands at the crossroads between the Middle East and Black Africa, has long been the setting for religious contacts, conflicts, and cross fertilization.[1] During the first millennium B.C.E., northern Ethiopia was the home of a developed polytheistic cult, which shared many features with the religions found across the Red Sea, in South Arabia. By the first centuries of the common era, strong Hebraic-Biblical influences had taken root in the country. These were rapidly followed by Christianity, and when the Ethiopian King Ezana converted to Christianity, in the first half of the fourth century, Ethiopia became the third Christian nation in the world. Three centuries later a number of the prophet Muhammad's early followers sought refuge in Ethiopia. Although the country was spared the jihad which Islamized the rest of the region, from the Middle Ages on Islam gained increasing support among the population. In none of these instances did the religions which entered Ethiopia retain their original foreign character. Rather, they were adopted and adapted, and emerged in a distinctively Ethiopian form. Thus, we find in Ethiopia a uniquely Biblical national church, a peculiarly non-Talmudic branch of Judaism, and a form of Islam

[1] On these external influences on the religious history of Ethiopia see for example C. Conti Rossini, *Storia d'Etiopia*, Istituto Italiano d'Artigrafiche: Bergamo, 1928; E. Ullendorff, *Ethiopia and the Bible*, Oxford University Press: London, 1968; J.S. Trimingham, *Islam in Ethiopia*, Oxford University Press: London, 1952.

which, at points, deviates considerably from the norm espoused in the great Muslim centers of the Red Sea region.

Historically, Orthodox Christianity has been the dominant religion in the Ethiopian highlands for over 1600 years. Moreover, the Ethiopian Christians were almost unique in their ability to compose written accounts of their country's history.[2] As a result, much of Ethiopian religious history, as it has come down to us, focuses upon either internal Church controversies or the interactions between Christians and non-Christians.[3]

Perhaps the most complex and interesting of all the inter-religious interactions which took place on the Ethiopian plateau are those which developed between the local Christians and the Beta Israel (''Falasha''). The purpose of this paper is to deepen our understanding of this interaction through the examination and comparison of several works of Christian and Beta Israel literature. However, before we turn our attention to this specific topic, it is necessary, by way of introduction, to offer a few brief comments regarding the major features of Beta Israel history.[4]

Anyone with even a superficial familiarity with the literature about the Beta Israel will have noticed that the question of ''Falasha origins'' has tended to dominate the debate. In the absence of hard data, theories have abounded.[5] Yet, despite their general lack of consensus, virtually all authorities would seem to agree that Jews or Jewish elements reached Ethiopia prior to the advent of Christianity in the fourth century. Our sources offer little information as to how the Judaized portion of the Ethiopian population reacted to

---

[2] Cerulli, *Storia della letteratura etiopica*, Nuova Accademia Editrice: Milano 1962, 1968, 2nd ed.

[3] Cf. Taddesse Tamrat, *Church and State in Ethiopia 1270-1527*, Clarendon Press: Oxford, 1972; S. Kaplan, *The Monastic Holy Man and the Christianization of Early Solomonic Ethiopia*, Franz Steiner: Wiesbaden, 1984.

[4] For a more detailed version of Beta Israel history to 1900 see my ''The Beta Israel: An Historical Introduction,'' in M. Corinaldi, *The Personal Legal Status of Ethiopian Jews* (forthcoming).

[5] A. Z. Aešcoly, *Sefer HaFalashim*, Reuben Mass.: Jerusalem, 1972, pp. 3-8. R. Hess, ''Toward a History of the Falasha,'' in *Eastern African History, Boston University Papers on Africa* III, ed. D. McCall, Praeger: Boston, 1969, pp. 107-132. S. Kaplan, ''The Origins of the Beta Israel: Five Methodological Cautions.'' (Hebrew) *Pe'amim* (1987) (forthcoming).

Christianity's success, and it is only a thousand years later, in the early fourteenth century, that we begin to receive reliable information concerning the "Jews" of Ethiopia. Although the reports in our possession tend to emphasize the series of battles which took place between the Beta Israel and the Christian kings, several texts also offer evidence of Jewish-Christian cooperation.[6]

Events which are attributed to the reign of the Christian emperor Yeshaq (1413-1430) appear to have been crucial in determining the later development of Beta Israel society and religion.[7] Yeshaq was the first emperor to wage war personally against the Beta Israel. Exploiting divisions within the local leadership, he was able to inflict the first in a series of devastating defeats upon the "Falasha." At the same time, and probably in response to the deteriorating military-political situation, Beta Israel society underwent an irrevocable transformation. Under the influence of Christian monks, the Christian institution of monasticism was adopted, radically altering the community's existing religious system. The same monks are also credited with the introduction of new laws of purity, literature, and liturgical forms. Indeed it is difficult to determine what elements of Beta Israel religious culture, as it appeared in the nineteenth centruy, pre-date the monastic revolution of the fifteenth century. While we may demur from the view put forward by some scholars, namely that the Beta Israel, as a people, only came into being in the Middle Ages, we must also admit that it is difficult to identify many elements in their culture which clearly preceded this period.[8]

During the two hundred years following Yeshaq's reign, the condition of the Beta Israel continued to deteriorate until during the

---

6 Cf. S. Kaplan, "On the Ethiopian Judeo-Christian Context of the History of the Beta *Pe'amim* XXII (1985), pp. 22-25 (Hebrew). Reprinted in English: *Israel Social Science Research* III (1985), pp. 9-20.

7 J. A. Quirin, "The Beta Israel (Felasha) in Ethiopian History: Caste Formation and Culture Change 1270-1868," Ph.D. Dissertation, University of Michigan 1977, pp. 54-63.

8 G. J. Abbink, *The Falasha in Ethiopia and Israel: The Problem of Ethnic Assimilation*, Nijmegen: Institute for Cultural and Social Anthropology, Social Anthropologische Cahiers XV, 1984, pp. 18-29; V. Krempel, *Die soziale und wirtschaftliche Stellung der Falascha in der christlichamharischen Gesellschaft Nordwest Äthiopiens*, Berlin: Freie Universitat, 1972, p. 9.

reign of Susenyos (1607-1632), they finally lost their independence. Although their skills as soldiers, blacksmiths and artisans enabled them to enjoy a degree of economic security during the Gondarine period (1632-1769), the chaos and disorder which characterized the "Era of the Judges" (1769-1855) hit the Beta Israel harder than most groups, and their social and economic status sank to a new low.[9] Thus, the Beta Israel encountered by European travelers such as James Bruce and Antoine d'Abbadie were neither the autonomous warriors of the Middle Ages nor the skilled artisans of Gondar, but rather a small declining "caste" group. Moreover, from the middle of the nineteenth century onward, a new challenge in the form of European Protestant missionaries faced the Beta Israel.

Joseph Halévy, who reached Ethiopia in 1867, was the first practicing European Jew to visit the Beta Israel. Although he had little success in convincing world Jewry to come to the community's assistance, his student Jacob Faitlovitch, who first visited Ethiopia in 1904, became a fervid campaigner on behalf of Ethiopian Jewry. He sought not only to bring them material aid and comfort, but also to close the gap between their belief and practice and that of normative Judaism. It is ironic to note, in light of Faitlovitch's steadfast opposition to the missionaries, that the demands he made of the Beta Israel were essentially the same as the missionaries': abandon sacrifice, monasticism, and laws of ritual purity and accept a religion which represents the true fulfillment of the teachings of the Old Testament. While many Beta Israel accepted Christianity as taught by Western missionaries and their disciples, about 30,000 remained within the borders of the traditional community. The religious culture of the latter group did not, however, remain unchanged, and, over the years, elements from "normative" modern Judaism were increasingly incorporated.[10] Although the schools opened by Faitlovitch were

---

[9] Quirin, pp. 95-254.

[10] Despite the plethora of books and articles on the Beta Israel, no adequate study of their modern history has yet been written. Abbink, pp. 72-102 contains some useful information, as does S. D. Messing, *The Story of the Falashas: Black Jews of Ethiopia*, Balshon Printing: Brooklyn, N.Y., 1982, pp. 54-93. In recent years, a number of case studies have appeared which attempt to document changing religious patterns in Ethiopia and Israel. See, for example, K. K. Shelemay, "A Quarter-Century in the Life of a Falasha Prayer," *Yearbook of the International Folk Music Council* X (1978), pp. 83-108; G. J. Abbink, "*Seged* Celebration in Ethiopia and Is-

closed in the aftermath of the Italian invasion of Ethiopia in 1935, a steady stream of Jewish and Israeli visitors after World War II ensured an ongoing connection between the Beta Israel and representatives of world Jewry. As a result, a gradual "normalization" of Beta Israel religion has taken place in some regions, and the gap between their Judaism and that of their brethren outside Ethiopia has slowly but inexorably become smaller. The massive immigration to Israel, during the period 1980-1985, had turned what had been a gradual evolutionary process into an irresistible revolution.[11] Moreover, as is so often the case, community traditions have been both consciously and unconsciously adjusted to bring them into line with this new reality. In some cases, the creation of new traditions has merely involved an emphasis on the community's pan-Judaic features at the expense of its pan-Ethiopian characteristics.[12] In more blatant instances, claims have been put forward that most of Beta Israel religion in Ethiopia reflected normative Jewish *halacha*. Small wonder that many knowledgeable authorities question the possibility of ever making an accurate reconstruction of traditional Beta Israel religion on the basis of these revised traditions.

In light of the above, it can be seen that the importance of Beta Israel literature to the historian of religion is multi-fold. As virtually the only documents on the Beta Israel which originated within the community, these religious texts offer invaluable insight into early Beta Israel religion. Indeed, as we shall see in detail, these texts are an especially important source for the evaluation of the influence of Ethiopian Christianity upon local Judaism. Moreover, they are among the few authentic sources on the character of Beta Israel religion in the pre-Faitlovitch period. While many community traditions, rituals, and beliefs have been radically transformed in the course of more than a century of change and upheaval, a few scattered manuscripts have survived intact. Within their pages we find an image of Ethiopian Judaism prior to its "normalization."

---

rael: Continuity and Change of a Falasha Religious Holiday," *Anthropos* LXXVIII 1983, pp. 789-810.

[11] S. Kaplan, "Falashas," *Encyclopaedia Judaica Yearbook 1983-85* Keter: Jerusalem, 1986, p. 243-247.

[12] Cf. Messing, and M. Waldman, *Yehude Etiopiya* Joint Distribution Committee: Jerusalem, 1985.

Te'ezāza Sanbat: An Original Composition?

Joseph Halévy was not only the first practicing European Jew to visit the Beta Israel, but also the first scholar to give their literature serious consideration. Towards the end of his life, in 1902, he published in Paris a volume containing seven "Falasha" literary works, entitled *Tĕ'ĕzāza Sanbat* (*Commandements du Sabbat*).[13] Although the title chosen by Halévy is certainly misleading — *Te'ezāza Sanbat* (hereafter *TS*) is after all only one of the works in the volume — it was probably not accidental. Halévy, and virtually every scholar since him, clearly viewed *TS* as the outstanding work in the corpus of Beta Israel literature. Even the great Italian Ethiopianist Carlo Conti Rossini, who was generally inclined to question the originality of any Beta Israel text, viewed *TS* as an exception: "In fondo, il *Te'ezâza Sanbat* è l'unico scritto sicuramente giudaico."[14]

Wolf Leslau, who published a variety of Beta Israel texts translated into English in his *Falasha Anthology*, also gives *TS* pride of place. Commenting on this, the first text presented in the book, he notes it "well deserves its first place in this collection, for it is one of the most attractive of Falasha literary productions."[15] His remarks on the works's originality are both cautious and ambiguous. On the one hand, he considers *TS* to be among "the most original [Falasha] productions" and notes that "on the whole Christian elements are insignificant."[16] On the other hand, he acknowledges "the presence of influence from Christian-Arabic quarters" and concludes: "It will be one of the tasks of future research to determine whether Jewish aggadic materials or Christian sources furnish any clues that would

---

[13] Librairie Émile Bouillon: Paris.

[14] "Appunti di Storia e Letteratura Falascia," *Rivista degli Studi Orientali* VIII (1920), p. 584 ff. Note, however, the continuation of the quote "pur avvertendo che la personificazione del sabato in un essere celeste di genere femminino non va al di là di analogue personificazioni che nei Midrašim." Cf. *idem*, "Notice sur les Manuscrits Éthiopiens de la Collection d'Abbadie," *JA* ser. 10, XIX (1912), p. 574, "Peut-etre le *Te'ezâza Sanbat* dont notre No. 219 permettra d'établir un texte acceptable, est-il le seul écrit, en dehors des prières, qui soit vraiment d'origine Falāšā."

[15] W. Leslau, *Falasha Anthology*, Yale University Press: London, 1951, p. 3.

[16] *Ibid.*, p. XXXVIII, 9.

make possible a more precise dating.''[17]

Despite the general recognition of the centrality of *TS* to the corpus of Falasha literature, it was only with the publication in 1963 of a detailed article by Max Wurmbrand that the similarities between the Falasha work and the Christian *Dersāna Sanbat* (*Homily on the Sabbath*) appear to have been documented.[18] In this lengthy, but strangely neglected, study Wurmbrand convincingly demonstrates the parallels between *Dersāna Sanbat* on the one hand, and the Falasha *Te'ezāza Sanbat* and *Maṣḥafa Malā'ekt* (*Book of the Angels*) on the other. He further argues that a Christian scribe composed the *dersān* (homily), by incorporating material from the two Jewish works and then falsely attributed the finished composition to the Syrian Church father Jacob (James) of Sarug. As I shall demonstrate below, Wurmbrand's arguments for the priority of the Beta Israel books are far from conclusive, and there are several factors which appear to favor the priority of the Christian work.

Before turning to a detailed discussion of Wurmbrand's thesis, however, a few general comments must be made concerning the relationship between the three works under consideration. *Dersāna Sanbat* (*DS*) is a lengthy work which can, for convenience, be divided into four sections: (1) An exhortation on the Christian Sabbath (Sunday); (2) An exhortation to priests and believers; (3) A homily concerning two angels; (4) Additional exhortations to priests. While section (1) presents very close parallels to *one* section of *TS*,[19] sections (2-4) bear no resemblance to any part of this Beta Israel composition. The question is accordingly not whether the whole Christian homily is based upon the Falasha work or vice versa. Rather, the issue at hand concerns the relationship of one section of *DS* to one section of *TS*. The authors of both works clearly also made use

[17] *Ibid.*, p. 10.

[18] ''Le *'Dersâna Sanbat'* - une homélie ethiopienne attribuée a Jacques de Saroug,'' *L'Orient Syrien* VIII (1963), pp. 343-394. Cf. *idem*, ''Falashas,'' *Encyclopaedia Judaica* VI, p. 1150. Cf. Getachew Haile and W. F. Macomber, *A Catalogue of Ethiopian Manuscripts Microfilmed for the Ethiopian Manuscript Microfilm Library, Addis Ababa, and for the Hill Monastic Library, Collegeville,*'' V Project Number 1501-2000 (Collegeville, minn., 1981), p. 12.

[19] *Ibid.*, pp. 362-70, Cf. Halévy, pp. 138-142 (tr.), 8-13 (tx), *Dersāna Sanbat* Tasfā Gabra Sellāse Addis Ababa, 1947 (E.C.), pp. 47-56.

of other material which they do not have in common.

Section (3) of *DS* presents close parallels to almost all of the *Book of Angels*.[20] If, as Wurmbrand claims, *DS* is later than the Falasha work, the Christian author of the homily incorporated the Jewish text virtually *in toto*. If, on the contrary, the Christian work is the earlier text, the Falasha scribe "composed" the *Book of Angels* by adapting section (3) of the *dersān*. In any event, the situation is clearly different from that which exists between *DS* and *TS*.

Perhaps the most telling point against Wurmbrand's position is his failure to distinguish between two independent issues: (1) the attribution of the *dersan* to Jacob of Sarug; (2) the relationship between the Beta Israel and Christian works. According to Wurmbrand (and to the best of my knowledge no evidence has appeared in the past two decades to contradict him), no Syriac version of *DS* exists.[21] There is, accordingly, a significant possibility that the Ge'ez homily is in reality a pseudepigraphic composition by an Ethiopian author, and not a translation of a work by a Syrian Church father. What Wurmbrand appears to have forgotten is that the alleged pseudepigraphic character of the *dersan* is of only minor relevance to the question of its relationship to Beta Israel literature. Certainly, if an earlier Syrian version of the homily is discovered, this will provide conclusive evidence that the Christian *Ge'ez* text is not based upon the Beta Israel compositions. However, the absence of as Syrian *Vorlage* does not prove that the *dersān* is dependent upon other texts. While it is certainly possible that *DS* was composed from earlier Falasha texts and falsely ascribed to Jacob of Sarug, it could just as easily be an original work ascribed to the Syrian and adapted by the Beta Israel. No logical connection exists between the issues of authorship and originality.

In fact, Wurmbrand offers no conclusive evidence for the priority of the Falasha works. Although Halévy, Conti Rossini, Aešcoly and Leslau all believed *TS* to be an original composition, none of them appear to have been familiar with the parallel Christian work.[22] As Stefan Strelcyn demonstrated in another context, even as great an

---

[20] *Ibid.*, pp. 93ff. Cf. Wurmbrand, "'*Dersâna Sanbat*," pp. 381-391, Halévy, pp. 173-175 (tr.), 51-54.

[21] Cf. Wurmbrand, "'*Dersâna Sanbat*," p. 346-347.

[22] Cf. notes 14, 16 *supra*.

Ethiopianist as Conti Rossini was liable to overestimate Falasha originality when he lacked the relevant Christian texts.[23] Moreover, Conti Rossini and Leslau both believed *Maṣḥafa Malāʾekt* to be based upon or influenced by Christian writings.[24] Under such circumstances, it is more than a little surprising to find that Wurmbrand assumes the originality of the Beta Israel works throughout. He repeatedly writes, for example, of the Christian author's substitution of "Christian Sabbath" for "Sabbath" and "Christ" or "The Father, the Son and the Holy Spirit" for "God."[25] At no point, however, does he offer any evidence to prove that this process took place as he described it and not in the opposite direction. Indeed, several cases are known to exist of Beta Israel books in which a Christian work has been adapted through just such a process of substituting "God" for "Christ" etc.[26]

One such composition which is of special relevance to our study is *Mota Aron* (*The Death of Aaron*), a fascinating work which exists not only in Syriac and Arabic Christian versions, but also in two Geʿez (Falasha) manuscripts.[27] Although no Christian Geʿez manuscript of *Mota Aron* has yet been found, the original Christian character of the work is certain and is testified to by both the foreign and the Beta Israel texts. In fact, the Beta Israel manuscripts offer valuable insight into the process whereby original Christian works

---

23 S. Strelcyn, "Sur une prière 'falacha' publiée par C. Conti Rossini," *Rassegna di Studi Etiopici* VIII (1949), pp. 63-82, Cf. Conti Rossini, "Appunti," p. 593.

24 *Ibid.*, p. 584; Leslau, *Anthology*, p. 51.

25 Wurmbrand, p. 353, 355, 365, n. 15. On the Ethiopian Christian beliefs and practices regarding the Sabbath see E. Hammerschmidt, *Stellung und Bedeutung des Sabbats in Äthiopien* (Stuttgart, 1963).

26 Strelcyn, "Une prière"; Halévy, "Baruch" in *Tĕʾĕzāza Sanbat*, p. 80-96; cf. Leslau, *Anthology*, p. 63; M. Wurmbrand, *Ardeʾet: Sefer Hatalmidim Ha-Falashi*, Gottenberg: Tel Aviv, 1963 (Hebrew). Wurmbrand also views the Christian *Ardeʾet* as a Beta Israel work, adapted by a Christian author. However,his case here is even weaker than that with regard to *TS*. I hope to explore the relationship between the two versions of the *Ardeʾet* in an article in the near future. For an important study of a Beta Israel work incorporating Arabic Muslim sources, see E. Ullendorff, "'The Death of Moses' in the Literature of the Falashas," BSOAS XXIV (1961), pp. 419-443.

27 M. Wurmbrand, *Mota Aron* (Petirat Aharon) Gottenberg: Tel Aviv, 1963 (Hebrew).

were adopted and adapted by Beta Israel scribes for use in their community. Not only have most Christological references been removed from the Beta Israel text, but in one manuscript the name of the author has even been eliminated.[28] The work's author is Jacob of Sarug!

Although Wurmbrand, who edited and translated, *Mota Aron*, passes over this point in silence, it is clear that his reconstruction of the history of *DS* assumes a truly amazing coincidence. On the one hand, the Beta Israel borrowed, adapted, and censored a Christian work, attributed to Jacob of Sarug. On the other, a Christian author having composed a Ge'ez homily, based in part upon two Beta Israel works and requiring a putative author of sufficient prestige to assure his compositions acceptance, chose, out of countless possibilities, the same Jacob of Sarug. While such a longshot cannot be totally ruled out, it seems much more likely that portions of the *dersān* were incorporated into the Falasha corpus in much the same fashion as *Mota Aron*, and that once again the attribution to Jacob was removed. Indeed, both works could even have been contained in a single manuscript of Christian homilies attributed to the Syrian author.

Far more troubling than either this coincidence or Wurmbrand's silence is his treatment of the problem of the quality of the texts in question. Even a superficial comparison of *DS* and *TS* reveals the superiority of the Christian text. Several passages which are incomplete, corrupt or garbled in the latter can be clarified by reference to the former.[29] Wurmbrand concedes this point, but draws a novel conclusion from this evidence: the compiler of *DS* worked from a text of *TS* superior to that found in any of the surviving manuscripts![30] Since we are still waiting for this "Ur-text" to surface, it is perhaps timely to offer some alternative solutions.

---

28 *Ibid.*, p. 13.

29 In addition to the passages discussed infra, see, for example, Leslau, p. 18-19 and p. 147, n. 91, n. 92 and cf. Wurmbrand, "'Dersāna Sanbat,'' pp. 366-369.

I am grateful to Dr. Getatchew Haile (personal communication August 13, 1985), for drawing my attention to a number of these examples.

30 Wurmbrand, "'Dersāna Sanbat,'' p. 352-353.

Both *TS* and *DS* contain a parable which compares a laden ship, which becomes maneuverable when unloaded, to a sinner whose burden is eased if he observes the Sabbath. In *TS*, the passage appears with no introduction and its relationship to the preceding passage is obscure.[31] In *DS*, the parable begins with Jesus speaking to the Sabbath and giving her the power to discharge the faults of sinners, who are like a laden ship...[32] Wurmbrand concludes: "Cette introduction provient sans doute [!] d'un manuscrit du *Te'ezâza Sanbat* plus ancien, plus complet et plus correct que les nôtres. L'homélie n'a fait que remplacer le terme originel de "Dieu" par celui de "Notre-Seigneur."[33] It is at least as likely that a Beta Israel scribe omitted the introduction because of its attribution to Jesus.

In a similar fashion, while both *TS* and *DS* recount the souls' exit from Hell on the Sabbath, only *DS* mentions their return at the end of the day.[34] Once again, Wurmbrand assumes that the missing material existed in the manuscript of *TS* utilized by the author of the Christian homily, but brings no evidence in support of this.[35] In fact, the souls' return is found in a section of the *DS* several times longer than those passages which resemble *TS*, and comes at a later point in the homily. Are we to assume that all this material existed in some early text of *TS*? Could it not just as easily represent original

---

31 Leslau, p. 17; "Pray to God, your Lord, you who have sins and faults, and you will be saved through the Sabbath. He who honors the Sabbath and the festivals, God will honor him in Heaven. Like a laden ship which none can move for the greatness of the goods therein but which when steered runs like a deer, even so will he be eased who has many sins, faults, and misdeeds but showed mercy and prayed on the Sabbath of God." Forced to explain why the landlocked Beta Israel should use the image of a ship, Wurmbrand (p. 365, n. 13) suggests they may have received the idea from Maimonides, through the Jews of Yemen!

32 *Dersāna Sanbat*, p. 50. Wurmbrand, "Dersâna Sanbat," pp. 364-65: "Our Savior said to the Christian Sabbath: 'I give to you power over he who believes in you, who observes the day of your commemoration on the day of the Christian Sabbath, who gives alms in your name and does not place resentment in his heart. If one is guilty of many sins and errors, he is like a laden ship which none can move because of the greatness of the goods therein. If one removes this merchandise and one puts in motion the vessel's oars, it runs like a deer. In the same way, I shall relieve of his numerous sins, he who shows mercy on the day of the Christian Sabbath.' "

33 Wurmbrand, "'Dersâna Sanbat," p. 353.

34 *Ibid.*, 369-70, Cf. Halévy 140-141 (tr.), 11-12 (tx), *Dersāsna Sanbat*, p. 57.

35 Wurmbrand, "'Dersâna Sanbat," p. 353.

material introduced by the Christian author, or material in the *dersan* which a Beta Israel scribe chose to omit?

Te'ezāza Sanbat: A Composite Composition

Thus far, in our discussion we have confined our efforts to criticizing Wurmbrand's thesis regarding the origins of *DS* and demonstrating a number of problematic points regarding his interpretation. It is perhaps now appropriate to turn our attention to the question of what evidence exists for an alternative explanation of the facts. We begin with a few comments regarding the character and composition of *TS*.

Virtually all commentators on *TS* have noted the work's repetitiousness and lack of clarity.[36] While no consensus has evolved with regard to the division of the work into sections or paragraphs, all authorities attempt to make some sense out of the book's frequent shifts of mood and subject matter. Rather surprisingly, little attention has been given to the implications this inconsistency and heterogeneity have for an understanding of the manner in which *TS* was composed, and the question of the work's authorship. In fact, ample evidence exists to suggest that *TS* is, at least in part, a compilation of previously independent works, and not a unified original composition.

To cite a few examples:

(1) Although the personification of the Sabbath is one of the most noteworthy features of *TS*, as Leslau has noted, "the personification is not carried through consistently in this text but occurs only intermittently."[37] While some sections of the work celebrate the Sabbath as a female personification of the heavenly, others make no attempt to convey this image.

(2) While the primary focus of *TS* is obviously the celebration of the seventh day, the text mentions the command to bring offerings on the fifth day (?) and the adoration of the Sabbath on Sunday![38]

---

[36] *Ibid.*, 364, n.9; 366, n. 15, 369, n.25; Leslau, *Anthology*, pp. 3-8; p. 143, n. 30, 31, 32, 53, 78, 91, 101, etc.

[37] *Ibid.*, p. 3.

[38] Halévy, pp. 156, 158 (tr.), 30, 33 (tx).

(3) The first section of *TS* contains a disjointed account of creation and man's fall which appears to be related to Arabic (Christian?) texts. Although the various manuscripts of *TS* vary at points, at least two different names ('Elyas and 'Elda) for the Garden of Eden appear.[39]

(4) With the conclusion of this passage, a new section of *TS* begins, with the statement: "This is the Book of Israel, concerning the greatness and the glory of the Sabbath of Israel."[40] It is difficult to escape the conclusion that what follows once represented an independent work, especially since it is only from this point (and in this section) that the parallels with *DS* exist.

Even more significant than *TS*'s composite character is the fact that at least some of the material incorporated appears to be Christian in character. These include, in addition to the aforementioned praise of Sunday and links to Christian-Arabic material, which do not appear in the section of *TS* parallel to *DS*, the following example which does appear in that section:

1. A reference to the twelve thrones [of the Apostles] *TS*:
"When God comes on the last day in the midst of earthquakes and thunderbolts, seated upon his twelve thrones to judge, He will be faithful to those who love him."[41]

DS: "And our Lord responded to the twelve Apostles saying: 'In truth I say to you that you will surely enter the Kingdom of my Father who is in heaven, and you will be seated upon twelve thrones to judge the people of Israel.' "[42]

Clearly this passage, strongly reminiscent of Matthew 19: 27-28, poses a major difficulty to any advocate of *TS*'s priority.[43] Halévy, who was not aware of the existence of *DS*, believed the twelve thrones meant one for each tribe.[44] Wurmbrand, unable to plead such

---

39 *Ibid.*, 136-38 (tr.), 5-7 (tx).

40 *Ibid.*, pp. 138 (tr.), 7 (tx). Cf. Wurmbrand, "Dersâna Sanbat", p. 384, n. 13.

41 *Ibid*, 141 (tr.), 12 (tx).

42 Wurmbrand, "'Dersâna Sanbat,'' p. 369; *Dersāna Sanbat*, p. 54.

43 "And Jesus said unto them [the Apostles]: 'Verily I say unto you, that ye which have followed me, in the regeneration when the Son of man shall sit in the throne of his glory, ye shall sit upon twelve thrones, judging the twelve tribes of Israel.' "

44 *Te'ezāza Sanbat*, p. 141, n. 1, but cf. Leslau, p. 147, n. 98.

ignorance and well aware of the New Testament parallels, simply pretended that the offending passage does not appear in *TS*![45]

2. A citation based upon Matthew 7:2 "They will measure you according to the measure which you have employed for others."[46]

3. A passage in praise of celibacy: "It [a seat in Paradise] is destined for those who kept their body in purity, for the virgin who knew not a man, and for the man who knew not a woman from his youth until the end of his days, and who married not."[47]

It is also significant to note that, in these cases, *DS* generally preserves a text superior to that of *TS*, revealing its author's greater familiarity with Christian material.

In light of the above, it appears plausible to suggest that the author of *TS* had at his disposal a variety of sources, including at least one section of *DS*. These materials were then woven together, not altogether successfully, but in a manner which sufficiently masked the Christian provenance of some of the sources.[48]

Who then was this author?

According to Falasha tradition, *TS* is attributed to the fifteenth-century monk and religious leader Abba Sabra, who is also credited with the organization of Falasha monasticism and the introduction of communal laws of purity known as *attenkuñn*.[49] It is interesting to note that most traditions claim that Abba Sabra was himself a

[45] P. 369.

[46] Wurmbrand, "'Dersâna Sanbat," p. 363; *Dersāna Sanbat*, p. 49; Halévy, p. 139 (tr) 9, (tx). Wurmbrand (p. 363, n. 5) suggests that the author of *TS* based himself not on the New Testament, but on Mishna *Sotah* I, 7.

[47] Wurmbrand, "'Dersâna Sanbat," p. 368; *Dersāna Sanbat*, p. 53; Halévy, p. 141 (tr.) 12 (tx). Wurmbrand, in opposition to Leslau, Ullendorff and the Beta Israel's own traditions (cf. Abbink, *The Falashas*, pp. 31-32, Quirin, pp. 61-63), denies that Falasha monasticism reflects Christian influences. His citation of *Fifth Baruch* in support of this argument is especially curious, since this work is of Christian origin (cf. Leslau, p. 62).

[48] The possibility should not be excluded that at least some of this source material was of Jewish provenance and reached the Beta Israel through a channel other than that of the Ethiopian Orthodox Church. Of particular interest is a section concerning the sacrifice of Isaac (Genesis 22), which associates the *Akedah* with the sounding of the *shofar*, a post-Biblical Jewish concept, not known to Christian Ethiopians (Cf. Leslau, p. 28, Halévy, pp. 25-26 [tx], p. 152 [tr].

[49] Wurmbrand, "'Dersâna Sanbat," p. 349.

Christian, who came in contact with the Beta Israel because of his attempts to convert them to Christianity. Eventually, he himself became a convert to Judaism and joined the Beta Israel.[50] Given the tremendous prestige enjoyed by Abba Sabra, we must, of course, be on guard against the tendency of traditions to exaggerate his importance and credit him with a wide variety of achievements. Nevertheless, it may well be significant that *TS* is attributed to a former Christian monk, who would certainly have been familiar with the type of Christian material contained in the work and discussed above.

Maṣḥafa Malā'ekt

One final piece of evidence should be taken into account, before we consider the general implications of our findings for the understanding of Beta Israel history and literature. As was noted above, Wurmbrand argues that the Christian author of *DS* made use of not only *TS*, but also the lesser known *Maṣḥafa Malā'ekt* (*Book of Angels*). Indeed, according to Wurmbrand, *Maṣḥafa Malā'ekt* was incorporated almost *in toto* into the Christian homily. Yet several passages in *Maṣḥafa Malā'ekt* would seem to support the view that here too Christian influences have been felt. These include:

(1) "Then the Angel of Darkness heard that they had sent Paraqlitos, the guardian of the sorrows of death"[51]

The mention of Paraqlitos (the Holy Spirit) can scarcely be of Jewish origin. Moreover, the idea of a "guardian of the sorrows of death" appears in Christian literature, such as the *Apocalypse of Paul*.[52]

---

[50] Quirin, pp. 54-67; Shelemay, "Historical Ethnomusicology: Reconstructing Falasha Liturgical History, *Ethnomusicology* XXIV (1980), pp. 233-258. S. Ben Dor, "The Holy Places of Ethiopian Jewry," *Pe'amim*, XXII (1985), pp. 41-45 (Hebrew); W. Leslau, "Taamrat Emanuel's Notes on Falasha Monks and Holy Places," *Salo Wittmayer Baron Jubilee Volume*, American Academy for Jewish Research: Jerusalem, 1974, II, pp. 624-26.

[51] Wurmbrand, "'Dersâna Sanbat," p. 385; Halévy, 174 (tr.), 53 (tx). Note that while the term *Paraqlitos* appears in *DS*, it is not in this passage!

[52] Leslau, p. 161, n. 26.

(2) "They clothe her [the soul] in white raiment from above and with their holy hands they put a sign upon her face"[53]

In *DS* the sign *of the cross* is put on the soul's face. Wurmbrand assumes, here and elsewhere, that the homily's author has added the phrase missing in the Beta Israel work. Yet he offers no indication as to the nature of the sign of the teaching which is being referred to in *Maṣḥafa Malāʾekt*. The phrase's obscurity can perhaps best be explained by arguing that the Beta Israel author deleted the offending word "of the Cross."

(3) God says: "Take this soul to Sheol [where there is] a gnashing of teeth."[54]

As Leslau notes this passage is reminiscent of Matthew 13:43[55] and the *Apocalypse of Paul.*

All three of these examples, and in particular the first, would seem to indicate that *Maṣḥafa Malāʾekt* is yet another example of a Beta Israel work with clear links to Christian literature. If this is in fact the case, then further difficulties exist for Wurmbrand's reconstruction.[56]

Conclusions

It now appears possible, on the basis of the evidence presented above, to offer a new hypothesis concerning the relationship between *TS* and *DS*. The author of *TS* was a member of the Beta Israel community, who compiled his work from a variety of sources. Among

---

53 Wurmbrand, "'Dersâna Sanbat," 382-83; *Dersāna Sanbat*, p. 46, Halévy, 173 (tr), 52 (tx).

54 *Ibid.*

55 "And shall cast them into a furnace of fire: there shall be wailing and gnashing of teeth."

56 No attempt has been made in this essay to undertake a detailed discussion of *Maṣḥafa Malāʾekt*. As has already been noted, even prior to the discovery of *DS*, most authorities viewed this work as being of Christian provenance (*pace* Wurmbrand). Many of the general arguments presented above, with regard to the priority of *DS* to *TS*, are of equal relevance regarding *Maṣḥafa Malāʾekt*. Nor need Christian influences on the latter have necessarilly been confined to those derived from directly *DS* (see note 48 supra.)

the material at his disposal, was all or part of a Geʿez homily on the Sabbath, attributed to the Syrian Church father Jacob of Sarug. (This homily was, in fact, one of several works by Jacob known to the Beta Israel).[57] The material from the homily was incorporated into *TS*, with minor changes, as the section of that work described as "the Book of Israel, concerning the greatness and the glory of the Sabbath."

While it would be incautious to draw too broad a set of conclusions from the examination and reevaluation of a single literary work, neither should the implications of the analysis presented above be minimized. *TS* has long been considered by even the harshest critics of Beta Israel originality to be an exceptional work and by far the most important composition in their corpus. In light of the reevaluation argued for above, its position must now be reassessed. While *Te'ezāza Sanbat*'s claim to originality is in a sense still intact (for no Christian equivalent exists for the work as a whole), it must also be recognized as a composition with close ties to the general body of Ethiopic (Christian) literature. In this, it is not substantially different from most other Beta Israel compositions. Moreover, and perhaps most importantly, it serves to demonstrate yet again that, whatever the origin of the "Israelite" self-identification around which the "Jews" of Ethiopia organized their religious life and their society, the building blocks from which the identification was constructed were almost invariably pan-Ethiopian in character.

Acknowledgments

I would like to thank the Harry S. Truman Institute for the Advancement of Peace and the Ben Zvi Institute for the Study of Oriental Jewish Communities for supporting my research. Drs. Roger Cowley and David Appleyard supplied materials not available in

---

[57] It is of interest to note that Mss. No. 9, 10, 12, 13, 14 of the "Falasha" manuscripts in the Faitlovitch collection contain homilies attributed to another Syrian Church father, Ephrem! Cf. Getatchew Haile, *A Catalogue of Ethiopian Manuscripts Microfilmed for the Ethiopian Manuscript Microfilm Library, Addis Ababa and for the Hill Monastic Library Collegeville* IV *Project Numbers 1101-1500*, (Collegeville, Minn., 1979), No. 1496 ff. 46a-59a.

in Jerusalem and Dr. Getatchew Haile encouraged me to pursue this project. Prof. Edward Ullendorff, Prof. Kay K. Shelemay, Prof. Olga Kapeliuk and Ms. Shoshana Ben-Dor provided valuable comments on earlier drafts of this paper. The opinions expressed and the errors which remain are, of course, my own.

RELIGIOUS VISIONS OF THE END OF THE WORLD

Joseph M. Kitagawa, Chicago

In the summer of 1958, I first met R. J. Zwi Werblowsky, then a very young faculty member of the Hebrew University, at the IXth Congress of the International Association for the History of Religions, held in Tokyo. Since then, I have seen him at all of the IAHR Congresses, except the one held in Lancaster (for I was in Australia and could not go) and in Israel, Japan, Europe, India, and North America as well. In my contacts with him I have, of course, learned much about Judaism and Jewish mysticism, for I knew little about these areas; but I also learned about religious change through his astute and sensitive remarks on this subject. One of his books, *Beyond Tradition and Modernity* (1976), with the revealing sub-title of "Changing Religions in a Changing World," is dedicated to his children, who, according to him, are "heirs, victims and re-makers of both tradition and modernity." The range of his concern is also seen in his article, "Crisis Consciousness and the Future" (*Diogenes*, nos. 113-114 [Spring-Summer 1981]), with another characteristic sub-title, "The Future of Religion, the Future of Mankind, the Dialogue of Religions." Now that he has decided to take partial retirement from a demanding teaching career, I hope that he will find more time to enlighten us with his global and futuristic orientation; and as one who has benefited all these years from Professor Werblowsky's work, I would like to dedicate the following remarks to him as a token of my esteem.

In December, 1982, a tragic event took place in the small community of Murphysboro, Tennessee, U.S.A. A police officer was held hostage for thirty hours by members of a religious cult and was finally beaten to death. This particular cult group apparently believes that the end of the world is imminent and that the Bible identifies the police as the anti-Christs and representatives of the devil prophesied by the Johannine Apocalypse.[1] When my students in Chicago heard about the incident, several of them shrugged their shoulders and dismissed it as one of many such bizarre cult-related happenings. I agreed with them that the fatal beating of a police officer by a presumably religious group is indeed bizarre; but I pointed out that religious visions of the end of the world, however they are understood, have been a persistent and important motif in various religions, both past and present, both in the West and in the East. In this paper, I will discuss how certain religious traditions have viewed the end of the world and how different perceptions of the end of the world have in turn shaped the religious and cultural outlooks of various peoples.

My reflections on this vast problem are based on a simple premise: every religion, every culture, and every civilization has a characteristic outlook toward the future and a characteristic way of recollecting the past; and these together influence the particular understanding of the meaning of present existence. St. Augustine expressed this premise in his statement of time: "There are three *times*: [first] a present of things past, [second] a present of things present, and [third] a present of things future." According to him, the "present of things past" is associated with memory, the "present of things present" with sight, and the "present of things future" with expectation.[2] These three foci — the expectation of the future, the recollection of the past, and the understanding of the present — are intricately woven into a kind of "mental prism" which extracts significant items from a mass of data and relates historical realities to fancies of fantasy and the imagination. Embedded in this prism are also the elements of forgetfulness and optical illusion.

---

1 *The Chicago Sun-Times*, January 16, 1983.

2 Augustine, "The Confessions," tr. by E. B. Pusey, *Great Books of the Western World*, vol. 18 (Chicago: Encyclopaedia Britannica, Inc., 1952), p. 52.

The persistent power of the past dimension of the mental prism, that dimension which recollects past experiences, is forcefully exemplified in our time by the Middle East conflicts[3] or the conflicts on the subcontinent of India. Equally powerful is the mental prism's angle of vision for the future, which is undeniably and integrally related to its angle of vision of the past. We are acutely aware that the future and the present are merely movable dots on the horizontal line of the continuum of time, as we read in the haunting words of Macbeth:

> To-morrow, and to-morrow, and to-morrow
> Creeps in this petty pace from day to day,
> To the last syllable of recorded time . . .[4]

In short, our daily existence assumes the existence of the future; and, in spite of the scriptural admonition not to be anxious about tomorrow, "for tomorrow will be anxious for itself" (Matt. 6:34), we feel that we must be concerned and prepared for the future. There are, certainly, psychological differences between optimists and pessimists, who clearly approach the future differently (despite a new definition that a pessimist is an optimist with experience). More significant, however, is the fact that one's perception of the future — whether that future be beneficial or detrimental — has a decisive impact on one's attitude toward the present; and, more often than not, our perception of the future is heavily influenced by our religious and cultural outlook.

Take, for example, the notion of progress, a word derived from the Latin *gressus*, "step," and connoting the act of stepping forward to a situation more desirable than the current. In our consideration we must first recognize the difference, as pointed out by Paul Tillich, between the "concept" of progress, which is an abstraction, and the "idea" of progress, which is an interpretation of an historical situation, with or without a verifiable basis, in terms of the "concept" of progress. The "idea" of progress thus involves our mental decision or affirmation; and it becomes a symbol as well as a way of life, a "doctrine" about the law of history, or even an unconscious "dogma" of progressivism.[5]

---

3 Cf. I. F. Stone, "Holy War" (review of "Le Conflit israelo-arabe"), in *The New York Times Review of Books* 9, no. 2 (August 3, 1967): 6.

4 William Shakespeare, *Macbeth* V. 5.

The notion that the future promises to be better than the present, leading to the culmination of all values at the end of the world, clearly is not based on empirical observation, but on speculation and affirmation. Such speculation and affirmation are often associated with a religious vision of the coming, at the end, of the cosmic ruler, the universal king or the world savior. In contrast to this positive form of progressivism, we find as well negative forms, which view the future in terms of the successive erosion of values, although they are still often associated with the belief in the coming of a supramundane figure who redresses all evils at the end of the world. Regardless of the positive or negative focus on progressivism, our perceptions of the end of the world, and of the character of the divine figure who appears at the end, as mentioned earlier, influence our attitude toward the present. In the history of religions, we have two prominent figures of cosmic saviors or rulers who have inspired a series of messianic ideologies, and who have thus influenced the future outlook of peoples in many parts of the world. The first is Saošyant of Iranian Zoroastrianism; the second is the Cakravartin of India.

Saošyant

According to the ancient Iranian religion, Zoroastrianism, history comprises a cosmic conflict between the just god, Ahura Mazdah, and the forces of evil. Human beings are destined to choose sides and to participate in the conflict. Zoroastrianism originally articulated the notion of the end of the world, *eschaton*, and the doctrine of the end, or eschatology: at the end of the cosmic cycle of 12,000 years, the savior and judge, Saošyant, born miraculously of a maiden and the seed of Zoroaster, will appear and rehabilitate creation, casting the Devil into hell and purging the human race from the stain of sin. The whole human race will then enter into a paradise, there to enjoy eternal bliss and happiness.

[5] Paul Tillich, *The Future of Religions*, ed. by J. C. Brauer (New York: Harper and Row, 1966), pp. 64ff.

"The significance of Zoroastrianism," writes R. C. Zaehner, "lies not in the number of those who profess it, but rather in the influence it has exercised on other religions [for example, all Gnostic religions — Hermetism, Gnosticism, Manichaeism] and particularly on Christianity, through the medium of the Jewish exiles in Babylon, who seem to have been thoroughly impregnated with Zoroastrian ideas." He states further that "Christianity claims to be the heir of the prophets of Israel. If there is any truth in this claim, it is not less heir to the Prophet of ancient Iran, little though most Christians are aware of this fact."[6]

Zoroastrianism exerted an especially strong influence on Jewish eschatology, including the beliefs in the Messianic era of national restoration, the coming of the new *aeon* of God's kingdom, and the celestial hereafter for the deceased; it influenced as well the Jewish comprehension of sacred history, which understands God, who had elected the nation of Israel, as one day fulfilling his promise by establishing his rule on earth. Christianity, which was born as a messianic movement within Judaism, inherited as a matter of course the Iranian-inspired Jewish eschatological perspective; but when early Christians recognized that the anticipated return of Christ (*parousia*, "arrival" or "presence") would not be realized as soon as they had expected — or that it had perhaps already been partially realized at the Pentecost — they were forced to come to terms with the social realities of the current situation. This example graphically illustrates, I think, how a change in the conception of the future causes changes in attitudes toward the present.

The Cakravartin

Indian religious lore gives us an ancient mythical ideal of a just and virtuous world monarch, the Cakravartin ("owner of the wheel, [*cakra*]"), a divinely ordained superman (*mahāpuruṣa*) who, due to his moral supremacy and moral power, has a special place in the cosmic scheme as the final unifier of the whole earthly realm.

[6] R. C. Zaehner, "Zoroastrianism," in *The Concise Encyclopedia of Living Faiths*, ed. by R. C. Zaehner (New York: Hawthorn Books, 1959), p. 209.

Heinrich Zimmer has traced the conception of the Cakravartin "not only to the earliest Vedic, but also the pre-Vedic, pre-Aryan traditions of India, being reflected in various Buddhist and Jain writings, as well as in the Hindu *purāṇas*."[7] The significance of the Cakravartin lies in the fact that his figure came to be accepted as the monarchical ideal in the later Vedic imperial ideology; in addition, it also provided a paradigm for Buddhist speculations on the person and mission of the Buddha.

Despite numerous legends about the founder of Buddhism, we actually know very little about the Buddha's life: we are not even certain which century he was born in — the sixth or the fifth century B.C. The canonical accounts of his life, written centuries after his death, portray the Buddha as a royal prince, accustomed in his youth to the splendor and luxury of the palace. Most likely, however, he belonged to a minor fighting aristocracy, wealthy according to the standards of the time. His spiritual quest motivated him to leave home to lead the life of a mendicant. We are told that, as he concentrated in deep meditation under a bodhi tree, he saw in a trance a vision of his previous existences. He also gained piercing insight into the meaning of existence and attained the path of emancipation from the transitoriness of the finite world. After his enlightenment experience, he preached the Good Law for over forty years. His mission was to establish a religious community of monastics and laity, the Samgha, which was not circumscribed by national, racial, or cultural boundaries.

In the course of time, the career of this humble mendicant came to be seen as a spiritual counterpart of the career of the universal monarch, the Cakravartin. Popular Buddhist piety held that the Buddha and the Cakravartin shared the same universal principle and that both had identical physical marks at birth — the thirty-two great marks. Buddhists believed further that when the Buddha was born, he had the choice to aspire to either the path of the universal ruler (Cakravartin) or the path of the world savior. They appropriated such symbols of the Cakravartin as the sacred wheel (*cakra*), the divine white elephant, the white horse, and the magic jewel (*cintāmaṇi*) for

[7] Heinrich Zimmer, *Philosophies of India*, ed. by Joseph Campbell (New York: Pantheon Books, 1951), p. 129.

use on their altars and in their relic mounds (*stūpas*), as symbols of the spiritual kingship of the Buddha.[8] They offered rhapsodic praises to the memory of him who is said to have given up an earthly kingdom to establish a spiritual kingdom:

> Unto this came I . . .
> for I will not have that crown
> which may be mine; I lay aside those realms
> which wait the gleaming of my naked swords:
> My chariot shall not roll with bloody wheels
> from victory to victory, till earth
> wears the red record of my name. I choose
> to tread its paths with patient, stainless feet,
> making its dust my bed, its loneliest wastes
> my dwelling, and its meanest things my mates . . .[9]

In the third century B.C., Buddhism, which had begun as an insignificant religion of mendicants and pious lay people in northeast India, was promoted by King Aśoka as the religion of his vast empire. Although Aśoka never claimed to be the Cakravartin, later Buddhists — especially Buddhist rulers in south and southeast Asia and China — came to regard him as a model of the Buddhist monarch, preshadowing the Buddhist image of the universal monarch (Cakravartin) yet to come.

The Cakravartin, Maitreya, and Amitābha

The Buddhist speculation about the person of the Buddha was not confined to identification with the Cakravartin. Since Buddhist tradition accepted the notion that the Buddha, seated under the bodhi tree, saw a vision of his previous existences, it was not difficult for Buddhists to speculate on the existence of previous Buddhas, or of the three bodies of the Buddha, or of multiple Buddhas, each residing in one of numerous Buddha-fields (*buddha-kshetra*), which together constitute the cosmos. Furthermore, the stream of foreign

---

[8] Ibid., pp. 130-31.

[9] Sir Edwin Arnold, *The Light of Asia and the Indian Song of Praise*, Bk. 4 (Bombay: Jaico Publishing House, 1949), p. 63.

religions and art forms that flowed into India from Bactria and Iran, shortly before and just after the beginning of the common era, greatly influenced the piety, imagination, and artistic sensitivities of both Hindus and Buddhists. Two examples of prominent Buddhist savior figures who emerged from this fascinating religious and cultural milieu, and who made a decisive impact on Buddhist outlooks on the future, deserve mention here. The first is Maitreya, the future Buddha; the second is Amitābha, the Buddha of the glamorous Western paradise.

Maitreya

The close association of the Buddha with the Cakravartin, the ruler who will unify the whole cosmos at the end of the world, forwarded the belief in Maitreya, the future Buddha whose coming would signify both the fulfillment of the Buddha's Law or Teaching, and the establishment of universal peace and concord. Many scholars believe that Saošyant, the Iranian cosmic savior mentioned earlier, inspired the Buddhist notion of Maitreya. In the opinon of A. L. Basham,

> under the invading rulers of Northwest India, Zoroastrianism and Buddhism came in contact, and it was probably through this that the idea of the future Buddha became part of orthodox [Buddhist] belief.... [And by the] beginning of the Christian era, the cult of the future Buddha, Maitreya, was widespread among all Buddhist sects.[10]

The Southern tradition of Buddhism — the Small Vehicle (Hīnayāna) or the Tradition of Elders (Theravāda), followed in Sri Lanka (Ceylon) and Southeast Asian countries — recognizes only the Buddha and Maitreya as Bodhisattvas, or "future Buddhas." According to legend, Maitreya (Metteyya in Pali), like the Buddha, had had many lives before being born as a prince. He, too, forsook his comfortable palace life and he attained Buddhahood under a dragon-flower tree. He now lives as the Lord of the *Tuṣita* heaven until the Buddha's teaching erodes. At that moment he will descend

[10] A. L. Basham, *THe Wonder That Was India* (New York: Grove Press, 1954), p. 274. For theories of the Indian origin of Maitreya, see P. S. Jaini's article in the forthcoming volume on Maitreya edited by Alan Sponberg and Helen Hardacre.

to the world and will hold three assemblies under a dragon-flower tree. Buddhists believe that, at his coming, Buddha's Law, peace, and justice will be restored, and all faithful followers of his path will be able to attain sainthood, or *arhat*ship.

Ironically, in the Southern tradition, the figures of Maitreya, the future Buddha, and the Cakravartin, the universal monarch who will appear at the end of the world, came to be seen as one and the same, and each was adopted by Buddhist kings as a way of legitimizing earthly royal reign. Moreover, many Buddhist kings aspired not only to ascend to Maitreya's heaven, but also to "become" Maitreya in future eras, and gigantic statues of Maitreya were erected throughout their kingdoms. Still and all, the Maitreyan ideal, conceived as a corrective to the ills of the empirical social and political order, never developed. Only in modern times has this idea been infused with a revolutionary impulse, as exemplified by various anti-colonial movements. After Burma's independence, U Nu, who was looked upon by many people as a Buddha in the coming, attempted to establish in Burma an earthly Nirvana, which was to become the dwelling place of the future Buddha, Maitreya, and of saintly hermits. Other attempts to actualize the Maitreyan paradise have been made in our time, and although they have failed, the fact that they have been inspired by the Maitreyan ideal is most significant. For those Buddhists, in particular, who now live in Cambodia, Laos, and Vietnam under regimes hostile to Buddhism, the anticipation of the "descent" of Maitreya may become an important basis for their outlook for the future.

Maitreya and Amitābha

In the Northern tradition — the Great Vehicle or Mahāyāna, that had spread to Central Asia, China, Korea, and Japan — Maitreya was rivalled by the savior figure of Amitābha (the Buddha of the Infinite Light), known also as Amitāyus (the Buddha of the Infinite Life), a Buddha not recognized by the Southern (Pali) Canon. Amitābha, too, emerged from the cross-cultural and cross-religious milieu that characterized the beginning of the common era, when the connection of divinity and light, or of divinity and the sun, became fashionable through the popularity of deities associated with light, such as Mithra, Helios, and Apollo in Central Asia and Northwestern India. Amitābha Buddha is the Lord of the Western Paradise — Sukhāvatī, the blissful Pure Land — the final home of the sun and all departed spirits. The figures of Maitreya and Amitābha followed the westward expansion of Buddhism first from Northern India to Central Asia to China, then to Korea and Japan — and their respective cults were closely intertwined in all of these areas.

In China, as in the Southeast Asian countries, the image born of the merging of Maitreya and the universal monarch, the Cakravartin, was appropriated and distorted by rulers eager to enhance their kingship by means of Buddhist symbols. Chinese popular piety developed two types of Maitreya cult, one stressing the motif of "ascent," and another the motif of "descent." Those who followed the "ascent" motif seriously aspired to be reborn in Maitreya's heaven at their death, while those who espoused the "descent" motif, believing that Maitreya might come very soon, hoped to prolong life until then, or to be reborn on earth after Maitreya's arrival, so that they could hear his preaching. The "ascent" motif was gradually eclipsed by the growing popularity of Amitābha, who was believed to have vowed to bring all sentient beings to his blissful Pure Land. Devotees of Amitābha were greatly influenced by the legendary theory of negative progressivism; they firmly believed that the era of the Buddha's true teaching was destined to be followed successively by the eras of counterfeit teaching and of the decline and decay of the Buddha's Law, and that the dreaded "last period" was coming soon — if, indeed, it had not arrived already. This sense of urgency, concerning the impending cosmic catastrophe, lent great intensity to their devotion to Amitābha.

Although the "ascent" motif of the Maitreya cult was superseded by worship of Amitābha, the motif of Maitreya's "descent" thoroughly penetrated the consciousness of the Chinese populace, especially that of members of the sectarian movements which arose outside of orthodox Buddhism. For those oppressed by, and dissatisfied with, social, political, and economic injustices, the Maitreyan eschatological vision was compelling, as attested by the series of rebel and revolutionary movements which have marked Chinese history from the seventh to the nineteenth centuries.

In Korea and Japan as well, the Maitreya cult attracted many devotees; but the movement soon lost its eschatological and prophetic character due to the rapid assimilation of Buddhism into the cultural and national fabric of both countries. In the twelfth and thirteenth centuries, Japan was beset by natural calamities, social unrest, and political instability, all accepted as confirmation of the arrival of the dreaded era of the decay of Buddhism. The cult of Amitābha, at this time, stimulated the growth of intense pietistic movements, for example, the Pure Land School, the True Pure Land School, and the Nichiren School. As the sense of impending doom lessened, however, Amitābha followers in Japan, not unlike the early Christians, lost their eschatological fervor and adjusted themselves to the realities of a mundane society. During the last century, when the foundations of a still-feudal society were shaken by both external and internal agents, the "descent" motif of Maitreya significantly inspired movements to rectify the social order, movements exemplified by an emergent series of messianic cults.

The Impact of the Modern West on Asia

The disintegration of the cultures of Asia during the past four or five centuries is beyond the scope of this discussion; we can only state that the slow process of internal stagnation in Asia was accelerated by the advance of the West during the eighteenth and nineteenth centuries. Since the Renaissance, Western civilization has acquired all the earmarks of a pseudo-religion of secularized salvation, and Westerners have become convinced that the West alone was the inventor and transmitter of true civilization, to be propagated for the edification of the "backward" peoples of the non-Western world. The combined forces of Western civilization, Christian missionary enterprise, and colonial expansion effected social, political, economic, cultural, and religious changes in much of Asia and Africa by the end of the nineteenth century. Democracy was the theology of Western civilization, and science its holy writ. The new gospel of secular salvation — liberty, equality and fraternity, and modernity — attracted both the intelligentsia and the iconoclastic youths in the non-Western world, who had "inhaled" the dogma of the modern West, the idea of "progress here and now," and had discarded the traditional ideas of otherworldly rewards, in the life to come in the heaven of either Maitreya or Amitābha.

When viewed from the perspective of the non-Western world, the significance of Wilson and Lenin, two secular saviors who emerged on the world scene after World War I, is readily apprehended. Each offered a universal program of peace and plenty; but Lenin's Russian Revolution did not achieve a world-wide utopia for the oppressed, and Wilson's League of Nations did not eradicate Western colonial imperialism. Deeply disappointed in both the Russian and the Western options, non-Western peoples were thus driven to find their own alternatives, alternatives which included political independence and the restoration of their neglected cultural and religious traditions. The emergence of independent nations in Asia after World War II — the Philippines (1946); India and Pakistan (1947); Ceylon (Sri Lanka), Burma, South and North Korea (1948); Indonesia and the Peoples Republic of China (1949); Vietnam (1954); Cambodia (1955); Laos (1956); the Federation of Malaya (1957) — to say nothing of the new nations in Africa — not only signified the end of modern Western colonialism, but also represented the beginning of a process by which peoples of the non-Western world could redefine their concepts of dignity, value, and freedom.

It is ironic that these new nations in Asia and Africa have attained political independence after the end of the era of the nation-state. Leaders of these nations increasingly understand that the real problems which confront them are not soluble within the confines of the egocentric sovereign nation, or within quarrelsome regional communities of nations. They cannot even approach the still rich and powerful Western nations to solve these problems because, as Walter Lippman warned us two decades ago, the great powers can no longer govern the affairs of the world. Trapped in this dilemma, we might indulge in romantic nostalgia for a lost paradise, and attempt to solve today's problems with yesterday's answers; or we might cling to both new and old forms of millenarian options. Our task, however, is to discern the real nature of our uncertain future, for it is as true today as it was yesterday that our perception of the future determines our attitude toward the present.

Some fifteen years ago, Claude Lévi-Strauss, the noted French anthropologist, stated in his comments on the unrest of the younger generation, the acceleration of population growth, the advancement of militarization, and the increased exploitation of energy that "man, who since the Renaissance has been brought up to adore himself," must learn a new meaning of modesty.

> He would do well to learn that if one thinks only man is respectable among living beings . . . he can no longer be protected. One must first consider that it is as a living being that [the human being] is worthy of respect . . .

Such a shift in our thinking, in Lévi-Strauss' view, will take "a spiritual revolution" of great magnitude.[11] While such a realization alone may not solve our problems, it might at least give us the courage to live responsibly in our time, without either indulging in wishful thinking or falling into despair. If not, our future is indeed bleak.

---

[11] Cited in John L. Hess, "French anthropologist, at onset of '70's, deplores the 20th century," *The New York Times*, December 31, 1969.

A SOCIAL AND RELIGIOUS REVOLUTION AMONG THE MAYAN TRIBES AS SUGGESTED BY MYTHOLOGY

Nahum Megged, Jerusalem

The way of religions is to change with the passage of time. Changes in essence, in worship, in interpretation of laws and in emphases are evident. Certain changes take place within a short period of time, and other processes require a continuum to breach the walls of tradition and take on a new form.

In numerous cases, the source of the changes is the appearance of another culture leaving its mark. This culture can penetrate forcefully or fill the void created when the former culture crumbles. Many such changes occurred among the tribes of ancient America. With the collapse of the Olmec culture in the gulf of Mexico, the Tehotihuacan cultures in the Mexican valley emerged and the cities of the Mayan tribes flourished. When Tehotihuacan collapsed, the Tula culture flourished, and so forth.

Similarly, tribes with an ethnic, lingual and cultural affinity experienced far-reaching internal changes. Such was the fate of the Mayan tribes. These changes took place when the tribes coexisted in an independent political framework or, as circumstances dictated, became subjects or servants of invaders. The tribes were not united under one statutorial structure, spoke different tongues and dialects and believed in different gods; nevertheless, common elements existed amongst them making possible their inclusion in one common reference group.[1] As a result of inter-tribal wars legitimate gods

[1] The first study of Mayan culture as a whole, written by Joseph Herbert Spinden in 1913, was called *Study of Maya Art*. In 1957, he compiled all his previous works

of one people were transformed into gods of darkness or false gods of other people. Even today, although different forms of Catholicism have been universally accepted, there is great diversity in belief, worship and emphasis.

---

into an anthology *Maya Art and Civilization*. For many years these books served as the basis for all scholars in the field. Despite the fact that many of Spinden's opinions have since been invalidated, certain elements are still widely accepted by numerous researchers, in particular the correlation between the Indian and the Gregorian calendar. In 1946, Sylvanus Morley published the most popular work on the Maya: *The Ancient Maya*. He discusses physical anthropology, culture, psychological guidelines, labour, society, dress, religion and belief. Later on most scholars rejected his allusions to tribal history, and after his death the book was republished, this time edited by George Brainerd who retained all epigraphic and anthropological data but suppressed most of Morley's historical reconstruction.

J. Erik Thomson, who stands out among researchers, incorporated in his studies archaeology (including field work), pottery, epigraphy, ethnology and linguistics. Already in 1927, he published his first book *The Maya Civilization*. At first, he accepted Morley's historical reconstruction but later retracted his opinion. In 1954, he wrote the most comprehensive work on the Maya: *The Rise and Fall of Maya Civilization*. Thomson outlines "the time philosophy" of the tribes on the basis of calendar studies. In his opinion, the spiritual foundation was the determining factor in this ancient culture, and scientific progress as related through priestly penmanship was ineffectual. As a factor contributing to the fall of the culture, Thomson concluded that barbaric peoples invaded the lands, bringing with them an adherence to the dogma of "human blood" as food for the gods. The priests accepted this religion, but the people rejected it, thus beginning the process of deterioration.

Rafael Girard, a Swiss researcher who lived for many years among the Chorti tribes of Guatemala, focused in his research on contemporary reality in the area of ritual worship. In his opinion, this reality of worship offers factual material no less significant than archaeological study.

Alberto Ruz, a Cuban-Mexican researcher, elaborated an overall theory following the Morley-Thomson studies. He was also the archaeologist who discovered the pyramid grave at Palenque, thus altering concepts of these peoples' burial rites. His conclusive study *El Pueblo Maya* was published posthumously.

Michael Coe, (*The Maya*), summarized the studies made by other researchers according to new archaeological findings (1966). I cannot mention here monographs, dealing with philosophical, ethnographic, archaeological, psychological or other issues.

Remnants of Popular Belief

If one explores the beliefs of the Mayan tribes alive today, especially remnants of religious elements and ancient gods, a vague picture is revealed: gods which existed on a popular level survived. To some degree, the names of the priesthood's or nobility's deities remained or filtered in, but only as far as their popular role was concerned. They became proprietors of miracles, rain givers, exorcists of spirits, and healers of the sick. The ancient significance of these images and the way of thinking associated with them have completely vanished. When the Yucatans, during the colonial period, mentioned their ancient religion they made no reference whatsoever to the ancient governing deities, but rather to beliefs in the wind, stream, mountain, etc.[2] Already then, only the popular level remained.

Today they believe in Yumtzilob, the "lords", gods of nature whose role is to guard the behavior of man in the forest or cornfield. They believe in Chac, the ancient god of water, and entreat him to bring them rain. They believe in gods or spirits who watch over animals and beasts. The ancient cross, affixed to the Christian cross, became a righteous interpreter between man and the supreme forces. Within the confines of the church, priests using ventriloquistic means "make the cross speak" and in this way pass the word to the believers. They believe in Nagual, the alter ego manifest in animals, and in witchcraft. In certain locations the dead are buried with food, as was the practice long ago, and they entreat the deceased to watch over the living. Certain gods underwent transformation into demons, even within the same tribe.[3] They believe in sacred trees and in the spirit of forest, streams and brooks. They associate "our father the sun" with Jesus and "Mother Earth" or the moon, who is also grandmother, with Mother Mary. In the depths of the jungle, the Lacandon tribes pray to Kin (sun), to Ixchel (moon) and to Kisin (the

[2] Tatiana Proskouriakoff, "El arte maya y el modelo genético de la cultura" *Desarrollo Cultural de los Mayas*, UNAM Mexico, p. 196.

[3] A classic example is the god Caixoc of the Cakchiquel's tribes, whose name became a synonym for the devil. On this topic, see Correa Gustavo "El espíritu del mal en Guatemala" *Middle American Research Inst.*, Tulane University, New Orleans 1955.

underworld), the entity transmitting diseases or watching over souls. Frequently, rituals connected with an agricultural or medical entreaty are enacted in the ancient cultural centers such as the shrines of Yachilan at Chiapas in Mexico without any awareness of the purpose which these shrines served.

There are instances in which an ancient figure of the past becomes a symbol of renovation of a messianic movement, much like the cross or images whose true function was forgotten. These movements anticipate the ancient days before the arrival of the white man. The great god Itzamna, creator of the gods, takes the form of a shamanistic god, as also happened to the ancient deity of the sun Kinik Kakmo.[4] We also hear of a pattern of an ancient world structure by which four gods support the world at its four corners, and are particularly fearful of the underworld. The religious new year "moves" to the first of January on which important ceremonies take place, such as the shifting of governmental rule, publication of a sacred book, and the like. Similarly, in the Christian New Year there is a survival of the popular elements of the renewal of the agricultural, religious or astrological year. In lieu of games of government, one would think that there is a continuation of "military theocracy" in certain villages,[5] but this theocracy, overshadowed by the "great shrine" — the church — has no connection with the ancient dynasty, just as the ancient divinity which became demonic does not indicate a continuum.

The transformation of the legitimate divinity into a demonic one is the consequence of the Spanish conquest in which the priests, through coercion or persuasion, turned the gods, especially those for whom spacious and breathtaking shrines were erected, into demonic figures.[6] A portion of the uneducated populace assimilated the

---

4 Luis Laffer, Marx Crevieux, Nahum Megged, *Cantos Mágicos del Chaman Uxom Kokon* (Piedra Jorobada, Yucatán), Etnomusica — Fondo de Cultura Economica, Venezuela 1976.

Anthropologists and ethnomusicologists collected, among other things, Shamanistic melodies from the year 57, including therapeutic chants. The shamans entreated the god Izamná who became a kind of divine spirit to whom one turned for special remedial entreaties.

5 Alfonso Villa Rojas, "Patrones culturales antiguos y modernos en las comunidades contemporaneas de Yucatan," *Desarrollo Cultural de los Mayas*.

6 The Spaniards or Indians who served as their scribes, when referring to the

doctrines of the priests and of the new lords, who took over the former position of the Indian nobility. A similar process had also taken place before the coming of the Spaniards: new peoples and religions obliterated the ancient deities or transformed them into false gods or gods of the underworld. The reality of modern times in which only popular ceremonies and beliefs survived is a consequence of the religious and cultural collapse and stagnation occurring as a result of the disappearance of the esoteric culturally-oriented leadership. Only popular memories of past ceremonies and of the images' roles and power remained. The memory of the use of a particular figure at a time of crisis or entreaty likewise survived. This recollection was not passed on by tradition from an official functionary to a clandestine one, but rather passed to the hands of people who functioned as believing lay worshippers rather than priests. This explains the great blurring of notions apparent already during the first generation.

It may be assumed that when a legitimate religious rule survived in the form of priesthood or of keepers of the great secrets, certain nuances of the conquered culture are retained even though new elements are added as a result of the conquest. Frequently, the conquered culture becomes predominant. The Aztecs contributed some of their deities to the Mexican pantheon but with this they accepted Toltecs' divinities and also saw themselves as their predecessors.[7] When the religious elite disappeared, only an obtuse memory and popular ceremonies remained.

The above-mentioned process recurred in different periods even when the rule passed from the known people of that region; all the more so when it passed to "the absolute divergence," "the absolute incomprehension" — as the Europeans were viewed by natives of the American continent.[8]

---

great gods, always wrote "demons" or "devils."

[7] The Aztec king even referred to himself as keeper of the seat of Quezalcoatl, who was — as is well known — the great god of the Toltecs.

[8] "An invention of the other person" due to an inability to understand him. See Miguel Leon Portilla, *La Vision de losencidos*, F.C.E. México 1971, O'Gorman Edmundo, *La Invensión de América*, F.C.E. México 1958.

Conclusion of the Classical Period

Researchers of Mayan culture divided the ancient period according to different criteria, using architectural or archaeological guidelines, such as writing and calendar, as the basis for period determination. In this way, following the Egyptologists, S. Morley conceived of the two concepts: Ancient Empire and New Empire.[9] This division deviates from the archaeological data and is based instead on considerations of political and governmental order. Later on, he changed his view, and suggested the following periods: pre-Classical, Classical and Post-Classical, at times making use of subdivisions such as ancient pre-Classical, late pre-Classical and so on; this is still the most widely accepted view.

Scholars have tried to understand what happened between the Classical and Post-Classical periods, and why a flourishing culture abruptly ceased to exist, but there are as many solutions as there are scholars. Sometimes the solution points to a way of thinking rather than to conclusive research. Mayan cities always indicated the end of the Katun period by a lengthy year-county.[10] At the end of the year 810, 19 cities marked the year (Katun 810). In 879, it was marked in only 4 locations and not in those locations which were most central. In 889, only in 3 cities, and in 909 indication of the year was found on a Jade pendant from South Quintana Roo in Mexico. This is the last documented date of the Classical Period. It is difficult to know how long the decline and degeneration lasted, how many years they continued to live in the cities after these ceased to serve as religious-cultural centers. When Cortes traversed the Peten forests (Guatemala) in the years 1524-1525, all centers were completely desolate. When the first Spaniards found their way to the big cities of the Classical Period: Tikal in Guatemala and Yachilan in Chiapas, Mexico (1696), the cities were completely covered by forest. The Classical Period went on for approximately 600 years (300-900), and if one adds the proto-Classical as well[11] this means 750 years from the

---

[9] See note 1 above.

[10] There were 13 different Katunes, each consisting of 20 years. This is the "short count." In addition, a method was devised for reading long-term dates called "the long count." For example, Alautun denotes 63,000,000 years. Naturally, this number was used only in reference to mythological intervals.

[11] According to the definition of Ruz A., *El Pueblo Maya*, Salvat 1981, p. 268.

beginning of prosperity until the final collapse. During this period the region underwent transformation - new irrigational techniques were introduced, magnificent buildings and shrines were erected, the calendar and hieroglyphs were created. Hundreds of breathtaking images were sculpted which stood in city squares and at the gates. The inhabitants triumphed over the jungle and its tendency to return and cover all available ground. All this development disappeared by a process lasting perhaps the span of the 9th century until the final collapse at the outset of the 10th century.

For explanation, natural catastrophes, environmental changes, have been mentioned. It is known that numerous regions in the center and north are not within the seismological range of Guatemala and Chiapas. What happened to them? No proof has been found substantiating the theory of torrential rains in the Peten region in north Guatemala, preventing the burning of fields which in turn prevented maize farming. In addition, no evidence has been found backing the theory of mass emigration.

Further reference has been made to diseases such as malaria and yellow fever. At the present time, two Florida researchers claim that it is the diseases brought over by Europeans which destroyed the Maya. They are obviously referring to the 16th-17th centuries. In this case, too, there is no historical or mythological mention of these diseases as is the case regarding documentation of the disease which wiped out almost all of México-Tenochtitlán. If diseases had been present in the lower-Southern countries as they claim, what happened to the mountainous region? Papers have been written on soil deprivation due to land fires which turned the forest into a Sabana. For this theory too evidence on the terrain is slim. The Sabana as it exists today is linked to topographical structure rather than to the burning of fields. In addition, in a region such as the Tikal's tropical forest, the jungle is quick to cloak the regions which were hitherto cleared or burned. This phenomenon is evident in Palenque (México) as well. Furthermore, there is evidence, albeit later, that maize was planted in the same area for a ten year cycle.[12] In other words, two consecutive years of land exploitation and eight years respite. Therefore, depletion is not a likely explanation.

---

12 Idem, p. 72, 83.

A problem arises regarding the basis of the version contending that the big urban culture could sustain itself from maize cultivation. From the 4th century on, so many cities and villages were built that there was no way they could subsist by means of conventional agriculture. Wolff claims that there were most certainly alternative branches of farming which enabled the existence of centers of government and of services.[13] Perhaps rafts or man-made islands as with the Mexicans, perhaps irrigation networks as exemplified by those found recently, may provide a partial answer. There are researchers who claim that the inhabitants utilized roots similar to potatoes from which they obtained rich flour.[14] In any case, there were not five hectares per family on hand to make ample provision by growing maize. In Tikal, for example, the land cleared for farming was approximately 1 1/2 hectares per family.

A different solution to the problems of subsistence has been offered by Puleston[15] who maintained that the Mayans grew a tree whose fruit was protein-rich (*Brosimum alicastrum*). According to his research, the same unit of land yielded ten times the flour by tree-growing than by growing corn, and the new flour was rich in vitamins and iron. No strenuous work was required either. Thus, according to his calculations, 3,000 pounds could be extracted within a 20-day work period. This production could enable leisure time for developing centers of worship and rule. By growing roots, in comparison, leisure time decreased by half in relation to tree-growing, and by 1/4 in relation to corn-growing. In any case, it was not agricultural difficulties which engendered the collapse. External causes still remained: Suggestion has been made of foreign invaders and influx of religious methods accepted by priests but rejected by the people, and so forth.

The opinions of Ruz, the scholar who discovered the grave in the Palenque Pyramid, and that of the Mayan Art expert T. Proskouriakoff, are unique in that they do not view what transpired as the consequence of a one-time or continuous catastrophe but rather as a

---

[13] Eric Wolf, *Pueblos y Culturas de Mesoamerica*, Era, Mexico 1967.

[14] *Ibid.*

[15] Puleston Dennis, "New Data from Tikal on Classic Maya Subsistence," *Annual of Society for American Archaeology*, XXXIII, Santa Fe, New Mexico 1968.

necessity stemming from the socio-religious political structure of the Mayan tribes. Elements such as land depletion or floods, if they occurred, could only have served as catalysts rather than as the main cause.

On the verge of collapse throughout the 9th century, widespread theocratic rule based on chiefdom was predominant, according to the Sanders-Price definition.[16] Towards the close of the period many secular buildings were erected, burial rituals were altered in such a way that women and children were also buried at the centers of worship. On steles one can see deification of the nobility, indicating a drastic polarization between the stagnating ruling nobility and the farmers who had to support them. When archaic ruling methods are used, polarization may cause ineffectual government. Wiley's[17] studies demonstrated a sudden transformation in art forms after the ruling class lost government control. At that time, construction was completely discontinued and many shattered images of leaders may be found. The reference is probably to the same leadership which degenerated and engaged in massive construction for their own ends at the expense of the centers of worship. This widespread construction was beyond the abilities of farmers, who were forced to produce food as well as to allocate time for construction work. In a case like this, an invasion by foreign powers, or popular internal rebellion such as that which took place against the ruling Cocom at Mayapán in 1441 (for which documentation is available), could cause widespread upheaval - as was the case at Mayapan despite the presence of Mexican mercenary troops who supported the city lords. Fresco paintings at Bonampac depict such a rebellion,[18] which took place most likely around the time of the debacle, and also describe the methods of suppression employed by the troops of the city lords.

We have a situation in which there existed an uncompromising class-defined society which centralizes all governmental resources, including religions and writing, in the hands of a privileged few. These constituted a group which established deities, interpreted their

---

[16] Barbara Sanders William-Price, *Mesoamerica: the Evolution of a Civilization*, N.Y. 1968.

[17] Gordon Wiley, "The Structure of Ancient Maya Society, Evidence from the Southern Lowlands," *American Anthropologist*, 58, 5, Menasha 1956.

[18] Ruz, *El Pueblo*, p. 276.

doctrines, read and wrote the ancient script, including agricultural guidelines or customs originating from the calendar. Upon the disappearance of this nobility, with the obliteration of the elite, the entire culture faced extinction. In such cases, what remains are only the popular expressions, those used, among other things, as a lever for controlling the farmer. And thus, until the Post-Classical period in the 11th Century, when the culture underwent transformation as a result of the Mexican invasion, a "parenthetic" culture emerged, in which the former culture was erased. The farmers seized the abandoned buildings. In the absence of a secular-religious leadership which was evicted, a leadership which monopolized both knowledge and authority, the new settlers could not cope with the jungle, which devoured chunks of settled areas. In this way, the forest emerged victorious and the magnificent buildings of yore were quickly engulfed.[19] With the desertion of the cities, agriculture reverted back to subsistence farming, in which there was no need to maintain more than the bare requirements of the farmers' families themselves. Authoritative evidence for these processes was found at different archaeological diggings in the main centers.

Have written recollections of this process survived, besides the Bonampac wall paintings?

Before this question is raised, mention must be made of the opposite theory, in order to prevent an unbalanced account. Harvard University researchers stayed in Zinacantán at Chiapas and on the basis of anthropological and archaeological study at Belice, they reached a different conclusion. In their opinion, during the Classical Period the Mayan population dwelled in scattered communities, while the center served as a place for religious gatherings. In small settlements the religious centers were small as well and the priests enjoyed the same economic status as the farmers. The majority of inhabitants had equal access to priestly and governmental positions owing to the rotationary method popular to this day in the villages. Today, for example, a villager serving as judge or village chief must revert in the following year to working the land. Since the priesthood and leaders, according to this theory, emerged from a farming background, this facilitated allocation of workers for the building of cities

---

[19] Proskouriakoff, "El Arte...," pp. 196-197.

and centers of worship while the training required for the priesthood did not deviate from the exigencies of our days as regards the fulfillment of economic or religious functions in the village. In other words, it was a classless society without a group of nobles who exploited the masses of farmers.[20]

Wall paintings, reliefs and diggings present a completely different picture.[21] Even in texts written in Latin characters, a world different from that depicted by the Harvard team is disclosed. The attempt to establish a model applicable to the 3rd-10th centuries on the basis of anthropological studies is questionable, since three periods have in the meantime elapsed, viz. 1) The Post-Classical Period, 2) the Spanish Period and 3) the period of Independent Mexican Rule. Furthermore, the architecture and monumental constructions are incongruous with a classless society or even a slaveless society.

---

[20] Evon Vogt, "Some Implications of Zinacatan Social Structure for the Study of the Ancient Maya," *Actas del XXXV Congreso Internacional de Americanistas*, I, Mexico, 1964.

Alberto Ruz, "Aristocracia o democracia entre los antiguos mayas," *Anales de Antropologiá*, I, Mexico, 1964.

William Havilland, "Social Integration and the Classic Maya," *American Antiquity*, 31, 5, Part I, 1966.

The attempt to focus on a concrete study in order to reach historical conclusions was not exclusive to the Harvard school. An attempt to erect a "psychological model" of the Mayan tribes was also devised. During eight research-seasons throughout the 1930's, a team led by Moris Steggerda of the Carnegie Institution in Washington tried to build such a model. The group sampling was very small and non-representative. During the first stage, 29 people were interviewed, 20 of whom worked on behalf of the researchers. Thirty-four additional respondents (Indians) answered questions of 50 interviewers, themselves Indians, and 38 answered questions of eight half-breeds. The method of research complied with accepted means of testing in the U.S. at the time. Steggerda himself was aware of the problems raised by employing a test drawn from one culture in order to understand a completely different one. The test determined, for example, the local inhabitants' IQ. In any case, even if the sampling had been sufficient in number and the method more effectual, the attempt to erect a psychological model of an entire culture on the basis of a limited study in one village, may be considered improper. On this topic see: Steggerda Morris, *Antropometry of Adult Maya Indians*, Lancaster, 1932.

[21] Ruz, *El Pueblo*, p. 283.

Problems of Script and Documentation

It must be assumed that the Mayan hieroglyphs provide solutions to different problems arising in cultural studies (not only this script, but the pictorial script as well which figuratively represents symbols and life stories). If it were possible to decipher the hieroglyphs this would enable us to understand events, beliefs, and governmental structure. Were one to add to this decoding the knowledge attained from deciphering paintings, the picture would be clarified, and it may be assumed that many of today's accepted theories would be invalidated. However, such is not the case in reality. A prominent scholar such as S. Morley has claimed that Mayan hieroglyphs were unique and that these hieroglyphs, the tribal chronological calendar, and clear architectural guidelines, characterize not only the Classical culture but Mayan culture as a whole. In his opinion, this script was the first on the continent (a strange deduction since already at the time of his publications there was some knowledge of the Olmeca script of the Veracruz coast which preceded the Mayan script). Mayans began to write with these characters in 353 B.C.E. or in the year 7.0.0.0.0. according to the Mayan calendar. Inability to decipher the complex script, especially in the absence of basic features, which were available when the Egyptian script was decoded, present difficulties which appear at this point to be insoluble. Bishop Landa, who interrogated and killed tribal members, found in his opinion a link between hieroglyphic characters and the 27 letter alphabet; in addition, he discovered the structure of the 18-month religious calendar in which each month comprises 20 days with an extra 5-days tacked on at year's end. Already 100 years ago, Ph. Valentini proved that what Landa thought to be an alphabet was characters possibly corresponding to Spanish phonetic values. In numerous paintings and pieces of writing some or most of the 27 symbols are not repeated; thus one may exclude the possibility that these form an alphabet.[22] The French priest Brasseur de Bourbourg, who studied one of the scripts (Codice Troano),[23] stumbled on a problem which

---

[22] Phillip J.J. Valentini, "The Landa Alphabet, a Spanish Fabrication," *Proceedings of the American Antiquarian Society*, 75, Worcester, 1880.

[23] Charles Brasseur de Bourbourg, *Manuscrit Troano, Etudes sur le système graphique et la langue des Mayas*, Paris, 1870.

puzzled the 19th century, i.e. the decline of the continent of Atlantis. A few years later, due to chronological decoding, it was found that the priest had read the symbols backwards. Everything may be found in this undeciphered script: wind directions, phonemes each of which denotes a day of the calender (W. Wolff), key words around which phrases are constructed. And there are many attempts at decipherment which are reminiscent of a fictional novel rather than a scholarly work.[24]

Studies employing new techniques have been made in the Soviet Union. Yuri Knorozow claims to have found a code instrumental in deciphering the script.[25] He refuted Bishop Landa's basic informative value. In his opinion, from now on, as a result of his method, it will be possible not only to decipher but to read the texts as well. According to newspaper reports (1976) (and one may anticipate a book on the latest research), Knorozow claims to have read the three existing codices and maybe even a fourth, the authenticity of which is questionable.[26]

An indepth study with completely different results was carried out at the Scientific Academy of Siberia,[27] where pictoral material and lexicographic material of the 16-17 centuries, and texts written in Latin characters, were run through a computer. In the researchers' opinion, a common denominator was found between all research components. But, as mentioned previously, the results are so different from those of Knorozow and Kosarev-Ustinov's studies that a long road still seems to lie ahead.

---

24 Antoon Vollenaere, "A Belgian Contribution to the World's historical Inheritances: the deciphering of Mayan Hieroglyphic Writing," *Views and Surveys*, 162, Brucelas, 1973.

25 Yurii Knorozow, "La antigua escritura de los pueblos de América Central," *Etnografía Soviética*, No. 3, Mexico, 1952; "The Problem of the Study of the Maya Hieroglyphic Writing," *American Antiquity* XXIII-3, Salt Lake City, 1958. He researched the Dresden, Paris and Madrid codices and a recently discovered table dealing with the planet Venus.

26 Ruz, *El Pueblo*, p. 163.

27 E.V. Eureinov, Y.G. Kosarev, V.A. Ustinov, *Investigación de la escritura de los antiguos mayas con máquinas y computadoras electronicas*, Novosibirsk, Siberian Section of the U.S.S.R. Academy of Sciences, 1961.

A few schools approached the hieroglyphs as a calendrical expression and an expression of calendrical values (Zimmerman).[28] Those refuting this theory (Proskouriakoff) found historical values expressed in the paintings. The struggle for chronological determination enable constructive scrutiny and further research. The numbers and also calendrical values have been deciphered. Already in the anthology of prophecies (Chilam Balam) in Codex Perez I-II[29] there is an exact description of the calendrical structure and signs denoting days. This is the reason why books and studies were compiled on the Mayan's obsession with time. The truth is, that the obsession was that of the researchers who deciphered only dates, and not of the Maya, who supposedly dealt with other issues as well.

A phenomenon similar to that which occurred with the Incanotted script (Kipu) recurred with regard to the Mayan script. In only one generation, that of the Spanish conquest, a writing technique hitherto popular was completely forgotten. No one could be found who would be capable of deciphering this script and who would make it possible on the basis of this reading to interpret the religious elements existing before the conquest. The differences between historians are numerous. It is necessary to return to the point previously emphasized: *In a class-oriented society where the reading of the script is in the hands of few people, as part of the state policy, and where there is a tendency towards a complex, as opposed to simple script, the disappearance of the elite or its close servants will eliminate the option of reading or deciphering this script.*

Texts in Latin Characters and Text Barrier

In order to try and gain a comprehensive understanding of the historical and mythical processes, one must base oneself on written texts, most of which appear in the original tongue and some of which appear in Spanish written in Latin characters. The penmanship was

[28] Gunter Zimmerman, "La escritura jeroglífica y el calendario como tendencias de la historia cultural de los Mayas," *Desarrollo Cultural*, pp. 243-257.

[29] "Explicacion del Calendario Maya,"*El Libro de los Libros de Chilam Balam*, F.C.E. Mexico, pp. 150-154.

executed by one of the groups proficient in writing, more specifically by the missionaries' aides (Chajales), who were also family representatives, the official scribes of the clans, the soothsayers, the village scribes and group chieftains who carried out ritual dance.

The material put into writing is relatively late. A book written in the 17th century hinders the understanding of 10th century processes. It is especially difficult to follow the changes taking place in the narrative. After the Spanish conquest, accounts directly influenced by missionary doctrine were written as apologetic texts aimed at protecting the inhabitants from the severity of the avengers of idolatry. Sometimes accounts were written in which a certain family proved its proprietorship over a certain piece of land. Furthermore, since it may be assumed that at that time the reading of the ancient script had been lost, and if the narrative was based on oral tradition, that tradition did not always emanate from a priestly or chieftain family, even if some of the scribes benefited from an initial decoding of the paintings. It is likely that a portion of the priesthood serving as dramatic ritual functionaries passed on the traditional familial roles to their offspring by custom. An interesting example is the surviving ritual play Rabinal Achi.[30]

Another question to be asked is, after the material was put into writing, what significance did it retain? Was it written for use and then shelved for fear of the Spaniards? Or did it possess a sacred value? Christian elements superficially appear in different texts, especially those aimed at proving proprietorship over land. In the Totonicapán[31] titles, for example, it is written that the ancestral scribes (Quiché) came from Babylonia across the sea and that they owe their lineage to Abraham, Isaac and Jacob, and Balam-Qitzé. In this case it is clear who was responsible for the written text. However in other cases where there occur elements tinted with Biblical themes (such as: chaos, creation, flood, tribal migration, promised land and so forth), these accounts do not necessarily imply later influence, but rather universal mythical elements. In addition, apologetic texts were

[30] *Rabinal Achi*, Trad. Georges Raynaud (French) and Cardoza y Aragon (Spanish), Editorial del Ministerio de Educación Pública, Guatemala 1953.

[31] *Memorial de Solola-Titulo de Totonicapán*, F.C.E. Mexico 1950, Trad. Dionisio Jose Chonay.

careful to play down ritual elements which might be viewed as divine. Here one may cite many examples. If the text was written naturally, it neither concealed nor particularly emphasized such elements (unless the intention was to maltreat the local population). If the accounts retained elements clearly emanating from periods considered antiquated in relation to the time of the conquest, this also indicates authenticity.

The Popol Vuh

The most comprehensive mythical text surviving to this day is the *Popol Vuh* or *Pop Vuh*,[32] found in the 18th Century by the monk Ximenez in the Guatemalan village of Chichicastenango or Chuila, as it was called in those days. The village is situated near the city of Utatlán which was the capital of the chiefdom of Quiché, one of the most advanced tribes in central America at the time of the conquest. It is likely that when Utatlan fell in 1524 and its people were massacred by Pedro de Alvarado, the nobles and priests escaped to the adjacent village and smuggled with them traditional chronicles which later served as a source for the Popol Vuh.

Concealment of ancient sacred texts was accepted as a mechanism for cultural self-defense. To this day, grave robbers are familiar with these hiding places (such as the caves near Copán), find the concealed texts and sell them to the highest bidder. The question is whether the text in our possession is a transcription of a former book or an oral tradition "suckled by the local inhabitants," in the words of the monk himself.

The original text was lost, and this fact presents difficulties as well. Only Ximenez's version remains, which he transcribed from the original and also translated. Ximenez's version contains erased sections relocated in other parts of the book. Did he read incorrectly and wrongly attempt to make corrections, or did he wish, for

---

32 *Book of the Council Popol Vuh* or *Book of Events Pop Vuj*. For quotations I have generally used the English translation of Adrian Recinos, Delia Goetz an Sylvanus Morley, *Popol Vuh: The Sacred Book of the Ancient Quiché Maya*, University of Oklahoma Press, 1969.

example, to amend fundamentals of belief? An additional question is to what extent could he or a different, anonymous author use an exact transliteration of the language characters. The word *Knik*, for example, means "today," but a stranger might pronounce it *Kanik*, meaning "death" — and this is only one example.

The author, actively involved as a popular narrator within the text itself, transforms the whole geographic scenario of events to the region of the chiefdom of Quiché *Are u xe oher tzih varal Quiché u bi*, "this is the beginning of the ancient tales of the place known as Quiché," or, according to Chavez's translation: "According to history, this place is called Quiché." Mention of a tribe's name is an anachronism, because this is relatively late in Mayan history. The author further adds that the text was written in the days of the Christians and that its goal is to preserve tradition:

> "This we shall write now under the Law of God and Christianity. We shall bring it to light because now the Popol Vuh, as it is called, cannot be seen any more..." (page 79)

In other words, the original text disappeared. In this vein, he adds:

> "The original book written long ago existed, but its sight is hidden to the searcher and to the thinker" (page 80)

In order to emphasize the fact that the text is no more, and to strengthen the version of the oral tradition, he further expounds:

> "Great were the descriptions and the account..." (page 84)

I have presented elsewhere evidence for the existence of a narrator who employed a popular technique in passing on myths by word of mouth; in the same way popular elements are found in the Bible, for example,[33]

Adrián Chavez, teacher of Quiché, who redeciphered the text with the help of his knowledge of the original language (which was his mother-tongue), found in 1973 an ancient hieroglyphic script at the archaeological museum of Chichicastenango, in what he claims to be the Quiché tongue, and texts like this could have served according to him as a genuine source for the contents of the Popol Vuh.[34] Logical as it may seem, his theory has yet to be substantiated:

---

[33] Nahum Megged, *Los Heroes Gemelos del Popol Vuh*, Ed. Jose de Pineda Ibarra, Guatemala 1979, pp. 154-158.

[34] Chavez, p. (4).

the ancient script he found cannot be read according to the text itself, a popular narrative is also involved — his is, indeed, undisputed. However, it is likely that the tradition took on a particular written form, even though it would be difficult to find a suitable candidate (a scholar or a wise man) who would have learned the ancient script in the mountain region. It is also likely that their script-writer copied ancient characters without understanding the content.

Manuscripts in Latin characters emerged to save the oral tradition, which was facing extinction. A text preserved in this form at Yucatan in Chumayel, the so-called tongue of Zuyúa[35] is particularly interesting since this is the only text which interprets esoteric terms and expressions put into writing for the first time. According to the narrator-priest, the true significance of the sayings and words was being forgotten; in one year (1628), no man would know what these signified.

Edmonson's theory that the Popol Vuh was written by the Kavék[36] family in order to prove proprietorship does not invalidate its interest as far as its contents are concerned. Dances and ritual fundamentals remain which can shed light on this magnificent text. The Swiss scholar R. Girard views the remnants of ritual expressions today as rudimentary material no less valuable than any precise archaeological finding.[37]

Religious Elements

What are the religious elements in the book which include cosmogony, law and religious ethics? Did these elements undergo transformative processes at the time of the Spanish conquest, or during the pre-conquest period?

---

35 "El lenguage de Zuyua y su significado," *El Libro de los Libros*, pp. 131-144.

36 Munro Edmonson, "Historia de las Tierras Altas Mayas, segun los documentos indigenas," *Desarrollo*, pp. 273-303.

37 Girard wrote numerous books on this topic, including studies on the Chorti tribes and research of ritual worship. We may especially note *El Esoterismo del Popol Vuh*, Mexico 1952; *Los Mayas Eternos*, Mexico 1962. *El Popol Vuh Fuente Historica*, Guatemala 1952.

In the Popol Vuh, there is a cosmogonic myth different from other written material from the same geographical region, which begins with the tribal migration of the 11th century. There are gods and not just tribal deities, there are cultural heroes, laws and religious ethics and changes to which one may relate in an historical context.

Already at the beginning of the book, mention is made of thirteen gods who plan and create the world by the spoken word. These thirteen gods are, according to the actual text, a transformation of four beings bearing different names. The names also indicate a separate essence, such as: the life-giving pair, the founders, images in the form of animals, etc. The heart of Heaven, the principal god, comprises three gods whose name is common — Huracan, i.e., the one-legged god. One of the heavenly god's names is reminiscent of the name of the almighty god of the Mayan tribes in Yucatan[38] (this also being the family of the culture heroes according to the actual text).

To these gods are added the patrons of "the old wise men" (Ixpiyococ Ixmucane) imbued with a divine-earthly identity. They are soothsayers and the gods use them to create men.[39] They are fathers, grandfathers and grandmothers of the culture heroes, and their habitat is earth. They are elders who come to the aid of heroes in need, especially at the time of crisis: when Hunaphu loses his hand in a struggle with a giant, or when the two twin brothers are sentenced to death by the lord of the underworld (Xibalba).[40] In other words, they can penetrate the earth's crust, without explaining how, and reach the world beyond at will.

The thirteen heavenly gods are identical in number to that of the heavenly gods of the other Mayan tribes (*oxlahun Tiku*), the lords of

---

[38] For example, Tzacol-Bitol are the creator and founder. The goddess mother: Alom. The god-patron: Qahalom. The big wild boar Nim-Ac, etc.

[39] The hunter Hunaphu is also the name of the 20th day of the Quiché calendar, name of a mountain, one of the culture heroes according to the *Popol Vuh*, in addition to resembling the name Hunab-Ku of Yucatan, the great god which was an almost-abstract figure.

[40] They are also the divine seers, creators of men from wood and corn. In addition, they served as parents of man, as grandmother and grandfather of the cultural heroes.

the number thirteen, corresponding to the calendrical value of 260 days (twenty days per month times thirteen months). In addition to the thirteen heavenly gods, as previously stated, there is the heart of Heaven comprised of three gods. The heart of Heaven, according to preserved beliefs, is apparently integrated into the system of "hearts" of the universe, i.e., "heart" of the earth, "heart" of the lake, "heart" of the mountain, and so forth. Among the other Mayan tribes as well, many gods existed in addition to the thirteen heavenly gods, each god with his particular heavenly department of authority.

Among the Yucatan tribes, counterbalancing the thirteen heavenly gods were those who loathed them and with whom they conducted an uncompromising struggle. The reference is to nine gods of the underworld, joining ranks with Cizim or Ah Puch, the god of death. The underworld of Popol Vuh includes six pairs of "lords," i.e., twelve gods, and not nine, as in the Yucatan tribes. The Pantheons are not identical.

Besides the gods, mention is made of the family of the "proud ones" those who declared themselves gods, sun, moon, and heroes, and who were finally exposed as false gods. The reference is to the Vucub Cakish family and their two giant sons. Culture heroes had parents as well (two twin male brothers along with a mother), and a pair of twin brothers. The brothers were a boon to the family, and an anathema to the gods, in the same way the heroes were a boon to the heart of Heaven and undesirable to the Earthly patrons, and in particular to the grandmother Xmucane, who, in a different context, is the divine soothsayer, assisting the gods in creating man.

From halfway through the book, after the creation of the true man from corn, the gods experience a reversal and the central stage is occupied by tribal gods, the predominant of which is the tribal chief of Quiché, Tohil, a cultivating guiding god, who also provides warmth, sun, light and rain. This god obliterates the importance of the gods preceding him in the book and especially that of the culture heroes, who are hereafter ignored. The god of the heroic period and of the migratory period forsakes the god who brought light and taught how to grow corn.

These chapters at the end of the book indicate the changes and reversal in religious, ceremonial and cultural perceptions. Not only were the gods' names obscured but in addition, the cultural, religious and geographical foundations were altered. It may be conjectured that a new cultural ethnic group emerged, foreign to the previously ruling group, which appears in the preceding chapters. The "new ones" may be identified with precision by the following characteristics. The tribes, it is told, migrated to Tulán later to leave it. They came to the city as one tribe with a single tongue, as it is written, and left the city as many tribes and tongues after the destruction. Thus, they were divided into different sections each of which had its own leader or a different god. Regarding Tohil, the great god, the narrator states:

> "Because, in truth, the so-called Tohil is the same god of the Yaqui, the one called Yolcuat-Quizalcuat" (page 189)

In other words, Tohil is the Mexican Quezalcoatl[41] and Tulan is Tula, the capital of his chiefdom; the migration referred to is that of the Toltecs who wandered southwards after the destruction of their city, opening in the south the period known as Post-Classical.

Following the appropriation of leadership by the four founding parents of the tribe, who were the parents of mankind according to the narrative, their sons turned northwards in order to seize rule. They aprpoached Nacxit, priest and leader of the Toltecs.[42] The pages which follow also mention the Mexican Tribes and Tepeu-Oliman — these being the Toltecs and Olmecs.

---

[41] Hunaphu is always losing a part of his body. In the battle against the giant Vucub-Kakish, he loses a hand. During the ball game in Xibalba, he loses his head, and during the rehearsal of body dismemberment he is the one sacrificed by his brothers. Inasmuch as the two twins became the sun and the moon, apparently personification of the ever-changing moon, as opposed to the sun which perpetuates its shape and form. In this case, the hero Ixbalamque. The name Ixbalamque comprises the word ***Balam*** meaning tiger. This animal, too, connotes the sun.

[42] Much has been written on Quezalcoatl, the legendary civilizer of the Toltecs. He is the white bearded figure who emerged from the sea in the direction of Tula and brought culture i.e., material and ethical refinement. Later on, following transgression, he goes into exile and according to one version, incinerates himself at the sea shore, promising to come back. On this subject, see Miguel Leon Portilla, *Quezalcoatl*, F.C.E. Mexico 1968.

According to characteristics of the *Popol Vuh* text, the god Tohil resembles to a greater degree the Mexican god Huizilopochli, and there are hints in the narrative as well. In later consciousness, the two foreign gods became united.

One of the characteristics of the period (according to other sources as well) was the revival of human sacrifice. The historian Herrera who followed the Spanish conquerors relates: "The ancients say that once, 800 years ago in this land, there were no idol worshippers and afterwards the Mexicans arrived led by Quezalcoatl... and among other things the commander taught them how to sacrifice hearts."[43] And elsewhere: "The number of sacrificial victims was great and this custom was introduced to Yucatan by the Mexicans."

The Popol Vuh, too, refers to this religious-ritual element:

> "What must the tribes give oh, Tohil... Well, are they willing to give their waist and their armpits? (page 179)[44]

and concludes saying that the god was brought there by the Mexicans:

> "Then they remembered their older brothers and their younger brothers, the Yaqui, to whom dawn came there in the land which today is called Mexico" (page 109)

The second portion of the book leaves no doubt as to its historic identity. In the 11th-12th centuries, inhabitants of the north invaded Mayan tribelands. They erected cities and transferred constructional and cultural patterns from the Tulan ruins, and, in addition, renewed human sacrifice which the Mayans had cast off or curtailed for many years. The legendary Quezalcoatl of Tula or one of his offsprings, or may be other priests who sustained the dynasty and bore its name, headed the leading group, although these did not necessarily follow his religious way, which was known to abhor human sacrifice. At the same time, the city of Chichén Itzá in Yucatán and the city of Mayapán were either restored or built. At that location, among other things, new ritual customs were concentrated. Quezalcoatl acquired various names — Nacxit according to the *Popol Vuh* and according to the prophetic anthology, *Chilam Balam*; Kukulkan in the Mayan

---

43 For Quezalcoatl, (the king or priest) had different names, this being one of them. Other narratives cite, for example, his daughter's murder in the wars of Guatemala. Cf. "Guerra común de Quichés y Cakchikeles," *Cronicas Indigenas de Guatemala*, Trad. Adrian Recinos, Edicion Universitaria, Guatemala, 1957.

44 Sylvanus Morley - revisado por George Brainerd, *La civilización Maya*, F.C.E. Mexico 1972, pp. 95-96, p. 201. Antoño de Herrera, *Historia general de los hechos de los castellanos en las islas* in tierra firme pp. 1726-30.

tongue of Yucatan where the figure corresponded with the god of ancient waters; and Gucumatz to the Quiché tribe; and thus, he appears in the Popol Vuh as an impersonation of the ancient god. Henceforth, the name Quezalcoatl, by undergoing various transformations, is connected with the history of the southern tribes. It is not difficult to see that the narrative presenting cultural beginnings after the creation of man from corn, deals with the outset of the Post-Classical culture in Guatemala[45] — a culture which itself disappeared in various locations, or was vanquished by the Spaniards.

Can the narrative of the chapters prior to the creation of man from corn (Book III) and the appearance of the Cavec family, serve as source material for the previous period (the Classical Period, especially the end of the period and the farmers' rebellion, according to the Ruz version)?

The key must be sought in the essence of the culture heroes, just as Tohil-Quezalcoatl's essence points to the Toltec Period.[46] The fundamental book dealing with the cosmogonic process up to the final creation of man after three futile attempts (animals as praying man, mud-man and wood-man) does not provide new gods, besides the gods of creation, the heart of Heaven and sorcerers who were also seers of the supernatural. This is not the case throughout the heroes' narrative, in which popular gods, to whom individuals turn in time of need, make their appearance. The central gods, to whom individuals turn in time of need, make their appearance. The central god is the heart of Heaven, to whom all requests are directed, including requests put forth by the seers of the supernatural who cast lots and decided how men would be created and from what substance (so as to sustain the gods with prayer, which was their nourishment). After the magic deed described therein, the sorcerers turned to the heart of Heaven with these words:

> "Come to sacrifice here, Heart of Heaven; do not punish Tepeu and Gucumatz" (page 89)

---

[45] A method of sacrifice popular with the Mexicans which included tearing out the heart of the sacrificial victim.

[46] It is interesting to cite the opposite theory of George Kubler, *The Art and Architecture of Ancient America*, The Pelican History of Art - Baltimore, 1962. In his opinion, the art of the Toltecs began in Chichen-Itza (Yucatan) and from there passed to Tula, rather than the opposite, as popularly conceived.

The heart of Heaven is the recipient of the sacrificial victim and the sacrificer. His non-participation in the ceremony is interpreted as punishment harmful to the other Heavenly gods, the gods of creation. That is, he is the almighty god and all are subordinate to him.

In the basic cosmogonic narrative there are many elements which could have emanated from priestly tradition by means of drawings or ancient script, or paintings dealing with the creation of the world; however, in this instance as well, there are symbols which provide differentiation — i.e., the man from corn, the farmer, who is the perfect cultural man. The manner in which this concept appears in the *Popol Vuh* is unique when compared with other Mayan sources.[47] In addition, the man from wood is unique, and so is the appearance of the "proud" family, which coincides with the flood that destroyed the wood-man. This family enjoyed a totem symbol in the image of a Guacamayan bird.

The religious-ethical characteristics of the fundamental text are: (a) The gods can err, just as the tribal Shaman may err in prediction, especially if the objective is the creation of something out of nothing. (b) There is no correlation between deed and punishment. The category of "sin" is unclear. In any case, it would be difficult to consider this an ethical category. The mud-man was punished for having been improperly created by the gods and for not having been granted an identity. The same verdict applies to the wood-men. The punishment is also inconsistent. In an etiological description, the

[47] The sanctity of corn was found among other tribes as well. According to chronicles of the Cakchikel tribe, *Memorial de Sololá*, man was first created of clay, later on of corn. But there is no significant difference between the two creations. On the other hand in the *Popol Vuh* the wooden-man who is transformed into an ape is inferior to the corn-man who is the genuine human being. The gods, too, were created from corn by the priests in a manner reminiscent of the Christian mass. Sahagún, *Historia General de las Cosas de la Nueva España*, pp. 1-72, relates that the Mexicans would mould the body of the god Huizilopochtli from corn and honey and afterwards eat it. And Fray Toribio de Benavente o Montolinia, *Memoriales* (pp. 32-33, 51-53) tells of the holy bread used in creating the god. Also Tezcatlipoca the Mexican was created from corn. Creation of the god from the crop sustaining men was an accepted practice in popular consciousness. The difference in *Popol Vuh* is in the significance of the creation of man from corn in relation to any other creation, and the superiority of this man over other creations, particularly art forms, which the narrator concedes.

animals, who could not pray, are sentenced to be used as food by future men. The primitive mud-man is condemned to destruction and obliteration. The wood-man is sentenced to die in the flood, whereas the flood, animistically perceived, involves domestic animals and household wares rebelling against man, upon whom injurious divine foam rains down. Surviving remnants of the remaining men are transformed into apes. (c) The text dramatically accentuates the gods' need for prayer for self-preservation. If the prayer did not appear before sunrise, before the dawn's light, the gods would vanish. The urgency may be viewed in a cultural-symbolic context through the motif of light, corresponding to the tribe's cultural dawn, and in a psychological context. In any case, it is clear that the gods are requesting a verbal and not a human sacrifice. The verbal sacrifice has to emerge from the mouth of the farmer, both corn-grower and conceived from corn, this being the true man. (d) The farmer is a creation preferred over all other fabrications, in particular artistic creations (pottery, man-made of wood or metal substance), and society is based on him. The essential difference in value is demonstrated by the dissolution of the wood-man, survivor of the flood, who becomes an ape. The ape is the god of artists or a totem symbol of them — the creature capable of mimicry, likened to a man without actually being one, whose power (like that of the artists) is in imitation and not in the creation of something out of nothing. Concurrently, the farmer repeatedly executes the miracle of creation year after year: the miracle of creating something out of nothing by transforming a seed into a food-bearing plant, and so on. All supernatural powers participate in the accomplishment of this great miracle: the Heart of Heaven, the rain-ruler, gods of the land, and the gods inside the earth, corresponding to the underworld. The real miracle is not in the construction or decoration of a city with paintings or statues, but rather in the production of food from the earth; (e) "Enter then into council grandmother, grandfather, our grandmother, our grandfather, Xpiyococ, Xmucane, make light, make dawn, have us adored, have us remembered by created man, by made men..." (page 87). The true man, the farmer, must pray and not offer sacrifice; this constitutes the religious-ethical foundation repeated throughout the heroes' narrative.

The heroes determine definite orientations which complement the basic narrative. Human sacrifice is forbidden, and only in one section do the heroes sacrifice the head of the underworld. This phenomenon, too, may be explained.[48] When the heroes' mother is accused of prostitution by the heads of Xibalba because she bore children of an unknown father, she is taken away to be sacrificed (according to the custom apparently accepted at that time) after an inquisition-like trial. The verdict would be carried out far from the settlement, in the forest or in an open clearing, as was apparently the custom later on during the Post-Classical Period, when according to the *Popol Vuh* narrative, the sacrificing priests hunted their victim at the crossroads. The gods' words:

> "Ahpcop, Achih, bring me her heart in a gourd and return this very day before the lords" (page 121)

Words of the princess to the messengers in a denunciatory tone:

> "Very well, but my heart does not belong to them. Neither is your home here, nor must you let them force you to kill men"

No more human sacrifice nor real blood. Instead of blood, they had to use the blood of a tree — ritual instead of actual sacrifice. This element returns during the fateful ball game between the gods of the underworld and the heroes. When the gods thought they had won, they unsheathed the sacrificial knives. When the heroes ultimately won, there is no mention of their desire to sacrifice (page 145).

The superiority of the farming man over the artists is exemplified clearly in the history of the heroes as well. The heroes' brothers were artists who were familiar with all arts and crafts, from playing instruments to smithery and construction, and who served later on as the gods of artists and craftsmen. That is, they gathered all the arts which were considered important during the Classical Period, the period of city-builders, when cities were adorned with statues and giant fresco paintings. In the construction of shrines as well, they employed all building materials: wood, stone, earth, metal and paint. Contrary to the contention that artists are superior (it is even said that artist-brothers are the eldest, the first) in a magic struggle against the younger brothers, the elder brothers, who are the artists, became apes just as the wood-men did. In addition, the great grandmother, seer of the supernatural, could not save them because she was unable to withhold laughter. There is reiterated emphasis on artists as apes,

[48] See further on.

who can only mimic, amuse and ridicule, as opposed to real men, the farmers, the men who are corn, corresponding to the heroes, i.e., the younger brothers; these men revitalize year after year the miracle of the creation of plants and manifest their true birthright by virtue of the gods.

Of the elder brothers, the narrative says:

> "They were invoked by the musicians and singers, and by the old people. The painters and craftsmen also invoked them in days gone by" (page 130)

In contrast, the younger brothers represent the spirit of the corn. Upon their descent to the underworld they planted two canes in the court yard of the house, the sacred site for earth rituals. When the twins died the corn wilted. When they were resurrected the corn sprouted. When they died, prior to their resurrection according to the narrative, their bodies were milled like corn flour and in this form they were cast into the water to emerge resurrected:

> "...if it dries, this shall be the sign of our death... But if it sprouts again: They are living"... (page 139)

In another chapter as well, the first chapter dealing with the lives of the heroes, reference is made to the primitives, those ostracized by the gods (the artist-brothers are also referred to as primitives), a family of giants headed by the bird Guacamaya, who is identified with the sun and the moon. The "proud one" (*Gucup Cakish* in the words of the narrative) derives his strength from his wealth which comprises precious stones, particularly jade and metals:

> "...For my eyes of silver, bright, resplendent as precious stones, as emeralds, my teeth shine like perfect stones"... (page 93)

This figure represents the wealth which accompanied the ritual to the gods, especially the sun god, corresponding in totem terms to Guacamaya. He is called Gucup Cakish (the 7th Guacamaya) in the Quiché language and Kinik Kakmo in Yucatan,[49] He and his sons are described as most primitive with respect to their ability to produce food efficiently. The proud one, the wealthy father, eats fruit off

[49] Many researchers have already related to the identity of the two figures, the sun god and the totem symbol of a Guacamaya bird. On this subject, see: Megged, *Los Heroes*, "El misterio de la familia de Vucub Caquix," pp. 59-83.

the tree because he is unable to produce food,[50] and his giant sons, capable of moving mountains and lowering the earth, gather crabs by the streams or depend on others to supply food. In other words, the rich figure, corresponding to the sun deity whose sons rule over the earth, is primitive and backward, while, in contrast, the wondrous miracle of food production is being carried out. Consequently, this whole family is wiped out by the heroes, and the story narrators speculate as to who is the truly rich man.

Poised opposite the proprietors of metals, feathers and precious stones, stands the heroes' mother, who resembles the agricultural goddesses, and in particular Ixcacao, the goddess of the cacao plant, whose crop served as legal tender in those days.[51] Many researchers have already related to the identity of the two figures, the sun god and the totem symbol of a Guacamaya bird. In other words, currency emanating from agricultural labour is opposed to metal, feathers or gems.

The inhabitants of Xibalba who were defeated by the heroes, apart from their role as gods of the underworld, also belonged to a definite social group. Others call them the lords. These same lords govern life and death, according to the narrative, because the real man from corn had not yet made his appearance. Regarding those same lords, the narrator states:

> "They were also false in their hearts, black and white at the same time, envious and *tyrannical*"... (page 162)

The labels are interesting: coloured (black and white), sacrificing priests (they would paint their faces before the ceremony) and *tyrannical*. In this way the rulers were described, those who governed within

[50] His inability to obtain food was a factor in his downfall. The twin heroes knew that he would always seek tree-grown fruit, and consequently found him and shot him with an arrow. His eldest son, giant and hungry, fell prey to the twins who informed him of the existence of crabs, his only food, which he would gather by the streams. The second giant, who ate birds prepared by the twins by means of special magic oath, was destined to the same fate. The family's wealth took the form of metals and precious stones and feathers; thus, according to the narrative, they could not obtain a divine category, or a category of heroes or nobles. They were dependent and secondary in respect to the farmer, provider of food.

[51] Oviedo Valdez, *Historia General y Natural de las Indias*, Libro 8 Cap XXX, Cevilla 1851, describes the cacao as tender; for example, they paid 10 cacao beans for a rabbit or a prostitute, 100 for a slave.

the earth, possessing that which the earth's belly yielded: precious stones and metals. In addition, they possessed legions of builders and craftsmen.

Opposite these stood the agricultural heroes, identified with corn. Corn, an entity sprouting from inside the belly of the earth, is also connected with the underworld, inasmuch as the twins' mother is daughter of the underworld (when the twins won in their struggle and the corn sprouted, the grandmother made the center of the house the fixed site for the corn rituals).

The corn-men as heroes in their struggle with the underworld return to the epic of the seed planted in the soil, which must overcome incalculable risks inside the earth until it finally manages to burst outwards. If it then succeeds in overcoming the obstacles of the outer world, food is created.

The heroes' parents would incorporate in their images the corn ritual and the ritual of the plant's yearly renaissance:

> "Green reeds growing in the plains was their name. And they were called the center of the House and the center, because in the middle of the house they planted the reeds. And the reeds, which were planted, were called the plains, Green Reeds growing on the plains. They also were called Green Reeds because they had resprouted" (page 162)

In the other hand, the Xibalba inhabitants, as past rulers, would no longer be eligible for privileges as far as the farmers were concerned:

> "... your rank shall be lowered" (page 161)
>
> "The noble sons, the civilized vassals, shall not consort with you."

They would also lose authority and privileges of the upper class, including the right to play ball: "Not for you shall be the ball game." And instead of lords, they would serve as slaves under the farmers, working at supplementary chores: "You shall spend your time making earthen pots and tubs and stones to grind corn."

The sacrifice of the two leaders Hun-Came and Vucub-Came may indicate this hostile attitude to the ruling leaders: no longer popular ritual sacrifice (extracting the heart) but dismembering bodily parts out of intense hatred:

> "... one by one his arms and his legs were sliced off: his head was cut from his body and carried away; his heart was torn

from his breast and thrown onto the grass'' (page 158)

Naturally, myths possess various, diversified meanings, both philosophical and psychological, such as hastening redemption, governing death, hoping for rebirth, and destroying the kingdom of evil. But one should not ignore historical and social implications — dissolution of the sect of lords, destruction, extermination, and enslavement, annulment of authority stemming from wealth, statues and splendid buildings, including the authority to decide men's fate at will. In opposition stands the man of corn, the farmer, at the top of the ladder. All this points to a far-reaching social change upon the destruction of the nobility who amassed all resources and authority and detached themselves from the labourers of the soil. This nobility might be the same class which began to establish its status as near-gods, in place of the popular gods. At the close of the Classical Period, at the time of the rebellion, the images which symbolized this nobilty, the steles and figures, were wiped out. According to Ruz, this indicates a victorious revolution as opposed to the crushed rebellion depicted in the Bonampac painting.

If we accept Ruz's rebellion theory, the Hunaphu-Ixbalamke narrative is the recollection which has survived during the later period and through mythological adaptation, of this strange period lost in the clouds of oblivion (darkness, according to the text). Thus, in a mythological sense, the great rebellion against the tyrants, whose rule could no longer be tolerated, was described and documented. And thus, during the Colonial Period, the Mayan informers related that before the coming of the Mexicans in the 11th century they knew nothing of human sacrifice as a form of idol worship (leader worship) and that they were devoted to the popular gods only, their only motive being to beseech these gods to assist them in the supply of food. This approach was contrary to the perception prevalent during the Classical Period, expressed through iconography, paintings and myths, whereby the artist stood at the top of the social ladder owing to his role as creator of deities and decorator of cities. In the eyes of the rebelling farmers, they were merely apes only capable of imitation and amusement, unable to bring about the miracle of corn.

Thus, it is only with difficulty that the narrative of theecond part of the book introduces the renewal of human sacrifice. The tribes rejected this practice, and waged war against the priests who renewed the ritual. They were defeated by the family of priests-sacrificers who brought Tohil and, according to the tribal memory, renewed the tyranny of days gone by, as well as human sacrificedentified with the underworld:

> "Then a man came before Balam-Quitze, Balam-Acab, Mahucutab and Igui. Balam and (this man) who was a messenger of Xibalba, spoke thus: 'This is in truth your God, this is your support; this is furthermore the representation, the memory of your Creator and Maker'' (177)... Ask Tohil... said the man of Xibalba...'' (178)

From this moment on, the twin heroes are pushed from focus and the narrative ceases to dwell on them. A vague memory survives of a world which existed for a short time, when the rule of the tyrants was abolished, the value of the rich men was dwarfed, the rulers (those who stayed alive), became slaves and human sacrifice was abolished, a time when the authority of those same individuals, who could determine working arrangements, the protection of the city against the jungle, irrigation methods, etc., was abrogated. In this way, the rebels maintained their position for a short time until the jungle again engulfed the cities which had previously belonged to the nobility and artists and in which they dwelled until the new culture emerging from out of the north brought back the ancient concepts and with them a new deity which demanded obedience, slavery and human sacrifice.

THE GOOD AND EVIL SHEPHERD

Wendy Doniger O'Flaherty, Chicago

(i) God and Animals

The metaphor provided by beasts in myths is often a valuable bridge between what we think we know (the nature of certain common animals) and what we think other people imagine ("fantastic" qualities attributed to certain common animals). For, although it is no longer believed, as it once was, that all mythology is somehow connected with totemism, it is certainly still true that divine animals and theriomorphic gods pervade most mythologies. Animals and gods are two closely related communities poised like guardians on either side of the threshold of our human community, two "others" by which we define ourselves. Aristotle remarked that a man who could not live in society was either a beast or a god.

The ways in which people think about themselves in relation to animals both reflect and are reflected by the ways in which they think about themselves in relation to God. The process works in two opposite directions at once. The observation of the local fauna provides images with which people may think of their gods; whether or not people get the gods that they deserve, they tend to get the gods (and demons) that their animals deserve. But the ideas that people have about the nature of the gods, and the nature of the world, and of themselves, will lead them to project onto animals certain human features, features that may seem entirely erroneous to someone from another culture observing the same animal (or the same god). It is the first of these two processes — imagining gods as animals — with which I will be primarily concerned, though it can never be entirely separated from the second process — imagining animals as people.

Though all animals can be mythical beasts, certain animals tend to be more mythical than others, more archetypal, if you will. Mythological bestiaries vary greatly, in part simply because certain numinous animals live in some places and not in others. The images of gods that grow out of the relationship between humans and animals take two forms: theriomorphic and anthropomorphic. The theriomorphic forms include all the gods who are depicted as animals; the anthropomorphic forms include the gods who are depicted as humans in relationships (such as hunting and herding) with animals. In addition, there are the combined images, humans with animal heads or (far less common) animals with human heads; these represent various kinds of syntheses between the human and animal worlds. On one level, we may see a sameness here that is significant, a universal; among all the things that gods might be likened to (a grain of sand, a star, a plant), many different cultures have chosen to represent their gods in terms of animals. This is not an arbitrary choice; the natural experience of the animal world, particularly the encounter with the killing of animals, is a deeply moving, one might almost say an archetypal, experience that has inspired many religious formulations. On this level, we might see a sameness in the image used as a metaphor: god is an animal. But if we look at what is signified by the same animal image in different cultures, the original sameness is dramatically colored, often entirely erased or reversed; the same image has a different meaning. And if we compare what two cultures see in the same animal, we are struck by the way in which one culture will ignore what we perceive, from the other culture, as a striking, almost an obvious feature of that animal. In this way, the comparison of animal images reveals to us what may be suppressed, repressed, or pointedly denied in a religion.

(ii) The Good Christian Shepherd and the Evil Vedic Shepherd

As an example of such a comparison, let us consider the image of the divine shepherd. The concept of the divine shepherd and the human sheep takes on two very different forms in Christianity and Hinduism. The image of the shepherd is familiar and beloved in the West in both Jewish and Christian traditions. We know it from the

King James translation of the Twenty-third Psalm in the Hebrew Bible: "The Lord is my shepherd; I shall not want. He maketh me to lie down in green pastures." And we know it from Christian uses, from Handel's *Messiah* — "For he shall feed his flock like a shepherd; and he shall gather the lambs within his arm . . . and gently lead those that are with you" — and from Christmas carols: "While shepherds watched their flocks by night . . ."

But Hinduism teaches us to look at the innocent image of the shepherd through more cynical eyes. For the Hindus call their God a herdsman, too: but he is a very different sort of herdsman. The Vedic god Rudra is a god of the wilderness, a god of mountains and jungles, a wild animal. Rudra is called Pashupati, the Lord of Animals. The first element of this epithet, *pashu*, (cognate with the Latin *pecus*, cattle) designates sacrificial and domestic animals. The second element, *pati*, literally "protector" or "lord," is ambiguous; it can mean lord in the sense of guardian (guardian of animals, or herdsman — a human) or lord in the sense of king (king of beasts, or lion — an animal).

There is a central myth that tells how Rudra came to be called Pashupati: he attacks someone who has taken the form of a wild beast (*mriga*):

> Prajapati (the Lord of Creatures, the Creator god) approached his daughter; some say she was the sky, others that she was the dawn. He became a male wild animal and approached her, as she had taken the form of a female wild animal. The gods saw him and they said, "Prajapati is now doing what is not done." They wished for one who would punish him, but they did not find him in one another. They they assembled in one place the most fearful forms, and these, assembled, became the deity Rudra; therefore his name contains the sound *bhuta* (*bhuta-pati*, lord of ghosts). The gods said to him, "Prajapati is now doing what is not done. Pierce him (or hunt him, *vyadh*)." "So be it," he replied, "and let me choose a boon from you." "Choose." He chose as his boon the overlordship of cattle; therefore his name contains the word cattle (Pashupati). And one who knows this becomes rich in cattle. He took aim and pierced him; when he was pierced he flew upwards; they call him "the Wild Animal" (*mriga*) [the constellation Capricorn, also called "Head of the Wild Animal," *mrigashiras*]. The

> piercer (or hunter) of the wild animal is called by that name (the hunter, Sirius), and the female wild animal is Rohini (designating a female gazelle or red cow, Alpha in Taurus). The arrow, made in three parts, became the Tripartite Arrow (the belt of Orion).
>
> [The seed of Prajapati was burnt.] The completely charred coals became the black cattle; the reddened earth became tawny cattle. The ash spread in various forms — the buffalo, the ox, the antelope, the camel, the ass, and tawny cattle. The god said to them, "This is mine; what remains here is mine." But they deprived him of a claim by reciting the verse addressed to Rudra: "Father of the Maruts, let your good will approach us. Do not separate us from the sight of the sun. Spare our swift horses, O hero. Let us increase in offspring, O Rudra." (*Rig Veda* 2.33.1).[1]

Rudra is created to become the hunter, and he hunts a god who has already become a wild animal (*mriga*, in particular a deer, but also the general term for any wild animal in contrast with a tame animal or *pashu*) in pursuit of a female wild animal. As a result of being hunted, both the male and the female wild animals become transformed into domestic animals: he is beheaded like a sacrificial *pashu*, and she becomes a cow (as well as a gazelle, often a domesticated pet of Indian noblewomen). It is in this domesticated form that they become eternally fixed in the sky. Rudra demands the leftovers, the leavings of the sacrifice, that are in fact usually given to Rudra; but he is explicitly denied any right to a share in the sacrifice itself. Yet he is made Lord of Pashus.

A later text deals explicitly with the way in which Rudra was given a share of the sacrifice. As a wild creature, Rudra was an outsider; the myth tells about this otherness and explains how the other gods dealt with it.

> No offerings were made to Rudra in the Vedic sacrifice, and the other gods divided among themselves the portions of the sacrificial animals (the *pashus*); Rudra cast his evil eye on them.[2] Infuriated by the denial of his worship in another

---

[1] *Aitareya Brahmana*, with the commentary of Sayana (Calcutta, 1896), 3.33-34; Wendy Doniger O'Flaherty, *Hindu Myths* (Harmondsworth, 1975), pp. 29-31.

[2] *Tandya Brahmana*, with the commentary of Sayana (Calcutta, 1869-74) 7.9.16;

> sacrifice, Rudra came to the Vedic sacrifice and killed and mutilated all the gods until they gave him a portion of the sacrifice and proclaimed him lord of beasts (Pashupati). The gods who had been mutilated at the sacrifice said that they had been reduced to the condition of beasts; when they humbled themselves before Rudra, and agreed to be his beasts (*pashus*) and to make him their lord (*pati*), he agreed to restore them all.[3] He reminded them that he had deformed them because they were like beasts in failing to acknowledge his divinity.[4] Thus the other gods became the tame beasts (*pashus*) in the power of the god who was a wild beast, the Lord of Beasts. Rudra is said to be lord of both *pashus* and *mrigas*.[5]

In another late variant, the sacrificer is a descendant of the incestuous creator, named Daksha; he is beheaded still in anthropomorphic form, but Rudra (now called Shiva) replaces the lost head not with the head of a wild beast (*mriga*) but with the head of a goat, the sacrificial animal *par excellence*.[6] And Shiva by this time is known not as a wild beast but as the god who rides on a bull, Nandi, a *pashu*, and indeed the most mild-mannered of bovines.

Thus the myths themselves make the transition from a story about hunting a wild animal to a story about the sacrificial slaughter of a domesticated animal. In these myths, there is a conflict between Prajapati, the creator god, who is the lord (*pati*) of creatures who are born (*praja*), and the destroyer god, Rudra, who is the lord (*pati*) of beasts who are slaughtered (*pashus* or *mriga*). Thus Rudra-Shiva demonstrates his dominion over both wild beasts (*mrigas*) like himself and tame beasts (*pashus*) like his subjects and worshippers.

Now, the Hindus recognize five basic kinds of sacrificial animal or *pashu*: goats, sheep, cows (and bulls), horses (perhaps including all other single-hoofed animals), and human beings.[7] Though human

---

Maitrayani Samhita, ed. L. von Schroeder (Wiesbaden, 1970), 4.2.12.

3 *Varaha Purana* (Calcutta, 1893), 33.3-24.

4 *Linga Purana* (Calcutta, 1812), 1.72.34-45.

5 See Wendy Doniger O'Flaherty, *The Origins of Evil in Hindu Mythology* (Berkeley, 1976), pp. 169-73.

6 *Mahabharata* (Poona, 1933-69), 12.274.2-58; Wendy Doniger O'Flaherty, *Asceticism and Eroticism in the Mythology of Siva* (Oxford, 1973), pp. 272-277.

7 *Atharva Veda*, with the commentary of Sayana (Bombay, 1895), 11.2.9, with Sayana's commentary. See my "The Case of the Stallion's Wife: Indra and

sacrifice may not have been a part of extant Vedic ritual, there is evidence that it preceded and continued to cast its shadow upon Vedic ritual.[8] Certainly it is significant that humans were, at least theoretically, among the beasts who were "kept" by God. Whenever a Vedic fire-altar was consecrated, there were placed within it five golden images of the five *pashus*, again including man. Some myths say that there used to be human sacrifice, and that animals came to replace humans. These myths are not Euhemeristic explanations of a transition from human sacrifice to animal sacrifice; they are about the nature of ritual symbolism, explaining how it is that the animal stands as a substitute for the human in the sacrifice.

The *Rig Veda* tells us of the cosmic man (Purusha) who was sacrificed so that his dismembered limbs could form the very substance of the universe and of human society.[9] This is certainly a myth about anthropomorphic sacrifice, if not, technically, human sacrifice; but the myth of Purusha never became a part of the Hindu temple ritual. Indeed, though the text speaks explicitly of the sacrifice performed of Purusha, by Purusha, and for Purusha, that sacrifice does not form the paradigm for other sacrifices (human or other) to be performed in imitation of the sacrifice of Purusha *in illo tempore*. For the myth of Purusha is a cosmogony, and explains a cosmology; it is not a ritual charter. It explains how it came to be that the universe *is* Purusha; it does not exhort the worshipper to continue to make the universe Purusha. Nor is it clear whether Purusha offered himself up *willingly* as human sacrifice, a factor that will play an essential role in our comparative enterprise.

The implications of the inclusion of humans as sacrificial victims were spelled out in later Hinduism: "Whoever among gods, sages or men became enlightened became the very self of the gods, and the gods have no power to prevent him. But whoever worships a divinity as other than himself is like a sacrificial animal [*pashu*] for the gods,

---

Vrsanasva in the Rig Veda and the Brahmanas," *Journal of the American Oriental Society* 105:3 (1985), 485-498.

[8] See the discussion of human sacrifice in Aasko Parpola, "The Pre-Vedic Indian Background of the Srauta Rituals," in Frits Staal's *Agni: The Vedic Ritual of the Fire Altar* (Berkeley, 1983), II, 41-75, esp. 49-53.

[9] *Rig Veda* 10.90; Wendy Doniger O'Flaherty, *The Rig Veda* (Harmondsworth, 1981), pp. 29-33.

and each person is of use to the gods just as many animals would be of use to a man. Therefore it is not pleasing to those (gods) that men should become enlightened."[10] Thus, human men and women are indeed God's sheep, his sacrificial sheep. God keeps his flocks, all right, and watches over them — to make sure that they don't get away from him, so that he can butcher them and eat them.[11] God herds us with all the other animals in order to devour us; he is the wolf (lion) set to guard the geese, in the old parable, or a wolf (lion) in sheep's clothing. This seems a far cry from the Good Shepherd of Christianity. The Hindu tends to identify his deity in this image with the animal — here a wild animal who herds tame humans, while the Christian tends to see this aspect of his God as analogous with the human — a human who is a herder of tame animals.

(iii) The Good Cowherd

But later Hinduism has another kind of herdsman. Krishna appears as the Hindu equivalent of the benevolent Christian shepherd: he is a cowherd (*gopa*), a word whose latter element (*pa*) we have already encountered in its extended form (*pati*) in the epithet of Pashu-pati. Krishna is a lovely young boy who tenderly and bravely (if, occasionally, mischievously) guards the cows and their calves from all predators. The mythology emphasizes the generosity of the cow in willingly and lovingly giving her milk to her own child, the calf, and to the infant Krishna, and to all of us. This image is as beloved by Hindus, and as popular in its iconographic representations, as the shepherd is among Christians. Indeed, as we shall see, the Hindu image of the cowherd is even more innocent than the Christain image of the shepherd; for the Hindu cowherd is always a vegetarian, while the dietary habits of the Christian shepherd are ambiguous.

---

10 *Brhadaranyaka Upanisad* 1.4.10; *Satapatha Brahmana* (Benares, 1964), 14.4.2.21-22.

11 For a discussion of Shiva as the Lord of Beasts, see my *The Origins of Evil in Hindu Mythology* (Berkeley, 1976), 171-173.

The special emphasis that Hinduism places upon the cow, the totem of *ahimsa* (non-injury), may be seen as a result of the fact that the cow is a transformation of the sacrificed *pashu*: the cow willingly and generously gives her milk. The question of the willingness of the sacrificial victim was broached even in the Vedic period; the sacrificial stallion was reassured, in several Vedic hymns, that he was going to heaven, and the priest whispered into the ear of the sacrificial goat, "do not be afraid; you are going the good going."[12] This uneasiness, perhaps even guilt, even at the time when animal sacrifice was the general rule, extends to present-day sacrifices to Durga. It is said that one does not usually eat meat because the animal does not want to be killed; it struggles and becomes angry, and so its body becomes full of tempestuous poisons that infect the meat so that it poisons anyone who eats it. But one can eat the meat of a goat sacrificed to Durga, for the priest pacifies the goat until it is willing to die; and so its meat has none of the poison of hate.[13]

The willingness of the cow to give not only her milk but her flesh is explicitly described in a myth that dates from a time when Hindus still ate beef, c. 900 B.C.:

> In the beginning, the skin of cattle [*pashus*] was the skin of a man, and the skin of a man was the skin of cattle [i.e., cattle then had the skin that men have now, and the reverse]. Cattle could not bear the heat, rain, flies, and mosquitoes. They went to man and said, "Man, let this skin of ours be yours, and that skin of yours be ours." "What would be the result of that?" asked man. "We could be eaten by you," said the animals," and this skin of ours would be your clothing." So saying, they gave man his clothing, and if he wears their skin, cattle do not eat him in the other world; for cattle do, otherwise, eat a man in the other world.[14]

Despite the apparent fairness of the bargain, the laws of retribution threaten anyone who eats cattle: such a person may be eaten in

---

12 *Rig Veda* 1.162.1-4; 1.162.21; O'Flaherty, *The Rig Veda*, pp. 89-91: "You do not really die through this, nor are you harmed. You go to the gods on the path pleasant to go on."

13 Ed Dimock, personal communication, March 1986.

14 *Jaiminiya Brahmana* (Nagpur, 1954) 2.182-83; Wendy Doniger O'Flaherty, *Tales of Sex and Violence* (Chicago, 1985), p. 40.

return when he or she dies and goes to the other world. According to this text, the danger of being eaten in return threatens anyone who eats (or, more generally, consumes) *anything*, including vegetables. But there is always a way to protect oneself against this potential danger, and the particular protection for one who eats cattle is wearing the skin of the cow. Thus, this text explains why (and how) it is all right to eat beef.

The "historical" solution to the problem of the evil shepherd — the transition from eating the cow's flesh to drinking the cow's milk — is described in a myth in which the cow comes to symbolize bloodless culture in opposition to bloody nature. In contrast with the Purusha myth, which is not about history, this myth seems to me to be genuinely Euhemeristic, to speculate upon a development in human history. The earliest variants of the story were recorded at approximately the same time as the myth of the exchange of skins:

> Prithu the son of Vena milked the cow of plenty, using Manu (man) as the calf; and from her he milked cultivation and grain. She was then similarly milked by demons, who milked illusion out of her; . . . by the gods, who milked strength out of her; and by the serpents, who milked poison out of her.[15]

The cow thus yields in place of her mere flesh whatever one desires; for mankind, it is cultivated grain, agriculture. Later Hindu texts added important details to this theme:

> King Vena was evil; he went hunting and killed all the poor wild animals; as a child, he would violently strangle children of his own age at play, as if they were beasts. Finally, he neglected to perform Vedic sacrifices or to pay the traditional fees to the Brahmins. The Brahmins killed him; but then they were faced with a terrible famine as a result of Vena's misrule and with the even more terrible threat of anarchy, since Vena had died without leaving an heir. The priests churned the body of Vena and churned out of him a black creature, a tribal hunter [Nishada] who went away into the mountains, taking Vena's evil with him. Then the priests churned Vena again; this time they churned out of him Prithu, the good king and the founder of the lunar dynasty of kings. Prithu set out to end the

[15] *Atharva Veda* 8.10.22-29; O'Flaherty, *The Origins of Evil*, p. 322.

> famine; he attacked the earth cow with his bow and arrow, but she begged him to spare her life. he spared her on condition that she promise to allow him to milk her of whatever his people needed, and she agreed to this.[16]

Vena, the evil father, kills children as if they were animals, but he is also said to be evil for killing animals as if they were animals. He is an evil hunter. He also neglects the Vedic sacrifice, but this probably refers to the later, bloodless form of sacrifice; his refusal to sacrifice is thus equated with his refusal to nourish Brahmins and cows, not with a refusal to kill cows. When the father dies, he is split in two: his evil leaves him in the form of a hunter (a particular non-Hindu tribe), and his good survives in his good son, Prithu. Then the evil mother appears in the form of the earth cow, who holds back the food inside her so that her children (Prithu's subjects) dies, until Prithu attacks her and transforms her into the good mother, the generous mother. Prithu is good, but he, too, begins, as a hunter: he sets out to attack the cow, presumably to slaughter her for beef. In the course of the myth, however, he is transformed into a herdsman (a cowherd) and into a farmer: he learns to use not only milk but the crops of a stable civilization — to make bread instead of beef.

David Shulman has noted certain telling parallels between the myth of Prithu and the myth of Rudra Pashupati:

> Prthu performs the sacrifice within his more limited role of patron and warrior-king, but also as the successor to Rudra in the ancient agonistic model of the rite. The myth contains an explicit progression from a monolithic to a dualistic conception of the king's sacrifical task . . . Prthu . . . opens up the doors that his father had sealed. He remains, it is true, closely linked to the sacrifice: even this ideal king has a violent bent to his nature, as we learn also from the explicit comparison of Prthu to Siva. Indeed, this comparison is used to underline an action — Prthu's pursuit of the Earth-cow — that implicitly suggests one of the basic myths of Rudra-Siva, the Vedic tale of Rudra's pursuit of the incestuous Prajapati (who has the form of a stag). Prthu's milking of the earth thus seems to

[16] *Bhagavata Purana* (Bombay, 1832) 4.13-15; O'Flaherty, *The Origins of Evil*, p. 324.

express the terrifying (*raudra*) side of the king's nature.[17]

Both Rudra and Prithu perform sacrifices of their fathers; both of them, too, begin by hunting domestic or sacrificial animals, *pashus*. The sacrifice itself might thus be seen as the ritualization of this paradox, the hunting of the tame animals; and the myths of Rudra and Prithu are myths about the shadowy side of sacrifice. Both of them end by transcending their own paradigms, arguing for a sacrifice which is no longer aggressive and martial but has become willing and pacific.

(iv) The Good-and-Evil Shepherd

The Hindu myths seem to split into two separate aspects of god two different sorts of herdsmen from two different stages of Indian religion. The shepherd, the earlier image, Pashupati, is the god who kills and eats his flock (a flock in which sheep and goats as well as cows supply the victims). The cowherd, the later image, Krishna, is the god who no longer kills his flock but merely utilzies their milks. But these two sorts of herdsmen may combine in the self-image of the human who herds and eats animals, though they may splinter back into polarized images held apart in the ambivalent mind of a single person. The kindly shepherd cares for the flock, trying not to think of the butcher who slaughters them (even when the shepherd may also double as that very butcher). Thus the Good (nourishing) Shepherd (Krishna) is also a Bad (devouring) Shepherd (Rudra).

The separation of the two aspects of the herder of domestic animals is reflected dramatically in the elaboration of roles in sacrifices in Hindu temples. The deity in the center of the temple (an aspect of Shiva or Vishnu or Kali), once probably carnivorous, is now said to be a strict vegetarian; he accepts no blood offerings, only rice, fruits, flowers, and so forth. He is the good shepherd. But his alter ego, the butcher, still casts his shadow in the same temple: the rice cakes are carefully "suffocated" before they are offered, a clear atavism from the Vedic sacrifice in which, as we know, a living

17 David Dean Shulman, *The King and the Clown in South Indian Myth and Poetry* (Princeton, 1985), pp. 83 and 85.

animal was suffocated;[18] and the whole coconuts that the deity fancies bear a suspicious resemblance to human heads (an oft noted resemblance that is sometimes explicitly mentioned in the accompanying liturgy). Moreover, while the Brahmin priest makes his vegetarian offering in the central shrine, an Untouchable priest in an outer corner of the temple courtyard, or outside the very wall of the temple compound, slaughters a goat and offers its flesh and blood to the God — or, if the distancing between the two personae is even greater, to a servant of the god, or to a demon whom the god had killed.

(v) The Sacrificial Lamb/Cow

The Good Shepherd by far outweighs the Bad Shepherd in Christianity; though a few counter-instances occur in European literature, they are not part of the liturgy or indeed of the mainstream of Christian thought.[19] But against this anthropomorphic Good Shepherd, Christianity sets its own central image of God as a sacrificial beast, the Paschal Lamb — that is killed and eaten. The Christian God thus plays a double role, like the Hindu God, but not the same double role; he acts both as the Shepherd and as the slaughtered Paschal Lamb. But he himself is not a lamb; he comes to replace the lamb precisely so that the lamb — symbolic of all that is vulnerable and pure — will no longer be killed:

> Neither by the blood of goats and calves, but by his own blood, he entered in once into the holy place, having obtained eternal redemption for us. For if the blood of bulls and of goats, and the ashes of an heifer sprinkling the unclean, sanctifieth to the purifying of the flesh: How much more shall

---

18 Frits Staal, in his *Agni*, II, 468-9, tells of the controversy that surrounded the intention to slaughter a goat in the Vedic sacrifice that he documented in India recently.

19 Benjamin Britten's *War Requiem* intersperses into the archetypal Latin mass a modern manifestation, Wilfred Owen's poems about Wold War I; before the traditional "Kyrie eleison" — Lord have mercy — the English text opens with a poem that begins: "What passing-bells for those who die as cattle?" These cattle are, presumably, murdered by the Bad Shepherd.

> the blood of Christ, who through the eternal Spirit offered himself without spot to God, purge your conscience from dead works to serve the living God?[20]

This text is a metamyth, reflecting self-consciously on the transition from the Hebrew Bible to the New Testament. So, too, Paul in Romans explicitly counteracts the Hebrew Bible, reminding his people that it was once said, "And you shall die like cattle." It might appear from the Christian text that a human victim has been substituted for an animal; or, rather, that the lamb that was a substitute (or scapegoat) for an original human victim has now been replaced by another human victim. A variant of this theme is the story of Abraham, about to sacrifice his son Isaac in place of the usual lamb when another, magic ram appeared in the bush.

But Christ does not fill the role of the sacrificed domestic animal; he denies and cancels that role. (In this, Christian religious symbolism makes possible a more subtle exchange than is represented by such systems as the Hamurabi code — an eye for an eye — or the Aztec sacrifice, in which human beings were killed in order that other human beings might live — ceremonies in which the thing signified *is* the signifier.)[21] And the ritual that celebrates this event sacrifices neither a lamb nor a man, but a wafer and a cup of wine. The Eucharist thus stands at precisely the same remove from human sacrifice as the "suffocated" rice cake in the Hindu ritual stands from the sacrifice of a goat. But, in another sense, the Eucharist *is* the flesh and blood, and the communion is indeed a cannibalistic human sacrifice. This is not the place, nor am I the scholar, to review the complexities of the arguments surrounding transsubstantiation. But it is, perhaps, the place to show that the same complexities can be applied to the Hindu ritual. The bread and wine are a transformation of the original body and blood of Christ, but they are also transformed back into that body and blood in the ritual; so too, the rice cakes that replaced the goat become the goat. (Indeed, even in

---

[20] Hebrews 9.12-14.

[21] Indeed, the Aztec ritual is a defining case in our search of the full range of the possible ways in which humans have visualized their relationship with the gods in terms of their relationship with animals. But that is another story, one that I am not qualified to tell. I am indebted to Kay Read for what little I do know about the Aztecs.

the Aztec ceremony, the human victims became the god.)

The parallels between the Christian Eucharist and both human and animal sacrifices have been noted by many sacrificers in the process of their conversion to Christianity. Early missionaries working among tribes where cannibalism was known but loathed found themselves in the awkward position of being regarded as proselytizers for cannibalism when they spoke of eating the body and blood of Christ. And in Papua New Guinea, where pig sacrifices were the central religious ceremony before Catholic missionaries began their work in the 1950's, the Papuan converts to Catholicism used to speak of the *Agnus Dei* as "the pig of god," a syncretism that startled the proselytizers but that some, at least, did not find inappropriate.[22]

It is significant that, in both the Hindu and the Christian rituals, the substitution consists of food substances that symbolize the triumph of culture over nature. For Christianity, bread is a symbolic transformation of flesh, but also an actual physical (one might almost say magical) transformation of wheat, and wine an alchemical transformation of the grape. For India, rice, that is planted and then picked and replanted several times, becomes a cultural symbol of semen and rebirth;[23] the complexity of its multiple plantings and reapings is taken as analogous to the complexity of the process of multiple rebirth. Balls of rice, called (*pindas*), are used in funeral ceremonies to supply a new body for the dead man and in birth ceremonies to guarantee a male child to a women who wishes to become pregnant.[24] In both cases, the foods that are regarded as symbolic transformations of living flesh are actual cultural transformations of crude substances into sophisticated foods that are taken as symbolic of the culture itself. They thus function as ritual expressions of the triumph of agriculture over hunting, a theme which we have seen in the myth of Prithu.

But the Christian god takes on, or at least symbolizes and replaces, an animal form that the Hindu god does not; Hinduism

[22] I am indebted to Mary MacDonald for her tales of Papua New Guinea.

[23] Wendy Doniger O'Flaherty, "Introduction," in *Karma and Rebirth in Classical Indian Traditions* (Berkeley, 1980), pp. xvi-xvii.

[24] Wendy Doniger O'Flaherty, "Karma and rebirth in the Vedas and Puranas," in O'Flaherty, *Karma*, pp. 5-10.

never fills the space created in Christianity for God as a substitute for the *willingly* sacrificed domestic animal, the Paschal lamb. With the possible exception of the Vedic Purusha, who *may* have been a willing divine victim, there are no Indian parallels. The Vedas expressed the pious hope that the sacrificial horse and goat were willing victims; and the goat does take upon himself the sins of the sacrificer, and carry off those sins,[25] just as Christ releases mankind from the stigma of death and the burden of sin. But the sacrificial goat and horse were not gods: they were sacrificed *to* the gods. And when lambs (or goats) are sacrificed in later Hinduism, the ritual is a sacrifice *to* God, never a sacrifice *of* God. In the metaphor of the shepherd and the sheep, Hinduism places the emphasis upon the negative side of the human protagonist (the Bad Shepherd, who actually does kill the lambs and calves) and makes god the aggressor rather than the victim in that relationship (the slaughterer of the Paschal Lamb rather than the slaughtered lamb).

A possible parallel to the Paschal Lamb might be seen in the animals in Indian literature who offer their flesh to starving people. In a famous story in this popular genre, King Shibi cuts off pieces of his own flesh to weigh in a scale in order to ransom the flesh of a dove that has been caught by a hawk.[26] This same theme resurfaces later in devotional Hinduism, particularly in South India, where devotees slice off their flesh and offer it to those who ask for it. But these devotees are not gods, nor is their action part of a reenacted ritual; it is part of their hagiography.

We might, finally, seek our parallel to the central Christian sacred animal in the central Hindu sacred animal, the cow, that is, as we have seen, a symbol of willing self-sacrifice. The cow is part of the mythology that supports the ritual structure of Brahmins and sacrifices. Magic wishing cows, like the cow milked by Prithu, are called Wish-milking (Kama-duh): they yield whatever their milkers think of while milking (not merely food, but *anything*). Such cows are often stolen from the great Brahmin sages who own them (a situation that provides the opening moves in the plots of many Hindu myths) and are identified with the fee that one pays to the priest who

---

25 *Rig Veda* 10.16.4; 1.162.2-4; O'Flaherty, *The Rig Veda*, pp. 49-51.

26 *Mahabharata* 3.131.30.

performs a sacrifice. And in the non-mythical world, cows are an essential part of the temple landscape.

Yet the cow is not actually a part of Hindu ritual. Nor are cows ever divine in India; indeed, the cow is one of the very few animals that are *not* divine. There are no temples for the worship of cows, nor are offerings made to cows. The cow may be sacred in a certain sense, as a cultural symbol (of motherhood, purity, generosity, and so forth), and is certainly sacred in the sense of not to be killed or eaten (that is, sacred in the sense of taboo); but the cow is not divine. (Indeed, it is generally the case that divine animals *are* eaten, particularly in the course of rituals). Monkeys, bulls, geese, peacocks, even bandycoots partake of divinity, often by virtue of the fact that they serve as vehicles (*vahanas*) for particular gods to ride upon; but not the cow. The cow does not, therefore, provide a true counterpart to Christ as the Paschal Lamb.

(vi) Hindu and Christian Lions

Let us now consider the Hindu and Christian images of god as a wild animal that hunts us. In the *Rig Veda*, Vishnu is described as lurking in the mountains in the form of a ferocious wild beast, identified as a lion by the commentator;[27] in later Hindu mythology, Vishnu becomes the man-lion, Narasimha, who disembowels a heretical demon. Rudra in the *Rig Veda* is, as we have seen, a wild beast who slays cattle and men; the worshipper prays to him, "Do not kill those of us who go on two feet, or those of us who go on four feet."[28] Pashupati, the evil shepherd, is a lion. The god Shiva is said to be called by the euphemism *shiva* ("auspicious") as an inversion of *vashi* ("controller"), since he controls everyone and no one controls him, just as the lion (*simha*) is so named as an inversion of the word for injury (*himsa*), because the lion kills all animals but cannot be killed by any of them.[29] The most notorious Hindu lion of all is the mount of the bloodthirsty goddess Durga; this lion attacks the

27 *Rig Veda* 1.154.2; O'Flaherty, *The Rig Veda*, p. 226.

28 *Rig Veda* 1.114; O'Flaherty, *The Rig Veda*, pp. 223-225.

29 *Siva Purana* (Benares, 1964), 1.1.18.75-76.

theriomorphic form of the buffalo demon Mahisha while the anthropomorphic form of the goddess attacks Mahisha's anthropomorphic form.[30]

To the same extent that Hinduism has no place for god sacrificed as a lamb, Christianity has no place for god as a lion who hunts men. The Hindu lion, with all its implications of mindless violence against mankind, plays no role in Christianity.[31] One might see overtones of the evil shepherd in the awesome image of Christ at the last judgment, separating the sheep from the goats, separating the good from the evil. But, though it may be implied that the goats are to be sacrificed, this is by no means a clear or necessary feature of this text; and, in any case, this is not the dominant liturgical image of Christ. Indeed, the image of the lion as a devouring beast is applied from an early period to the Enemy of god rather than to God. The Hebrew Bible story of Daniel in the lion's den, protected by God, was enacted in history by the early Christian martyrs whom the Romans threw to the lions. But the leonine enemy *par excellence* was none other than Satan himself: Peter warned, "Be sober, be vigilant; because your adversary the devil, as a roaring lion, walketh about, seeking whom he may devour."[32] So, too, the requiem mass prays that the worshipper be delivered "from the mouth of the lion" (*de ore leonis*) — the lion who is Satan.

Just as early Christian observers mistook many Hindu gods for demons, since Hindu gods incorporate powers of evil that Christianity usually relegates to an Other Power,[33] so the ravenous beast is a god in Hinduism and a devil in Christianity. Thus Liturgical Christianity does not find a use for the category of God as an active wild animal, a devouring, hunting beast who takes us for his prey. This category that Christianity largely ignores is, however, filled by Judaism: for the same Hebrew Bible that presented us with the original image of the good shepherd also presents us with the Lion of Judah,

---

30 Wendy Doniger O'Flaherty, *Women, Androgynes, and Other Mythical Beasts* (Chicago, 1980), pp. 81-86; see also O'Flaherty, *Hindu Myths*, pp. 64-69.

31 This image, like that of the Bad Shepherd, does occur in literary manifestations of Christianity, such as T.S. Eliot's "Christ the Tiger," but it is not the dominant doctrinal image.

32 I Peter 5.8. I am grateful to Mary MacDonald for this citation.

33 O'Flaherty, *The Origins of Evil*, pp. 57-173.

the God of Job. In this (as in many other ways),[34] Judaism is closer to Hinduism than Christianity is. More precisely, Hinduism's vision of its relationship to Vedism is in many interesting ways similar to Christianity's vision of its relationship to Judaism.

The sacrifice of a divine wild beast, a divine lion, does not find a central place in Christianity. But it does occur, by implication, in the Book of Revelation, in the midst of many apocalyptic inversions (and many other mythical beasts), where the lion is identified with the sacrificial lamb: "And one of the elders saieth unto me, Weep not: behold, the Lion of the tribe of Judah, the Root of David, hath prevailed to open the book, and to lose the seven seals thereof. And I beheld, and, lo, in the midst of the throne and of the four beasts, and in the midst of the elders, stood a Lamb as it had been slain, having seven horns and seven eyes, which are the seven Spirits of God sent forth into all the earth."[35]

A twelfth century bestiary spells out many of the surprising implications of the identification of Christ with the lion:

> When [the lion] sleeps, he seems to keep his eyes open. In this very way, Our Lord also, while sleeping in the body, was buried after being crucified — yet his Godhead was awake. As it is said in the *Song of Songs*, "I am asleep and my heart is awake," or, in the Psalm, "Behold, he that keepeth Israel shall neither slumber nor sleep." . . . When a lioness gives birth to her cubs, she brings them forth dead and lays them up lifeless for three days — until their father, coming on the third day, breathes in their faces and makes them alive. Just so did the Father Omnipotent raise Our Lord Jesus Christ from the dead on the third day. Quoth Jacob: "He shall sleep like a lion, and the lion's whelp shall be raised."[36]

This text explicitly invokes the lion of the Hebrew Bible, an active, aggressive lion, only to transform it into a passive, sacrificed lion. This image of the sacrificed lion eventually finds its way into

---

[34] Wendy Doniger O'Flaherty, "The Uses and Misuses of Other Peoples' Myths." 1985 Presidential Address, American Academy of Religion; *Journal of the American Academy of Religions*, Summer, 1986, pp. 1-15.

[35] Revelation 5.5-7.

[36] *The Book of Beasts*, being a translation from a Latin Bestiary of the Twelfth Century, made and edited by T.H. White (London, 1954), pp. 7-11.

contemporary Christian mythology through the back door of children's literature: Christ appears as the Paschal lamb in one brief episode of C. S. Lewis' Narnian epic,[37] but throughout the cycle he appears far more powerfully as the Lion, Aslan — a Lion who is sacrificed in the place of a sinner and who is subsequently resurrected.[38] And, as Lewis keeps reminding us, "He is not a *tame* lion."[39]

(vii) Humans Among the Animals

Both Hinduism and Christianity have theriomorphic images that explain simultaneously the brutality of god and the protectiveness of god, but not the same images. The image of the shepherd is shared, but Christianity emphasizes the positive aspect of the shepherd while Hinduism emphasizes the negative. And against the Hindu image of God as a devouring beast, Christiantiy sets the image of God as a willing substitute for the sacrificed domestic animal. When God becomes flesh and blood, human or animal, he may sanction the killing of animals; indeed, in the *Bhagavad Gita*, God become man sanctions the killing of men in war. But in Christianity, the mystical celebration of the killing of the lamb is taken as a reassurance that god is not only so benevolent as *not* to kill us like so many cattle, as the Hindu lion does, but indeed, that he will go to the other extreme, giving himself up to allow us to slaughter him like a lamb. Here is an irreducible difference between two distinct manifestations of the archetype of the relationship between man and god expressed through the metaphor of the relationship between humans and animals.

There is also a difference in the degree to which animals function as metaphors in the myths of Hinduism and Christianity. Just as, as we have seen, the metaphor of the ritual involves complex transsubstantiations in both cases, so too the metaphor of the myth is so

---

[37] C.S. Lewis, *The Voyage of the Dawn Treader* (Harmondsworth, 1952), chapter 16.

[38] C.S. Lewis, *The Lion, The Witch, and the Wardrobe* (Harmondsworth, 1959), chapters 13-15.

[39] *Ibid.*, chapter 8.

complex as to defy any confident interpretation. But the Hindu attitude to actual living bulls, for instance, does suggest that the god Shiva is regarded as being present in those animals to a degree that Christ is not present in all lambs.

At the still center of this corpus is a theme that must be noted as an implicit (and often explicit) contrast with all other myths of animals: it is the ever enchanting myth of people who live among animals neither as hunters nor as shepherds. This is the myth of a magic time or place or person that erases the boundary between humans and animals: the ancient time when humans spoke the language of animals; the magic place in the Looking-Glass forest where things have no names, where Alice could walk with her arms around the neck of a fawn; or the person who lives at peace among animals (Enkidu in the *Gilgamesh Epic*, or Francis of Assisi, or the child who is raised as a cub by an animal or a pack of animals — Romulus and Remus, or Mowgli, or Tarzan). The time of this animal paradise finds a close parallel in the myth that tells of the time when gods walked among people, or people among gods; the place is like the high mountains where people mingle with the gods; and the particular individual with these special powers finds a parallel in the myth of a particular person (often a shaman or a priest) who has the special ability to traffic with the gods.

In these stories, the gods do not become human; a human becomes one of the gods. So, too, the ideal state of humans among animals is not one in which wild animals become tame (as they often do in reality). The strongest form of the myth is the one in which wild animals remain wild and speak their own language, and humans become wild, humans become once again innocent of civilization, and can speak with lions. It is a world where wild and tame have not yet come to have any meaning for people, or therefore for animals. The Garden of Eden is such a paradise in the past, and another is described in the Hebrew Bible as existing in the apocalyptic future.

> The wolf also shall dwell with the lamb, and the leopard shall lie down with the kid; and the calf and the young lion and the fatling together; and a little child shall lead them. And the cow and the bear shall feed; their young ones shall lie down together; and the lion shall eat straw like the ox. And the sucking child shall play on the hole of the asp, and the weaned child shall put his hand on the cockatrice's den.[40]

[40] Isaiah 11.6-8.

In this magic time, the only companions of the animals are *innocent* human beings, children, still wild, still unpolluted by civilization.

Many mythologies of animals are haunted by this lost or unattainable paradise. To be with the animals (or the gods) in this way would be to transcend our human condition entirely. In contrast with the rituals of cultural transformation in which we cease to eat flesh by becoming quintessentially cultural and eating bread or rice instead, these are myths of natural transformation, in which we become quintessentially natural and eat what animals eat (food that may in fact include other animals). In Jonathan Swift's myth of Gulliver among the equine Houyhnhnms, he finds that he is unable to survive on their vegetarian fare; but after living among them he is also unable to eat the flesh that is the food of the horrid Yahoos, the deformed humans that are the beasts of the civilized equine Houyhnhnms. The solution appears: "I observed a cow passing by; whereupon I pointed to her, and expresed a desire to let me go and milk her."[41] Henceforth Gulliver survives, in perfect health, on a diet of milk and a bread made of oats — the two civilized alternatives to the two natural extremes of grass and raw flesh.

In the Hindu myths of this genre, the humans among the animals eat "fruits and roots;" in the Buddhist variants, they eat nothing at all (not being true humans yet) or they eat the earth itself, which is delicious and nourishing — another form of the earth-cow, made of food, that Prithu milks.[42] These two strategies, one realistic and one fantastic, provide natural alternatives to the food that men do in fact share with *unmythical* animals: meat. Often, the myth does not tell us what the people and animals eat (though the author of *Isaiah* goes out of his way to tell us that those lions are no longer carnivorous); yet it always tells us how they manage to speak to one another, and how they manage not to attack one another (two closely related problems). It is language, not food, that ultimately separates us from the animals, even in myths.

41 Jonathan Swift, *Gulliver's Travels* (London, 1726), part 4, chapters 1 and 2.

42 O'Flaherty, *The Origins of Evil*, pp. 17-26.

(viii) Other Peoples' Animals

We can learn much about animal gods in a particular religion by watching for the category that is *not* filled. Sherlock Holmes once solved a mystery by using a vital clue of omission. When Inspector Gregory asked Holmes whether he had noted any point (in the case of Silver Blaze, a race-horse) to which he would draw the Inspector's attention, Holmes replied, "To the curious incident of the dog in the night-time." "The dog did nothing in the night-time," objected the puzzled Inspector. "That was the curious incident," remarked Sherlock Holmes.[43] Only when we see the Christian animal through Hindu eyes, and the reverse, does it occur to us to ask why the Christian dog does not bark at the image of god as a devouring wild animal, and the Hindu dog does not bark at the image of god as a domestic animal who offers himself up for sacrifice. It is easier to understand the role of an animal in one culture if we can see where it does *not* appear in another; and we can notice the lacuna left by an animal in one culture if we see where it does appear in another. To borrow the Zen koan, we cannot hear the sound of one hand clapping.

Hinduism and Christianity share the metaphor of the shepherd. By focusing upon this one metaphor, one is able to focus on a point in which the two religions might appear to be the same. When we look at what is symbolized by the shepherd in the two religions, we see how different they are. This is not merely to say that Hinduism and Christianity are two different cultures — that their animals are not the same (Indian cows are far more beautiful and spiritual looking, gazelle-like, than Friesians), that their animal-herding techniques are not the same, and that their attitudes to their animals are not the same. This we knew anyway. It is to say, rather, that once having made the decision to say that God is like a shepherd, all the possible sorts of shepherding were potentially available to both Christians and Hindus to flesh out the theological metaphor. From Christianity we know that it is possible to have a God who sacrifices

[43] Sherlock Holmes, "Silver Blaze." The fact that the dog did not bark when someone entered the house at night was evidence that the criminal was someone familiar to the dog.

himself as a lamb; but Hinduism systematically excludes this insight from its meditations on the theme of shepherding. From Hinduism we know that it is possible to have a God who devours his own sheep as if he were a wild beast; but Christianity systematically excludes this insight from its meditation. In this way, we can see the cultural blinkers that each culture constructs for its archetypes. In this way, a look at *their* divine animals makes us see things that we never noticed in *our* divine animals — either because in fact those things aren't there or because it troubles us to see that they are.

THIS-WORLDLY BENEFITS IN SHIN BUDDHISM

Michael Pye, Marburg

Shin Buddhism (Jōdo Shinshū[1]) , it is usually said, takes an unusually severe attitude towards any expectations of this-worldly benefits (Japanese: *genzeriyaku*) accruing from religious faith and practice, and in the context of Japanese religion in general this is, broadly speaking, true. At the same time the relationship between Shin Buddhist teaching and the idea that religious faith is beneficial in this life is not without its subtleties. It should not be forgotten that the founder of Shin Buddhism, Shinran Shōnin, lived as long ago as the twelfth and thirteenth centuries (1173-1262). While he was a pioneer in espousing a disenchanted, demagicised world view by summing up religious faith into a single principle, namely reliance on the "other-power" (*tariki*) of Amida (Amitābha) Buddha, the manner in which he did it (and the manner in which modern exponents view the matter) is not precisely parallel to the comparable process set in motion by Western Protestantism.

Because of this the question of the relationship to this-worldly benefits may be regarded as a touchstone of the Japaneseness of Shin Buddhism. The general question "How Japanese is Shin Buddhism?" arises because of the fact that Shin Buddhism is gradually

---

[1] The term "Shin Buddhism" is used in the title of this paper for the sake of convenience to refer to the Buddhist tradition known as Shinshū, identified above all with the teaching of Shinran Shōnin (1173-1262), and organised as a religious institution active today. Although the term "Shin Buddhism" is not without difficulties, its use as a name seems to be justified by its appearance in adjectival form in the name of the International Association of Shin Buddhist Studies, under whose auspices this paper was first presented.

acquiring an international role. Because of this, those engaged in the propagation of Shin Buddhism must be concerned about the translatability and communicability of Shinshū in non-Japanese terms. Indeed, at the level of the actual translation of texts, much excellent work has been done.[2] However, there is a deeper question as to what actually is being transmitted when Shinshū is removed from one culture to another. This is a deeper question because it involves making new judgements about the essential nature of this faith in relation to the formative period in Japan, in relation to its matrix in early Mahāyāna Buddhism and indeed to early Buddhism, and in relation to the features of religion in modern Japan, where Shinshū clearly is at home. Ideally these matters should be considered with respect to the various dimensions of religion, the conceptual, the ritual, the social and the subjective aspects, and, last but not least, the traditional-dynamic dimension. This paper however is limited to one brief example, which links conceptual and subjective aspects. If one wanted to discuss the social dimension, one might consider the relevance of the hereditary principle, widespread in Japanese religion and prevalent also in Shinshū, to Shin Buddhism outside Japan. If one wanted to discuss the ritual dimension, one might consider the use of house-altars (*butsudan*), the style of funeral services (in which the deceased is addressed by the living) and connected matters. These too are clearly continuous with other Buddhist practice in Japan, but it may be debatable how essential they are in non-Japanese contexts, if it is really the practice of the *nembutsu* (the invocation of Amida's name) and faith in the original vow which are to be transmitted.

In the case of "this-wordly benefits" (*genzeriyaku*) we have a concept which is familiar in many types of Japanese religion, but less common in some non-Japanese contexts. Since Shinshū doctrine, based on the works of Shinran shōnin, displays a critical attitude towards *genzeriyaku*, it is of particular interest to ask just how far it remains within the Japanese religious world at this point and how far it achieves a level of universalisable religious sensibility.

---

2 Particular mention should be made of the Ryūkoku Translation Series with their excellent format showing the original text, transliteration, translation and annotations on the same page, and now including several of the most important texts of Shin Buddhism. See e.g. notes 8 and 28 below.

The concept of *genzeriyaku* is well known to students of Japanese religion. As a reminder of what is ordinarily understood thereby, in contemporary Japanese religion, we may take as a convenient random example the "ten benefits of Ebisu Daijin" as set out in the booklet of the Shichifukujin Meguri of Hawaii.[3] This "Pilgrimage of the Seven Gods of Fortune" is a direct and hardly transmuted import from Japan for the Japanese population of Oahu island. The use of a Hawaiian example is particularly poignant, as religions of Japanese origin are there experiencing a problem of acculturation even within the ethnic Japanese, but increasingly Americanised or culturally neutralised, population. The ten benefits of the pilgrimage are as follows:

safe voyage
successful fishing
prosperous business
family fame
family harmony
traffic safety
good health and long life
fulfillment of happiness
good fortune
peaceful world

This is a typical list of this-worldly benefits for the common man in modern times. Naturally, there are others which appear in other contexts, and historically the details could vary interestingly, as will become clear below. However such variations are of minor importance. The major question is, when it comes to *genzeriyaku*, what is Japanese, what is Buddhist, what is Shin Buddhist?

Now the simple view of this matter is that Shinshū rejects prayers for this-worldly benefits and hence the whole issue simply falls to the ground. However, the simple view is too simple. It is not for nothing that Mikogami Eryū had a whole chapter entitled "Riyakuron" in his work *Shinshūgaku no komponmondai* (Fundamental Problems in Shinshū Studies).[4] Nor is it irrelevant that one of

---

[3] This is an otherwise unclassifiable booklet available in Hawaii at the time of the Second Conference of the International Association of Shin Buddhist Studies (August 1985).

[4] Kyōto 1962.

the *wasan* composed by Shinran shōnin is devoted to this theme. (A *wasan* is a song of praise composed in Japanese.) It will shortly be considered in detail. This *wasan* is included in modern collections of Shin Buddhist liturgies, e.g. in *Ishaku Shinshū Gongyōshū*.[5] (It is also found in the liturgical book of the Honganji Temple, Honolulu.) As the name implies, this is a collection of liturgies (*gongyōshū*) which is accompanied by interpretations in small print. At the beginning of the book, we find a page devoted to the chief marks of the Jōdo Shinshū faith (*Jōdo Shinshū no kyōshō*), these being the name: Jōdo Shinshū Honganjiha (Nishi Honganji); the founder: Kenshin Daishi Shinran Shōnin; the object of reverence (*honzon*): Amida Nyorai; the sutras: *Jōdo Sanbukyō*; and then a short statement of the teaching and the mode of life. The teaching of Shinshū is summarised as:

> "To believe the teaching of Namu Amida Butsu, rejoicing in the happiness of knowing that one will be brought to Buddhahood without fail, and thus to live for the world and for others."

The "mode of life" is slightly longer, and runs:

> "This denomination (*shūmon*) is a fellowship (*kyōdan*) of like-minded people united in the joy of a common faith, and thus believers are discreet in word and deed, humanitarian and law-abiding, and they join forces to work for the spreading of the true law of life (*nori*) in the world at large. Having a deep discernment of the nature of cause and effect, they do not perform this-worldly prayers or incantations and do not depend on superstitions such as divination."[6]

Now the question is, why do this-wordly prayers, or rather their denial, figure so prominently in this Shin Buddhist prayerbook? The answer must surely be that, in this respect, Shin Buddhism stands in an ambivalent relationship to the wider context of Japanese religion. This will become clear if we turn our attention to the *Genzeriyaku Wasan* ("Hymns on the benefits in the present life"). The *Genzeriyaku Wasan* is also contained in the English-language work *The Shinshū Seiten, The Holy Scripture of Shinshū* published in Hawaii.[7]

---

[5] Kyōto 1969.

[6] *Ibid.* Translations by present writer.

[7] Honolulu 1955.

However, the translation in the work *Jōdo Wasan*, in the Ryūkoku Translation Series, will be used here.[8]

According to Mikogami, the benefits referred to in the stanzas of the *Genzeriyaku Wasan* can be classified under four headings, namely:
(i) *turning evil into good* (stanzas 3 and 4)
(ii) *protection of beings in the five lower realms* (stanzas 5-12)
(iii) *continuous protection by the mind of light* (stanzas 13-14)
(iv) *protection by all the Buddhas* (stanza 15).[9]

This classification, significantly, disregards the first two stanzas of the *Wasan* on which brief comment may, however, first be made. Stanza 1 runs as follows:

> "Amida Tathāgata came into this world
> And, in order to end misfortunes and lengthen our life,
> Taught the chapter on the Measurement of life
> In the *Sūtra of the Golden Splendor.*"[10]

The significance of this is as follows. Firstly, as is explained in the footnote to the text, Amida Buddha is claimed as the teacher of the *Juryōhon* (the chapter on "Measurement of Life"), because he appeared with three other Buddhas to testify to the immeasurability of Śākyamuni's life. But there is more to it than this. The import of this allusion lies in the great popularity of this sūtra in the early period of Japanese Buddhism. Since it did not become the basis for one of the later schools (and as the longer Chinese version has not been translated into English),[11] this is often overlooked, although it has been amply documented in de Visser's *Ancient Japanese Buddhism.*[12] Apart from its function in protecting the state, expressed in the chapter on the four heavenly kings, it was popular because it was believed to have the power of "eliminating the miseries and

[8] Fujimoto, R. Inagaki, H., and Kawamura, Leslie S. (trans.) *The Jōdo Wasan, The Hymns on the Pure Land*, Kyōto 1965.

[9] *Op. cit.*, p. 290.

[10] Stanza 96 in the Ryūkoku translation (see note 8 above), p. 130. The sūtra in question (Japanese title: Konkōmyōkyō) is otherwise known as the *Sūtra of Golden Light*. See also next note.

[11] Nobel, J. (trans.), *Suvarṇaprabhāsottama sūtra, Das Goldglanz Sutra. Ein Sanskrittext des Mahāyāna-Buddhismus*, Leiden 1958.

[12] De Visser, *Ancient Buddhism in Japan*, 2 vols., Leiden 1935.

sufferings of sentient beings,"[13] and of course, as it says in the *wasan* itself, to lengthen life, these two points being succinctly formulated in the phrase *sokusai enmei*.

Now there is no doubt that these two benefits are benefits which accrue within the present world, that is, they are literally *genze riyaku*. Thus, in this allusive *wasan*, without criticism or dialectic at this point, Shinran picked up a leading theme in the Japanese Buddhism of his time.

As if to make sure that there was to be no mistake, the second stanza refers to Dengyō Daishi, the towering patriarch of the Japanese Tendai tradition, as authority for reciting the *nembutsu* for the elimination of the seven calamities. The stanza runs:

> "Dengyō Daishi of Mt. Hiei,
> Pitying the people of the land,
> Taught the recitation of 'Namu Amida Butsu'
> As the incantation for removing the seven calamities."[14]

These were essentially natural calamities, namely: (i) eclipses of sun and moon (ii) astronomical changes (iii) lightning and fire (iv) heavy rain and flood (v) strong winds (vi) drought and (vii) war.[15] Again, protection from such disasters must be construed as a *this-worldly* benefit, and here too there is no doubt that Shinran was consciously seeking to link his exposition with a widely recognised theme.

For the whole background of *nembutsu* practice as linked to the securing of this-worldly benefits one may compare Hori Ichiro's 1965 Haskell lectures, published under the title *Folk Religion in Japan, Continuity and Change*.[16] He puts special emphasis on the practice of the *nembutsu* in the context of Tendai Buddhism, the emergence of the so-called *nembutsu-hijiri* or *Amida-hijiri* and the use of *nembutsu* to pacify the fierce, wandering spirits known as *goryō*. By contrast, the *nembutsu* practice of Hōnen and his followers, especially Shinran, represented a rationalisation and an interiorisation. As Hori put it:

---

13 Fujimoto *et al.*, *op. cit.*, p. 130, n. 1.

14 *Ibid.*, p. 131.

15 *Ibid.*, p. 131, n. 3.

16 Hori, Ichiro, *Folk Religion in Japan*, Chicago 1968. See especially Chapter III, "Nembutsu as Folk Religion," pp. 83-139.

> "Shinran severely criticised ritualism, magic, divination and the worship of the old pantheon. The worship to Amida did not consist of prayers for health or temporal welfare or any petitions. After a man has once obtained faith in Amida, he commits all to his power, and his worship consists of nothing but thanksgiving."[17]

However it is strange that Hori does not mention the *Genzeriyaku Wasan* at all, even though he mentions the *wasan* composed by Shinran in general. It appears therefore that the picture is not quite so simple as might first appear from Hori's account, which reflects Shin Buddhist doctrine in all brevity.

Clearly, any interpretation of the teaching of Shinran on *genzeriyaku* must stress change rather than continuity. But what else does the *wasan* itself say? As was said before, following Mikogami, stanzas 3 and 4 are about the benefit of turning evil into good. Admittedly this is a spiritual process. But what kind of spiritual process? Take stanza 1 first. It runs:

> "If one utters 'Namu Amida Butsu,'
> which surpasses all other virtues,
> All of his heavy sins of the three periods
> will surely be altered and become light."[18]

Why should one wish one's sins to become light? The reason is surely that one fears their karmic effects, that is, in this life. To have one's grave sins made light does not in itself produce salvation, rebirth in the Pure Land, or nirvana. Hence the footnote to the Ryūkoku translation seeks to press forward to a religious teaching more in line with the central emphasis of Shinshū doctrine by commenting: "Grave sins are made slight and little. In reality, however, all the sins are destroyed with one utterance of the *nembutsu* which follows faith."[19] While this may be the central emphasis of Shin Buddhist teaching, it does not appear to be the import of the text at this point.

By contrast, the interest in karma and its ill effects, probably much stronger in Shinran's time than it is nowadays, is emphasised

---

[17] *Ibid.*, pp. 131-32.

[18] Fujimoto *et al.*, *op. cit.*, p. 132.

[19] *Ibid.*, p. 132, n. 3.

in stanza 4, which runs:

> "If one utters 'Namu Amida Butsu,'
> Benefits gained in this life are unlimited,
> Sins of his samsaric existence are erased
> And the determinate karmic effects and
> untimely death are avoided."[20]

It will be noted that the stanza is concerned with "determinate karma," that is karma which has definite effects in actual life unless alleviated. Also avoided, through the practice of *nembutsu*, is "untimely death," something which clearly belongs in the realm of disaster and calamity, and the avoidance of which is also without doubt a *this-worldly* advantage.

Thus in these two stanzas, which go beyond the mere reference to traditional authority, the value of mitigating the unpleasant effects of past karma in the present life is clearly accepted and the possibility of doing so is linked to the utterance of the *nembutsu*.

The next eight stanzas (just over half of the fifteen stanzas in all) are all to do with the protection of beings in the five lower realms of rebirth (that is, the traditional six realms omitting the deva realm).

Stanzas 5-11 all specifically refer to protection (*mamori*) and link it explicitly to the practice of the *nembutsu*. The protection is given by *devas* and *nagas*. Specifically mentioned (stanza 6) are the four heavenly kings, an important group in early Japanese Buddhism, linked especially with the famous Shitennō Temple, in present-day Ōsaka. Also important are the "wardens of the five realms"[21] which administer the realms of warring spirits, humans, animals, hungry ghosts and karmic purgatories, at the command of Yama (Emma Hōō), the king of the deceased. One who recites the *nembutsu* however is respected by Yama and therefore protected by the wardens of the five realms.

Stanza 12 is entirely consistent with stanzas 5-11. It happens to be formulated the other way round in that it says that evil spirits fear the faith (*shinjin*) endowed by the inconceivable power of the vow of Amida. Thus, here too protection is assured against evil spirits. It is impossible in the phrase *tenchi ni miteru akkijin* ("evil spirits

---

20 *Ibid.*, p. 133.

21 *Ibid.*, p. 138 (stanza 9).

swarming throughout the heavens and earth")[22] not to think of the belief in and fear of *goryō*, which was still widely prevalent in Shinran's time.

With this whole section it is important to remember that the five worlds, indeed the six worlds if we include the world of good heavenly beings who afford protection, are all part of a single, pre-enlightenment system. If we make use of the sociologically popular distinction between "this-worldly" and "other-worldly" (*diesseitig* and *jenseitig*), then the karmic relations which pertain between these worlds, or realms, are all *this*-worldly. All of these realms of rebirth are understood to be interrelated through an elaborate karmic exchange, which simply becomes more evident to humans in the human realm. Thus the protection throughout all these realms, which is granted to one who recites the *nembutsu* is properly applauded in the *Genzeriyaku Wasan*[23] and should be regarded as a this-worldly benefit.

Returning to stanza 12 for a moment, it may be noted that here, for the first time, it is not the *nembutsu* which is referred to but the "inconceivable power of the vow" (*ganriki fushigi*). The full phrasing is: "Faith of the Vow-power inconceivable, Being the Great Bodhi Mind"[24] so that we have here a bursting forth of central Shin Buddhist concepts (developed fully in the footnotes of the Ryūkoku translation). The point is that while stanza 12 belongs to the previous sequence from 5-11 in one sense, in another it introduces stanzas 13-15. This is because it opens up the whole *transcendental* frame of reference so characteristic of Shin Buddhism, which, until this point in the *wasan*, had not been at all clearly expressed. After this reference to the power of the vow, stanza 13 brings in the companion bodhisattvas Kannon and Seishi (Avalokiteśvara and Mahāsthāmaprāpta) and innumerable other bodhisattvas which "follow (him) like the shadow which follows one's body."[25] They represent the compassionate expression of transcendent power. Stanza 14 provides a different image of Amida's saving splendor, by

---

22 *Ibid.*, p. 141.

23 See note 8 above.

24 *Ibid.*, p. 141, " *Ganriki fushigi no Shinjin wa, Daibodaishin nari kere ba.*"

25 *Ibid.*, p. 142.

declaring that "In the rays of the Buddha of Unhindered Light, There dwell innumerable Amida Buddhas." These are transformed Buddhas (*kebutsu*), perhaps better described as projected Buddhas, appearing in order to "protect the (man of) true faith."[26] Finally stanza 15 completes this picture of a radiant and protective Buddha-world, by referring to the "innumerable Buddhas of the ten quarters."[27]

Thus in these last few stanzas it is the Buddha-world which is allowed to take over. Protection remains the unifying theme, but almost imperceptibly the believer is led from an ambiguous, possibly manipulative, understanding of the *nembutsu*, to a transformed reliance on power which arrives from without, by means of the *nembutsu*. Looked at in this way it does not seem necessary to separate stanzas 15 from stanzas 13 and 14, as in Mikogami's analysis. It seems preferable to analyse four groups as follows: (i) stanzas 1-2; (ii) stanzas 3-4; (iii) stanzas 5-12; (iv) stanzas 12-15, with stanza 12 playing a double role as a hinge leading to the climax of the *wasan*.

Approximately the same sequence of ideas may be found in the *Kyōgyōshinshō* which speaks of obtaining ten kinds of benefit in the present life[28] (*genshō ni jisshu no yaku*). These ten are traditionally explained as falling into three groups of three, with the tenth ("the benefit of entering the Group of the Rightly Established State") being in a class of its own in that it represents the religious goal of Shinshū. The others, however, are not thereby denied, and of particular interest in the present discussion are some of the earlier ones, cutting across the grouping in threes. Three are to do with protection. These are (1) "the benefit of being protected by unseen divine beings," (4) "the benefit of being protected by all Buddhas," and (6) "the benefit of being always protected by the Buddha's spiritual light."[29] Also of interest is the third, "the benefit of having evil turned into good,"[30] which here too is given a spiritual interpretation in the footnote. Of course it can bear a spiritual meaning, and it

---

26 *Ibid.*, p. 143.

27 *Ibid.*, p. 144.

28 *Genshō no jisshu no yaku.* Ishida, M. *et al.* (trans.) *The Kyō Gyō Shin Shō* (Ryūkoku Translation Series V), Kyōto 1966, p. 120.

29 *Ibid.*, p. 121.

30 *Ibid.*, p. 121.

is likely that it did for Shinran. However in his time it must also have carried the meaning of transmuting the otherwise deleterious effects of bad acts in this present life, thus being in tune with stanzas 3 and 4 of the *Genzeriyaku Wasan* as explained above. What does this understanding of the *Genzeriyaku Wasan* mean for the questions referred to at the outset? It is easy enough to say that Shin Buddhism accepts neither a manipulative nor a wonder-working understanding of the *nembutsu* and that it rejects irrational superstition. It would appear however that Shinran, in his own time, was much closer to this "magical" mode of understanding religious practice, even though he went beyond it, than modern (or perhaps one should say modernist) thought finds comfortable. The view of religion with which he deals in the *Genzeriyaku Wasan* permeated the Japanese religion of his own time. In many circumstances it reappears in modern Japanese religion, which explains the sharpness of the comments in the Shin Buddhist literature of today. Shinran, however, *aligned* himself with the idea of this-worldly benefits before transcending it. This may be understood as being distinctively Japanese in a double sense. Firstly it implies recognition of a theme generally current in Japanese religion, even though the interpretation is a special one. Secondly the dialectic of aligning and then discarding apparent in the *Genzeriyaku Wasan* is a classic example of the skill applied by leading Japanese teachers of Buddhism. This latter point is indirectly documented by the introductory comment to the *Genzeriyaku Wasan*, given in the *Shinshū Kangyōshū* referred to above. This runs:

> "The *wasan* extols the fact that the *nembutsu* practitioner enjoys this-worldly benefits furnished by ultimate reality, the ultimate reality of Dharma, even though the expectations of the man in the street are not permitted."[31]

This modern statement is true to Shinran's thought by displaying, for all the dialectical tension, a close affinity with generally current Japanese religious ideas. Fascinating though this is, it is not easy to see how this aspect of Shin Buddhism can be internationalised except by being left to lapse into oblivion.

---

[31] *Op. cit.*, p. 47.

THE HISTORY OF RELIGIONS (*RELIGIONSWISSENSCHAFT*) AND THE RELIGIOUS SITUATION IN EASTERN EUROPE: SOME COMMENTS*

Kurt Rudolph, Marburg

i

Problems in the history of religions are not religious but scholarly problems; that is, they are historical, philological, sociological, or psychological. Nevertheless, "religion," the religious situations, and the history of religions are connected. If we examine the beginnings of the discipline, we see everywhere that a certain distance from one's own tradition opens one's eyes toward the foreign world; on the other hand, contact with a foreign tradition affects one's own tradition in such a way that very soon reflection begins, reflection which thematizes this contact, often with the result of producing an awareness of self through a new awareness of others. It is well-known that as a discipline, the history of religions is a product of European *Geistesgeschichte*. It was and still is accompanied by the midwives who assisted its birth: tolerance, humanitarianism, and a critical attitude toward tradition. Whenever the history of religions

* Translated by Dr. Gregory Alles, Associate Professor at South Western State University, Springfield, Missouri. Based on a lecture delivered at the 25th Anniversary Meeting of the American Society for the Study of Religion in Chicago, April 28, 1984.

has found itself in the dangerous waters of religions and theology, it has consistently chosen to swim in liberal, antiorthodox, and "enlightened" currents. To this extent, it has preserved a religious heritage which theology itself has often lost. Whether this heritage has always been a blessing to the history of religions as an independent, non-theological discipline is a question which I will not pursue further here.[1] In any case, the history of religions has in its own history both an objective and a subjective relation to the religious situation, to the various religions.

My theme exemplifies this relation, but perhaps in a slightly novel way. Here, in addition to religious and theological motives, political ones have a much stronger role to play than previously. Unfortunately, I am not in a position to write about the entire Eastern European situation, since I am familiar only with a subjectively conditioned portion of that situation. Accordingly, I will mention only several particulars which I feel are typical. First I will outline the religious situation in Eastern Europe, then the history of religions and its relation to the religious situation.

I will be concerned here with Eastern Europe defined politically, or more precisely with those countries which today consider themselves socialist and stand under the leadership of the Soviet Union. To say nothing of their very different histories, these countries do not form any sort of religious unity. This is not without importance for the situation of the history of religions here, at least in those lands where the history of religions exists at all.

Countries with Orthodox religious traditions, such as Russia, the Ukraine, Bulgaria, and Rumania, do not have long-standing traditions in the history of religions. Even today the history of religions as known in the West is not cultivated there. Theologians are educated in special schools where historical-critical research is of peripheral concern, so that the history of religions has had no chance to become acclimatized. Beginnings of religio-historical work can be found only outside the ecclesiastical-theological educational systems, in either the philological or the historical sections of the humanities faculties at state universities.

---

[1] Cf. my 3rd and 4th Haskell Lectures: *Fundamentals of the Study of Religions*, New York: Macmillan 1985, 41ff., 59ff.

Those countries with a strong Catholic population — Hungary, Croatia, Czechoslovakia or Poland — have in some ways relatively old traditions in the history of religions, but these traditions are marked by strong Catholic influence, as, for example, at the Catholic University of Lublin in Poland. The history of religions is practiced most significantly in areas which are traditionally Protestant, that is, in the German Democratic Republic and at the Protestant schools of Czechoslovakia and Hungary (for example, the Comenius faculty at Prague). For now, let me simply stress that the different ecclesiastical traditions have always been and still are important in Eastern European countries for determining whether the history of religions is cultivated as an independent discipline or not.

As for the religious situation as such in Eastern Europe, I am, of course, no expert.[2] My personal knowledge does not extend far beyond the boundaries of the German Democratic Republic. The situation in Poland is too well-known to go into it here in detail. Polish Catholicism, strict and very traditional, is the strongest religious power in Eastern Europe; it exercises significant influence on Poland's internal politics. Poland thus provides a counter-example to Marx and Engels' thesis that religion dies off after economy and society are reorganized on a socialist basis. The connections between "Polish-ness" and the Catholic Church through the past centuries have been very close. Since the Poles were politically oppressed for much of their history, Catholic ideology was the tie which held Poles together, in addition to their common language and culture. Just as the Russian Orthodox Church was the religious ideology of Old Russia in the East and the Protestant religion that of Prussia, or, rather, of Germany, in the West, Catholicism distinguished and continues to distinguish the Polish people spiritually.

No other traditionally Catholic land in Eastern Europe can match the strength of Poland's tradition. In Hungary, the Catholic church is not so strong. Catholicism, however, retains more influence in Hungary than it does in Czechoslovakia, where from 1948 on, the state has financed the churches, including paying the salaries of priests

[2] A former brief overview is provided in *Western Religion*, ed. by Hans Mol, Mouton, The Hague 1972 (Religion and Reason 2), 83ff. (Bulgaria), 117ff. (Czechoslovakia), 213 (East Germany), 277ff. (Hungary), 403ff. (Poland), 565ff. (USSR), 507ff. (Yugoslavia).

and pastors. As a result, it can and in fact has wielded some direct control over the church. Nevertheless, a true theological education is available in Czechoslovakia, and some lectures are given on topics in the history of religions.

I personally do not know much about the situation of the Orthodox Church in Bulgaria and Rumania. In Bulgaria the Church has served as an ancient bulwark for preserving the Bulgarian people against Islamic infiltration. As a result, it has probably earned more than mere toleration from the government. The situation in Rumania appears to be similar, although by contrast, the Church of the German-speaking Lutherans in Transylvania stands under stronger government supervision. Of course, the activities of the Russian Orthodox Church are closely watched. In recent decades, though, it appears to have won a certain amount of respect, especially because of the part it played in protecting the Soviet Union during the German invasion in World War II. The prudent diplomacy of the Russian clergy and their support for the official national policy has procured for the Russian church even more influence. Observers continually report growing interest in the often endangered but never extinct religious tradition of the Russian people, interest which is connected with the powerful movement to resurrect older Russian culture and art (for example icon-painting) even outside the Church. This interest is evident in recent Soviet literature, for example, in the writings of Solouchin and Kopelev. In the case of religious minorities such as the Jews, Protestants, and Catholics (the latter predominately in Lithuania), tensions with the state are great. The strongly atheistic education provided in Russian schools and universities allows churches and religious communities little room to grow. Religious education is above all a family matter, supplemented by actual participation in religious services. Probably none of the churches or communities exercises any public influence.

The situation in the German Democratic Republic is somewhat different. Since the end of the second World War and liberation from the Nazi regime, the Protestant churches, above all the Lutheran churches, have experienced a resurgence of vitality. Their new life manifests itself in several different directions, such as the *Kirchentage*, church academies, and the youth movement. The strict separation of Church and State after the war was a radical break with the German situation previously. But already during the Nazi period such a separation had taken place in practice if not in name (in, for example, the *Bekennende Kirche*). The political situation was, of course, new to the East German church; for the first time in its history it encountered in the regime and in the socialist party an outlook which was consciously and emphatically antireligious, anti-theistic (not merely a-theistic), and Marxist-Leninist. Tensions soon arose, especially after the founding of the German Democratic Republic in 1949. On the ecclesiastical side, they were promoted by Otto Dibelius, the bishop of Berlin. But in the 1970's, or actually beginning in 1968, tensions began to diminish due to official contacts — the first since the G.D.R. was founded — between ecclesiastical and political authorities. A "gentleman's agreement" was the result, which is still in effect today. Its latest manifestation was the celebration of the Lutheran quincentenary in 1983. After Poland, the religious and ecclesiastical situation in East Germany is on the whole the most favourable in Eastern Europe. Not only are theologians trained in both the ecclesiastical and the old state universities, and not only do theological students have the same rights and duties as other students; the churches are allowed a significant if limited amount of freedom in which to operate. They have their own academies, *Kirchentage*, hospitals, nursery schools, and nursing homes. In addition, contact with churches outside East Germany have been steadily increasing. Youth display a growing interest in religious and quasi-religious problems, not only in the search for an international and bilateral policy of peace, but also in questions of protecting the environment and of ethical-moral responsibility in a technological age.

This brief overview of the religious situation in Eastern Europe has been, I should point out, purely subjective and incomplete. The actual religious attitudes of the populace, for example, can be apprehended in detail only through sociological investigation. Still, it may be worth noting that in the last official census of East Germany, some 40% of the population, or 8 million out of East Germany's 17 million citizens, identified themselves as members of a religious community.

ii

As I have already said, the religious situation in the countries of Eastern Europe has important implications for the status and character of the history of religions as an academic discipline there. I would like to outline three different types which illustrate this point. They will at the same time give glimpses of the roles of the history of religions in three Eastern European countries: the Soviet Union, Poland, and East Germany.

1. For the situation in the Soviet Union I can supplement my own information with that provided by the Scottish historian of religions, James Thrower.[3] It is well-known that the official ideology of the Soviet Union is a unified *Weltanschauung*, so-called Marxism-Leninism, Lenin's forced interpretation of Marxist theory. Soviet citizens are given no real alternative, for religion plays no official role. It is required that Marxism stand at the foundation of all the humanities, although the natural sciences are nowadays less touched by it. Lenin employed Marxism's indubitable atheism as a fundamental characteristic of propaganda and education.

In such a setting, there can be no "objective," factually-oriented history of religions. "Religion" is a superstition which belongs to the former, bourgeois stage of development. The end of religions as an expression of a perverted or false consciousness was declared in theory by Marx and then allegedly accomplished in the Soviet Union. From the Marxist perspective, there is no value-free research, especially not in the history of religions, that is, in the scientific study of religion and atheism. In the Marxist conception, atheism is the actual object of the study of "religion." It is the alternative, non-religious tradition which stands opposed to religious traditions. Of course, religion is an obvious part of the history of ideas even for Marxists, a part which is still active today, and therefore needs to be studied.[4] But it must be studied not in a neutral, objective fashion

---

[3] "The Study of Religion in the USSR," *Religion* 13 (1983), 127-136; *Marxist-Leninist 'Scientific Atheism' and the Study of Religion and Atheism in the U.S.S.R.*, The Hague/Berlin 1983 (Religion and Reason 25).

[4] Cf. also my brief remarks about the Marxist conception of 'ideology' in my 4th Haskell Lecture: 'The History of Religions and the Critique of Ideologies,' *op. cit.* 62-66.

but from a partisan standpoint. In the end, such study must serve the goal of demonstrating religion's dispensability. At the least, it must demonstrate that religion as religious people understand it does not exist; that is, religion is only part of the ideology of an earlier form of society, a weapon of the exploiters in the class struggle.

The concerns which the Western history of religions has with religion are found only to a limited degree. As Thrower says, the slogan is: "Historians of religions have hitherto sought to understand religion in various ways: the point is to overcome it."[5] In recent years a relatively large amount of material has appeared in two areas:

(1) special research in the so-called regional sciences (Indology, Assyriology, Islamic studies, and so on), and
(2) the theory of a Marxist history of religions.

The first is in essentials philological and historical research. It is concentrated above all in the old stronghold for philology and history, Leningrad. But religio-historical work in a more precise sense is centered more in the philosophical area, that is, in the field of study known as "scientific atheism" (*nauchnyj ateizm*), an expression which is used officially for any undertaking concerned with religion and atheism. This field of study has academic chairs, institutes, and its own organs of publication.

History of religions, then, is possible in the Soviet Union only in the sense of a Marxist sociology of religion. Religion is seen as a product of social processes and can only be understood as such, provided that one employs historical materialism or some other sociological theory. In this sense, courses have been organized in schools of higher learning in the last few years. Their goal is not only negative (to criticize religious worldviews) but also positive: to contribute to constructing a "scientific outlook" and to the "spiritual" (*dukhovnyj*) renewal of the human personality. Soviet historians of religions by no means consider their work a case of "art for art's sake." They serve not only the party and society, but also humanity itself. That is, they see themselves as liberating humanity from the yoke of the obsolete, out of date, life-inhibiting concepts which

[5] Thrower, *The Study*, p. 117. Illustrated by S.A. Tokarew in the introduction to his well-known book *Religion in the History of the Peoples of the World*, Moscow 1976 (in Russian).

religions preserve.[6]

In the Soviet Union, then, the history of religions, insofar as one might wish to use this Western term, is part of a large-scale educational program, which serves the state-fostered Marxist ideology. Because of its place and its connection with scientific atheism, the history of religions in the Soviet Union has acquired since the end of World War II a whole series of new institutions and organs for publication, which allow it not ony to work but also to disseminate and to "propagate" its results. The old "Museum for the History of Religions and Atheism" in Leningrad, founded in 1930, was re-founded in 1956 and began a publication series in 1950, *Problems of the History of Religions and Atheism.* This series appeared until 1964 and contained several pieces worthy of attention, such as those on text-editions and themes in the historical study of religions. Between 1957 and 1963, the same museum brought out another journal, the *Yearbook of the Museum of the History of Religions and Atheism*, which, although it had the official orientation, nevertheless contained good bibliographies of relevant Soviet work. Since 1961 there has appeared, at irregular intervals, a bibliography devoted to Russian and Western works on atheism and religion, but it is selective and poorly balanced.

Other pertinent publications in the Soviet Union include: *Problems of scientific atheism (Voprosy nauchnogo ateizma)* published under the auspices of the Institute for Scientific Atheism of the Soviet Academy of Social Sciences; *Sbornik trudov* (Collection of works), which publishes ethnological reports on North-Asian hunting peoples; *Znanie* (Knowledge), a popular journal of atheistic propaganda, critical of religious traditions; and various monograph series, which contain, for example, studies on the history of the critique of religions, on free-thinking and atheism, and on the Inquisition and witchcraft.

Among individual Soviet scholars, the ethnologist S. Tokarew is perhaps the best known. His *Religija v istorii narodov mira* (1965 *et passim*) is the standard Soviet handbook on the history of religions.[7]

6 According to a standard textbook called *Nauchnyj ateizm*, 1974, 4f., quoted by Thrower, *The Study*, p. 116.

7 It has been translated and published in East Germany (Berlin 1965); there exists also a Spanish edition from 1972. The last known Russian 'Introduction to the

A. J. Klibanov has written several significant books on the history of Russian religion. N.A. Smirnov published in 1954 a work on the study of Islam in the Soviet Union, which is still a standard work. Among his other publications, the great Russian Arabist, Kratschkovsky has translated the Qur'an into modern Russian. Various Jain and Islamic texts, such as Hasan an-Naubakhti's history of Islamic sects, have also been translated.[8] It is regrettable that Soviet scholars do not participate in the international congresses of the I.A.H.R. The only sizeable participation has been at the second study conference on religio-historical methods, held in Warsaw in 1979.

2. In Poland, the place of the history of religions is totally different from that which exists in the Soviet Union, because, in my opinion, of the totally different religious situation there. The strength of the Catholic church prevents state and the communist party from launching an aggressive propaganda campaign against religion and in favour of atheism. As a result, the history of religions certainly has more room to operate than it has elsewhere. But it is typical of the Polish situation that the history of religions works within a certian political frame, which confers upon it anti-Catholic and secularizing tendencies. The history of religions in Poland is an a-theological and anti-theological discipline. It is concerned with the history and role of religions and religious traditions. It is firmly anchored in the Polish Academy of Sciences — to be specific, in the Institute for Philosophy and Sociology — and also in most Polish universities (Warsaw, Lublin, Krakow). Since there are no theological faculties at Polish universities, the history of religions is the only discipline which treats questions of religions. Thus, a non-theological, historical-critical treatment of religions contributes to "laicization," that is, in Catholic lands, to the overthrow of "clericalism." To this extent, the history of religions is not strictly value-free but serves speciifc goals. Of cousre, this is not the official view, and it is not so deep-seated that the history of religions is practised as a means to oppose religion directly. In the Polish situation, this anti-clerical direction is

theoretical Religionswissens chaft' by D. M. Ugrinovitch (1973) is more an introduction to the Marxist sociology of religion for undergraduates than a work of Western standard.

[8] Cf. the survey article by M. Batunsky, "Recent Soviet Islamology," *Religion* 12 (1982), 365-389 (rich bibliography).

thoroughly appropriate to the history of religions. It corresponds completely to the discipline's early self-understanding in the West, especially in 18th and 19th-century France, where the history of religions found itself in a similar situation.

The center for the history of religions in Poland is Warsaw, where the only Polish periodical on this subject, *Euhemer*, has been published since 1957. It is practically the only periodical of its kind in Eastern Europe. Its contents — all in Polish, but recently with Russian, English, and German summaries — give a good impression of the range of Polish religio-historical work. Next to often outstanding works written by philologists and historians, there are studies in the sociology, psychology and phenomenology of religion, as well as studies on problems of atheism and the critique of religion, especially by Professor Nowicki in Lublin. There is also a series which publishes monographs in the history of religions. It has included Polish translations of Joachim Wach's *Sociology of Religion* and G. van der Leeuw's *Religionsphaenomenologie*. Moreover, Poland can boast of having the only East European society for the history of religions, a recognized affiliate of the I.A.H.R., headed by Professor W. Tyloch, an orientalist at the University of Warsaw. In 1979, the first and, up to now, the only session of the I.A.H.R. ever held in East Europe took place in Warsaw.[9] It continued the methodological discussion begun in Abo/Turku, Finland, in 1974. As already mentioned, a five-member Soviet delegation took part in these discussion, as did delegates from Israel, Italy, North America, Holland, East Germany, and Sweden. One hopes that these contacts will continue.

Much has been done for the current situation of the history of religions in Poland by Zygmunt Poniatowski of Warsaw, a former pupil of Adam Schaff and colleague of L. Kolakowski. He directed the translation of J. Wach's and G. van der Leeuw's works and himself wrote an *Introduction to the History of Religions* which has gone through several editions. He has also produced a single volume entitled *History and Religions* and a widely distributed *Dictionary of Re-*

---

[9] Cf. now the printed papers of this conference: W. Tyloch, (ed.) *Current Progress in the Methodology of the Science of Religions*, Warsaw, Polish Scientific Publishers, 1984.

Religions. From time to time, Poniatowski has also concerned himself with questions of biblical exegesis and the history of early Christianity. I should also mention T. Margul's *Habilitationsschrift, One Hundred Years of the History of Religions*, a history of the discipline from the time of Max Mueller.

In addition to Warsaw, the Catholic University of Lublin (the only one of its kind in Eastern Europe, founded in 1918) has a professor of religious history, but his bent is strongly theological and he stands on the uncertain ground of Pater W. Schmidt's theory of primal monotheism. Much has also been accomplished in Poland in many of the historical and philological specialities (Egypt, Greco-Roman Antiquity, Gnosis, Islam, Buddhism). These works appear in the journal *Rocznik Orientalisticzny* (Journal of Oriental Studies).

3. The German Democratic Republic contributes yet another image to our theme. As part of Germany with its five old universities (among them Leipzig, one of the oldest German universities, and Humboldt's model university at Berlin, dating to the beginning of the 19th century), East Germany possesses a respectable reservoir for religio-historical work. In Leipzig, for example, this tradition extends back to the first half of the 19th century. Max Mueller spent his first years as a university student there. I have discussed the history of the Leipzig tradition in a publication of the Saxon Academy of Sciences,[10] so I will be brief here and proceed quickly to the situation today.

Because of the strong Protestant, especially Lutheran, background of this part of Germany, the study of religious history has an old tradition which still continues, even if in more recent times changed political relations have caused new points of view to assume prominence (namely, Marxist history or sociology of religion and research on atheism). In any case, Leipzig has a chair in the history of religions, which has been filled continuously since the days of its first incumbent, Nathan Söderblom, by H. Haas, W. Baetke, and myself (till 1984). Until 1946 this chair was located in the

---

[10] *Die Religionsgeschichte an der Leipziger Universität und die Entwicklung der Religionswissenschaft*, Berlin 1962 (Sitzungsberichte der Sächsischen Akademie der Wissenschaften zu Leipzig, Philol.-Hist. Kl., 107, Heft 1). Cf. the short outline in my 1st Haskell Lectures 'The Leipzig Tradition of Religionswissenschaft,' *op. cit.*, p. 3-20.

theological faculty. In addition, Leipzig's humanities faculty had an associate professor in the history of religions, beginning with Joachim Wach in 1924. After Wach's exile from Nazi Germany in 1934, the position was filled by the ethnologist F.R. Lehmann until 1939. For a time, then, Leipzig had the good fortune, unusual in Germany, of having two professors of the history of religions. The strong Leipzig tradition persisted also after 1945, and even after 1949, the year of the founding of the German Democratic Republic, and for many years after World War II Leipzig was the East German centre for religio-historical research. Along with Baetke, J. Leipoldt and S. Morenz continued to work in this field. Only with the second reform of higher education in 1958 did the situation change. Then an attempt was made to transform the Institute for the History of Religions into a center of atheistic research and propaganda after the Soviet model. Baetke and Morenz were able to fend off the attack, but the influence of the Institute declined, and its pedagogical activity was confined almost exclusively to students of theology. With the University reforms of 1969 all independent institutes and their libraries were abolished. The history of religions was given its own chair in the newly founded historical section of the university, with virtually no teaching duties in the area of history. Work became concentrated on research (Iran, Gnosis, Manichaeism, The Mandaeans, Islam). The gradual dying off of the older generation of professors, a lack of younger blood, and changes in the structure of fields traditionally related to the history for religions such as Egyptology, Assyriology, Indology, Sinology, and Tibetology, have prevented a renaissance of the old Leipzig school of the history of religions. Only in 1982, following the uprising in Iran, was a *Dozent* for Islamic studies appointed in the Department of African and Near-Eastern Studies.[11] In the last several years, an attempt has again been made to introduce, from philosophy, a history of religions which is atheistic or strongly Marxistic in orientation. Courses have been given, with total disregard of the chair in the history of religions, by thorough Marxist scholars who had received a part of their training in the Soviet Union.

[11] According to my information, this young scholar (H. Preissler) has now been appointed as a successor to my former chair, after I decided to remain in the U.S.A. in Spring 1984 and not to return to East Germany.

Apart form Leipzig, the theological faculty at Jena has a chair in the history of religions (Th. Lohmann), but it is certainly not very influential. For years it stood in the shadow of the chair for atheism, the only one of its kind in East Germany, until it was abolished in 1969. A short while ago Berlin acquired a *Dozent* for the history of religions (K.-W. Troeger) in its theological section. Other East German universities do not teach the history of religions as such, but the latter does appear as part of oriental studies, as in Halle. The history of religions has received no influx of young blood even in the ecclesiastical seminaries. This is quite deplorable, especially because East Germans today are increasingly interested in and receptive to dialogue with other religions.

Research in areas of significance for the history of religions still continues in individual academic institutions, such as the Academy of Sciences of the German Democratic Republic, formerly the Prussian, and then, in the Nazi period, the German Academy of Sciences. Especially thriving is research in the field of Greek and Roman Antiquity, carried out in association with the Commission for the History of Religions in Late Antiquity, formerly the Church Fathers Commission, directed by J. Irmscher and K. Treu. Also quite active is the research group on the Turfan texsts in which are especially active W. Sundermann and P. Zieme (the study of Manichaean, Iranian, Turkish, and Buddhist texts). In other academic fields, the history of religions receives only sparse attention.

It is unfortunate that East Germany still has no organ devoted to the history of religions. J. Irmscher and myself have tried repeatedly to begin anew the old *Archiv für Religionswissenschaft*, but to date we have had no success. As a result, work in the history of religions has only a limited outlet in three journals somewhat related to the discipline, the *Theologische Literaturzeitung*, the *Orientalistische Literaturzeitung*, and *Altorientalischen Forschungen*. Some work can also be published in two theological series, either that issued by the Evangelische Verlagsanstalt or that issued by the Union-Verlag, both located in Berlin.

I will add now only a brief glance at Hungary and Czechoslovakia. In Czechoslovakia, the philological and historical institutes and chairs, especially those at Charles University in Prague, produce every now and then special studies in the history of religions, especially in the fields of Assyriology, Egyptology, and Iranian studies.

Such studies are published in the *Archiv orientalni*, which has been well-known for some time. History of religions *per se* does not, so far as I know, exist in Czechoslovakia, nor does research on atheism seem to be much fostered. I should mention, however, O. Klíma, the Nestor of East European Iranianists, who is well-known in history of religions circles for his works on Manichaeism and Mazdakism. Jan Heller works in the Comenius faculty at Prague (associated with the Moravian Brethren) as an Old Testament specialist and religious historian. He has published in Czech a history of religion in the Ancient East.

The situation in Hungary in similar to that in Czechoslovakia. The center for religio-historical work, as for so many things, is Budapest. Work in the history of religions is divided between several cultural specialties, especially Egyptology (Kakośy, Luft), Assyriology (G. Komoroczy) and classical philology (F. Hahn, who has published a popular history of religions). The great Hungarian figure in the history of religions after the second World War was Imre Trenczenyi-Waldapfel), who combined his great work in classics and folklore with a moderate Marxist-Leninist orientation. He has written a great book on classical mythology, *Die Töchter der Erinnerung*, and he has published a collection of essays under the title, *Untersuchungen zur Religionsgeschichte* (Budapest, 1966). To my knowledge, Hungary has no professor for history of religions proper, not even in the theological seminaries, whether Protestant or Catholic.

Thus, the picture of the history of religions in Eastern Europe is just as unbalanced as the religious situation — indeed, just as unbalanced as it is in other countries and on other continents. The major difference is that in Eastern Europe, under the "banner of socialism" (as the official expression runs), religions (the churches) and the history of religions as a science remain more under the spell of a modern materialistic outlook than is the case in Western Europe and America. Even in Western Europe and America, however, one finds a creeping materialism among the general public. In any case, religion and the history of religions have to follow each its own course: for revealed religion, supernatural truth is acquired not by knowledge but through faith. For the history of religions, the ideal of research and knowledge, as objective and factually oriented as possible, has religion, with its faith and traditions, as its object.

SOME REMARKS ABOUT MUSLIM NAMES IN INDO-PAKISTAN

Annemarie Schimmel, Cambridge, Mass.

As the name carries with it a *baraka*, a blessing power, and is almost identical with the named one, it is extremely important to choose an auspicious name for the newborn. Islamic tradition is no exception to this old custom, for did not the Prophet himself admonish the faithful: "Call yourselves with graceful names!"? The implications of this *ḥadīth* for early Islamic nomenclature have been discussed lucidly, some years ago, by Professor M. J. Kister. It has been obeyed, to our day, in most parts of the Islamic world, and its results are particularly interesting, and fascinating, in non-Arab regions, especially in Indo-Pakistan.

From the Middle Ages it is attested that the people of Iran and east of it have delighted in the use of fanciful *alqāb*, especially those connected with *ad-dīn* — so much so that visitors from the Maghrib found these highsounding titles (which often were no longer used as nicknames but became part and parcel of the "real" name) quite overwhelming if not shocking. Religious treatises from eighteenth century India, then, such as the *Nāla-i 'Andalīb* by the Delhi mystic and founder of the *ṭarīqa muḥammadiyya*, Nāṣir Muḥammad 'Andalīb, and even more the *'Ilm ul-kitāb* of his son, the noted Urdu poet Khwāja Mīr Dard, surround the heroes of their stories (projections of themselves!) with more than a hundred sonorous names. But even in normal upper middle class families, especially in the Deccan, it is customary to give a whole string of names to men and women, combining *kunya*, *ism* and several *alqāb* into one grand name. A friend from Hyderabad, Deccan, Dr. Ziauddin A. Shakeb, to whom I owe much information about Deccani customs, mentioned a person called Abū'l-maḥākim Muḥammad Iḥsān Afżaladdīn Yūnus 'Abdal-Muḥīṭ Shāhid Allāh Khān, who had seven sons, all of them named according to the same pattern, e.g., Abū'l-maḥāsin Muḥammad Muḥsin Rashīdaddīn Mūsā 'Abdal-Muḥṣī 'Ubaydullāh Khān. And when another gentleman in Hyderabad learned that his future wife's name was not less than Amat al-jāmi' Juwayrīya Jawāhir Jāsmīn he asked in despair whether this was a name or rather a recipe for some exotic medicine...

Indeed, Muslim names in the Subcontinent have always been interesting as they enlarge the simple early Islamic patterns almost endlessly. The above example shows that the Prophet's name, heavy with *baraka*, must definitely form part of every male Muslim's name, and that the names of the Qur'anic prophets, like Mūsā and Yūnus, are equally used, as is suggested in a *ḥadīth*. Names composed of *'abd* and one of the Divine Names, recommended as well in a *ḥadīth*, also occur. *Kunyas* pointing to some hoped-for noble qualities and a *laqab* showing the bearer's relation with his religion are also not lacking.

Especially the *laqab* seems capable of being expanded and altered considerably in India, and one has the impression that almost any noun could precede *ad-dīn*. One finds names like Iṣrār ad-dīn, and more often than not combinations of Persian nouns with *ad-dīn*, such as Aghāz ad-dīn, "beginning of religion," a name attested for the early 14th century. Āftāb ad-dīn instead of the Arabic Shams ad-dīn is found; and in former times the article of *dīn* was left out and Persian *iżāfa*-constructions were built, such as Fīrōz-i dīn or Chirāgh-i dīn — though often the i of the *iżāfat* was left out, as is usual in Indo-Pakistani names and titles. Thus one would pronounce the name Chirāgh Dīn. One can find that in the course of three generations such names are slowly Arabicized and reach via Chirāgh ad-dīn the correct Arabic Sirāj ad-dīn. Among the strange combinations of this kind is Alif dīn, a man who wrote a religious book at the turn of the century and was praised by the noted satirist Akbar Allāhābādī for having done a good job and not like a *bē-dīn*, that is, "without religion." The use of Persian nouns can also be seen in names like Khurshīd al-Islām, "Sun of Islam."

Especially colorful are names which parents invent out of gratitude for the birth of a healthy child, mainly a boy. These names are very common all over the Muslim world, and correspond to our Theodor, Isadore etc. When a family in Arab countries called their son 'Aṭā'Allāh or Hibat Allāh, "God's gift," the Persian might call him Khudādād, Allāh bakhsh, or Yazdāndād, with forms denoting "giving"; and in Turkish areas the verbal form *birdī, bardī, werdī* "he gave" is used, as in Allāhverdī, Taghrī birdī (the Turkish *tengri*) or Jabbārberdī. The Sindhi and Panjabi might use the same device by naming the boy Allāhdiyā or Allāhvarāyō. Often, however, the feeling of gratitude is directed not so much at God but at the Prophet, the imam, or a special saint thanks to whose intercession the child is born: hence the numerous Rasūlbakhsh or Nabī-bakhsh, or, in Shia families, Dād-'Alī or Imāmbakhsh, while families with strong Sufi connections might use names like Ghauthbakhsh, "given by The Help, i.e., 'Abdul Qādir Jīlānī" or Qalandarbakhsh (referring to Lāl Shahbāz Qalandar in Sehwan, Sind). In Turkey, I know a girl Pīrden, "From the Pīr," that is, in this case, Maulānā Jalāladdīn Rūmī. In the Indian environment one preferred — at least in upperclass or *sayyid* families — to call children with more elaborate names, and instead of naming the boy simply with the classical Faḍl Allāh, "bounty of God," one adorned the names and made Fażl ar-Raḥmān, Fażl(-i) Rabbī, Fażl-i Bari, Fażl-i Ḥaqq or Fażl-i Mannān, all of them using different Divine names. Names combined with *In'ām* "granted by" or *Luṭf*, "kindness of" as well as *'Ināyat* "grace" occur in such combinations, such as In'ām ul-ḥaqq, Luṭf al-Bārī, 'Ināyat al-Ḥaqq.

The Divine name used most frequently in these combinations is ar-Raḥmān, favorite from the days of the Prophet, and thus one finds people called Dalīl ar-Raḥmān, 'Azīz ur-Rahmān, Ẓill- (Shadow), Mustafiż- (taking grace from), Asad- (lion) I'jāz (inimitability), Tanzīl- (Sending down) — the latter two connected in common theological parlance with the Qur'ān and its inimitable style and its being sent down to the Prophet; Nasīm ar-Raḥmān, the "Breeze of the Merciful" and many more combinations can be gleaned from newspapers and personal connections. Other names that sound somewhat unusual are Khalīq as-subḥān, "appropriate, in keeping with, the Most Glorious," Anwār al-Karīm, "Lights of the Generous," Najm al-Ghanī, "Star of the Rich" or Nūr al-Bāqī, "Light of the Eternal."

These beautiful names are only part of the spectrum. Families connected with a Sufi order — and a large majority of Indo-Pakistani

Muslims are — will not only express their gratitude to their patron saint by naming a child Qādirbakhsh, "given by ['Abdul] Qādir," but connect themselves and the children with the blessing power of the saint. Thus one finds among the Qādiris, who are strongly represented in South India and in parts of the Panjab, names like Ghulām Qādir, Ghulām Muḥyi' ddīn (this is one of 'Abdul Qādir's honorific titles) or, frequently, Ghulām Dastgīr, for he is the one who "takes man's hand." Similar combinations are found with the surnames of other saints, such as Ghulām Shihābaddīn (i.e., Suhrawardī) Ghulām Rabbānī or -Mujaddid, both pointing to Aḥmad Sirhindī, or Ghulām Mu'inuddīn (Chishti). Such names are also given to women and assume their grammatical forms which are difficult to believe for an Arabist. Certainly, Ghauthīya or Jīlānī Begum are acceptable for women in the Qādiriyya tradition, but there exists even the name Ghulām Muḥyiuddīn an-Nisā' Begum, or Mu'īnaddīn an-Nisā' Bānū, or Dastgīr Bī. The former examples show that in the Indian environment the word *an-nisā* can be prefixed with almost every other noun or, as in these cases, half sentences. While forms like Sharaf un-Nisā' or Nūr an-nisā' are perfectly understandable, it becomes more difficult to accept Raḥīm an-nisā' or, in many families who admired the poet-philosopher Iqbāl, Iqbāl an-nisā'.

Special rules are of course observed in the Shia community in India as elsehwere, and, as in Iran, the names of the first two caliphs are absolutely tabu. (Strangely, I met an Ismaili by name of Fārūq; the family was apparently unaware of the fact that this is a nickname of the caliph 'Umar). Combinations with 'Alī (and to a smaller extent, his honorific name Murtażā) abound, and not only is the parents' gratitude to him expressed in names like Dād-'Alī, Iḥsān 'Alī or Karam 'Alī, but one wishes the child also to assume the "qualities" or "virtues" of the first imam: Auṣāf 'Alī, Fażā'il 'Alī. And one shows one's love for him in names like 'Āshiq 'Alī (parallel to 'Āshiq Muhammad), Muḥibb 'Alī and, in Pakistan, Piyār 'Alī; rather, one goes so far as to call one's child Kalb 'Alī, " 'Alī's dog" or his ram, Qoch 'Alī, and in Mughal history, one Kafsh 'Alī, " 'Alī's shoe" appears.

'Alī's famous sword Dhū l-fiqār is part and parcel of Shii nomenclature, as names like Qilich 'Alī, " 'Alī's sword" are also found. The Muslims are particularly fond of combinations of 'Alī with one of the names of the lion, for he was called Asadullāh, "God's Lion" and his mother had called him first Ḥaydara after his maternal grandfather Asad, as was the custom in pre-Islamic Arabia. This accounts for the numerous Shīr 'Alī or 'Alīshīr, Ghażanfar or Amīr Arslān.

Similar trends can be observed in combinations with the names of the following Shia imams. Ḥusayn, of course, takes pride of place; but there is no lack of Zayn al-'Ābidīn (sometimes cut into two names, Zaynul and 'Ābidīn), Ḥasan 'Askarī or Mahdī. All these names can be combined with Ghulām, "servant of" or with the suffixed *qūlī*, "servant," like Shāhqūlī, Murtażāqūlī or Ḥaydarqūlī. Even *'abd* with the names of the imams occurs in Shia areas as it does sometimes with the name or titles of the Prophet, although it should be restricted to combinations with names of God. But as one finds 'Abdur Rasūl and 'Abdun Nabī, one also encounters, though less frequently, 'Abd 'Alī, 'Abd al-Ḥusayn and even 'Abd al batūl, "servant of Fatima" — names which will arouse the wrath of every strict Sunni Muslim. Sometimes, the second and third imam are taken together, and their servant is called Ghulām-(i) Sayyidayn, or hopes to be Ḥasanaynnawāz, "cherished by Ḥasan and Ḥusayn." Now and then, the reference is to the imam or imams or to the "innocent martyrs," *ma'sūm*, as in Fakhr-i Imām, Kalb al- a'imma, or Ghulām Ma'ṣūm.

The custom of choosing names not only from the sacred history of Islam but from its very sourcebook, the Qur'an, is widespread, especially in the Subcontinent, and leads sometimes to strange results. One can mention here the numerous Bismillāh, Māshā'Allāh and Inshā'Allāh Khāns in the northwestern part of the Subcontinent, and Qul huwa Allāh (Sura 112/1) was the name of the ancestor of a *sayyid* family in Sind.

One way of finding an appropriate name is to open the holy book and to take the first letter of the first word on the page as initial letters for the names: thus, if the first word should be *dhākirīn*, the name has to begin with a *dh*, such as Dhakā' Allāh or Dhahānat son of Salāmat. One can also take a full word — noun or verb — from the page, and thus names like Yusrā (Sura 87/8 and 92/7) or Asrā (Sura 17/1) appear as women's names. Sometimes a fitting expression lends itself to the family, as in the case of *Al-'urwat al-wuthqā* (Sura 2/257) son of Ahmad Sirhindī. But sometimes the outcome is not very acceptable to those who know Arabic, and are familiar with the Qur'ān: the eighteenth century polyhistor Āzād Bilgrāmī tells that one day a man came to visit him in Aurangabad. When asked his name, the poor man said, it is *Ba'du bi'd-dīn* (Sura 95/7), following which the learned writer refused to talk to him on account of the terrible context, which is "And what makes you deny *after that the Judgment*?" The Mirza *A-lam nashraḥ* "Did we not expand..." (Sura 94/1) in the *Fasāna-i Āzād* may be a fictional name but could as well be taken from life. For who can imagine my shock when a headline in the *Pakistan Times* announced: "Naṣrum min allāh dies in road mishap." *Naṣrun min Allāh* (written with m due to the pronunciation, Sura 61/13), "Help from God" is difficult to combine with any mishap — and even Pakistani friends found this name definitely embarrassing.

The full range of "graceful" and blessing names in Indo-Pakistan, which express the pride of belonging to the community of the faithful and distinguish one's self from the surrounding non-Muslim people, can never be measured. A single glance into a newspaper or into a telephone directory in Pakistan, Delhi, Hyderabad of Bangladesh shows that the imagination of the Muslims is still very creative where beautiful new names are concerned. Although a name like Nād 'Alī — the beginning of the famous Shia invocation *Nādī 'Aliyyan*, "Call Alī, the one who manifests miracles" — occurs as early as the sixteenth century in Mughal history, daring combinations seem still very common, and one is happy to find a Farzand-i tauhīd, a "child of the confession of God's Unity" or some Ṣubḥ-i azal, "Morning of Pre-Eternity" as well as a lady Nūr al-hudā, the Light of Right Guidance (which is originally a name given to the Prophet). And our driver in Delhi, good Muslim but certainly no major saint, is basking in the radiance of his name, Shams ul-'Ārifin, "the Sun of the Gnostics."

POST-MORTEM IMMORTALITY

or:

THE TAOIST RESURRECTION OF THE BODY

Anna Seidel, Kyoto

> Scandit ad Aethera
> Virgo puerpera,
> Virgula Jesse.
> Non sine corpore
> Sed sine tempore
> Tendit ad esse
>
> *Legenda Aurea*

Western students of Chinese religions are often tempted to pursue questions which are pertinent in the Judaeo-Christian frame of mind but have little relevance in the context of Chinese religions and therefore lead to no significant new insights — such as the question concerning the different sects or creeds into which Chinese religion can be divided. This essay will deal with a question that does not seem to make much sense from the Western point of view, but has been a crucial issue in China: what happens to the physical human body after death?

Every religion has its own answer to this question. Seen from a Far-Eastern perspective, Christianity "blurred" this issue by the dualistic concept of spirit and matter, soul and body. The survival of an eternal soul (of which the body is, more often than not, considered to be only the prison) consoles the Christian over the decomposition or even cremation of his body; on the other hand, a belief in the rising of the dead from their tombs on Judgment Day assures the faithful of the creator God's *omnipotentia* to resurrect and transfigure even the most completely annihilated body.

For a Buddhist, the only advantage of an existence in the human body is the chance it offers to improve one's karma so that one may, in the optimal case, not be reborn ever again in a human or any other body. This chance of advancement toward non-corporeality, offered only by the human existence (among the Six Ways or existences), and the interdiction of killing are the only inhibitions against the willful destruction of one's own body — inhibitions that have at times broken down, giving way to bodily destruction in religious suicides (still very recently in Vietnam), or to the offering of one's body to feed or cure other beings.[1] This thoroughly negative view of corporality made the annihilation of the physical body a desirable goal for the Buddhists, and cremation has always been their logical favourite among funeral customs.

In China, the Buddhist *Leibfeindlichkeit* encountered serious opposition. Whereas in Japan cremation was introduced and accepted without any question as soon as Buddhism became firmly established (seventh-eighth centuries AD), the Chinese have always been horrified by any willful mutilation or destruction of the body. The majority even of the early Buddhist patriarchs in China, Hsuan-tsang (AD 602-664) for example, were interred by their disciples. The conflict is illustrated in the story of the Chinese monk whose corpse was found still intact after cremation — a Chinese proof of saintliness — and swiftly turned to ashes only after having been reminded of his Buddhist goal: "If you have indeed achieved the Way, you should disintegrate!"[2]

---

[1] Cf. the article on cremation in *Hōbōgirin, dictionnaire encyclopédique du bouddhisme*, fasc. VI, Paris/Tokyo 1983, pp. 573-585: "*Dabi*"; Étienne Lamotte, "Le suicide religieux dans le bouddhisme ancien," *Bulletin de l'Académie Royale de Belgique (Classe des Lettres)*, tome 51 (1965): 156-168; Jacques Gernet, "Les suicides par le feu chez les bouddhistes chinois," *Mélanges de l'Institut des Hautes Études Chinoises* II, Paris, PUF 1960, pp. 527-558; Jean Filliozat, "La mort volontaire par le feu ...," *Journal Asiatique* CCLI,1 (1963):21-51. On Kuan-yin's offering of her eyes and arms, see Glen Dudbridge, *The Legend of Miao-shan*, London 1978 (review *JAS* 38.4 [1979]:770f). One fascinating case of Buddho-Taoist self-immolation is described by Eric Zürcher, "Buddhist Influences on Early Taoism," *T'oung Pao* LXVI, 1-3 (1980):103-04. For a unique case, in the history of Jewish piety, of the "desire to be burned alive 'for the sanctification of the Name'," see R.J. Zwi Werblowsky, *Joseph Karo, Lawyer and Mystic*, Philadelphia 1980, pp. 152-154.

[2] *Ch'u san-tsang chi chi* 13, in *Taishō Daizōkyō* vol. 55, no. 2145, p. 97b10-12.

The obstacle to Buddhist cremation in China was the deeply ingrained concept of the human being as a perfectly homogeneous entity in which 'soul and body' form an inseparable continuum, not a karmic prison of debasing desires and illusions, but a potentially perfect microcosmic realisation of the primordial life force *ch'i* (neither 'matter' nor 'spirit'), which animates the universe in an harmonious and dynamic *creatio continua*. This most basic of all Chinese axioms is still today the rationale of Chinese religion, of Chinese medicine and even of Chinese *cuisine*, since food is medicine and medicine is long life and immortality is the name of the game in all Chinese religion.

As Needham has said with regard to alchemy: "...in Chinese culture alone, ... the eschatological conditions were right for the origin of real belief in the existence and efficacy of macrobiogens, chemical and physiological elixirs of material immortality."[3] The belief that certain physiological practices, diets and pharmaka can render the body imperishable is attested in China since the fourth century BC. The Taoist search for the avoidance of death and the indefinite prolongation of life in a perfected physical body is a much discussed subject on which I do not intend to dwell,[4] except to remind readers of recent evidence which illustrates the practice. What will interest us here are the beliefs such an utterly this-worldly culture could have concerning the fate of those 99.9 per cent of men who did die — a question which scholars of Taoism, fascinated as they are with immortality, have so far neglected. A large majority of the sites excavated in the course of the present-day archaeological boom in China are richly furnished tombs built for those who did not avoid death. So it might be timely to ask the question as to what hope the religion of material immortality could offer to those whose bodies went to the grave.

After what was said above, we can see that the hopeless condition of him whose life force has fled, whose 'spirits' have scattered and whose body decomposes was, in the Chinese context, a greater dilemma than in other cultures. How unsatisfactory the solutions of this dilemma were felt to be is revealed in the readiness with which the Chinese popular religion adopted the Buddhist belief in the transmigra-

---

3 Joseph Needham, *Science and Civilisation in China*, V:2, Cambridge 1974, p. 71 (in the introductory passage of the most complete and up-to-date presentation of Taoist immortality theory and techniques, pp. 71-154).

4 Needham, *op. cit.*

tion of "karmic residue" understood as soul. Thus, from about the fourth century AD onward, Chinese Buddhists, as well as many Taoists who despaired of the arduous path to immortality in *this* body, prayed for an advantageous rebirth in *another* physical body. In doing so — but that is another question — they of course thoroughly misunderstood the Buddhist doctrine of the non-existence of the soul, as we know from the famous *Shen-pu-mieh* ("The spirit does not perish") controversy.[5]

In order to get a clear focus on this problem we will consider the period in Chinese history when immortality was already considered an attainable goal but Buddhism had not yet propagated its, in a way, facile solution to the problem of what happens to those who do not attain it. This period roughly coincides with the Han Dynasties (206 BC-AD 220) and the Three Kingdoms (221-264).

The beliefs and burial customs of the aristocracy during this timespan have been studied. There is no single accepted belief concerning the afterlife. As Loewe has pointed out: "In discriminatingbetween recognised motives it is of some importance to realise that the Chinese themselves did not necessarily believe that they were mutually exclusive."[6] The ideas of the lettered class have up to now been understood to have been roughly the following. At the moment of death one (or later three) pneumatic, more refined *Yang* component of man, the *hun* (let us not call it a 'soul'), escapes from the body, is ritually summoned back in the *chao-hun* ceremony, is then guided by careful steps to the realm of the deified ancestors, and was perhaps thought to descend to the clan's ancestral temple on the occasion of sacrifices. Three (later seven) vital or vegetative *Yin* energies of man, the *p'o*, follow the corpse back into the earth and have to be appeased with grave goods.

---

[5] It was the Buddhist Hui-yüan who wrote the treatise *On the Indestructibility of the Soul*; see Kenneth Ch'en, *Buddhism in China*, Princeton 1964, pp. 138-42. With or without the doctrine of the non-existence of the soul, the belief in the transmigration of souls through different bodies posed no problem to the Buddhists since their final goal was nirvanic extinction. Problems arise only when the idea of reincarnation enters a religion that believes in the resurrection of the dead. Medieval Judaism had to reconcile its belief in metempsychosis (*gilgul*) with that in the resurrection. Which of its bodies would rise with the soul? This question was solved by multiplying man's soul into three components which, in an intricate play of joining and separating, produce a soul (*nefesh*) for each of the three resurrecting bodies; cf. R.J. Zwi Werblowsky, *Joseph Karo*, p. 243.

[6] Michael Loewe, *Chinese Ideas of Life and Death*, London 1982, p. 114.

Alternatively, they may find their way into the corporate existence of the "Yellow Springs" (*huang-ch'üan*).[7] These and similar very abstract notions do not seem to have had as wide a currency as we assumed up to now. They are due for a reappraisal in view of all the new data concerning Han religion provided by the archaeological work on Han tombs. Richly furnished upper-class tombs contain clear indications of a transition to a heaven or paradise through the tomb. The modality of this transition has yet to be understood but surely the *hun* spirits of the deceased would not be excluded from this passage through the earth to new life. The famous funerary banner found on top of the coffin of the Marquise of Tai (Ma-wang-tui, tomb No. 1, 168 BC) shows the ascension of this lady to a paradise. Two centuries later, the frequent representation, on tomb reliefs, of the foremost life-granting deity, the Queen Mother of the West (Hsi Wang Mu), and of paradises of the immortals attests to a belief in some yet to be explained means to achieve what one can only define with the contradictory phrase of *post-mortem* immortality.[8] That these tokens of immortality in Han tombs were more than a futile "pious" hope against hope is indicated by the remarkable state of preservation of some of the corpses found in these tombs.[9] The preservation of the physical body from decomposition was of the utmost importance, as we know also from literary sources. A Han record of *Popular Traditions and Customs* speaks of burial rites intended to protect the grave from demons who "like to eat the liver and the brain of the deceased."[10]

---

[7] For a less superficial presentation of these ideas, cf. Needham, *op. cit.*, V:2, pp. 85-93.

[8] Loewe, *op. cit.*, pp. 114-26, the most recent and dependable Western survey of Han funerary culture; for more details cf. also Michael Loewe, *Ways to Paradise, The Chinese Quest for Immortality*, London 1979, *passim*, and my review article of this book in *Numen* XXIX, 1 (1982):79-122.

[9] Cf. Needham, *op. cit.*, V:2, pp. 303-04, and Timoteus Pokora, " 'Living Corpses' in Early Mediaeval China," *Religion und Philosophie in Ostasien*, Festschrift für Hans Steininger, Würzburg 1985, pp. 343-57. Preservation was also the motive for enclosing the corpse inside a magnificent suit made of jade discs which, of course, did not prevent putrefaction, cf. Needham, V:2, pl. CDLII.

[10] *Feng-su t'ung-i t'ung-chien, i-wen*, p. 88 (Peking ed., Taipei 1968 repr.); cf. also Anna Seidel, "Traces of Han Religion" (at note 48), forthcoming in *Dōkyō to shūkyō bunka*, volume in honour of Professor Akitsuki Kan'ei, Tokyo 1987.

With this text we are already in a more popular milieu where the hope for bodily immortality beyond the tomb did not yet exist in the second century AD. This we know from funerary texts recently discovered in more poorly furnished Han tombs. These documents are extremely interesting for the historian of the Taoist religion. They show that, in the first two centuries of our era (if not before), the Chinese underworld was not any more the dark She'ol of the Yellow Springs deep down in the earth (as in the earlier Chou religion) but already the bureaucratised netherworld society inside the sacred mountains of China, the "earth-prisons" (*ti-yü/jigoku*) which the Buddhists were to transform into their gory hells. In the Han funerary texts the emphasis is not yet, as later in Chinese and Japanese Buddhism, on the ethical issues of retribution, expiation and the concomitant sadistic phantasies of torture. The dead, whether good or bad, are simply locked away in a subterranean replica of the Chinese empire, with its bureaucratic hierarchy, its tax offices, tribunals and prisons. There they lead a gray and resentful existence, exiled from the world and without any hope of ascent to the realms of the immortals.

The function of the funerary texts is that of a passport or letter of introduction by which a plenipotentiary of the highest celestial deity, the "Envoy of the Heavenly Thearch," recommends the deceased to the netherworld authorities, thus assuring the newly arrived shade of a satisfactory integration into the subterranean society. The real motive behind these *documents de passage* concerns, of course, the living members of his family. They must assure themselves that this utter calamity of death will not taint their own future destiny because death, especially early death, in this proto-Taoist milieu, is the absolute disaster. The funerary texts make it quite clear that the *hun* as well as the *p'o* components of man, his whole social persona and individual being must descend under the earth, while his body becomes the prey of the demons of putrefaction. With the loss of the body, all is lost and the living rightly fear the boundless resentment and wrath of the deprived shade. He is placated with funerary goods (duly inventoried in 'grave goods lists', often joined to the funerary documents), he is given "sacred pharmaka" (*shen yao*) to delay the decomposition of his cadaver (most funerary texts are in fact written on the surface of pottery jars containing these drugs), and, above all, he is sternly ordered, with all kinds of commands, invocations and threats, to go away and never come back. Some texts contain almost poetic couplets insisting on the necessary separation of the dead from the living, such as this ordinance written on a jar in the year AD 175:

> "Azure is Heaven above, limitless is the Underworld.
> The dead belong to the realm of Yin, the living belong to the realm of Yang.
> [The living have] their village home, the dead have their hamlets.
> The living are under the jurisdiction of Ch'ang-an in the West,
> the dead are under the jurisdiction of Mount T'ai in the East.
> In joy they do not [remember] each other,
> [in grief] they do not think of one another."[11]

Other documents are more coldly bureaucratic:

> "All misfortune emanating from the earth be banished and annihilated! We order that calamities are to happen no more! After receipt of this document, the netherworld officials are obligated by oath never again to annoy or disturb the Chang clan! Promptly, promptly, in accordance with the statutes and ordinances!"[12]

And one incantation is outright cruel:

> "The subject deceased on the *i-szu* day has the demon name 'Heavenly Brightness.' The Divine Master of the Heavenly Thearch has already been informed as to your name. Promptly remove yourself three thousand leagues away! Should you not go away, then the [...] of Southern Mountain will be ordered to come and devour you. Promptly, in accordance with the statutes and ordinances!"[13]

The disembodied dead have become demons, strangled life force deprived of its support and seeking frantically for a way back. "Demon, ghost, wraith" (*kuei*) is cognate to "return" (*kuei* — written with another character); the dead are terrifying revenants who inflict disease and misfortune, and extort propitiatory offerings of slaughtered animals to nourish their baleful energies. They have to be securely locked away.

---

11 Ikeda On, "Chūgoku rekidai bokenryakkō," *Tōyō bunka kenkyūjo kiyō* 86 (1981):273, no. 7; cf. also Seidel, "Traces of Han Religion."

12 AD 173. Ikeda, *op. cit.*, p. 273, no. 6. Cf. also A. Seidel, "Geleitbrief an die Unterwelt—Jenseitsvorstellungen in den Graburkunden der späteren Han Zeit," *Religion und Philosophie in Ostasien*, Würzburg 1985, p. 168.

13 *Kaogu* 1960.10:20-21. For Han funerary texts the reader is also referred to my more comprehensive (than the articles cited above) study and translation forthcoming in *T'oung Pao* (1987-88?).

In the late second century AD, the first popular Taoist movements appeared on the scene. Among the reasons for their success was no doubt the fact that they proposed a way out of the dilemma of physical death. What is more, they eventually came to devise means to save even those who had already become wretched demonic shades.

The deathless immortality of the hermit sage, who simply leaves the society of men to ascend to the stellar palaces, was of course out of reach for the villagers of a Taoist community. To take the sting out of the visible death of the Taoist parishioners, especially of those who were just and saintly in a now increasingly ethically polarized religion, the idea of an only "apparent" death arose. We find it expressed in the earliest religious commentary to Lao tzu's *Tao te ching* passage: "He who stays in his proper place can endure; he dies and does not perish, this is longevity":

> "The [good] actions of the man of the Tao are perfect and the spirit of the Tao gathers about him. When he retires from the world, he *simulates* death and passes over into the realm of the Extreme Yin (T'ai Yin). There he revives, goes forth anew and thus does not perish. This is meant by "longevity" [in the *Tao te ching*'s phrase]. The profane, however, those who have no good deeds [to their credit], when they die, they come under the jurisdiction of the nether-world administration. They indeed perish."[14]

This belief in a feigned death appears already in the *Discourses* by Wang Ch'ung (AD 27-97), where this method is, for the first time, called by its rather strange name "liberation from the corpse" (*shih chieh*).[15] Needham renders it as "release from the mortal part." "Corpse" means here all the corruptible aging factors of the physical body. In modern ecological language, one could say that the Taoist rids his body of all 'biodegradable' elements or of his 'built-in obsolescence,' in a way which is often likened to the moulting of the cicada.[16] The superior Taoist accomplishes this in his lifetime, and ascends in a perfected body without passing through death. Less advanced adepts seemingly die like any other mortal, but in reality achieve purification

---

[14] *Hsiang-erh* commentary to *Tao te ching*, chap. 33; cf. Jao Tsung-i, *Lao tzu Hsiang-erh chu chiao-chien*, Hong Kong 1956, p. 46.

[15] *Lun Heng*, chap. *Tao-hsü*, transl. by Alfred Forke (as "separation from the body"): *Lun Heng, Wang Chung's Essays*, vol. I, New York 1962, p. 345.

[16] Described (and criticised) by Wang Ch'ung, cf. Forke, *loc. cit.*

of their body by a smelting process in the Extreme Yin palace, in the high North of the universe, as described in the *tao te ching* commentary; they perform "liberation from the corpse." This leads them to a grade of inferior immortals in the invisible mountain paradises of this world, or of presiding officials in the underworld, or of candidates in the lowest echelons of the heavens.[17] On whatever low a rung, they have thus entered the ladder of the immortal hierarchy in which they can continue to advance in divine perfection and into high office for aeons to come.

Needham and Robinet have shown that the phenomenon of "deliverance from the corpse" is very complex. For our concern — the restoration of the body after a real death — suffice it to clarify two points.

1° It is not one or several 'souls' that go to be purified and then return to revive the corpse — it is unmistakably the physical body that undergoes restoration in the Northern Citadel of Extreme Yin. As a fourth century text puts it, the body (*shen*) passes through the Three Offices of the netherworld protected by various deities who

> "summon the *p'o* energies, guard the skeleton, protect the life force (*ch'i*), collect the *hun* pneumata, so that flesh and bones will not rot and the five viscera not decay."

The adept will feel as if he had only slept for one night and already he is outside the coffin.[18]

To profane eyes, this process appeared as it is described in the Taoist hagiographies. The departing Taoist lends to some personal object - his sandals, sword, staff or robe — the appearance of a corpse for the eyes of those who perform his funeral. If the coffin of such a saint is later opened, the discovery of a pair of sandals instead of a decomposed corpse serves as proof that he has indeed become immortal.[19]

---

17 On *shih-chieh*, the recent short study by Isabelle Robinet is most illuminating: "Metamorphosis And Deliverance From The Corpse In Taoism," *History of Religions* 19.1 (1979):57-70. Equally important for the more alchemical aspects: Needham, *op. cit.*, V:2, pp. 301-04; also Michel Strickmann, "The Alchemy of T'ao Hungching," H. Welch and A. Seidel eds., *Facets of Taoism*, New Haven, 1979, pp. 180-185.

18 *Chiu-chen chung-ching* A.10a-b, in *Tao-tsang* fasc. 1042, *Harvard-Yenching Index* no. 1365; Robinet, *op. cit.*, p. 63.

19 Cf. Max Kaltenmark, *Le Lie-sien tchouan*, Peking 1953, pp. 40, 45, esp. 52 note 6; Robinet, *op. cit.*, p. 62. We will see, *in fine*, that this legendary theme is not unknown in the Christian West.

2° Most if not all methods of "liberation from the corpse" imply preparatory techniques, be they meditation and macrobiotic exercises, alchemical labours with ingestion of drugs,[20] or just "accumulation of good deeds," as in the *Tao te ching* commentary. Taoism is — in Japanese Buddhist terms — a *jiriki* religion, where one has to achieve salvation by one's "own power;" faith is not at issue.[21] The *post-mortem* immortality of the corpse-liberated Taoist thus reveals itself as one more technique to bypass death, one more variation on the theme of the all-important corporeal continuity.

This means that we still do not know what Taoism could possibly have devised to help the truly dead, those whose body did not even preserve the tiniest pilot flame of the primordial *ch'i* force, apt to burst into a new blaze of life in an incorruptible body smelted in the womb of Extreme Yin.

The answer is liturgy. Ritual communication with the gods takes, in Taoism, the form of bureaucratic procedure since, as we have already seen above, the unseen world is an administrative hierarchy or, to quote Strickmann's quick tongue, a "paperwork empire."[22] Thus it does not surprise us that the liturgy to save the dead is modelled after the judicial paperwork necessary for freeing a condemned prisoner.[23] Gifts (with a flavour of bribes) are prepared, and an official petition is drawn up humbly submitting the case to the highest celestial gods, with an appeal for amnesty. Such petition formulas are perserved in the *Petition Almanac of Master Red Pine*, a liturgical *Briefsteller* in the tradition of the Han funerary texts, but already influenced by Buddhism and therefore difficult to date (third-fifth century AD).

The action is initiated by the descendants of the deceased who are motivated by something much more vital than "filial piety" in its usual moralistic Confucian sense. Genealogical continuity as one aspect of

[20] Needham, *op. cit.*, V:2, p. 294sq.; Strickmann, *op. cit.*, pp. 182-84.

[21] For an exception that confirms the rule, see Robinet, *op. cit.*, pp. 62-63.

[22] In the English manuscript of "Therapeutische Rituale und das Problem des Bösen im frühen Taoismus," *Religion und Philosophie in Ostasien*, Würzburg 1985, pp. 185-200. This short essay is a concise and vivid portrayal of the early Taoist scene with regard to the dead, their pathogenic role and the liturgies of healing.

[23] Already Wang Ch'ung had likened the dead to criminals condemned beyond appeal, cf. *Lung Heng* 23, Forke, *op. cit.*, II, pp. 372-73; Seidel, "Traces of Han Religion."

physical permanence is taken so literally in Taoism that a bond of collective responsibility is believed to link the Taoist with seven generations before and after him. The merits of an ancestor can contribute to his descendants' prosperity and advancement toward immortality, just as a "truly dead" ancestor undergoing trial in the netherworld can be the cause of sickness and death among his children and grandchildren to the seventh generation. Strickmann points out the psychologically interesting fact that, generally, good-fortune-producing merit was attributed to distant ancestors, whereas disease causing misdeeds were imputed to the immediately preceding generation.[24] This purely Chinese concept of inherited guilt (*ch'eng-fu*) became entangled with the Buddhist idea of bad karma accumulated in one's *own* past lives, so that we find, in Master Red Pine's petitions, appeals for pardon of the ancestors' misdeeds and of the load of guilt resulting from one's own "previous bodies" (*hsien-shen su-yüan*).[25] The immediate motive for such a liturgy is a disease in the family, which the priest is called upon to cure by intervening in the ghostly lawsuit and effecting the acquittal and redemption of the dead ancestor, whose plight has caused the affliction.

Now let us see what kind of salvation the petitioner hopes to achieve for his "truly dead" ancestor. In a "Petition for release from banishment, ransom of misdeeds, confession and repentance for a deceased [forebear of the afflicted patient]", the Offices of the Three Heavens are asked to repeal the conviction of the spectral defendant by issuing an "Imperial Decree" (*Nü-ch'ing chao-shu*) to the spirits in charge of the grave (the Deputy of the Burial Mound, the Tomb Provost, the twelve Cemetery Spirits...) and to the governors ruling over the various infernal mountain fortresses, such as the Twenty-four Prisons of Mount T'ai, the Great Jail of the Central Citadel and the Three Tribunals of Heaven, Earth and Water, etc., ordering them to

"release forthwith the *hun* and *p'o* spirits of so-and-so [name to

---

24 Strickmann, "Therapeutische Rituale...," pp. 194-97. Strickmann does cover himself by adding (p. 196): "Historiker und Anthropologen sind gut beraten, sich einer psychologischen und, vor allem, einer psycho-analytischen Erklärung zu enthalten. Es ist ein todsicherer Weg, sich seine Karriere zu ruinieren, und ich möchte auch nicht mein bescheidenes Erstgeburtsrecht als Historiker für ein freudianisches Linsengericht verkaufen."

25 *Ch'ih-sung tzu chang-li* 6.13a4 (also 5.1b1 *et passim*). *Tao-tsang*, fasc. 336, *HY Index* no. 615. The influence of the ideas of karma and retribution on early Taoism is discussed in Zürcher, *op. cit.*, pp. 135-41.

> be filled in], *to return his corpse to him and reassemble his bones*, to discharge him from the suffering of penal servitude and let him ascend and join celestial officialdom in the Land of Harmony and Joy. Shut off all sickening miasmas [affecting the living descendants] and strike his name from the Registers of the Dead.''[26]

So it has indeed become possible to span the great divide between the terrestrial and celestial world of life and the world of the truly dead. A similar petition words the request somewhat differently. The netherworld agencies

> ''are to release forthwith the *hun* and *p'o* spirits of so-and-so, shred the list of his indictment, erase his condemnation, discharge him from penal servitude; bathe him and garb him in [the proper official's attire with] cap and belt, and let him ascend to the Hall of Happiness. May he revert to the state of embryo and be reborn in a good household. May all lethal miasmas emanating from the Six Palaces [of the dead] be shut off, and his name entered on High in the Cinnabar Registers of Life.''[27]

This passage is a typical example of the nonchalance with which the Taoists adopted Buddhist beliefs, without much concern for consistency or, in most cases, any basic change in their attitudes. The immortal official's admission into the celestial hierarchy of the Cinnabar Register is juxtaposed with reincarnation; the cleansed body attired in the official's cap and belted gown is prayed for, as well as the return to the embryo in a respectable family.

As Zürcher has pointed out, some areas of Taoism absorbed more Buddhist influence than others.[28] The fundamental notion of *ch'i* and the cluster of immortality beliefs and practices, for example, were not affected at all. However, the dilemma discussed in the preceding pages made the Taoist beliefs concerning the world *d'outre tombe* a ''soft area'' where the Buddhist concepts of rebirth, transfer of merit and compassion were readily accepted, because they provided answers to questions of vital concern.[29]

---

[26] *Ch'ih-sung tzu chang-li* 6.12a-b.

[27] *Ibid.*, 6.14a.

[28] Zürcher, *op. cit.*, p. 121.

[29] Strickmann (''Therapeutische Rituale...,'' p. 199) dates the Taoist change from the *battle* against the dead (as we have seen it in the Han funerary texts) to the *salvation*

None of these Buddhist notions were completely alien to the Chinese mind. The sentiment which moves the "Great Tao to commiserate with the living, to take pity on the dead" and to free the spirits fettered in the dark, is *tz'u*,[30] the "parental kindness" which had been stressed by Mo tzu as the counterpart to "filial piety."[31] But *tz'u* is also the translation which the Chinese Buddhists chose for *maitrī*. Thus one might wonder if the Taoist gods did not accord a gift as thoroughly non-Buddhist as physical immortality to the hopelessly dead — inspired by the great Bodhisattva virtue of compassion.

As a concluding vignette, I would like to mention a Christian case of "liberation from the corpse" (*shih-chieh*), which starkly illuminates the unfathomable difference of context in which strangely similar motifs can occur.

In 1951 Pope Pius XII proclaimed the dogma of the bodily assumption of the Virgin Mary into Heaven. As is usual in the case of a new dogma, the belief in the newly proclaimed doctrine was said to have existed in the Catholic Church since many centuries. Indeed, the thirteenth century *Legenda Aurea* by Jacobus a Voragine collates a number of legends concerning the *assumptio* of the Mother of Christ. There we find several interesting themes, such as the Virgin Mary's fear lest her soul, once outside the body, be confronted with demons (*ut anima mea de corpore exiens nullum spiritum teterrimum videat nullaque mihi Sathanae potestas occurrat*), her fear of the Jews who, *malitiae obstinati*, plot to steal her body and burn it (*venite, omnes discipulos, occidamus ac corpus illud, quod seductorem illum portavit, ignibus comburamus*). At the moment of death, her soul, leaving her body, is wafted aloft in the arms of her son who had descended from heaven *cum angelorum ordinibus, patriarcharum coetibus, martirum agminibus, confessorum acie virginumque choris*; the scene brings to mind the descent of the Buddha Amida and his multitude of Sages to welcome a dying soul to the Western Paradise, as depicted in Japanese *Shōjuraigō* paintings[32] (except that the Buddhist version lacks the strong hierogam-

of the dead as late as the fifth century. I would suggest that, outside the Mao Shan tradition, both systems coexisted much earlier.

30 *Ch'ih-sung tzu chang-li* 6.13b *et passim*.

31 *Mo tzu*, Book 4.14; transl. (as "liebevolle Gesinnung" or "liebevolle Güte") by Helwig Schmidt-Glintzer, *Mo Ti, Solidarität und allgemeine Menschenliebe*, Diederichs, Düsseldorf 1975, pp. 137sq.

32 Icons depicting the descent of Amida were shown to the dying in order to fix this

ic overtones of the *Legenda Aurea*, Her corpse radiated such a dazzling light that the virgins who washed it could only touch but not see it.

After three (or forty) days, Jesus redescends *cum multitudine angelorum*, the Virgin Mary's soul reunites with the body coming forth in glory from the tomb, and she is received into the Heavenly Palace (*statimque anima ad Mariae accessit corpusculum et de tumulo prodiit gloriosum sicque ad aethereum assumitur thalamum*). When the tomb is later opened, it contains only the robe and the shroud (*tandem sepulchrum aperientes corpus minime invenerunt, sed tantum vestimenta et sindonem repererunt*). The robe became a miracle-working relic and is said to have been used by the Bishop of Chartres as a standard in a battle against the Normans.

To the question why, of all mortals, solely the Virgin Mary was granted *in anima simul et corpore assumptio* or, in Chinese terms, achieved physical *post-mortem* immortality, the *Legenda Aurea* gives several answers: her motherhood of God, her own *conceptio immaculata (ut, sicut per coitum labem non sensisti criminis, sic in sepulchro solutionem corporis minime patiaris)* and, last but not least, the fact that her *virginitas inviolata permansit*.

As our friend Zwi Werblowsky so aptly wrote: "The more a male culture is (consciously or subconsciously) obsessed by its dubiously controlled sexual desires, the more it is also obsessed with ... the need to guard the virginal purity of their womenfolk."[33] In the imagination of thirteenth-century Christian monks, this virginal purity could become even the *conditio sine qua non* for the physical body's everlastingness.

However, Werblowsky also reminds us that, compared with the more rigorously misogynist Buddhists, orthodox Christianity (for whom the *Legenda Aurea* is not a very comfortable text) has dealt less harshly with the mother of their saviour. Queen Maya had to die seven days after giving birth to the Buddha because "the idea of a mother of flesh and blood co-existing with the Buddha" was intolerable to the Buddhists,[34] whereas Mary was allowed even to outlive her son and to per-

---

vision in their minds at the moment of death, cf. Gail Chin Bryant, "A Vision of Salvation: *The Coming of Amida and His Multitude of Sages*, a Painting of Mount Kōya," (ms.).

33 "Women ... And Other ... Beasts or 'Why Can't A Woman Be More Like A Man'", *Numen* XXIX.1 (1982):125.

34 *Ibid.*, p. 131.

sonify those aspects of womanhood Christianity felt safe to valorise: as virgin and mother she was exalted above all humankind by her bodily translation to heaven.

> *Non est derelicta anima tua in inferno, nec corpus tuum vidit corruptionem. Decebat autem Dei sacrarium, fontem indefossum, agrum inaratum, vineam non irrigatam, olivam fructiferam terrae gremio non teneri.*[35]

---

[35] Jacobi a Voragine, *Legenda Aurea*, recensuit Dr. Th. Graesse, Otto Zeller Verlag, Osnabrück 1969 (editio tertia 1890), Cap. CXIX, pp. 504-527; Jacques de Voragine, *La légende dorée*, trad. J.-B. M. Roze, Paris, Garnier-Flammarion 1967, vol. II, pp. 86-92. I owe the discovery of this theme in the *Legenda Aurea* to the indeed "catholic" erudition of my esteemed colleagues Lothar von Falkenhausen and Hubert Durt. Last but not least, I should like to thank the great Han specialist Michael Loewe, who did me the honour of reading this paper, during his brief visit to Kyoto, and offered valuable comments and corrections.

FIRST MAN, FIRST KING

Notes on Semitic-Iranian Syncretism and Iranian Mythological Transformations

Shaul Shaked, Jerusalem

In the original Indo-Iranian period Yima (Indian Yama) was probably a First Man figure. This trait of his personality is not preserved with any clarity either in India or in Iran, but certain hints in late Iranian literature show that he may have been considered as the originator of humanity and of civilization.[1] Several myths connected with his figure suggest that he was the first mortal, for at his time humanity knew no death. His connection with death is also a prominent feature of the Indian figure of Yama.[2] As the first mortal, he is the originator of proper human existence. If it is true that he was in one early layer of tradition the first human, he may have lost that position in Iran with the advent of Zoroastrianism. This could have been the result of a reshuffle of functions, caused, among other things, by the fact that Gaya Maretan assumed the role of the first Man.

Gaya Maretan (later Gayōmard) belongs to the specific Zoroastrian terminology, and is thus part of the novel religious conception introduced in Iran by Zoroastrianism. The main argument in favour of this assumption is the observation that his name has a structure similar to that of several other Zoroastrian innovations: Angra

---

1 Cf. Christensen 1934:35; also the recent and interesting study by Kellens 1984.

2 For details see lately Kellens 1984:279ff.

Manyu "the Evil Spirit", Vohu Manah "the Good Mind", Aša Vahišta "the Best truth", etc.[3] The name Ahura Mazdā "Lord Wisdom" itself falls in the same category. The structure of this divine name serves, I believe, as a powerful argument in favour of the Zoroastrian origin of this deity, although the issue is still disputed.[4]

Yima, representing an older layer of tradition, has had to be accommodated as a secondary figure, one whose function, in part overlapping with that of Gayōmard, is not entirely lucid. It is by no means clear where he fits in within the Zoroastrian history of humanity. He does not form part of the cycle of creation stories, but occurs separately, both in the Avesta and in the later literature, in a series of independent episodes.[5] Only in mediaeval texts is there an attempt

---

3 This is an opinion already expressed by Christensen 1917:41f.; Schaeder 1926:211f.; Lommel 1930:137. Hoffmann 1957 argues that the myth of Gayōmard continues an ancient Indo-Iranian story, attested in India for the figure of Mārtāṇḍa, a suggestion which makes good sense. (He does not make the identification, but Boyce 1975:97 regards Gayōmard as identical with Mārtāṇḍa.) Hoffmann further assumes that the epithet Gaya Maretan, which became the proper name of the First Man figure in Iran, goes also back to Indo-Iranian times, since it corresponds closely to the epithets *amartya-gaya-* "immortal life", attested in the Rigveda (cf. Hoffmann 1957:100). The last point is important, but does not prove the existence of the Avestan epithet in the ancient period or of the person to which it was applied. It only shows that such an epithet was in use. The Avesta contains numerous expressions and themes which continue pre-Zoroastrian usage; for establishing the continuity of a divine figure we want to know that it existed in the Indo-Iranian period, but evidence for this is lacking. Lincoln 1975/6 assumes, on the basis of the Scandinavian parallel, that Gayōmard takes the position initially occupied by Yima. Again, whether this is correct or not, this would not affect our judgement as to whether Gayōmard is a creation of the Zoroastrian religion. If there was an ancient myth of the sacrifice and dismemberment of Yima, memory of it was no longer alive either in India or in Iran by the time of the beginnings of Zoroastrianism.

4 Cf. Kent 1933; Konow 1937; Thieme 1970; Humbach 1957; Boyce 1975:38ff. The issue is not capable at the moment of proof, the arguments in either direction being undecisive. The fact that, like the abstractions which later became the Ameša Spenta, and similar Zoroastrian deities, Ahura Mazdā too was not yet a fixed proper-name in the Gāthās shows, I believe, that at the time of Zoroaster it was still an innovation. In the pre-Zoroastrian period an earlier process had taken place by which abstract notions had become divine proper names (cf. e.g. Mitra=Mithra, Varuna, Aryaman; Thieme 1970:402ff.). The Gathic list constitutes the beginning of a new layer of notions which were to undergo the same procedure. See also lately Lincoln in Colpe 1974:352-354 s.v. "Gayōmart".

5 An example of the embarrassment caused to Zoroastrian commentators by the position of Yima with regard to the couple Mashye and Mashyāne may be seen in

made to combine and harmonize the various stories and bring them into a seemingly continuous narrative. This is seen in the Islamic works, and is particularly typical of the Shāhnāme, where both the harmonization process and the euhemeristic tendency are given full expression.

Yima (Jamshīd, as he is called in the later literature) is one of the most ambiguous figures in Iranian mythology. In a religious civilization where a clear-cut distinction between good and evil is so important, and which is not prone to admit the existence of intermediate shades between light and darkness, Yima, who combines in his person something of the two opposites, stands out as an unusual phenomenon. There are of course also some other subtle ambiguities in the Iranian mythical accounts. Ohrmazd himself emerges as a de facto collaborator with Ahreman in the myth of creation, for without an agreement concluded between them the world would not have come into being, and in this sense the world is in effect the result of the joint effort of both powers. Another case of ambiguity, to be discussed further on, concerns the first human couple, who are also the first sinners according to the account of the Bundahishn; the nature of their sin is also somewhat hazy. But in their case the sin is part of their human character, a result of the intervention of the demonic powers in the world, which has turned the creation of Ohrmazd into the mixture that it presents nowadays. As we shall try to show, Yima's case is different. A third type of ambiguity is caused by the occurrence of different third-party figures in the myth, whether it is Mithra as a judge and mediator, or Vayu, an ancient deity with ambivalent associations in Zoroastrianism.[6] Yima belongs to none of these categories. He is, in Iranian mythology, a semi-divine figure with a flaw.

Yima is not the First Man in Iran, but belongs rather to the type of founders of civilization and archaic heroes. He is specifically the first King;[7] indeed, he is the model virtuous king and an originator of

---

the discussion of *Dk* III 12 (French translation in Menasce 1973:36).

[6] Cf. Shaked 1980:16ff.

[7] Kellens 1984 has argued against taking Yima as a royal figure. He sets out from the tripartite framework of Dumézil, which I believe tends to distort the proper understanding of the texts, because it imposes on them questions which are not always demonstrably part of their own background. While it is true that some of the epithets and appurtenances of Yima have agricultural and especially pastoral associ-

religious obligations. At the same time, he is also a sinner, perhaps the first transgressor.[8] Thus he is said to have established incest marriage (*xwēdōdah*), one of the most important of religious precepts; he invented the idea of *paymān*, the Right Measure, a virtue which is considered by Zoroastrians to be a central trait of their religion;[9] he is credited (in late sources) with the foundation of the Nowrūz, the New Year holiday, which has strong associations with the beginning of human civilization and with eschatology, and which also serves as the prime symbol for the permanence of royalty and of the good order of society; and he is mentioned as the originator of the *kustīg*, the sacred belt which symbolizes one's adherence to the Zoroastrian faith. Besides, as the founder of civilization, he is said to have established the production of weapons and the weaving of textiles, the division of society into classes,[10] the hewing of stones for the construction of buildings, and similar skills and exploits.[11]

---

ations, only a firm faith in a rigid tripartite division of society and in the essential incompatibility of pastoralism with royalty can lead one to reject the numerous references to Yima's royal position as irrelevant. Other distortions which sometimes occur as a result of the way in which Dumézilian conceptions are imposed on the texts will be pointed out in the following. It may be noted that Dumézil himself gave a different interpretation of the enigmatic figure of Yima (1971:282ff.). Cf. also the remarks by Gnoli 1980:150ff.

[8] Something like a concept of original sin occurs in the story of the first human couple, Mashye and Mashyāne, but this is part of a different cycle of stories, and the sense of this fall is different; cf. further on.

[9] On this concept see Shaked (forthcoming).

[10] This point has as its basis the Avestan text Yt. 19:34-38, which was interpreted by the later Zoroastrian literature as referring to the three classes of society. The text itself does not say that. It merely speaks of the *khvarenah*, the divine splendour, which left Yima three times (or less likely: of three splendours that left Yima) as a result of the fact that he found joy in lying words; it states that the splendour was received successively by Mithra, Thraētaona, and Kbresāspa. *Dk.* VII 1:25-37 applies these successive transfers of splendour to the three social classes, although it puts Oshnar in the place of Mithra (cf. Molé 1963:462f.). Darmesteter 1892-93, II:624ff. interpreted the Avestan passage in this light as referring to the social classes, and his idea was endorsed by Molé (ibid.) and Dumézil 1971:284ff., despite the obvious difficulties of this interpretation. Kellens 1984:275, whose approach is also Dumézilian, has had to admit that the passage defies explanation from this point of view. Lincoln 1975/6:132 n. 41 gives a new explanation which seeks to retain the idea of an original tripartite version of the myth, by assuming that one of the names was changed at a later date.

[11] Cf. e.g. Ṭabarī, *History*, I:179; translation in Christensen 1934:85.

At the same time, Yima is also presented as a man who committed some grievous offence against the deity. While his virtues are manifest and clearly described, the cause or circumstances of his collapse are shrouded in some mystery. The mode of his fall is also recounted in several conflicting versions. The nature of Yima's sin is often not described at all. This is the case with the Vendidad account of his reign, where it is said that after a period of great welfare and expansion under Yima's reign, a flood was brought over humanity, and was about to annihilate a large part of it, but the reason for this is not specified. In another Avestan allusion to his person, in the single unequivocal reference to Yima in the Gathas (Y 32:8),[12] where he is mentioned as one of the early sinners, it is hard to tell what his sin consists of. The obscure Gathic verse has been the subject of numerous attempts at interpretation.[13]

When Yima's sin is mentioned in clear terms, different versions give a bewildering number of conflicting accounts of it. It is said in one place that Yima lied (Yt. 19:33). But this is hardly a specific sin, for lie is a general term for sin in Zoroastrianism.[14] The accusation

---

[12] Humbach 1974 has tried to argue that Y 30:3, the famous Gathic verse which mentions the two primeval spirits as twins (yemā), is actually concerned with Yima, but this seems doubtful; see the criticism by Insler 1975:330ff. On the other hand, it does not seem excluded that the two primeval spirits were in some way related to the Indo-Iranian myth of the twins of whom one was attacked and killed by the other; a more direct echo of that myth is found in the late story of Gayōmard, as recounted in the ***Bundahishn***, if the reconstruction proposed by Lincoln 1975/6 is to be accepted.

[13] See lately Insler 1975:204f.; Boyce 1975:93. Apart from establishing the nature of Yima's sin, there is the problem of understanding why he was regarded as tainted by sin. It seems barely sufficient to explain Yima's sin on general grounds by stating: "In a mythology where there is already the figure of a creator, Yima...has some traits of the antagonist, in conformity with a fairly widespread phenomenon" (Gnoli 1980:150). Boyce 1975:93 regards the motif of the sin as a priestly attempt to explain in moral terms why death had to befall Yima.

[14] The verb "to lie" as a general designation for sin is used, for example, in the account of the sins of the first human couple, where every sinful action committed by them is described as a lie, although some of these actions did not necessarily involve saying untruthful things (*GBd*, translation in Christensen 1917:19). That it was used in this sense not only in religious contexts, but also in the political language, may be seen from the great inscription of Darius in Behistun, where every act of disobedience to the king is called a lie. Boyce 1975:93f. assumes that the theme of Yima's sin is secondary in the story. We are here chiefly concerned with Yima's history in Iran, and the question of the origins of the various themes in the story are therefore of lesser importance in this context.

that Yima taught men to eat flesh may be merely the result of a wrong interpretation of the Gathic verse Y. 32:8 (cf. Christensen 1934:49). We have no way of telling whether the praise bestowed on Yima for refusing to make a certain substitute for cattle, as the demons wanted, has anything to do with the sin mentioned in the Gatha.[15] It is often said of Yima that he was seduced by a female demon.[16] The final outcome of this seduction story is good, for he discovers the virtue of consanguinous marriage, when he abandons the female demon and cohabits with his sister.[17] Very often he is said to have become haughty and to have regarded himself as a god.[18]

Sometimes what is wrong with Yima is not a sin deliberately committed by him, but some circumstantial association with demons. The act which entails this contact is done with the best of motives, and yet is harmful, because it carries within it a kind of contagious effect. Thus, when he descends into the realm of Ahreman and extracts from there that valuable commodity, the *paymān*, the Right Measure,[19] he acts in an outrageous manner; besides, the implication that there are certain beneficial qualities which are hidden in the realm of evil and which may be extracted from there for the good of humanity is essentially alien to Zoroastrianism.[20] Another instance for the peculiar involvement of Yima with Ahreman is provided by the episode in which he puts his hand through Ahreman's buttock in order to wring out from Ahreman's entrails his brother Tahmurath;

15 The passages where this episode is alluded to are *PRiv*, p. 102f.;*MX* 26:33. Early translations of the passage in *Mēnōg ī Xrad* have rendered the word **pyl** "an old man" (i.e. *pīr*). Cf. West 1885:60; Christensen 1934:24. Tafazzoli 1354H:125ff., and 1975, has recently argued that the word should be read *pīl* "elephant". In the absence of supporting textual evidence, it is difficult to accept the suggestion that the elephant was substituted to cattle as a sacrificial victim (or as provider of meat?), and one would welcome a different reading of the word.

16 *Dd* 39:16.

17 *PRiv* 14-16; cf. Christensen 1934:28f.

18 *'Ulamā-i Islām*, ed. Mohl, 6; Christensen 1934:63. Also Firdawsi, *Shāhnāma*, translated in Christensen 1934:103.

19 On this episode cf. Shaked (forthcoming).

20 Such a conception is typical of gnostic thinking, and is current in Manicheism, which may have influenced the myth under consideration. It is equally possible that this is a pre-Zoroastrian motif which re-emerges in this late story.

here again he acts unconventionally, and is accordingly punished by having his hand, where it touched Ahreman, covered with leprosy. The final point of that story is aetiological: Yima discovers the purifying effect of bull's urine, the substance considered in Zoroastrianism most beneficial for ritual cleansing, and can impart this knowledge to mankind.[21]

Running through the Yima stories is a theme with an almost tragic ring to it, since Yima's association with the powers of evil is inadvertent or inevitable, but the results are disastrous. This duplicity in his character may well be an early Iranian feature of the cycle of stories connected with his person, as allusions to it are found in the Avestan references to Yima. It was presumably suppressed, or at least toned down, in the classical Zoroastrian accounts, and has mostly survived in the more popular versions of the mythology, those which often preserve for us ancient features we might otherwise have disregarded.

As noted above, the story of the first human couple, Mashye and Mashyāne, who fell into a life of partial sinfulness (representing the actual situation of mankind), also contains within it an element of fall. But there are marked differences between the fall of Yima and that of Mashye and Mashyāne. These latter are not superhuman or quasi divine. On the contrary, they are the very models of humanity as it really is. Their story is that of the human condition: from initial innocence and purity, they fall into the ways of the actual world, where good and evil are mixed. They go through this, because this is how humanity is constituted. Yima the Luminous, in contrast, is a conspicuous solar figure.[22] During his reign, humanity does not know of death. He symbolizes divine power and presence in the world. When he falls, in the Iranian stories, his fall does not represent the devolution of human existence, but a divine failure in the world. It hints at the possibility that dualism may be inherent in the bright luminosity of divinity itself, though this is a possibility that goes against Zoroastrian doctrines, and is vehemently denied and rejected in other contexts.

---

[21] This occurs in a Zoroastrian *Rivāyat* in Persian; translation in Christensen 1917:188.

[22] Cf. Kellens 1984:277.

The extensive survival of Yima's ambiguities in the popular versions of the Iranian mythology seems to suggest an internal Iranian syncretism, a syncretism which operates vertically, between different layers of the religion, and diachronically, by letting ancient themes filter through and imbue the later formulations of the Iranian view of the origins of the world. A different kind of syncretism is seen when we consider the accounts of the Iranian religion in the Islamic books. Yima, according to the ignorant among the Persians, says Ibn al-Muqaffa',[23] is the same as King Solomon, son of David. "The ignorant among the Persians" may have made this identification because they wanted to integrate their mythology to that of their Arab conquerors. It seems however possible to assume that they had already made it earlier, at the time of the Sasanians, in order to harmonize their traditions with those of their Semitic neighbours. The process of syncretistic adaptation of Iranian materials to the surrounding Semitic world may have begun long before the advent of Islam.

If we turn to examine the vicissitudes of the story of Gayōmard, we find a situation which is different in certain respects. There is no pre-Zoroastrian layer here, since Gayōmard appears to be a Zoroastrian creation.[24] But within Zoroastrianism the figure underwent a series of ramifications, in addition to the changes which took place later, in the Islamic sources.

There is a marked contrast between the story of Gayōmard in the official Zoroastrian cannon and the more popular stories preserved by the Islamic authors. The figure of Gayōmard and those of Mashye and Mashyāne are presented in the Zoroastrian books as forming part of the grand scheme of divine origins from which the whole world and humanity came about. The creation of humanity fulfils a definite function within a larger plan. There is a well-defined theology which lies behind the mythological story. The name Gayōmard, interpreted to mean "mortal life", or "life and death", or "life, death and reason",[25] is certainly a direct reference to his human existence; it may

---

[23] Dīnawarī, 9. A similar opinion is reported by Ibn al-Nadīm, 309; Tha'ālibī, 10 (who objects to this opinion and remarks that Yima is separate from Solomon by a period of more than two thousand years). a discussion of these identifications is in Christensen 1934:119.

[24] See above, note 3.

[25] Pahlavi *zīndagīh gōwāgīh mērāg<īh>*, (*DkM* 230:8-9); and the Arabic

be noted that the cognate terms *martya, mašya* in India and ancient Iran also describe Man primarily as "mortal". Gayōmard's features are reminiscent of humanity, but his character and dimensions are super-human. He belongs however also to the vegetable world by virtue of the fact that he grew from the earth like a plant. His position is strictly parallel to that of the Bull, *Gāw ī ēwag-dād*, and in this sense he constitutes the human counterpart to the animal world. The account of Gayōmard is thus clearly that of a composite figure, carefully designed to represent, in a symbolic way, the characteristics of the main forms of existence. The germs of human existence, as symbolized in the person of Gayōmard, contain within them the chief elements of all the other forms of being, both in the material and in the divine world, but Gayōmard does not represent human existence as it was constituted after it was attacked and defiled by the Evil Spirit: he lacks nourishment, particularly the more problematic kind of food, which is meat; and he lacks sexuality (his descendants are born from his sperm, ejected at his death, but without the application of sexual differentiation and contact); and deceit, the archetypal form of sin in Iran, is never connected with his person.

The account of the first human couple, the indirect descendants of Gayōmard, Mashye and Mashyāne, is, by contrast, one of gradual development from the elements characteristic of Gayōmard (initially they have an undifferentiated, vegetable, immutable shape) to those which are identifiably human, containing movement, sexual differentiation, and the basic human cravings and failings. They grow as a single stalk of a rhubarb plant, but are subsequently separated to become a human couple, and eventually they come to discover their biological human needs. They begin to consume milk and flesh, and they discover sexuality. This, in Iran, as in the Jewish and Christian traditions, is regarded as a fall from perfection.

The accounts given in the Muslim sources, for the most part, show no familiarity with the imaginatively mythical aspects of the figure of Gayōmard, but portray him simply as one of the ancestors

---

equivalents: *al-ḥayy al-nāṭiq*, which occurs in several sources (e.g. Shahrastānī, *Milal*, 233). "The ability to speak" is an epithet attributed to Man, presumably by influence of Greek philosophical terminology, where speech (*logos*) is equated with reason. Bailey's erroneous interpretation of this phrase (1943:83f.) is corrected in the introduction to the second edition, p. xxxiv f.

of mankind. He is viewed as either a first man or a first king; in the latter version, in which his functions overlap with Yima's, he marks the beginning of human society, creating its institutions of government and civilization.

The changes which the Iranian themes underwent in Islam were probably caused by a number of different reasons. In some cases it may be assumed that Islamic writers elaborated on the material they received from their Iranian informants. Since many of them were themselves of Iranian origin, they might have actually served as their own informants. Often they may have supplemented their own answers to unformulated speculative questions which were never explicitly formulated in the Iranian material. In other cases they may have put together stories which they had received separately, and combined them into a continuous narrative.

We can occasionally spot textual errors which betray the fact that the Islamic accounts derived from literary sources written in the highly ambiguous Pahlavi script. Two examples may be quoted. The epithet of Gayōmard is recorded in two different manners: in some versions it is said to be Gil-Shāh, "King of Clay", while according to other authorities it is quoted as Gar-Shāh, "King of the Mountain". The confusion cannot be explained by oral transmission; it can only arise when one reads the epithet in the Pahlavi script, where -l- and -r- are expressed by the same letter, and where the vowels are not marked.[26] The second example is derived from the Islamic accounts of the creation of Gayōmard. This is sometimes said to be associated with perspiration coming on the forehead of Ohrmazd,[27] but one cannot help feeling that this is not an original detail of the story, but is the result of a textual error. When the pain of death was brought upon Gayōmard by Ahreman, it is said that Ohrmazd caused sleep to come to Gayōmard in order to alleviate the pain which he was suffering. In the Pahlavi script "sleep", *xwāb*, and "perspiration", *xwey*, can have an identical appearance; it seems likely, as Schaeder has shown,[28] that the perspiration of Ohrmazd owes its

[26] Various confusions have taken place with regard to *gil* in Pahlavi. Cf. Christensen 1917:27; Nöldeke 1879:xxv, and, in a different context, Bailey 1944:29f. Further notes relevant to this point are in Shaked 1971:92 n. 6.

[27] Bīrūnī, *Āthār*, 99:7.

[28] Schaeder 1926:217 n.1 and 351f.

existence to this confusion. Once "sleep" was misread as "perspiration", it was moved to the stage of creation, where it seemingly made better sense.

Such confusions appear however to be of minor importance. They do not account for the major differences that exist betweeen the story of Gayōmard as transmitted by the Muslim authors, and that of the Pahlavi tradition. What emerges is that we have basically two kinds of reports in the Muslim sources: one, based essentially on the known Iranian literary traditions (e.g. Shahrastānī, Bīrūnī), results in the two conflicting views of the origins of humanity — the Iranian view and the Muslim (i.e. Judaeo-Christian) one — being presented side by side; and another one, the result of a harmonization, tries to reconcile the Iranian view to that of Judaism and Islam by interspersing the figures of Iranian mythology within the genealogy of the early forefathers of mankind according to the Biblical account.

Whatever the origins of the representation of Gayōmard, the fully developed Zoroastrian story, as it is given in such late Zoroastrian sources as the *Bundahishn* and the *Selections of Zādspram*, forms part of the well-conceived organic whole which constitutes the scheme of Zoroastrian cosmogony. According to this theological mythology, the world is planned by Ohrmazd as a trap, following the agreement made by him with Ahreman: it is an agreement in which both deities stand to lose, but which Ohrmazd is clever enough to turn to his ultimate advantage. The initial power of Ahreman is equivalent to Ohrmazd's, and there is no way of overcoming him, since in *mēnōg* both spirits are eternal and invincible. The pact which set a temporal and spatial Limit on the battle between the two deities may have seemed fair to Ahreman, but it contained the promise of his final destruction, because he would have to fight on alien territory, and within a time limit which was not his own. The result is that his fate is determined from the start. In another episode of the story he is said to be extremely dejected, to lie prostrate and incapacitated for a long period of time, until he is comforted and cheered up by the promise made to him by Jeh, the Primal Whore, that she would arouse sexual desire in Man — a promise that stamps sexuality with a taint of impurity. This conclusion is not invalidated by the observation that the story is directed at giving an aetiology to the demonic origin of menstruation.[29]

[29] The statement that Ahreman suffered a total loss of consciousness following the discovery of his ultimate defeat by the hand of Ohrmazd occurs also in the main

The creation of Man in this narrative is part of the grand scheme of Ohrmazd, devised for the purpose of fighting and overcoming Ahreman. The figures of Gayōmard, of Zoroaster, and of the Final Redeemer, the Saošyant, merge into each other as we are given to understand that they are basically three different representations, or stages, of the same function in universal history, the function of vanquishing the devil. The generic term which hides behind all three is that of the Righteous Man (*mard ī ahlaw*), the potent symbol of that power which is capable of defeating evil in the world. This is associated with the idea that evil has no place of its own, indeed it has no reality of its own in the world, and so it survives in this world by clinging to mankind. Once it is cast away from humanity, it has been virtually banished from the whole world. None of this implied theology is present in the Islamic versions, where the tale of Gayōmard is given merely as a curious story.

In a monograph on Gayōmard, Sven Hartman (1953) argues that there is a distinction in the Avesta between two figures: Gaya and Gaya Maretan. In the later literature those two persons fell together, according to Hartman, in the single figure of Gayōmard. The evidence for this hypothesis is not entirely convincing. The term *gaya*, which means "life", is used in the Avesta sometimes on its own, as an abstract notion, but it also occurs in a number of passages as a shorthand designation for the full epithet "Gaya Maretan". The name Gaya, in this usage, appears as the counterpart of Gav "the Bull". The pair Gaya and the Bull are exactly equivalent to the pair Gaya Maretan and the Bull (Y. 13:7), just as in the late formulation of the cosmogonic story, Gayōmard and the Bull constitute a constant pair.[30] In the Avesta, Gaya occurs as one of the "elements" of the world, indeed as the final item in a list which contains the sky, water, earth, plants, the Bull and "Gaya" (Yt. 13:86). Its place in this list indicates quite clearly that we are dealing with the figure of the Primordial Man, whose full name elsewhere is Gaya Maretan.

version of the story, where Jeh does not figure. See *GBd*, p. 7 and *Zs* 1:24 (translation in Zaehner 1955:314, 342, respectively).

30 In the late version, which exists in several forms, both in Pahlavi and in a number of Islamic sources, Gayōmard, "Mortal Life", and the Bull (Gāw) are parallel creations of Ohrmazd and also parallel victims of the assault of Ahreman on the world.

The obvious conclusion is that the two terms are interchangeable. The assumption that there could be two such separate figures in the Avesta, each one associated with the Bull as its pair, both called by practically the same name and yet belonging to two different traditions, seems tenuous.[31]

The attempt to distinguish in the Avesta between two concepts, Gaya and Gaya Maretan, is unfortunately associated with a hunt for texts which supposedly contain Zurvanite elements. One is invited to accept the hypothesis that the Avesta as we have it is a composite of two sets of religious texts, Zurvanite and non-Zurvanite, and that even supposedly non-Zurvanite passages may contain traces of tampering by Zurvanite editors. Such a conception, evidently inspired by the hypotheses and methods used in Biblical criticism (where this approach seems also to have lost some of its glamour), has not yet proved to be useful for the study of the Avesta. No one would deny that the composition and redaction of the Avestan corpus stretched over an extensive period of time. As a result, the Avesta certainly contains several distinct chronological layers, which reflect, it may be assumed, different stages in the history of the religion. It is however far from proven that it also embodies the conflicting views of diverse theological schools.

In the course of his arguments, Hartman (1975; 1983) refers also to the fact that the name of the supreme deity of Zoroastrianism does not occur in the Gāthā in the same shape as we know it from the Younger Avesta.[32] This does not mean to say that it does not occur at all: it only means that its usage is somewhat different from that of the later period. It often consists of only one of the two elements of the name; when both are present their order is often reversed, they may be separated from each other by the interposition of other words, or they may occur in two different hemistichs separated by a

[31] Hartman's strongest argument is the observation that both Gaya and Gaya Maretan occur in the same Avestan text (Yt. 13:86-87, cf. Hartman 1953:13). This fact is however as damaging for Hartman's theory of a conflict of schools as it is for any other view of the matter; for it is difficult to explain how and why both designations are present in one text, when the assumption is that each designation belonged to a different school.

[32] This had already been noticed by Bartholomae 1904, col. 292, and Kent 1933. See also Kuiper 1976 and Kellens 1984a.

caesura. This shows, to my mind, nothing more than that it took some time for such a Zoroastrian innovation as Ahura Mazdā to become established as a proper name in the full sense of the term. Zoroaster himself apparently treated it as an epithet rather than as a proper name, and its usage in the Gāthā still displays a great deal of fluidity. The same situation may apply also to the Avestan Gaya Maretan.[33]

As developed in late Zoroastrianism, probably in the Sasanian period, the two sets of First Man figures, Yima (Jamshīd) with his associates (e.g. Thraētaona=Farīdun) on the one hand, and Gaya Maretan (Gayōmard) with the Bull and the first human couple Mashye and Mashyāne on the other, found themselves complementing each other, despite the obvious inconsistencies and duplications in their functions and symbolism caused by their divergent origins. Thus, for example, both Yima and Gayōmard are distinctive solar figures; both are associated with the major Zoroastrian festivals; both mark the beginnings of humanity; and both are said to have been the first to receive the divine message of Ohrmazd.[34] At the same time, each one of the two sets belongs to a different symbolic field. Gayōmard and his set symbolize humanity as a passive instrument in the cosmic battle. They are marked by initial innocence, by subsequent transgression (for the first human couple), and by ultimate death and suffering (for Gayōmard), without any connection between the two last points. Jamshīd represents a semi-divine presence in the world, indicated both by a superhuman splendour and abundance and by a gigantic fall. His style of action, even during his period of decline, is active and heroic. From another point of view, however, the two sets of myths developed in parallel fashion in two different Sasanian milieus. In the official, priestly, Zoroastrian religion, the roles were very much as formulated here, while in popular, non-theological circles, there developed, through a combination of euhemerism and harmonization, the tendency to describe both sets of

[33] Indeed, not only Gaya but *maretan* too may have served in the Avesta as a shorthand designation for the whole name, if one adopts the suggestion made by E. Lehmann and endorsed by Schaeder 1926:213 for the interpretation of the Gathic verse Y 30:6.

[34] This is most clearly visible in the account of Shahrastānī, *Milal*, 240, 242, which is definitely derived from a written Zoroastrian source.

figures as those of early kings and heroes, and to seek to establish for them an appropriate place in the biblical genealogies.

That there used to be considerable diversity in the mythological data transmitted in Iran is a manifest fact. Some diversity of this kind is visible even in the extant Zoroastrian sources, although they seem to represent on the whole a single school of priestly teaching, the one that prevailed and that has survived in late orthodox Zoroastrianism. Extraneous sources, however, were not bound by the same restrictions, and they often give us more than one account of various Iranian mythical events. It is from them that we can most often reconstruct some of the popular, uncanonical views of Zoroastrian mythology which we possess. On the basis of these deviant versions we may try to understand the other reality of Zoroastrianism, that of the popular religion. Although it was probably believed in and practised quite widely, very little of it survived, because it was not included in the teachings of the priests who were ultimately responsible for the transmission of the religion. If the religion transmitted to us in the literary canon of scripture and in the mediaeval Zoroastrian tradition is mainstream Zoroastrianism, it was certainly not the only form of religion, perhaps not even the most widespread one, in the Sasanian period.

Popular Zoroastrianism was apparently more open to syncretistic relationship with the neighbouring religious cultures than was the official religion of Iran. The tendency to harmonize Iranian traditions with those of the Semitic world belongs, one may assume, to this layer of religion. Under the general term harmonization, it may be useful to distinguish two types, one consisting of a genuine fusion of conflicting traditions, and the other representing a process of translation. The first one is caused by the wish to smooth over the conflict caused by divergent traditions. This may be motivated by different aims. It may, for example, reflect a desire to endow one of two cultures with the respectability of the more prestigious one; or it may represent the aim of creating a unified history, free from the internal contaradictions caused by the different sources of transmission. As a result, one tries to combine the exclusive claims of the different versions about the origins of humanity into a unified, albeit artificial, tradition.

The other type of harmonization is not so much concerned with a fusion of two traditions, as with an act of translation. In the Islamic context it involves, for example, equating Gayōmard with Adam, which signifies that in the Iranian story Gayōmard fulfils a function similar to that of Adam. Taxmuraf is equated with Noah (Mas'ūdī; v. Christensen 1918:194). This conveys the sense that Taxmuraf is one of the ancestors of mankind, although not the ultimate beginning of humanity; it further denotes that he is responsible for the foundation of much of human civilization. This is basically the method already employed by Mani, when he caused the figures of his elaborate mythology to be translated into terms available in each one of the cultures in which his religion was propagated.[35] This is not syncretism in the proper sense of the term. It does not necessarily represent a desire to combine two cultures and does not directly affect a change of contents. Starting off from an awareness of the affinity of concepts in different cultures (and probably from the former existence of syncretism), it treats the religious language as a collection of mere labels which point at certain realities, but are not to be confused with those realities themselves. It conveys the implicit message that sheer names may be disregarded, and that one should concentrate on the meanings behind the names. The technique of translating the names of one mythology into those of another was widely practised in the Greek and hellenistic periods, but Mani may have been one of the first to use it in the creation of a whole religious system. In contrast, most prophets and founders of religions before and after Mani, especially in Judaism, Christianity and Islam, regarded the name as essential to the deity. Even when one deals with a mere translation of divine names, however, the activity probably entails also some far-reaching change. In other words, it may be assumed that some genuine syncretism takes place even though what is affected is seemingly only a set of names.

Through the data given by the Islamic authors we may form an idea of the activity of what may be labelled "les mages sémitisés".[36] Both forms of cultural contact, that of assimilation

---

35 For a penetrating discussion of this point cf. Schaeder 1926:281ff.

36 The term is used by Bidez and Cumont 1938 I:68. In the context in which they apply it, however, the grounds for attributing this particular piece of tradition to Semitized Magians seem to me erroneous. They refer to a text of Theodore of Mopsuestia as quoted by Photius, *Bibliotheca*, where the name of Zoroaster is given in the form Zarades. From this form they conclude, on the basis of the -d- which replaces the original -t- of the name, that the origin of the information received by

through harmonization, and that of name-translation, were evidently pursued in what looks like the popular forms of the Iranian religion. In fact, the two processes cannot be easily distinguished. While adopting Semitic labels which they deemed to be interchangeable with the labels carried by the Iranian mythological heroes, the character of the Iranian figures may have changed. This process seems to have had its beginnings in the Sasanian period, and it may well have paved the way to the overwhelming encounter Iran was to have with Semitic culture following the Islamic conquest.

References

[Pahlavi texts are quoted as in the abbreviations to my *Wisdom of the Sasanian Sages*, Boulder, Col. 1979.]

Bailey, H.W. 1943. *Zoroastrian problems in the ninth-century books*, Oxford. (Reprint with new introduction, 1971).

Bartholomae, Christian. 1904. *Altiranisches Wörterbuch*, Strassburg. (Reprint, Berlin 1961).

Bidez, Joseph and Franz Cumont. 1938. *Les Mages hellénisés. Zoroastre, Ostanès et Hystaspe d'après la tradition grecque*, I-II. Paris (Reprint: Paris 1973).

Bīrūnī, Abū al-Rayḥān Muḥammad b. Aḥmad, *Al-āthār al-bāqiya 'an al-qurūn al-khāliya*, ed. E. Sachau, Leipzig 1923.

Boyce, Mary. 1975. *A history of Zoroastrianism*, I (Handbuch der Orientalistik, I, 8, 1, 2), Leiden-Köln.

Christensen, Arthur. 1917. *Les types du premier homme et du premier roi dans l'histoire légendaire des Iraniens*, I (Archives d'Études Orientales, 14), Stockholm.

—. 1934. Idem, II, Leiden.

Colpe, Carsten (ed.). 1974/82. "Altiranische und zoroastrische Mythologie", in H.W. Haussig (ed.), *Wörterbuch der Mythologie*, II, Stuttgart.

Darmesteter, James. 1892-93. *Le Zend-Avesta*, I-III (Annales du Musele Guimet, t. 21, 22, 24), Paris (Reprint: Paris 1960).

Dīnawarī, Abū Ḥanīfa Aḥmad b. Dāwūd, *Al-akhbār al-ṭiwāl*, ed.V. Guirgass, Leiden

Theodore was Semitic, since this change, according to them, took place in Syriac (Bidez and Cumont 1938 I:37). This is a mistake. The phonetic change -t->-d- in postvocalic and postsonantic position is a feature of Middle Persian and Parthian, not of Aramaic or Syriac. It is true that the form Zarathushtra should have resulted in Middle Persian not in -d- but in -h-; and such a form is actually attested in Manichaean Middle Persian. But a form derived from a putative *Zaratushtra is also attested: it is the form underlying the spelling in Pahlavi **zltwxšt**, as well as that of New Persian, Zardušt.

1888.

Dumézil, Georges. 1971. *Mythe et épopée, II. Types épiques indo-européens: un héros, un sorcier, un roi*, Paris.

Gnoli, Gherardo. 1980. *Zoroaster's time and homeland. A study on the origins of Mazdeism and related problems*, (Istituto Universitario Orientale, Seminario di Studi Asiatici, Series Minor, VII) Naples.

Hartman, Sven S. 1953. *Gayōmart. Etudes sur le syncretismedans l'ancien Iran*, Uppsala.

—. 1969. "Les identifications de Gayōmart à l'époque islamique", in S. Hartman (ed.), *Syncretism*, Stockholm, 263-294.

—. 1975. "Der Name Ahura Mazdāh", in: A. Dietrich (ed.), *Synkretismus im syrisch-persischen Kulturgebiet*, Göttingen, 170-177.

—. 1983. "Datierung der jungavestischen Apokalyptik", in: D. Hellholm(ed.), *Apocalypticism in the Mediterranean World and the Near East. Proceedings of the International Colloquium on Apocalypticism*, Tübingen, 61-75.

Hoffmann, Karl. 1957. "Mārtāṇḍa und Gayōmart", *Münchener Studienzur Sprachwissenschaft* 11:85-103. (Reprinted in: K. Hoffmann, *Aufsätze zur Indoiranistik*, II, Wiesbaden 1976, 422-438.)

Humbach, Helmut. 1957. "Ahura Mazdā und die Daēvas", *Wiener Zeitschrift für die Kunde Süd- und Ostasiens* 1:81-94.

—. 1974. "Methodologische Variationen zur arischen Religionsgeschichte", in: *Antiquititates Indogermanicae. Gedenkschrift für Hermann Güntert*, Innsbruck, 193-200.

Ibn al-Nadīm, *Kitāb al-fihrist*, ed. Gustav Flügel, Leipzig 1871/2 (Reprint: Beirut 1964).

Insler, S. 1975. *The Gathas of Zarathustra*, Leiden-Tehran-Liège. (Acta Iranica 8).

Kellens, Jean. 1984. "Yima, magicien entre les dieux et les hommes", *Acta Iranica* 23 (Orientalia J. Duchesne-Guillemin emerito oblata), Leiden, 267-281.

—. 1984a. "Mazdā Ahura ou Ahura Mazdā?," *MSS* 43:133-136.

Kent, R.G. 1933. "The name Ahuramazdā", in: *Oriental studies in honour of C.E. Pavry*, London, 200-208.

Konow, Sten. 1937. "Medhā and Mazdā", *Jhā Commemoration Volume*, Poona, 217-222.

Kuiper, F.B.J. 1976. "Ahura Mazdā 'Lord Wisdom' ?," *IIJ* 18:25-42.

Lincoln, Bruce. 1975/6. "The Indo-European myth of creation", *History of Religions* 15:121-145.

Lommel, Herman. 1930. *Die Religion Zarathustras nach dem Awesta dargestellt*, Tübingen [Reprint, Hildesheim-New York, 1970].

de Menasce, J. 1973. *Le troisième livre du Dēnkart*, Paris (Travaux de l'Institut d'Etudes Iraniennes, 5; Bibliothèque des oeuvres classiques persanes, 4).

Molé, Marijan. 1963. *Culte, mythe et cosmologie dans l'Iran ancien*, Paris (Annales du Musée Guimet, Bibl. d'études, t. 69).

Nöldeke, Theodor. *Geschichte der Perser und Araber zur Zeit der Sasniden*. Aus der arabischen Chronik der Tabari übersetzt..., Leyden.

Schaeder, H.H. 1926. "Iranische Lehren", in: R. Reitzenstein and H.H.Schaeder, *Studien zum antiken Synkretismus aus Iran und Griechenland*, Leipzig and

Berlin, 199-355.

Shahrastānī, Abū l-Fatḥ Muḥammad b. 'Abd al-Karīm, *Al-milal wa-l-niḥal*, ed. Muḥammad Sayyid Kīlānī, Cairo 1967.

Shaked, Shaul. 1971. "The notions *mēnōg* and *gētīg* in the Pahlavi texts and their relation to eschatology", *Acta Orientalia* 33, 59-107.

—. 1980. "Mihr the Judge", *Jerusalem Studies in Arabic and Islam* 2, 1-31.

—. (Forthcoming). "Paymān", *Studia Iranica*.

Tafazzoli, Ahmad (tr.). 1352H. *Mīnū-ye xerad*. (Enteshārāt-e Bonyād-e Farhang-e Irān, 201.) Tehran.

—. 1975. "Elephant: a demonic creature and a symbol of sovereignty", *Acta Iranica* (Monumentum H.S. Nyberg, II), Leiden-Tehran-Liège, 395-398.

Tha'ālibī, Abū Manṣūr 'Abd al-Malik b. Muḥammad. *Ghurar akhbār mulūk al-furs wa-siyarihim. Histoire des rois des Perses*. Ed. H.Zotenberg. Paris 1900 (Reprint: Tehran 1963).

Thieme, Paul. 1970. "Die vedischen Āditya und die zarathustrischen Amešа Spenta", in: B. Schlerath (ed.), *Zarathustra*, Darmstadt (Wege der Forschung, Bd. 169), 397-412.

Zaehner, R.C. 1955. *Zurvan. A Zoroastrian dilemma*, Oxford.

THE SECULARIZATION OF THE HISTORY OF RELIGIONS

Eric J. Sharpe, Sydney

A couple of years ago, the Canadian scholar Donald Wiebe published an essay, provocatively entitled "The Failure of Nerve in the Academic Study of Religion,"[1] in which he began by stating that:

> the academic study of religion on the methodological level jeopardizes the very existence of such an academic study for it opens to debate once again who and what it is that ought to set the agenda for, and therefore to control, such a study; is it the scholar-scientist or the scholar-devotee, the church or the academy, the procedures of science or the (supposed) transcendent subject-matter of that science...?[2]

Turning back the clock to the years around 1959-1960, which I still see as marking the initial skirmishes in that major (though often confused) passage of arms we call the modern methodological debate, in 1959 Zwi Werblowsky was asking very similar questions. In his celebrated review of Joachim Wach's *The Comparative Study of Religions* (ed. Kitagawa, 1958),[3] Werblowsky had accused Wach of, in effect, confusing theology with *Religionswissenschaft*, perhaps not to the detriment of theology, but certainly to the detriment of *Religionswissenschaft* (the history of religions, the science of religion, the comparative study of religion, or whatever).[4] In 1960

---

1 *Studies in Relgion/Sciences Religieuses* 13/4 (1984), pp. 401-422.

2 *Ibid.*, p. 401.

3 *Judaism* 8/4 (1959).

4 Cf. Sharpe, *Comparative Religion: a History* (1975), p. 275 f.

precisely the same issue was raised at the tenth international congress of the International Association for the History of Religions, meeting in Marburg; aside from the debate itself, one consequence was the putting forward, on Werblowsky's initiative, of the closest thing to a *confessio fidei* the IAHR has ever professed, which stressed, among other things, that personal ideals on the individual scholar's part must "... under no circumstances be allowed to influence or colour the character of the IAHR."[5] It was this statement which Wiebe, almost a quarter of a century later, was to take as his point of departure for a discussion of what he termed a "retreat to theology" — by direct implication, a movement *away from* the secular ideals for which Werblowsky and others were fighting in 1960. Wiebe has in this and other contexts sought to show that in the present-day study of religion in the West, "... the hidden theological agenda present in religious studies has now, so to speak, come out of the closet"[6] — and that this cannot be other than to the detriment of the academic study of religion as such. In this, Werblowsky and Wiebe are in general terms of the mind. Nor do I wish to argue that either is wrong. I do, on the other hand, suspect that the question of what I have here chosen to call "the secularization of the history of religions" — within which is also contained the possibility of its desecularization or resacralization — is in need of further discussion, since it is by no means a straightforward matter. In particular, I see the relationship between the history of religions on the one hand, and (largely Protestant Christian) theology on the other as having been a complex one from the very beginning. In this paper I shall examine briefly some of its complexities and ambiguities and offer my own tentative analysis.

Terminology, I might say before proceeding further, has been a bugbear to the non-confessional study of religion from the very beginning. What is it to be called? I was brought up on the term "comparative religion" (shorthand for "the comparative study of religion"), and still in many ways prefer it to the common alternatives *Religionswissenschaft*, "the history of religions" and "religious studies."[7] However, in this context I shall stick as far as

[5] *Ibid.*, p. 278.

[6] Wiebe, *op. cit.*, p. 411.

[7] Cf. Sharpe, *Understanding Religion* (1983), p. vii f.

possible to "the history of religions" on the grounds that without the element of sound and sober history, the whole enterprise dissolves into insubstantiality. The "whole enterprise" has however never excluded — at least not deliberately or as a matter of principle — the critical study of the Judaeo-Christian traditions to which the vast majority of its representatives have belonged. That "comparative religion" in particular has generally been taken outside the Academy to mean the study of "comparative (i.e., non-absolute, non-normative) religions" is strictly irrelevant. Images, however, may be hard to live down, and both "the history of religions" and "religious studies" have come to be interpreted in the same way, not least by the theological community at large. When for instance the Catholic theologian Bernard Lonergan wrote that "Theology and religious studies need each other..."[8] he was at the very least acknowledging that the two have not generally walked hand in hand, still less that they are Siamese twins. Low-level criticism has to concur. As the two have moved across the academic stage over the past century or so, they have been separated, not so much by subject matter (for each has trespassed freely on the other's preserves), but by a fundamental difference of attitude to the material under consideration.

There is, I fear, no fully satisfactory way of expressing the difference I have in mind, though in general it is the age-old difference between Science and Faith, domination and submission, control and obedience. The way of religion (though not necessarily the way of theology in all its modern forms) is the way of faith, submission and obedience to transcendental authority; the way of the Academy is the way of science, knowledge, domination and control — and of course the way of reason. When from the point of view of the Academy we speak of the need to observe, understand, interpret, explain, translate and edit as essential to the history of religions enterprise, we are presupposing that we (whoever "we" may be) occupy a rather special point of vantage from which we are able to carry out these functions, a position that we have attained through our own academic training and abilities, rather than through the deliverances of divine revelation or supernormally-induced insight. Revelation and insight we treat with the utmost caution, not because they may not be real,

8 *Studies in Religion/Sciences Religieuses* 6/4 (1976-7), p. 354f.

but because they form no part of the Academy's working methods.

But what is true of religion is not necessarily true of theology. Doubtless a fair proportion of those who would classify themselves as theologians, and still more of those who merely happen to be employed by theological seminaries and colleges, divinity schools and faculties of theology, will rise up in wrath and deny categorically that their scholarly work is conditioned in any such way. Some may well point out that they have had trouble with the governing bodies of their seminaries precisely on account of their reluctance to conform to confessional norms. Others again will claim that, in their sphere, they work under precisely the same academic conditions and restraints as do historians of religions in theirs — textually, historically and as objectively as is humanly possible. And it would be most ungenerous of me not to allow that this is indeed the case. Acknowledging all this, it would seem that the controversy does not really lie between scholars working in secular universities and those employed by religious agencies. At least it does not lie there in principle. Nor is it necessarily a matter of method as such: relatively few scholars on either side of the divide cultivate methods to any very high level of consistency — for real methodological determination we must look to ideological conservatives in theology and the social sciences, rather than to historians of religions as a class or to theologically trained experts in religious studies.

However, it can hardly be denied that the way of religion does involve certain assumptions about the nature of the world, the place of men and women in the world, and the processes of human history; or that it presupposes that those assumptions (faith, beliefs) will lead to the taking up of a certain life-style. To this end it protects itself, its affirmations and denials, by fences of doctrine and less obvious, but none the less real, barriers of custom and convention.

I scarcely need to add that the emergence of comparative religion in the nineteenth century was made possible in part by the lowering (if not the complete removal) of those control mechanisms, especially in the new phenomenon of the secular university. Here the one overriding factor was that, in the new milieu, no community of faith was in a position to be able to insist that the study of religion should follow a pattern determined in advance by the contents of confessional writings, or that it should lead to a predetermined result. All this is tolerably well known.[9]

What is less frequently remembered is that religion itself (and hence also academic theology) was at precisely the same time passing through a period of profound reappraisal, with the emergence in Europe and America of various forms of liberal religion (Jewish and Catholic, as well as the better-known Protestant liberalism).[10] As in education, so in the churches and synagogues, there was a passionate demand for the discarding of outworn authorities, for the scrapping of confessions that had outlived their usefulness, for democratization and for the creating of new forms of religion in which the human reason would have the full play that restrictive educational practices hitherto had denied it. Viewed from a Christian perspective (which was where most of those involved stood) this meant, among other things, that history itself took on a new aspect. In a word, the history of Religion gave way to the history of religions as an aspect of *Weltgeschichte*. The tracing of the single Judaeo-Christian thread in the world's religious tapestry was complemented, a little at a time, by the attempt to describe and plot the design of the tapestry as a whole.

It is extremely easy in the late 1980s to overlook the fact that practically the whole of the comparative religion establishment in the half-century between about 1889 and 1939 was made up of scholars very much involved in the practice as well as the study of religion. It is slightly startling to reflect that, for instance, all five pre-1937 incumbents of the Uppsala chair of comparative religion (though it did not have this name), von Schéele, Ekman, Söderblom, Reuterskiöld and Andrae, became bishops in the Lutheran Church of Sweden. Elsewhere in Europe during the same period Tiele, Chantepie de la Saussaye, Kristensen, Lehmann, Heiler, Otto and van der Leeuw; in Britain Moulton, Peake, James and Bouquet; in Australia Elkin — all professed one or other form of comparative religion from a position well inside the liberal wing of Christianity. Not, it must be emphasized, in spite of their theology, but as an important and indeed integral part of it.

---

[10] I am not here using the term "liberal Protestantism," which convention decrees to be a label for a much more limited phenomenon. In intellectual terms, the chief distinguishing feature of all such forms was that they claimed to work on the inductive principle, though how far they actually did so is open to question.

Two observations may be added. First, that the names quoted include a number of those commonly counted among the founding fathers of the phenomenology of religion. I do not propose to go into this in more detail, except to emphasize that the phenomenology of religion in its original form (whatever may have happened to it since the 1940s) was *both* a scientific *and* a theological enterprise, and cannot be understood unless both aspects are taken into consideration. And secondly, that at various times, in books, articles and notably inaugural lectures, most of them tackled the intractable question — still unresolved today — of the relationship between comparative religion and theology.[11] All came to more or less the same conclusion, that *confessional* theology and comparative religion are incompatible, but that, in Nathan Söderblom's words,

> Every scientific study of religion, provided that it is carried out with competence and directed toward a worthy object, must — with or against the will of the scholar, consciously or unconsciously — serve the cause of religion.[12]

True, these words date from as far back as 1901; nonetheless I believe them to represent a liberal consensus on the subject: or rather an idealist consensus that the human quest is a quest for wholeness, and that the more one learns of the fragments of human experience, the more they will prove to fit together into a comprehensible picture as part of the *ratio aeterna.*

Now the significant thing is not that liberal theology in these years was prepared to admit (with however many reservations) comparative religion into the *sanctum sanctorum* as confessional theology was not; it is rather that comparative religion made its entry at a time when theological liberalism was in the process of finding its identity. It is my impression therefore, that in the interplay between the two, comparative religion may well have been the dominant partner, exercising far greater influence on liberal theology than the reverse. Certainly, there was a secularizing process at work within the communities of faith, and the fires of controversy burned high.

---

[11] Chantepie de la Saussaye at the Stockholm "Science of Religion" Congress of 1897; Söderblom and Kristensen both in 1901; van der Leeuw in 1918. Later such inaugural lectures included those of Hendrik Kraemer in 1959, Ninian Smart in 1968 and my own in 1977. Doubtless there were many others.

[12] Reprinted in Söderblom, *Om studiet av religionen* (1951), p. 24.

But liberal religion, whatever its faults, had a high level of intellectual integrity, and was open to persuasion as confessional religion was not. To the disgust of conservatism, it modelled a new theology on the inductive principle, taking its cue from comparative religion (among other things) in so doing. It set up universals in place of specifics, "essences" over culture-bound manifestations, experience in direct opposition to conformity, cultivated to the best of its ability an interest in psychology, valued mystics more highly than functionaries — and in some cases dissolved into a wash of useless generalizations.

"Secularization" of course means different things to different people.[13] As I have been trying to show, the formative years of comparative religion in the West marked a secularization of the study of religion in the sense of the liberation of that study from institutional religious *control*. That most of those involved were in no way disposed to abandon their individual religious *concern* was another matter entirely — added to which most held as a part of that concern a deeply-felt desire to establish a principle of free religious inquiry on "scientific" principles within the churches to which they belonged. Such matters as these cannot be legislated out of existence. Religious tests having been happily abandoned, there can be no question of their reintroduction — in either direction — as a condition of employment. The formula "of any faith or none" must be protected. But because personal religious concern continued to be voiced whenever the occasion demanded, or when a professor or lecturer in comparative religion became a bishop (most recently, I believe, in the case of the present Bishop of Ripon), or when a scholar in the field ventured into the dangerous area of apologetics, some were unable to disguise their disquiet. For aside from the "theological" comparative religionists, there were the classicists, the historians, the anthropologists, the ethnologists and the rest, often living lives altogether free from the kind of personal and institutional concern from which the theologian could hardly escape. In their view the secularization process had not proceeded far enough. Religious concern is all very well, provided that it remains private and is not allowed to intrude into public — or in this case educational and

---

[13] Cf. Sharpe, *Understanding Religion*, pp. 108-124.

scholarly — life. Secularization necessarily leads to the privatization of religion, and hence to its neutralization.

There were a number of factors motivating the secularist-empiricist stance in the history of religions against the "speculative" tendencies of theologians and philosophers — for by the 1950s and early 1960s an ill-defined "philosophy" had joined theology as a focal point of empiricist opposition, typically in the work of the late C.J. Bleeker.[14] To a certain extent what was operative here was a generation shift, away from comprehensive idealism and toward the quest for analytical precision. Local *Realpolitik* was sometimes a factor, as in those cases in which small university departments of the history of religions were forced to defend themselves against the attacks of colleagues who insisted (often for very bad reasons) that the modern secular university is no place for the teaching of religion in any shape or form - to which the historian of religions had little choice but to retort that he/she was teaching not religion, but history, not (non-rational) religion or theology, but (rational) historical science. In more recent years pressure has been felt from the direction of the social sciences, the representatives of which have come to devote a fair amount of attention to the study of the forms and functions of religion, without needing to concern themselves with anything whatever of a "transcendental" nature (with which they cheerfully admit that their methods are unable to deal). Yet another factor has been the much smaller, but not unimportant, impact of analytical philosophy and its long-running feud with "metaphysics." Although more characteristic of the 1960s than of the 1980s — the lines today are by no means as clearly drawn as they were twenty years ago — the distance has never been long between anti-idealist, anti-metaphysical, anti-theological and anti-religious. Donald Wiebe's critique of theology stems to a certain extent from this source.

Realpolitik, the social sciences and analytical philosophy aside, some historians of religions have also expressed a certain fear of the diminution of standards in their field due to the intrusion into the area of those who have *not* been properly trained in philological,

---

14 Bleeker always insisted, *contra* van der Leeuw, that the phenomenology of religion was "an empirical science without philosophical aspirations" (*The Sacred Bridge*, 1963, p. 7).

archaeological and historical methods and techniques. This however has no obvious connection with the secularization process *per se*, though it might perhaps be argued that it is not unconnected with the dominance of populist theories of education in the post-war years. It is a real enough danger where it exists, but here is no obvious correlation between religious or theological concern on the one hand and slipshod scholarship on the other. Perhaps it would be better to say that there is no easily quantifiable correlation. In a moment I shall suggest one reason why a certain kind of religious and theological involvement *may* militate against sound historical scholarship.

Those who appear at the present time to be most concerned with what it has become somewhat fashionable to term a "crisis of identity" in the study of religion are less historians of religions as such than those who are employed by secular universities in departments of "religious studies." There, the controversy is far less a matter of methodology (though it is often made to appear in that light) than a question of diverse backgrounds and conflicting states of presuppositions at various points along a sliding scale of secularization. In the energetic and innovative 1960s and early 1970s it seemed only reasonable in view of the obvious upsurge of popular interest in matters of religions and a period of (as it transpired, short-lived) affluence in the little world of the publicly-funded Western universities, to create new departments of religious studies, in which the proverbial principle of "many hands make light work" could be put to the test. But there is a counter-proverb that says "too many cooks spoil the broth" — especially when they insist on working to different recipes. The new departments had perforce to be "secular," like the universities within which they were placed, as a condition of being funded in the first place. And a considerable number of new departments *were* created (my own department in Sydney, which enrolled its first students in 1978, would seem to have been the last). Faculty members were recruited from Oxbridge colleges, SOAS, Harvard, Yale and Chicago Divinity Schools, departments of anthropology, history, sociology, pyschology and philsophy; where Judaism was to be taught, a Jewish scholar was hired; where Hinduism was to be taught, a Hindu; where Islam was to be taught, a Muslim; and so on.[15] The principles and intentions involved in the exercise could not

[15] In very many cases older departments, journals and associations, previously

be faulted: tiny in comparison with departments of sociology and psychology, nevertheless in the 1970s departments of religious studies — secular departments in which the world of religion as a whole could at least be brought under examination — brought together a range of professional competence that the study of religion in the West had never previously known under one organizational canopy and one label.

However, all was not sweetness and light. The departments as such were "secular" — all well and good. No chairperson or head of department was likely to be chastised by an Archbishop, Imam, Chief Rabbi or Shankaracharya for not "keeping the faith" (though some, myself included, were pestered for what the advertising world calls "endorsements" by the Hare Krishnas, Scientologists and Moonies: some capitulated). Far more serious was the difficulty experienced by those employed to teach in the new departments in communicating with one another on matters of larger professional concern. Some departments overcame the difficulty more successfully than others: farther than that it would not be safe for me to go. The reason for the difficulty was not far to seek. The very ideals — thoroughly secular educational ideals — that had assembled the religious studies teams under the headings of multidisciplinary, polymethodic and interdepartmental studies, recruiting faculty members as subject specialists, had the unwanted side effect of making a common disciplinary matrix extremely difficult to establish.

It may be objected that, at this point, I have ceased to talk about the history of religions as a coherent sub-department within the study of religion, and have slipped into the wider field of the study of religion generally. In actual fact, however, the history of religions has scarcely ever existed in such total isolation as to remain unaffected by what colleagues in other subdisciplines have been doing. Historians of religions have very often "doubled" in other fields — philology, psychology, sociology, ethnology and many more. A similar principle has frequently operated in reverse among professional historians, ethnologists, sociologists and others. To this extent, it might

---

one-sidedly Judaeo-Christian in their emphasis, were reorganized in accordance with the new ideals. There were relatively few entirely new departures, though departments in Lancaster, Santa Barbara and Sydney may be mentioned among the exceptions.

be argued that the present-day "religious studies" pattern has merely institutionalized a principle that has long been operative on the unofficial level. The International Association for the History of Religions has never actually functioned as a guild of historians of religions, and over the past twenty or so years has broadened out more and more to embrace virtually every field that has found a place under the "religious studies" canopy. The name, however, has not been changed: to the argument that "history" ought to be replaced by "study," the general response (of Zwi Werblowsky, among others) has been that the term "the history of religions" has always been a blanket term sufficiently wide to embrace every *secular* arm of the study of religion, and that change therefore is strictly unnecessary.[16]

But does "the history of religions" also embrace theology? Or is the conflict of principle (control *contra* submission) we have mentioned too profound for any such alliance to be possible?

Were "theology" an unambiguous term, a decision might be easier to arrive at. But it is not, and much depends on what *kind* of theology finds its way into the religious studies team, and how the "theologians" in question go about their business. Provided that certain obvious standards of thoroughness, accuracy and professional competence are adhered to, there is no reason to cry wolf. That is not the issue. Nor do we need to worry overmuch, it seems to me, about the disruptive influence of exteme conservatives (of any tradition: fundamentalists are of more than one kind), who are unlikely to want any part of the secular religious studies enterprise. Lurid images of what confessional theology might be at its worst doubtless disturb the sleep of many a liberal seminary president; but in the religious studies departments I have known, it is more often encountered at the student level than among the teaching staff.

There are, however, two genuine causes of nervousness in the history of religions/religious studies ranks where "theological" participation is concerned.

One I have already mentioned. It concerns the academic standing of the subject, particularly in face of the methodological and

[16] Cf. Wiebe, "A Positive Episteme for the Study of Religion," in *The Scottish Journal of Religious Studies* VI/2 (1985), p. 95, n. 42.

practical expectations of the social sciences. Still the gap between theology and the social sciences is a wide one, and there are few signs of it being narrowed.

More serious, while at the same time being less easily quantifiable, has been the recent impact on the world of religious concern of an attitude for which I can find no better term than "existentialist" (in which connection we might do well to recall the historical links between existentialism and phenomenology). Existentialism, in the sense in which I am using the word, is less a system than an anti-system, less a method than a comprehensive vote of no confidence in the very possibility of arriving at a coherent method. It makes much of "the present moment," of "experience," "paradox" and the need to be constantly revising moral standards. It claims the superiority of intuition over reason — for which reason it is deeply subjective, and may be profoundly anti-intellectual and anti-historical, with a notable impatience with what little it understands of the past. One who has absorbed this attitude takes nothing consciously for granted, except his or her own autonomy — an egregious error, since the attitude as such is highly contagious.

My point here is not that this species of crude existentialism has ever exercised a baneful influence on the history of religions. On the whole it has not, though it has been known to throw student seminars into confusion. It has, on the other hand, found a safe haven on the liberal wing of Christianity, both Catholic and Protestant, where it coexists happily with the pursuit of Causes. It is hardly a system or a method: but is the closest thing to either that a good many religious studies students — those, that is, who enter the field from a Christian direction — possess. In a curious sense it has come to resemble a form of Gnosticism. If we should wish to settle upon this as the most recent protest against the secular ideal of rational discourse, then there may be genuine cause for concern here.

Twenty years ago, the secularization process seemed both unidirectional and irreversible. Since the 1970s we have learned that it is neither. And since the study of religions cannot but reflect what is taking place in the world of religion as well as the world of the intellect, we have also been forced into the realization that the historical empiricism of the kind so confidently announced in the 1960s is very much open to challenge. The post-1960s "existentialists" certainly reflect the latest stage in a secularization process. The "secular theologies'' of the 1960s are no longer a living issue. Neo-conservatism and neo-existentialism are. And of the two, it is the latter which poses the greater threat to the history of religions, since it calls in question practically all the principles on which the history of religions enterprise operates.

To return finally to the point from which I began, I must confess myself puzzled by Donald Wiebe's assertion that the raising of the question of theology's relationship to the academic study of religion should jeopardize ''the very existence of such an academic study.'' On the contrary, the discussion is one that is well worth pursuing — as doubtless it will be pursued for a good many years to come. But if it is to prove fruitful, it is more than ever necessary that it be given a firm basis in the history of ideas, and that it should take with the utmost seriousness whatever is to be learned from the sociology of knowledge. The sociology of knowledge, according to Peter Berger,

> isolation from the social context within which particular men [and women] think about particular things. Even in the case of very abstract ideas that seemingly have little social connection, the sociology of knowledge attempts to draw the line from the thought to the thinker to his social world.[17]

The history of religions has begun to apply these principles to its own varied history, as have most other branches of the humanities. In the case of theology the task has scarcely even been begun — and in addition, behind the academic theologian there is the vast company of devotees who are seldom deferred to but who cannot be argued out of existence.

Therefore let the dialogue continue by all means. But let it above all be firmly grounded in the full awareness of where we have been, and the reasons for the positions we currently occupy — some of them in all probability rather different from what is claimed. The history of ideas and the sociology of knowledge will not solve all our problems; what is tolerably certain, on the other hand, is that without their contribution, used judiciously, the secularization process, as it applies to the Academy, will not be even charted satisfactorily, much less understood in respect of the history of religions.

---

[17] Berger, *Invitation to Sociology* (1963), p. 111.

THE ANTHROPOLOGY OF THE AVATAR IN KAMPAṈ'S *IRĀMĀVATĀRAM*

David Shulman, Jerusalem

That one god who is lord
over all the gods
has transformed himself,
taken birth,
and come here
as a man—
now Śiva, who holds the river[1]
in his matted hair,
together with Brahmā
and all the other hosts of deities
have been defeated
by humanity.[2]

This is the conclusion reached by Sugrīva, forlorn king of the monkeys and newly-found friend of the divine hero Rāma, as we meet him in Kampaṉ's twelfth-century Tamil version of the *Rāmāyaṇa*, the *Irāmāvatāram*.[3] Rāma and his brother Lakṣmaṇa, wandering through the forests in search of Rāma's kidnapped wife Sītā, have just been introduced to the exiled Sugrīva by the latter's minister, Hanuman, who has already discovered for himself the delights of spontaneous devotion (*aṉpu*) to Rāma.[4] Now it is Sugrīva's turn, and his meeting with Rāma

---

[1] The Ganges, which flows upon Śiva's head.

[2] *Irāmāvatāram* of Kampaṉ (Tiruvallikkeṇi, Madras, 1967), 4.3.19. I have used the edition with commentary of Vai. Mu. Kopālakiruṣṇamācāriyar. The final phrase of the verse reads: *māṉuṭam veṉṟat' eṉṟe.*

[3] On Kampaṉ, see D. Shulman, "The Cliché as Ritual and Instrument: Iconic Puns in Kampaṉ's *Irāmāvatāram*," *Numen* 25 (1978), pp. 135-55.

[4] See 4.2.11-15. Watching the two heroes walking through the wilderness, where hot

produces the famous statement that we have quoted — embodying a somewhat unusual example of a definite notion of "humanity," sometimes said to be conspicuously absent in India.[5] In fact, Kampaṉ's anthropology is stated with particular clarity and emphasis in this part of the work, the opening chapters of Book IV (*Kiṣkindhākāṇḍa*). As we shall see, the poet's vision of man is not a simple one, categorically dividing him from other beings or, for that matter, imposing a special burden on his consciousness (as others, e.g. the Buddhists, tend to do). The focus of the verse cited above is rather on the peculiar state of a divine identity paradoxically and rather uneasily encased in human form. It is in examining this alluring paradoxicality of the human-divine hybrid avatar that Kampaṉ consistently transcends and transforms his model, the Sanskrit *Rāmāyaṇa* attributed to Vālmīki.

We shall look at a short but very striking illustration of this transformation, the dramatic passage where Sugrīva reveals to Rāma the jewels that Sītā had desperately cast to earth while she was being carried off to Lankā by the demon Rāvaṇa. The jewels had fallen in the vicinity of the monkeys' kingdom of Kiṣkindhā, in the forest where Sugrīva was hiding from his brother Vālin, and Sugrīva had gathered them up and saved them — for just this moment. The episode constitutes a separate canto, the *kalaṉ kāṇ paṭalam*, in Kampaṉ's text, roughly corresponding to chapters 6 and 7 in Vālmīki's *Kiṣkindhākāṇḍa*. We begin with a brief summary of the Sanskrit prototype.

Here the emphasis is on the friendship that has sprung up between Rāma and Sugrīva (in this epic of ideal-types, Sugrīva exemplifies the very notion of a perfect friend). Hanuman brings the two brothers to Sugrīva and, partly to calm the latter's fears — for the monkey-king's first reaction was one of panic — explains that they come seeking friendship; he also recounts a capsule-history of their exile and loss of Sītā. Sugrīva declares himself honored by this request for friendship and extends his hand, which Rāma warmly grasps. As a sign of this

rocks become like flowers beneath their feet, while fierce animals follow them lovingly, and the birds shade them with their wings, Hanuman feels as if he were approaching someone from whom he had been separated long ago (11): "My bones melt, limitless passion rises within me, there is no end to the love I feel" (15).

[5] See the fine survey by W. Halbfass, "Man and Self in Traditional Indian Thought," in press.

bond, Hanuman lights a fire, which the two new friends circumambulate, insatiably staring at one another in joy. Sugrīva and Hanuman break off branches to serve as seats for the guests. Now Sugrīva tells his own story of woe, with special emphasis on that part of it that links him so closely with Rāma — the loss of *his* wife, Rumā, to his brother Vālin, Sugrīva's mortal foe. The parallelism is not lost on Rāma, who smiles and promises at once to kill Vālin for Sugrīva — for friends must certainly help one another (*upakāraphalaṃ mitraṃ viditaṃ me*, 4.5.26[6]). Sugrīva is pleased by this promise and counters with one of his own: he will find Sītā, who is doubtless languishing in sorrow in her separation from Rāma, and bring her back to her husband, "as if he were restoring the stolen Veda" (*naṣṭāṃ vedaśrutiṃ yathā*, 4.6.5). He uses a typically simian, gastronomic metaphor to reassure Rāma: Sītā may have been stolen, but like food made of poison, no one, not even the gods or demons, could digest her. So Rāma need worry no longer: he, Sugrīva, will recover Sītā; moreover — this is the sudden, stunning revelation that Sugrīva springs upon his guests — it turns out that he actually saw Sītā as she was carried off, writhing like a serpent, screaming "Rāma, Rāma! Lakṣmaṇa!" Then, as Sugrīva and four of his companions stood watching, she tore off her upper garment (*uttarīya*) and her jewels and threw them to earth, where the monkeys found them. Sugrīva would be happy to show them to Rāma for identification.

Rāma is understandably overcome: "Bring them quickly, my friend; why are you delaying?" Sugrīva at once goes to a deep cave in the mountain and returns with the ornaments and the *uttarīya*. Rāma clutches them to his breast, weeps copiously — like the moon enveloped by mist[7] — and, crying "O, my beloved," falls helplessly (*dhairyam utsṛjya*) to the ground. In the throes of his lamentations, he shows the ornaments to Lakṣmaṇa, and the latter, in a famous verse, lives up to his role as the devoted brother who has never even raised his eyes above his beautiful sister-in-law's feet: "I do not recognize the armlets, nor do I recognize the earrings; but I can attest that these are, indeed, her anklets, for I saw them each time I worshiped at her feet."[8]

---

[6] I cite the edition of K. Chinnaswami Sastrigal and V. H. Subrahmanya Sastri, Madras, 1958.

[7] *nīhāreṇeva candramāḥ* — possibly an allusion to the hero's full name, Rāmacandra.

[8] *nāhaṃ jānāmi keyūre nāhaṃ jānāmi kuṇḍale/nūpure tv abhijānāmi nityaṃ*

Now Rāma begs Sugrīva to tell him where it was that he saw Sītā, and where that demon lives who kidnapped her and thus, swears Rāma, brought death upon himself. Sugrīva gives a somewhat evasive answer: he does not know where Rāvaṇa lives, or what his real strength is, but in any case Sugrīva will definitely kill him. The important thing now is for Rāma to gain control of himself again: "Enough of this despondency; remember your powers of self-control; behavior like this does not befit someone like you." Next comes a gentle boast: "Look at me: even though I, too, suffered the misfortune of losing my wife, I have not given way to grief, nor lost my self-mastery, even though I am only a simple monkey (*prākṛto vānaro 'pi san*) — how much less should you do so, being the great person that you are!" Rāma must control his tears; the wise man does not become depressed even in moments of disaster, or even death (here Sugrīva seems to echo the *Gītā*); only a fool sinks down in sorrow, like an overloaded ship at sea. And so on — Sugrīva shames, cajoles, and comforts Rāma to the point where, at last, the hero returns to his normal state of self-possession. The clinching plea is based on the new bond between the two: "I speak to you," Sugrīva says, "for your own good, as a friend, not to teach you anything; please respect my friendship and stop grieving." And this note immediately recurs in Rāma's first words after his attack has passed, as he wipes his eyes with his garment: "You have behaved exactly as a good, dear friend should...; such a friend (*bandhu*) is hard to find, especially at a time like this." The scene closes with a reaffirmation of Rāma's promise to help the monkey: Rāma has never lied and never will, and Sugrīva can rely on his word completely.

There is irony here: Rāma's promise to Sugrīva will soon involve him in perhaps the most problematic event of his epic career — his cowardly, unfair slaying of Vālin from an ambush behind a tree.[9] In keeping his word, the perfect hero will severely compromise his perfection. But the more immediate and more pervasive irony of the chapters we have just summarized is a gentler one — the irony inherent in the incongruous relationship of the human paragon and the lowly, somewhat pitiable monkey. Vālmīki points to this strangely asymmetrical and

---

pādābhivandanāt (4.6.22).

9 This episode is discussed at length in D. Shulman, "Divine Order and Divine Evil in the Tamil Tale of Rāma," *Journal of Asian Studies* 38 (1979), pp. 651-69. This context is also highly relevant to our understanding of the present passage in Kampaṉ.

surprising bond in several verses addressed by Lakṣmaṇa to Hanuman, immediately *before* the meeting with Sugrīva: "He who was once the lord of the entire world seeks Sugrīva as his lord... The embodiment of *dharma* for all the world, he who was ever a refuge to all, my *guru* Rāma, has come to Sugrīva for refuge...." (4.4.18, 20). This, perhaps, our text suggests, is what friendship is all about — not a "reasonable," calculating movement of self-interest, but an unpredictable inner process that follows an overriding logic of its own. Thus it turns out that Sugrīva, despite his obvious limitations and the great disparity in status, is indeed able to help Rāma out of his misery. Note, too, that the thrust of this assistance, at least in this passage, is toward bringing Rāma's unseemly grief under control. This stress on circumscribing and containing sorrowful emotion would be wholly alien to the prevailing atmosphere of Kampaṉ's Tamil version of the poem.

Such, then, is Kampaṉ's Sanskrit model. As always, the Tamil poet has introduced highly significant changes on at least two levels — that of the narrative (the "human" level of the story) and that of an implied theology. For we must remember that, however, we seek to understand Rāma's identity in the Sanskrit epic — as essentially and primarily human and heroic, or as already veiling an avatar — for Kampaṉ there is no doubt that Rāma is God in human form. The great power of the poem, and its hold over the Tamilians from Chola times until the present are largely derived from the complex and subtle play, evident throughout, between this definite understanding of Rāma's identity, and the inherited narrative structure with its all-too-human demands upon the hero. Or, to put this somewhat differently: the tensions implicit in the notion of the avatar have here become essential elements of Kampaṉ's poetic technique, which consistently embodies them in ironic figures and other forms, and which also points to these same tensions as a central part of the text's semantic concerns. The result is often a somewhat unsettling double-focus: Rāma's human experiences and reactions, exquisitely and exhaustively portrayed in passage after passage, are suggestively transferred to the god as coherent and serious statements about his nature, thoughts, and emotions.[10]

[10] In terms of Sanskrit poetics, it is as if we were witnessing a vastly extended, literally understood *utprekṣā*.

Let us examine this consistent merger of planes in the passage we have selected. We should recall that Sugrīva has already had some intimations of Rāma's divine identity, though it is unclear if he is capable of retaining this awareness throughout.[11] The canto begins innocently enough, with Sugrīva's first mention of Sītā's jewels:

Some time ago, while we were somewhere here,
a woman far away — was it your wife? —
looking straight at us,
screamed in sorrow
as the cruel demon carried her away. (1)

Even the monkeys could sense Sītā's sorrow, *kavvai*; the word echoes Hanuman's first, beautiful blessing of welcome to Rāma and Lakṣmaṇa in the forest — *kavvaiy iṉṟ' āka nunkaḷ varavu*, "may your coming be without sorrow" (4.2.16). But, of course, sorrow is just what awaits the hero here, of a new and intense kind.

We couldn't understand what was in her mind —
perhaps she thought these jewels
could serve as messengers.
She cast them off, together with a flood of tears
from her eyes, dark as a raincloud,
and we found them here. (2)

At this point Sugrīva, "whose heart is like milk mixed with ghee," brings out the jewels and shows them to Rāma. Suddenly we are plunged into an ambiguous and overpowering inner world of emotion:

He looked at the jewels that had graced his wife's body,
and understood.
We cannot say that his body melted,
like wax in a burning fire.
Nor can we say that he drank in sustenance for his spirit.
What, then, can words convey? (4)

Note the explicit statement of the incapacity of language, which must fail to confront the powerful inner reality of such a situation. This, together with an emphasis on *understanding*, apparently of a special kind, is the leitmotif of this section:

What can I say? —

---

[11] Sugrīva has also been informed by Hanuman of Rāma's apparent identity: "Who can he be who took this body/ except he who is worshiped/ by all the great gods?" (4.3.11).

that these jewels called up
his forgotten understanding (*viṭṭa per uṇarvu*)?
that they attacked his spirit?
that they cooled him
    like the soothing touch of sandal-paste,
or, rather, burned him
like flames? (6)

Clearly, it is a mixed and baffling experience that Rāma must undergo; the poet himself, remarkably present in these verses, can only offer tentative and mutually contradictory metaphors, which he then immediately undermines by pointing to the failure of language. But what is the "forgotten understanding" that the ornaments call up in Rāma's mind? At this point, we can merely surmise that we are dealing with a strong feeling (*uṇarvu*, "understanding," often connotes an emotional, intuitive perception, as opposed to the "hard," cognitive act, *aṟivu*)[12] that both torments and comforts the hero, at once burning him and cooling him, weakening him and sustaining him. The more specific content of this *uṇarvu* will be made clear in subsequent verses. But the general context is that of separation (*pirivu*), one of the major themes of the *Irāmāvatāram*[13] — the painful separation of Rāma from Sītā, of God from his beloved. Here, clasping Sītā's jewels, the hero at once recovers a tangible sign of her presence, and is made to feel even more poignantly the burden of her loss. Each ornament conjures up before him the image of that part of her body where it was worn; he sniffs at them, and they become flowers in his arms, or a cloak of light enveloping him (5, 7). Sītā herself eludes him, and, in the longing that now overwhelms him, Rāma momentarily loses consciousness (*uṇarvu*) altogether:

The flood from his red eyes
swept all before it.
Bristling hairs covered his entire body.
Did he break out in a drenching sweat?
Did he rage within?
What can I say
    about that pure lord (*tīrttaṉ*)? (8)

[12] See M. T. Egnor, "The Sacred Spell and Other Conceptions of Life in Tamil Culture," Ph.D. dissertation, University of Chicago, 1978, pp. 60-64.

[13] See D. Shulman, *The King and the Clown in South Indian Myth and Poetry* (Princeton, 1985), p. 43.

Like poison spreading through his system,
heat overcame him;
for a long while, he lost consciousness
and ceased to breathe —
but *he* (Sugrīva) supported him,
touching his body
with his heavy hairs. (9)

Again, the poet doubts the power of his words, but the external picture, at least, is clear, and, indeed, delicately drawn — the inner storm has its outer counterpart in the flood (*vĕḷḷam*) of tears;[14] the feeling or understanding we have been exploring has become an incandescent force, which Rāma can no longer contain; and the hairy monkey-king, Sugrīva, who is not even mentioned by name, catches the hero's refined and delicate body as it falls. This moment concludes the initial section of the canto; the next eight verses present Sugrīva's response and his address to Rāma (here Kampaṉ condenses and reworks the major part of Vālmīki's version, discussed above).

Typically, Kampaṉ begins by directing attention to Sugrīva's own inner state rather than to his approaching speech of encouragement:

He (Sugrīva) steadied him,
but his own heart, unable to bear that suffering,
moaned within him as he said in sorrow,
"Mighty lord, it is I, with my evil deeds (*viṉai*),
who have taken your life
by bringing you these jewels." (10)

Like many of Kampaṉ's characters, Sugrīva reveals a hidden capacity for self-reproach. It is all his fault for showing Rāma the ornaments; the suffering is too much to bear; he fears he has already killed his new friend. But then, after all, Rāma is God, as Sugrīva seems slowly to recall as he proceeds with his address: he promises to search the entire universe, as well as whatever lies beyond it, for Rāma's wife, immediately afterwards described as "the lady of divine chastity like Tirumakaḷ (Śrī)" (12). Note the simile: Sītā is, in fact, none other than the great goddess Śrī! Sugrīva has not, perhaps, yet fully assimilated this knowledge. But he reminds Rāma that all the three worlds must fol-

---

[14] This verse may also recall the opening canto of the *Irāmāvatāram*, the *āṟṟuppaṭalam*, which describes the great flood of the Sarayū River and suggests certain of the major themes of the poem.

low his, Rāma's, commands; why, then, does he humble himself in this way (*ciruka nokkal ĕn̲*, 14)? Not even the three gods of the Trimūrti — Brahmā, Viṣṇu, and Śiva — can equal Rāma (16); moreover, there is Rāma's identification with *dharma*:

The truly great
never speak of greatness.
Their deeds alone
bear witness.
Does *dharma* exist
apart from you?
What is too difficult for you?
Why stand here in such pain?

In short, Rāma's real powers should save him, in Sugrīva's view. Perhaps this is a monkey's-eye vision after all, which does not really come to grips with the god's inner experience of pain. In any case, the tactics which Vālmīki ascribes to Sugrīva — his attempt to bully and shame Rāma out of his unmanly mourning — are wholly absent here. They have been replaced by a combination of empathy, self-reproach, and partial awareness of Rāma's divinity. Sugrīva concludes his remarks by magnanimously offering to postpone the straightening out of his affairs — his quarrel with Vālin — in the interests of recovering Sītā quickly (17). Now it is time for Rāma's response.

This is the central section of Kampan̲'s presentation of the episode, where meaning and emotion are most highly concentrated and most complex. It is important to observe that this section has no true parallel or prototype in Vālmīki's text. The Tamil poet follows his own interests here, elaborating the themes implicit in his earlier depiction of Rāma's state upon seeing the jewels. The opening verse raises once again the issue of the hero's "understanding:"

As the son of the brilliant sun[15] spoke thus,
the god with Śrī upon his breast
opened his flooded eyes
and looked at Sugrīva with love;
and, as consciousness returned
and, with it, a sort of understanding (*ŏru vakaiy uṇarvu*),
he began to speak. (18)

[15] Sugrīva is the son of Sūrya, the sun-god.

The epithet has been carefully chosen: Rāma is "the god with Śrī upon his breast," i.e. Viṣṇu, incarnate in the human hero. Whatever he will now say will reflect, in some sense, a divine reality. It is thus of considerable importance for us to follow Rāma's exposition of his new-found understanding, as developed in the next six verses:

It is *I* who am loaded with deeds:
she tore off her jewels
while I was still alive, with a bow in my hand —
what other chaste woman would do that? (19)

Rāma echoes Sugrīva's self-reproach in verse 10, cited above; evil *karma* (*viṉai*) clings to him, in this case the *karma* of helplessness and passivity. Normally, only widows remove their ornaments; Sītā has acted the part of a widow, while her husband was still alive! This rather shocking statement, imbued with inauspicious associations, points the way to the violent self-laceration in which Rāma now indulges:

She is waiting for me to come,
watching for me with her eyes long as swords —
while I have passed the time
weeping
over high mountains, beside forest pools,
and now here, with her jewels.
I have not even been ashamed
to wander about, carrying this bow
with its long string.[16] (20)
There are those who would give their lives
defending soft-spoken women who are perfect strangers,
molested by others on the roads —
but I am unable to allay the sorrow
of that woman
who relied on me. (21)

In my lineage of worthy kings,
there are those who dug the sea,[17]
who brought down the Ganges to earth,[18]

---

16 There is an untranslatable pun here on *nāṇ*, "bowstring" and *nāṇ*, "shame": *nāṇĕṭuṉ-cilai cumant' uḻala nāṇ aleṉ*. On the latter sense of *nāṇ*, see discussion below.

17 The 60,000 sons of Sagara dug the ocean's pit in their search for their father's sacrificial horse, stolen by Indra.

18 Bhagīratha performed penance to bring the Ganges to earth.

who made the deer drink with the tiger;[19]
and after them came I,
who failed to save my wife from sorrow. (22)

My father did away with Indra's distress
and wiped out the fierce demon[20]
whom even Death could not combat.
Here am I, who came from him:
my bow has brought nothing
but cruel suffering and disgrace. (23)

I thought that if my great father's word
were to fail,
there would be a disgrace —
so I rejected the crown.[21]
But when the enemy seized my wife,
whose words are sweeter than sugar-cane,
disgrace itself became my crown.
Now there is no escape. (24)

So the god-man feels trapped, in a situation for which he assumes personal responsibility, in a manner which must surely seem exaggerated in the context of the inherited *Rāmāyaṇa*-plot. It was hardly Rāma's fault, alone, that Sītā was kidnapped, yet he blames only himself. As we have seen, this is a general tendency of Kampaṉ's heroes: Sītā, languishing in captivity, tortures herself with very similar self-accusations.[22] In the present case, however, the charge is connected to a wider series of perceptions and feelings which, together, might even be said to define the essential nature of the divine avatar. Rāma sees himself as shamefully impotent and, therefore, passive; he has a most pronounced inclination to waste time (*pŏḻutu pokkiṉeṉ*, 20) in lamentation and the sweet delights of yearning for his lost beloved; he has wan-

[19] Māndhātṛ, a conventional figure in Tamil versions of the solar genealogy: cf. 1.11.7; *Kalinkattupparaṇi* of Cayankŏṇṭār, 8.12.

[20] Śambara.

[21] Daśaratha had promised his wife, Kaikeyī, two boons; she chose to have her son Bharata crowned in place of Rāma, and to have Rāma exiled for 14 years to the forest. Rāma accepted this loss of the throne without demur, in obedience to his father and in order to safeguard the latter's word.

[22] 5.3.12-16.

dered about ineffectually, not even aware of how ashamed he should feel, still carrying his great bow. Here, Rāma seems to comment upon his own most common iconic guise, Kodaṇḍa-Rāma, "Rāma with the bow;" it is this form that one encounters repeatedly in South Indian temples, and that Kampaṉ, too, must have known and constantly visualized. But the usual suggestion of nobility and heroism has here been transformed; the poet isolates the icon, animates it, and then allows its own subject to attack it bitterly, on the basis of a new conception of his epic experience. The hero sees himself as weak, wanting, and unaware. He is given to despair, doubts that there is any escape from his predicament (which is, we stress again, more of an inner state than an external problem). Above all, he feels a terrible burden of disgrace (*paḻi*); this is the theme which recurs relentlessly in these few verses.

The term itself has a venerable history in Tamil. In the bardic culture of the so-called "Caṅkam Age" (roughly the first three centuries A.D.), *paḻi* constitutes the hero's nightmare. His entire life is predicated on the possibilitiy of *pukaḻ*, "fame," "glory," and on his horror of *paḻi*, "blame." Like other heroic cultures, notably those of Homeric Greece and of the Icelandic sagas, the Caṅkam world is one of violence and physical struggle, regulated by notions of honor, pride, and, on the negative side, the sense of shame before one's fellows. The hero who is wounded in the back, no matter under what circumstances, starves himself to death in shame. The bard, who immortalizes the heroes, is also the guarantor and exponent of these values; his application of the terms *pukaḻ* and *paḻi* is, perhaps, his most powerful weapon in his relations with potential patrons; he invokes these concepts explicitly in constructing the heroic world:

> They would give their very lives for fame (*pukaḻ*),
> but they would refuse the whole world,
> if the cost were blame (*paḻi*).[23]

Similarly, the Caṅkam hero is motivated by his sense of *nāṇ*, "rightness, honor," applied only to one's own actions (whereas *paḻi* reflects the judgment of others). In short, the social universe depicted in the classical bardic poems can undoubtedly be classified among the various "shame-cultures" familiar to the anthropologists.[24]

---

23 *Puṟanāṉūṟu* 182.5-6.

24 See discussion by K. Kailasapathy, *Tamil Heroic Poetry* (Oxford, 1968), pp. 87-93; and cf. comparative Greek material in E. R. Dodds, *The Greeks and the Irrational* (Berkeley, 1961), pp. 17-18, 28-63. Kailasapathy notes the analogy between *pukaḻ* and

Both *paḻi* and *nāṇ* are used by Rāma in our passage, in his description of his sorry state, but here the terms function within the transformed moral universe of medieval South India. As happened in Greece, Tamil society underwent a gradual transition from the early "shame-culture" to the medieval "guilt-culture," characterized by a far-reaching moralization of values, a far greater complexity in the understanding of the forces at work upon man's fate, and a deep internalization of critical standards — so that one's own self-judgment now counts for more than that of one's peers. The transition is already evident in works of the Pallava period (third to ninth centuries), which also saw the disintegration of older forms of social organization and their replacement by the complex state and social formations of the medieval culture.[25] The change is particularly conspicuous in Kampaṉ. Although Rāma retains something of the ancient Tamil hero and, indeed, makes use of the latter's characteristic vocabulary, he is, above all, the embodiment of the concept of *dharma* (Tamil *aṟam*), and a visible form of God. It is not by chance that he accuses himself — first of failing to feel shame (*nāṇ aleṉ*, 20; note the semantic change form the Caṅkam usages of *nāṇ*), then of bringing *paḻi*, not simply blame but a more pervasive, inwardly motivated sense of disgrace, upon himself. He repeats this several times: by comparing himself first, implicitly, to the unnamed, chivalrous "others" who rescue women on the roads (21), and, more to the point, to his own illustrious ancestors (22); then, explicitly, in verse 23, in relation to his father; and again, most strikingly, in the climactic image of the "crown of disgrace" in verse 24. There is an unusual, ironic twist in this verse: Rāma first claims, rightly, to have saved his father, or, perhaps, his entire lineage, from *paḻi* by his self-abnegating exile and renunciation of the throne; but, contrary to what one might expect from this strict adherence to a severe *dharmic* norm, in the end *paḻi* affects him nonetheless, the direct result of the tragic events of his exile. *Dharma*, it seems can at times reveal a darker side; this, indeed, is one of the lessons of the next episode of our text, Rāma's slaying of Vālin.[26] The god's mournful encounter with Sītā's jewels leads directly into still more unhappy and ambiguous circumstances. Clearly, we have come a long way from the archaic,

timē, *paḻi* and (Homeric) *nemesis*.

[25] See *The King and the Clown*, pp. 31-32, 342-43, 372-73.

[26] See the study cited in n. 9 above.

Caṅkam notion of *paḻi*, even if Rāma's self-accusation still revolves around a failure of "heroism" in relation to his enemy Rāvaṇa. It is also interesting to observe Rāma's stance of assumed inferiority vis-à-vis his father, Daśaratha, whose authority and greatness seem beyond reproach (at least to his devoted son!). Rāma remains the ideal son, always obedient and reverent, even — or especially — in the context of undeserved suffering inflicted on him by his father. He refers to Daśaratha as "great" (or "beautiful" or "powerful," *virump' ĕḻil*, 24), obviously humbling himself accordingly, perhaps as the culminating, decisive note in this tirade of self-abasement. For Daśaratha himself, of course, things look rather different; he is quite as capable of berating himself as is anyone else in Kampaṉ's poem, as one can see from the beautiful verse, from a much earlier point in the narrative, which may well have been the model for our verse 24:

> No sooner had I ordered you to put on the crown
> that is yours by right
> than, cruel creature that I am, I invested you
> with a crown of matted hair. (2.4.57)

We now have three crowns — the royal one that properly belongs to Rāma (*uṭai mā makuṭam*); the ascetic's crown of matted hair (*caṭai mā makuṭam*) that Rāma assumes by leaving for the forest at his father's command; and, at this moment dwarfing them both, the "crown of great shame (*pĕrum paḻi cūṭiṉeṉ*, 24), that Rāma now claims to have acquired by his inaction and general incapacity in the face of the personal disaster that has befallen him.

Nor is this the last appearance of *paḻi* in this passage. After Sugrīva, touched to the quick by Rāma's terrible suffering (*paiyuḷ*, 25), again seeks to comfort him — this time without words — Rāma stirs himself and says:

> My lord, could I go on living
> without your words of comfort?
> What other power (*uṟuti*) do I have?
> To wipe out this disgrace (*paḻi*) in the world
> I must die —
> but not before I carry out my promise to you. (26)

In Rāma's eyes, only death can redeem him; but, ever the ideal hero, he is still conscious enough of duty to remember his promise to Sugrīva, which he is determined to fulfil before dying. Sugrīva's friendship now appears to him as his only support and source of power. As in Vālmīki, this reaffirmation of Rāma's promise brings closure to the episode — but how different is the emotional atmosphere surrounding Rāma's statement! In Vālmīki's text, Rāma emerges, thanks to Sugrīva's blustery speech and to everyone's relief, from the supine state of helpless mourning to which he had been reduced; the renewed promise is a sign that he has come back to his senses. For Kampaṉ, the promise is dramatically wedded to Rāma's continuing despair, which still absorbs him to the point where only death holds out a hope of release. He will carry out his pledge and then let go of life, in the only possible atonement he can conceive for his disgrace. There is, we observe, no real resolution of the emotional crisis brought on by Sītā's jewels.

At this point we may cease following the text verse by verse and resume our initial concerns. The remainder of the canto is taken up by two sections: first, a short, practically oriented speech by Hanuman about the serious difficulties awaiting them in the search for Sītā, and the need to get started at once; this apparently convinces Rāma, who simply says, "Good (*cātuv ām*), let us go to Vālin" (33). Then follow the final nine verses of the canto depicting, in ornate *kāvya* style, various scenes on the mountain slopes that the heroes begin to traverse together with the monkeys. We will return shortly to these last vignettes. We should also note in passing one suggestive line put into Hanuman's mouth: Rāvaṇa's home and hiding-place is unknown, he states — it could be in heaven, or on earth, or on a mountain, or in the world of the Nāgas — "because we are embodied in the state of being human" (*ūṉ uṭai māṉiṭam āṉaṭ' uṇmaiyāl*, 29). Again, the poet sounds the note of a unique, in this case uniquely limited and problematic, human situation. This is the theme we must now pursue. What have we learned from this passage of Kampaṉ's divine anthropology?

To begin with, the Tamil poet has extended and transformed one of the basic themes of the *Rāmāyaṇa*-literature generally, a theme I have elsewhere described as "anamnesis" — in the literal sense of a non-forgetting, a negation of the negative process of amnesia.[27] The Sanskrit *Rāmāyaṇa* is largely concerned with the problem of memory — or, more precisely, with the forgetfulness that permeates so much of our awareness, and that sometimes finds its remedy in our listening to a story. At several points in the Sanskrit text, one of the heroes hears a part

[27] "Toward a Historical Poetics of the Sanskrit Epics," in press.

or a version of the *Rāmāyaṇa* story, and suddenly recognizes himself, or recovers some aspect of his life that had been lost, denied, or endangered. This is especially true of Rāma himself, who hears his own story — including the circumstances of his future death! — from the mouths of his sons (whom he recognizes only through their telling this tale), and who indirectly learns in this way of his hidden identity as the god Viṣṇu, an identity he had forgotten or repressed.[28] But in Kampaṉ's text, the process is reversed: if, in Vālmīki, the hero discovers, at certain crucial junctures, that he is really a god, in Kampaṉ God discovers what it means to be a man. This take us beyond the obvious assertion that Kampaṉ's Rāma is simply God, and that this constitutes the major difference between the Tamil text and the Sanskrit prototype. The point lies in the content of the understanding triggered by the sight of Sītā's jewels, an understanding that has all the marks of a *recovery* of former knowledge. The god suddenly sees himself in all his human limitations — helpless, guilty, amnesiac, disgraced. He discovers despair: separation appears to be his lot. He has delayed, wasted time lamenting, failed to live up to his, and the world's, demands upon himself. There is no way out, no simple resolution to his suffering; the resort to action — the slaying of Vālin — will only enmesh him further in painful ambiguities. He is lonely, lost, at fault, burdened with ambivalent emotions. And such, too, it would seem, is the state of man, especially — so the poet suggests throughout his long *kāvya* — of the ideal man and hero who carries divinity within him.

Let us sum up the differences we have noted between the texts of Vālmīki and Kampaṉ. In Vālmīki, the jewels precipitate an intense crisis that passes by means of Sugrīva's intervention. In Kampaṉ, the crisis is permanent, inherent in the world or in the god's relation to the world; the jewels merely reveal this truth. Vālmīki stresses the incongruous association of man and monkey; Kampaṉ paints a picture of empathy and shared emotions between the two, including the most prominent emotion of self-reproach. Incongruity here rests on a different level, that of the inner experience of the divine avatar. In Vālmīki, the hero's attack of lachrymose weakness is considered inappropriate and eventually suppressed; in Kampaṉ, it persists as an enduring feature of all existence, human or divine. Vālmīki's Sugrīva shames

[28] See especially 7.98.12-13.

Rāma into abandoning his mourning; Kampaṉ's Rāma speaks obsessively of shame from the much more difficult perspective of internalized personal guilt. Vālmīki uses this context to exemplify Lakṣmaṇa's ideal devotion to his brother; this element is completely missing from the scene in Kampaṉ. The Tamil version is also far more open-ended and unresolved than the Sanskrit episode. More generally, the hero of the Sanskrit epic moves, in his consciousness, from the level of man to that of god; indeed, this is the classical direction of change recommended by Hindu texts, which stress the hidden reality of the divine within the human being and the need to realize this identity practically through an expanding awareness.[29] The Tamil text, with its theistic axiology, stresses the opposite direction — that of God's similarity to man, at least in the vision of the avatar, when, for whatever reasons,[30] the god assumes a human form and, with it, such basic human emotions as longing, the need for friendship, sorrow, helplessness, remorse. Moreover, these emotions are no mere accidental accretions to divinity. Given the assumption of the god's transcendence and power, they cannot but be seen as paradoxical; but, if the poem is to be taken seriously, we must concede that they are no less real and substantial for all that. The god suffers in his sorrow and loss and yearning no less than his devotess, trapped, together with him, in the world.

Let us conclude with a verse from the final scene of this canto, which shows the hero's progression over the wilderness landscape of Kiṣkindhā. As so often in Kampaṉ (as in Tamil poetry generally), this verse, seemingly devoted to a wholly external landscape, effectively

---

[29] *Bhakti* texts also assert that this process is a necessary part of worshiping the deity: *nādevo devam arcayet*, "only God can worship God."

[30] Perhaps in play (*līlā, tiruviḷaiyāṭṭu*), the aspect of divinity stressed by Kampaṉ in the initial verse of the *Irāmāvatāram* (*taṟciṟappup pāyiram* 1):

We take refuge
with that god
of endless games,
who creates, sustains, and destroys
all the world.

One thinks also of the theology of paradoxical self-limitation by the deity in the temple-image (*arcāvatāra*), according to the medieval Vaiṣṇava commentators: see Friedhelm Hardy, "Ideology and Cultural Contexts of the Śrīvaiṣṇava Temple," in B. Stein (ed.), *South Indian Temples: An Analytical Reconsideration* (New Delhi, 1978), pp. 119-51.

suggests an inner reality and at the same time recapitulates, *in nuce*, the themes of an entire episode:

The slopes of that bewildering mountain
became slippery beneath their feet
as maddened elephants, blind with passion,
hurled themselves at the black aloe and sandal trees
which shattered, fell, and rolled downhill,
spilling viscous streams of honey
from the broken honeycombs.

Rāma picks his way over the wild and eery mountain covered with thick streams of honey and the broken trunks of the aloe and sandal trees assaulted by elephants in rut. Remember that this is a picture of god in the world — a world of slippery slopes, of bewildering beauty, of drunken passion and consequent destruction, of blindness and breakage and, in the end — as the unexpected result of this violent movement — of an enticing, entangling sweetness flowing at our feet.

THE IMPORTANCE OF DIASPORAS

Ninian Smart, Santa Barbara and Lancaster

The Jewish diaspora is the most important diffusion of people and ideas in the history of the world to date. But there are other diasporas that have hardly attracted the attention of students of religions, although they are playing a more and more vital part in the revivification of their home religions. Thus there are diffusions of Hindus overseas from India, often substantial in number, in such places as Fiji, South Africa, Kenya, Guyana, the U.K. Also, there are important groups of Sikhs in Canada and the U.K. and elsewhere, who have had a financial and ideological role in recent stirrings in the Punjab. Because of the oppression of Buddhist religion in Tibet, we have witnessed, in the last quarter of a century, the arrival of significant numbers of Tibetan refugees in India, Nepal, Britain, the U.S.A., Canada and elsewhere. In some places, the most likely form of Buddhism a Westerner is likely to encounter at home is Tibetan. There are, outside of the main Islamic territories, significant minority communities of Muslims, e.g. in parts of Europe, in other Western countries, in South Africa, East Africa and the Caribbean, and elsewhere. Chinese and Japanese, Korean and Vietnamese forms of Buddhism are widely dispersed in North America, and Chinese religious culture is central in Singapore and important in Malaysia and Indonesia, etc.

In many of these diasporas, there is an element of exile. In some cases, it is the consequence of the harsh economic realities in which overseas communities have grown up (as in the case of the indentured laborers of the post-slavery British Empire). In other cases political persecution has driven folk abroad. But sometimes it is a more casual matter; people have migrated without extreme pressures. Thus many Algerians in France and Turks in Germany have found it attractive to go to the host countries for reasons of economic opportunity. Migration has, for some, been a matter of opportunity rather than life-or-death necessity. Even so, there remains a sense of exile when persons come out of their own culture and settle in among an alien majority in an adopted country.

These diasporas are important for us to study, and this for several reasons. The first is that it can provide a clue to patterns of religious transformation. You may find similar developments in different communities, which reflect parallel solutions to parallel problems. Such changes may also pinpoint problems in the religion which make its adaptation to a new environment difficult. So the first reason has to do with adaptation. Second, diasporas may themselves affect the home-based religion. Thus Sikh militancy is strong in Britain, and this helps to stoke the fires of passion in the Punjab. Migrants often become wealthier than those left behind, and they may also be more exposed to education and foreign influences, and can export such influences back home. Third, the phenomenon of the diaspora is important because of its great incidence in the modern world. In Los Angeles, California; in Birmingham, England; in Sydney, Australia; in Frankfurt, Germany, and numerous other major cities of the world multiethnicity is now commonplace.

Incidentally, this diaspora phenomenon is also a great opportunity for students of religion. It is possible, up to a point, for students to do much of their fieldwork at home. You do not have, in many areas, to go far to meet Tibetans or Iranian Shi'is, or Japanese Pure Land Buddhists. This presence of other religions may help us, by the way, to be more realistic in appraising Western homegrown religions, that is Christianity and Judaism especially: we may be more open to seeing how they work on the ground, rather than just in the text. (Generally speaking, in my opinion, Christianity and Judaism are the religions least well taught, because of seminary-type assumptions still guiding our curricula. A strong dose of sociology and anthropology, or history of religions on the ground, would inject color and realism into religious studies in relation to these "homegrown traditions.") Recently, at the University of California Santa Barbara, we have instituted a program called "Religious Contours of California," funded substantially by the California Council for the Humanities. This seeks to encourage the teaching of world religions by beginning with the forms of religion found in California itself: Hinduism, Buddhism, Catholicism, and so on, exemplified in various ways through the influx of Hindus, East Asians, and

Mexicans, as well as more traditional migrants into the State. This is a way of using diasporas as bridges to their native or classical manifestations. It has incidentally revealed extensive areas for research. All this focuses on the diasporas, and does not take into account the way some religions have jumped their more traditional boundaries and taken root among new ethnic groups: Buddhism among Anglos or White people, Islam among American Blacks, an so on.

However, it is to the more theoretical aspects of the study of diasporas that I wish to draw attention in this paper. What are the kinds of religious changes one might expect? And what changes are found on the ground? Much obviously depends on the host societies. The migration of Christianity into India, in ancient times, and its survival in South India to the present time would imply some degree of adaptation to the most important structural feature of Indian society, that is to the caste system. In fact this assumption seems borne out by experience. However, we may note in the modern period a special feature of the intercultural contact implied by the creation of diasporas — that because of European and American power during the colonial experience, certain powerful ingredients of Western life and values became a pervasive presence virtually throughout the world. Even countries such as Japan and Thailand, which did not fall under Western rule, had to absorb many Western values in order to retain their independence; China, though not formally conquered, was nevertheless greatly penetrated by Western economic and educational forces. So, when new diasporas were being created, either during or shortly after the colonial period, the people involved had already had some experience of the host societies before they migrated. Or else they migrated from one area of Western domination to another, as with Indian laborers going to the sugar plantations of Natal or Guyana. In any case, there was a powerful exposure to Western values, either directly in the colonizing host countries or, at some remove, in Western-colonized countries.

In the last twenty-five years a different dynamic has also been important. Travel has become much easier, so even rather poor communities can maintain cultural contact with the homeland more easily. This has combined with other factors to encourage a kind of ecumenism. There are world organizations for every major tradition and subtradition. There is a sign of this, for instance, in the recent emergence of the paper *Hinduism Today*, which styles itself as "an international bimonthly newspaper fostering Hindu solidarity among 650 million members of a global religion.'' Such a consciousness of belonging to a world community has grown considerably in very recent times. Consequently, the divergences between diaspora and home communities are diminishing.

The need of other cultures to cope with Western values (or things perceived sometimes as Western, though in principle of universal scope, such as science and technology) meant that sometimes new religious movements from the homeland, also directed towards dealing with this problem, could flourish in the diaspora. Thus, in Fiji, Natal and elsewhere, the Arya Samaj has great vigour. Its nineteenth century religious fundamentalism (''back to the Vedas'') gave it a conservative, even nationalist, attraction which served overseas communities well. Because of the peripheral character of exiles, they often feel the need to be more patriotic or traditional than the traditionalists. On the other hand the simplification of Hinduism from a ritual perspective could be helpful in a situation of exile, where the maintenance of traditional rituals is difficult. It was difficult in the Hindu case for a number of reasons. First, indentured laborers were a relatively deprived group who nevertheless needed elite Brahmins for the proper performance of public rites. Second, the Hindu system is not one of much formal training. Customs and rituals are handed down from one generation to another by a kind of social osmosis. The rupture of this osmosis, implied by transportation overseas, proves to be a problem in Hindu education. Until recently, overseas Hindu groups were inadequately served for public rituals. Only in the last twenty-five years (what we may call the Global Period of world history) have provisions for ritual performance improved. Also, diaspora Hindus have begun building temples: *Hinduism Today*, in its January 1, 1986, issue, lists 47 temples in the U.S.A., but the list is very imcomplete. In a period of consolidation, then, there may be some revival of Hindu practice; but before the Global Period there was a long stretch when the survival of orthodox Hinduism was more problematic. Indeed, social changes — in Natal, for example, those brought about by a housing policy based on units suitable for accommodating the nuclear but not the extended family; and the growth of individualism, already favored by capitalist and consumer values, and by urbanization — have provoked a crisis for traditional Hinduism. There is an increasing proportion of ex-Hindu Indians who have become Pentecostal Christians. This allows them to adapt *bhakti* religion to a more consciously individualistic religious pattern. We may also note that traditional Hinduism, in losing its old osmotic potential, has become somewhat unintelligible to a new class of young people growing up in a modern environment.

But, as we have seen the Arya Samaj has grown in vigour in these circumstances, as have other new movements, including — for the better educated — the Ramakrishna Vedanta Math and Mission. So we may say that some of the pioneering movements of the nineteenth century, which involved reaction to Western values then present in India through the British occupation, have had an important role to play in helping the diaspora Hindus to adapt themselves to a new environment.

It might also be an interesting research project to see how far the various themes of the Hindu tradition are present in a non-Indian environment — themes such as caste, yoga, *bhakti*, pilgrimage, temple rituals, austerity (*tapasya*), wandering holy men, instruction in the scriptural traditions, regional variation, pundits, a strong sense of purity and impurity, household rituals, veneration of the cow, the practice of astrology, belief in reincarnation, the importance of acquiring merit, etc. These themes, which are woven together into the complicated fabric of Hinduism in India, do not all travel equally easily to new environments. The very act of going overseas implies something about purity and loss of caste, for instance. Though caste is not absent as a phenomenon in the diaspora, it is less rigidly observed (or, as an Indian sociologist told me wryly in Fiji: "If a Fijian Indian tells you that there is no caste in Fiji, you can be sure that he will be of lower caste.") Cow veneration does not have the wide social outreach it has in India itself. Pilgrimage and wandering holy men are hardly in evidence. Temple rituals are, as we have seen, less easy to maintain, but experiencing a revival. Regional variation at one time was more important overseas, because it implied a linguistic basis of division without the overarching presence of a Brahmin superstructure; but in later generations this variation loses vitality because of the decay of the homeland languages. Most of the Hindu diaspora has to transact its communications in English. This already implies a certain sophistication, and the erosion of folk Hinduism. It is a further factor in the importance of the post-British Hindu movements, including some recent phenomena, such as ISKCON, which have a strong presence overseas; in effect, these movements reflect a second main wave of religious developments in overseas Hinduism. Such English- speaking movements have also led to a revival of interest in the practice of yoga. Generally, new revivals emphasize the importance of religious experience and thus of the yoga-*bhakti* polarity, even during a time of reconstruction of ritual Hinduism in an overseas context.

I remarked earlier that, during the Global Period, there is the tendency toward the consolidation of world religions, however dispersed. Thus we have the formation of such institutions as the World Fellowship of Buddhists. This facilitates the evolution of a kind of ecumenical Buddhism, and is in part the consequence of a new feeling of identity, since Buddhism perceives itself as a world religion. This concept is itself important, and I shall return to it below. The diasporas in the Global Period become somewhat more orthodox in tone. We have noted the case of Islam, and the convergence of Black Islam with Sunni orthodoxy. A similar evolution happened with the Bahai in the United States. But the case of Hinduism is itself peculiar: some scholars would deny that there is such a thing as Hinduism at all, or would argue that, even if we can speak of Hinduism, it does not have a single unitary set of beliefs or practices. This thesis of the non-existence or dis nity of Hinduism has much to commend it, if we wish to represent realistically "religion on the ground" in India; it is however no longer correct. For the fact is that Hindus have perforce had to define themselves over against a number of traditional rivals — the Buddhists (here the distinction between *astika* and *nastika* was important); then, more seriously, the Muslims; and, finally, European modes of Christianity. Important here is what may be called "the modern Hindu ideology," pioneered by Vivekananda and developed by Radhakrishnan and others, affirming that Hinduism preaches the unity of religions and the unity in diversity of the Hindu tradition itself. Now, to some extent, this ideology, a powerful ingredient in the Indian nationalist movement, prepared the way for a pluralist state and, at the same time, provided a relatively convincing reply to criticisms launched at Hinduism by missionaries, social reformers and British administrators during the colonial period.

This modern neo-Vedantin kind of exposition of the nature of Hinduism has taken strong root among English-speaking Hindus, and though it neglects the tensions between differing forms of Hinduism on the ground (e.g. between Saivism and Vaishnavism), it serves as an important platform for self-understanding, especially among diaspora Hindus. A more complex model could be espoused - viz. that there are four main movements among Hindus: Saivism, Saktism, Vaishnavism and Smarta Hinduism. The modern Hindu ideology, as I have called it, is largely a Smarta account. The more complex "fourfold" understanding of the Hindu tradition, nevertheless, usually implies mutual toleration and a sense of unity among the branches of the religion, and so in practice comes to approximate the neo-Vedantin version.

From all this it may be observed that the diaspora itself contributes to the process of self-definition an ecumenical spirit and a kind of new orthodoxy. This is especially so in the Hindu case. So we may reply to those who say that there is no such thing as Hinduism: "Maybe over much of its history there was no such clearly demarcated '-ism' as Hinduism; there is now." In a sense Hinduism is a new religion, although its roots are of course very ancient.

The diaspora religions must exist, by their very nature, typically as minority groups (though sometimes, as in Fiji, they may come to constitute a majority). Those that are a "minority at home" have no special difficulties, but there is a question as to how a faith which dominates its home environment, such as Islam with its concept of *dar al-islam* or homeland of the faith, will work out its affairs in the overseas environment. This is in part because the home arrangements give the tradition unfettered opportunity to exercise its law. In a modern bureaucratic State there are further problems, such as regulations about the slaughter of animals and the conflicts between supposedly hygienic arrangements and the demands of traditional law.

As there is a growing consciousness of the Global Period, it becomes apparent to every religion that globally it is, however dominant in a region, a minority. In this sense the diaspora manifestation of a dominant religion can provide experience which will, in due course, become relevant to the global situation.

Another interesting aspect of diaspora religion concerns the degree to which it may expand from an ethnic basis. While a diaspora group may originally have migrated for economic or political reasons, it may eventually acquire some degree of mission, if only at first osmotically. Thus Tibetan Buddhism, which at first was more concerned to preserve Tibetan traditions abroad—in India, the U.K. and elsewhere — has become an active presence; so that, like other Buddhist groups and institutions, it is attracting growing interest and converts among Anglos in the English-speaking Western countries. Similarly while much of Hinduism in South Africa is ethnic and disinclined to proselytize, the Ramakrishna Vedanta had a more outward-looking and missionary face. Hinduism there stands in an intermediate position between the more or less non-missionary minority religions, such as the Parsees, Sikhs, Jains and so on, and the more active and traditionally missionary groups such as the Buddhists, the Muslims and the Christians, and smaller groups such as the Bahai. But, as is well known, even Sikhism, which has been largely ethnic in basis, has gained some Anglo converts in the United States. So the distinction between missionary and non-missionary groups may gradually blur and fade away. At any rate, we can see that the impulse to spread and the need to present the teachings in a modern and clearly articulated manner will favor the adaptation, especially the linguistic adaptation, of the diaspora faiths.

There is a factor that the rather conservative minor religions have in practice to bear in mind; that diaspora reinforces contact with major world cultural forces. This factor underlines the need for the faith to express itself in the face of universal religions and secular values. The same problem is faced by a limited ethnic religion (limited, say, to a tribal group) when it comes in contact with universal proselytizing faiths. Each such religion needs to give a universal account of itself, and to articulate its teachings, perhaps under some general principle — e.g., that every group is entitled to its own cultural and religious traditions, and such traditions can, like the universal faiths, point to some aspect of the truth. Admittedly such an argument gets away somewhat from tradition, which needed no defence. This new account of a religion's doctrines is an innovation. Maybe the ethnic group will fuse with others of a similar cultural affiliation, to produce some larger entity: thus it is common these days to talk about "Native American religion," as if there are common values distributed through the varieties of cultures that go to make up, and have gone to make up, the traditional small-scale mosaic which preceded European conquest in North America. Such Native American religion is now held to ally itself with certain universal values of the modern Western milieu, such as environmentalism. The lesson seems to be that you can only deal with the universalist intruder by adopting a universal-type defence. It is thus a natural thing for diaspora religions, even if they have no great missionary pretensions, to evolve universal-type explanations of their teachings and practices. Often they may follow the lead of Western traditions and publish translations and editions of their scriptures, or adopt other external models of operation borrowed on the whole from the West. This degree of adaptation also makes their teachings accessible to the host community. Given that this is a Western style of community, and especially in the United States, attitudes to religion will be in general individualistic and privatized; and so it will not be unusual for religious searchers to hit upon a diaspora religious group and come to belong to it, whether that group is explicitly missionary or not. All this contributes to the cosmopolitan character of religion in major diaspora areas. Yet, at the same time, we have noted the tendency for diasporas in the Global Period to have a greater sense of self- definition because of increased communication, to and fro, between the homeland and the places of the diaspora.

All this represents the beginnings of blending. Apart from the adaptation of diasporas to host cultures, there are the possibilities, inherent in cultural interfaces, of new forms "betwixt and between," constituting religions in the making. Part of the Hindu diaspora are the migratory gurus, who have pioneered varying forms of religion which absorb elements from both East and West in new syntheses. We may differ as to their value or staying power, but it may well turn out that from among these various Eastern blends there will emerge a strong new religious tradition.

Another factor in the life of diasporas is that members of a transethnic religion will find new ways to work together, for mutual protection and the like. Thus Cambodians, Vietnamese, Sri Lankans, Koreans, Chinese, Japanese, Tibetan and other Buddhists are found in substantial numbers in Southern California, and, through such organizations as the Sangha Council of Southern California, they cooperate in various ways. So it may turn out that the diaspora situation will enhance ecumenism, even apart from the easier communications of the Global Period. There is, as we have seen, the analogous cooperation between Hindus of different languages in the Hindu diaspora, partly due to the decay of the linguistic heritage.

From time to time, I have touched on the phenomenon of the diaspora of subtraditions. Here the classical case I have in mind is where an "alien" subtradition of a dominant religion migrates into the area of that religion. In England, for instance, there are West Indian Christians, various kinds of Eastern Orthodoxy, largely ethnically based, etc. Gradually ecumenical tendencies soften the edges between such a group and the dominant kind or kinds of Christianity. This example leads us to wonder whether in a pluralistic society the diaspora religions themselves may not begin to belong to some kind of pan-religious ecumenism. It would be interesting to analyse the attitudes of believers in such societies. For instance, in Sri Lanka, despite the religious and cultural conflicts between Tamils and Sinhalese in recent times, there appears to be a tendency, especially among the Muslim leadership, to accept a worldview in which different religions have value if pursued with sincerity. This is a worldview which encourages a pluralistic *modus vivendi*. It is an attitude of "Islam within the wider framework of sincere religion." That already is a modification of traditional Islam which, where it is dominant in a society, leaves only a limited place for alternative religions. There are signs in some diaspora societies of the desire for a world religion or world outlook. However, such a new development (finding echoes in neo-Vedanta and Islamic Sufism, etc.) can itself create a particularist backlash among the religions, and this in effect has already happened in Christianity, with works such as Kraemer's *The Christian Message in a Non-Christian World* (1938) and evangelical affirmations of the uniqueness of the Gospel. Liberal interpretations are often faced with conservative countermoves; this, by the way, helps to increase the variety of types of religion.

These, then, are some thoughts about the study of diasporas, an area of research in religion which has been somewhat neglected. Some of the phenomena to which I have drawn attention in this essay have already been looked at by some scholars, including Zwi Werblowsky, to whom this volume is dedicated. It may be time for some worldwide systematic studies. This may also be a field which implicitly heralds important changes in world religions. We are entering, in the Global Period, a new era, not just of religious researches but of religious life. Not all the traditional religions, nor many scholars, have yet come to terms with these changes.

THE PARABOLIC USE OF NATURAL ORDER IN JUDAISM OF THE SECOND TEMPLE AGE

Michael Edward Stone, Jerusalem

The purpose of this article is to set forth some changes in attitudes towards natural phenomena that may be observed in Jewish writings of the Second Temple period. The argument is constructed of three elements. First, particular aspects of such attitudes in the literature of the Hebrew Bible are set forth, but only in the most summary fashion. Second, the views evinced in selected sources of the Second Temple period are expounded, and, finally, these are compared with the views set forth in the Fourth Book of Ezra.

It is freely admitted that at the genesis of this essay lay the material in the Fourth Book of Ezra. Initially I was intrigued by the fact that in that work natural phenomena are used in parables as paradigms of regularity. This brought to mind some previous observations about the way certain apocalypses describe the relationship between the astral bodies, and these two elements combined to provide the stimulus for the present paper. Although thus originating from a rather narrow base, the observations made here seem to have wider implications.

The Biblical Background

"The Hebrew vocabulary includes no word equivalent to our term 'Nature.' This is not surprisng if by Nature we mean 'The creative and regulative physical power which is conceived of as operating in the physical world and as the immediate cause of all its phenomena.' The only way to render this idea into Hebrew would be to say simply 'God.'''[1] So begins one of the best studies of the concept of nature in the Hebrew Bible.[2]

It is, of course, impossible within the confines of this article to analyse all the various ways in which nature is treated in the Hebrew Bible, not to speak of the complex modes in which it was understood in Ancient Near Eastern religion.[3] Some brief comments are called for, however, to sketch the background for the ensuing discussion.

Natural phenomena serve in certain parables in the Hebrew Bible, such as the trees in the parable of Jotham (Jud 9:7-16) or the ant in Prov 6:7-8. Such instances are comparatively rare and in them it is not the orderliness or regularity of the phenomena that provide the parable with its moral. This is not to deny that ancient Israelites perceived a regularity in the succession of the seasons or the sequence of the rains, even though the continuation of this regularity was often said to be dependent on God's will and human action.[4]

In a different vein, other texts talk about natural phenomena in such a way as to imply that they carry out actions normally only attributed to animate beings. Thus, in a number of instances heaven and earth are summoned to witness a prophetic or similar pronouncement. The background of such passages, which include Deut 32:1, Isa 1:2 and differently Deut 4:26 and 30:19, usually lies in covenant

---

[1] H. Wheeler Robinson, *Inspiration and Revelation in the Old Testament*, (Oxford: OUP, 1946) p. 1 citing the definition from the *Shorter Oxford English Dictionary* s.v.

[2] *Ibid.*, 1-48. Robinson's remarks are penetrating. In them, he tends to subsume the apocryphal writings under those of the Hebrew Bible as minor witnesses. His analysis of Biblical ideas is executed in contrastive dialogue with surrounding paganism. The present article has benefitted particularly from his pages 9-11.

[3] An overly systematic attempt at treatment is J. L. McKenzie, "God and Nature in the Old Testament,"*CBQ* 14 (1952) 18-39, 124-145. It is perhaps indicative of the neglect that this topic has suffered that in neither the *Interpreters Dictionary of the Bible* nor in the *Supplement Volume* to that work is there an article on it.

[4] Robinson, *Inspiration and Revelation*, p. 9f. This is clearly related to the idea, which emerges from numerous passages, that human action can disturb the orderliness of nature. Such are, e.g., Deut 11:14-17, 28 (particularly v. 12 and contrast vv. 23-24). This concept was, in turn, crucial in the development in later times, of the idea of the Messianic woes and the great disturbances of nature which precede the eschaton, as we shall demonstrate elsewhere.

ideas.[5] Nonetheless, they refer to the phenomena of nature in a fashion not dissimilar, in some ways, to that in which the Psalmist talks of the works of creation that praise God. A striking instance of this is Ps 19:1: "The heavens are telling the glory of God; and the firmament proclaims his handiwork" (cf. *ibid.* vv. 2-6). Another example is Ps 148. It may even be that, with H. W. Robinson and J. Pedersen, we might talk of nature being alive in such Biblical thought, of the extension of anthropomorphism to nature, and we might even refer to it as responsive "to the rule of its Creator and Upholder on whom it directly depends."[6] Yet, for all this, the various natural forces are not separate or individual personalities endowed with their own consciousness or will. Thus, again, although the great recital of creation in Psalm 104 is rife with personification as a literary device, it contains no hint at true attribution of separate personality or will to the various forces of nature.

The Regularity of Nature in Some Later Sources

The situation is strikingly different in documents of the Second Temple period. One sort of paradigmatic use of nature is to be found in *1 Enoch* 2-5, where the order of nature serves as an exemplar of regularity and faithfulness. In particular, the cyclical character of the natural order serves as the point of the comparison.[7] Even more significant, in *1 Enoch* the regularity of nature is invoked in a paraenetic passage which is reproving mankind for lacking those very characteristics of faithfulness and regularity that nature epitomizes. Thus we read: "5:1 And understand in respect of everything and perceive how He who lives for ever made all these things for you; 5:2 and (how) His works (are) before Him in each succeeding

[5] Thus in Hittite treaties, forces of the natural world were included with the gods in the list of witnesses; see *IDB* s.v. "Covenant," 1.715a. The Biblical texts show a pale reflection of this sort of usage (*ibid.* 720b). The mountains and hills are similarly invoked in Mic 6:1-6.

[6] Robinson, *Reason and Revelation*, p. 16.

[7] These five chapters of *1 Enoch* have been the object of an extended study by Lars Hartmann, *Asking for a Meaning: A Study of 1 Enoch 1-6* (CB, New Testament Series 12: Lund: Gleerup, 1979); see particularly pp. 66-70.

year, and *all His works serve Him and do not change, but as God has decreed, so everything is done.*" Behind this statement lies a view which regards the various powers of nature as independent personalities. This is expressed, again, in the next verse: "And consider how the seas and rivers together complete their tasks."[8]

A similar view of nature is a prominent characteristic of a slew of sources that deal with the heavenly bodies. The regularity of the heavenly bodies, of course, was greatly admired in antiquity. "By establishing the unchangeable character of the celestial revolutions the Chaldeans imagined that they understood the mechanism of the universe and had discovered the actual laws of life."[9] Although, as fitted his argument, denying their ultimate reality, Plato refers to the stars as "the finest and most perfect of visible things" (*Republic* 529), and this general estimation prevails in many sources.[10] Frequently in Jewish literature of the Second Temple period, we find references to the order of the heavenly bodies as paradigms of action. One of the earliest is Ben Sira 16:26-28:

> The works of the Lord have existed from the beginning by
> His creation,
> and when He made them, He determined their
> divisions.
> He arranged His works in an eternal order,
> and their dominion for all generations;
> they neither hunger nor grow weary,
> and they do not cease from their labours.
> They do not crowd one another aside,
> *and they will never disobey his word.*

---

[8] *1 Enoch* is cited from the translation of M. A. Knibb, *The Ethiopic Book of Encoh. 2, Introduction, Translation and Commentary* (Oxford: OUP, 1978).

[9] F. Cumont, *Astrology and Religion among the Greeks and Romans*, (1960, repr of 1912 edn.; New York: Dover Publications), p. xiv. The attitudes to the astral bodies in Hellenistic antiquity form, of course, a large and complex topic into which we will not enter here. Some indicative references are: W. Jaeger, "Greeks and Jews," *Journal of Religion* 18 (1938), esp. pp. 132-134; cf. also *idem., Diogenes von Karystos* (Berlin: 1938), p. 139; M. Stern, *Greek and Latin Authors on Jews and Judaism* (Jerusalem: Israel Academy of Sciences and Humanities, 1974) 1, p. 11 (with further bibliography and sources there); see note 11 below.

[10] See preceding and following notes.

Note the observation I have underlined. This passage is bracketed by an invocation to pay attention and by a description of the creation of humankind. The latter concludes in 17:14 with the demand that humans act with the regularity and obedience that we find celebrated of the heavenly bodies in 16:26-28. The attribution of personality and will to the heavenly bodies, which is expressed both in their mutual relations ("they do not crowd one another") and in their regular obedience to the Creator, is an essential element of the view given here. Exactly the same appears in other sources.

In *The Testament of Naphtahali*, a document which by all accounts is much later than Ben Sira, a similar idea is encountered: "Sun, moon, and stars do not change their order; so you also do not alter the Law of God by the disorderliness of your activities" (3:2).[11] This view of the phenomena of nature as distinct personalities is carried to an extreme in the passage in *The Similitudes of Enoch*, unfortunately fragmentary, which describes the oath by which creation is regulated. There each of the elements of creation is discussed in this personal fashion. "And through that oath the sun and the moon complete their course and do not transgress their command from (the creation of) the world and for ever. And through that oath the stars complete their course, and He calls their names, and they answer Him from (the creation of) the world and for ever" (69:20-21). The text goes on, in vs. 24: "And all these make their confession and give thanks before the Lord of Spirits, and sing praises with all their power; and their food consists of all their thanksgiving."[12] That these verses refer to the stars is evident from

---

[11] Translation from H. W. Hollander and M. de Jonge, *The Testaments of the Twelve Patriarchs* (SVTP 8; Leiden: Brill, 1985). They adduce numerous pagan, Jewish and early Christian parallel sources in their commentary. These witness both to the prevalence of admiration of the regularity of the heavenly bodies and, in Jewish and Christian sources, to the moral or paradigmatic force of this siderial regularity from the human perspective. The animate heavenly bodies were not always regarded positively as is evident from some Gnostic sources.

In quite other terms, it is worth noting that the Greeks designated the world, from the fifth century on, by the term *kosmos* which is "the cosmic system in the sense of cosmic order. Only later does *kosmos* come to denote the totality which is held together by this order, i.e., the world in the spatial sense, the cosmic system in the sense of the universe" (H. Sasse, art. *kosmos* in *TWNT* 3.870).

[12] The idea that the various parts of nature give praise to God is to be found in later writings, such as the documents published by M. Beit-Arié, *Pereq Shira: Intro-*

the following: "And this oath is strong over them, and through it they are kept safe, and their courses are not disturbed." The view of the powers of nature, and particularly of the luminaries, as independent personalities is absolutely indubitable here.

The same oath may be referred to in *1 Enoch* 41:5: "And I saw the chambers of the sun and the moon, whence they go out and whither they return, and their glorious return, and how one is more honoured than the other, and their magnificent course, and (how) they do not leave the course, neither adding (anything) to, nor omitting (anything) from, their course, *and (how) they keep faith with one another, observing (their) oath.*" Other texts refer explicitly to the angels or spirits that guide the luminaries. Such are *1 Enoch* 43:2: "...and (I saw) their revolutions according to the number of the angels, and (how) they keep faith with one another."[13] *2 Enoch* 40:3 speaks of the "guides or the guided ones" of the stars. Further texts could be adduced to this point. The most instructive is perhaps the creation recital in *Jubilees* 2, which refers throughout to the angels or spirits of the various natural creations.

---

duction and Critical Edition (dissertation; Jerusalem: Hebrew University, 1966) and M. E. Stone, *Armenian Apocrypha Relating to the Patriarchs and Prophets* (Jerusalem: Israel Academy of Sciences and Humanities, 1982), pp. 58-77. On the calling of the stars by name, see detailed discussion in M. E. Stone, "Lists of Revealed Things in the Apocalyptic Literature," *Magnalia Dei* (Garden City: Doubleday, 1976), pp. 426-428 and notes. The roots are Biblical, of course, cf. Ps 147:4-5 and Isa 40:26. In those Biblical texts, however, although God calls the stars by name, they do not respond! This they do in the later texts, see *1 Bar* 3:34-5, *1 Enoch* 43:1. M. Greenberg has commented (orally) that in the Hebrew Bible, the heavenly host, alone of natural phenomena, seems to retain a measure of animation.

13 The continuation of this passage reads "And I asked the angel who went with me and showed me what was secret: '(What) are these?' And he said to me: 'Their likeness has the Lord of Spirits shown to you; these are the names of the righteous who dwell on the dry ground. . . .'(43:3-4)"

The "likeness" must resemble "parable" in some sense. What is interesting is not just the existence of the angelic patrons of the luminaries, but the connection, in this text, between the luminaries and the righteous: see Stone, "Lists" 430-1 and *idem, Features of the Eschatology of IV Ezra* (unpublished dissertation; Cambridge, MA.: Harvard University, 1965), pp. 206-211. This usage, drawing ultimately upon mythological ideas, is different from the employment of nature in the parables of The Fourth Book of Ezra.

The Parabolic Use of Natural Order in The Fourth Book of Ezra.

Particularly interesting is the way the idea of the regularity of the natural order is used in the Fourth Book of Ezra. This work, also called the Apocalypse of Ezra, was written in Hebrew probably in the last decade of the first century C.E. by a Jewish author.[14] It is profoundly concerned with issues of divine justice as they arose out of the destruction of the Second Temple. The book is presented in seven visions, the first three of which are sustained dialogues between the searching and sceptical seer and an *angelus interpres*. In these dialogues, in order to illustrate his discourse, the author often has recourse to images and parables in which the various phenomena of nature or the world serve as a basis for comparison. Such parables are set in the mouth of the angel and serve to instruct the seer.[15]

The chief instances in which nature is used in parables are the following: 4:19, the forest and the sea; 4:48-50, the furnace and the clouds; 4:41-42, 5:46-55, cf. 8:9-13, the womb and the mother; 7:3-9, the sea and the city; 7:52-57, 8:2-3, base matter and precious stones; 8:41-44, cfr. 9:17, seed and sowing. Certain natural phenomena are utilised only once in the book, while others recur a number of times.[16]

---

[14] For a conspectus of the critical problems associated with the book see M. E. Stone, *Jewish Writings of the Second Temple Period* (Compendia Rerum Iudaicarum ad Novum Testamentum, 2.2; Assen and Philadelphia: van Gorcum and Fortress, 1984), pp. 412-14 and further bibliography there.

[15] Our formulation in the text makes the use of such parabolic symbolism a literary device, as it surely is. Yet, in The Fourth Book of Ezra, there are also some parables which are presented as visionary experiences. In these, instead of the interlocutor or instructor telling a parable in order to make his point, a vision is granted, in which the parabolic symbols appear to the recipient. The interpretation of the vision symbolism is equivalent to the drawing of the moral of a parable. Such, in The Fourth Book of Ezra, may be observed 4:48-50, the parabolic vision of the furnace and the rain in the first vision. This may be contrasted with the functionally identical use of a true parable in the corresponding context of the second vision, in 5:48-55. We include these "parabolic visions" in our corpus of parables.

[16] Naturally, some of these parables may draw on older traditional themes and imagery. Thus, the mythological conflict of the sea and the dry land probably lies in the background of 4:15 (so H. Gunkel, "Das vierte Buch Esra," *Die Apokryphen und Pseudepigraphen des Alten Testaments*, ed. E. Kautzsch [Tübingen: 1900] 2.356). Likewise the theme of the "two ways" may be generative of 7:8 (see the

What is striking is that in nearly all these parables the comparison with the natural phenomenon serves to stress the fixed order of the world, or of nature, or of creation. That this is the moral of these parables is well illustrated by the concluding lines of various of them. So 4:21 epitomizes the message of the parable of the sea and the forest: "For as the land is assigned to the forest and the sea to its waves, so also those who dwell upon earth can understand only what is on the earth, and He who is above the heavens what is above the height of the heavens." Or again in 4:50: "Consider for yourself; for as the rain is more than the drops, and the fire is greater than the smoke, so the quantity that passed was far greater." A further example is 5:49: "For as an infant does not bring forth, and a woman who has become old does not bring forth any longer, so have I organized the world which I created." The same is true of the other examples mentioned. Thus, when the author seeks to stress the regularity of God's plan or of some aspect of cosmic order, he takes a feature of nature as his paradigm. From this we may infer that according to his notion, nature is the very best example of that which is regular, harmonious and orderly.

The same attitude is expressed in 6:1-5. That passage is not a parable, but a recital of the work of creation set in the mouth of God. In it the divine rule and power, evident from the acts of creation, serve as an overall demonstration of God's control of the eschaton: "I planned these things, and they were made through Me and not through another, just as the end shall come through Me and not through another" (6:6).[17]

Attitudes to Natural Order Expressed by the Seer

In contrast with this use of nature in parables which are always set in the mouth of the angel, other instances are to be found in

---

writer's forthcoming Commentary).

[17] See also 7:70 and compare 7:26-27. Rabbinic literature often presents lists of those things that were prepared before creation. Such are in *b. Nedarim* 39b; *b Pesahim* 54a; *Pirqe de R. Eliezer* 1; *Midrash Tehillim* to 72:6, 90:12; *Seder Olam Rabba* 31 (160); *Genesis Rabba* 1:1 (Theodor-Albeck 6) and other sources. Views on these matters varied widely in contemporary and earlier texts.

which the seer expresses his wonder at the works of creation. The seer's extended praise of God as Creator in 6:38-54 exhibits clear similarities in many details to God's discourse on his own creative activity in 6:1-6. The seer's praise of the Creator in 6:38-54 is permeated by a feeling of the awe and wonder experienced by a human being who contemplates the magnificence of the divinely created natural order. A no lesser sense of wonder is dominant in 8:8-11, the quite extraordinary passage on the creation of human beings. The formation of an embryo in the womb, its development, nurture, birth, growth, and education truly astound him. This process is due to God's creative action. In both passages, 6:38-54 and 8:8-11, the seer employs the marvellous complexity of natural phenomena, and *a fortiori* of their genesis, as an argument for the working of divine providence.

There is in this book an apparent contradiction, implicit in arguments based upon the order of nature, or the magnificence of the creative act of the growth of an infant in its mother's womb. The contradiction is with the view, also put forward in the book, that human life is a fleeting thing and that the order of creation is hastening to its end: "This age is full of sadness and infirmities" (4:27); "a creation which already is ageing and passing the strength of youth" (5:55); this world is corruptible, mankind is "corrupt in a corrupt world" (4:11). For one holding such a view of the world, one might argue, the order of nature is not a convincing paradigm for human action or divine providence, nor are the mysteries of conception and birth particularly enticing. Yet our author seems to be quite innocent of this, as he is innocent of a dualism of matter and spirit.[18] This innocence, it may be remarked in passing, should serve as a warning beacon to those who would characterize the author's thought as thorough-going pessimism about this world and the course of its history.[19]

---

[18] See Stone, *Features* pp. 147, 182f., 200-202.

[19] When formulated in terms of history, this becomes a major theme in certain modern approaches to the book. See, e.g., W. Harnisch, *Verhängniss und Verheissung der Geschichte* (Göttingen: Vandenhoeck und Ruprecht, 1969) *passim*, and particularly pp. 55-57. If the author did express a thoroughly pessimistic view at some points, he did not carry it through systematically, as the implications of his statements about nature make evident.

We have seen that nature is used very differently by the angel and by the seer. Yet it is quite striking that both uses share a very markedly positive attitude to nature. Nature is paradigmatic of divine order and of divine providence. This is true, as we have said, in spite of and in tension with the stress on the imperfection of nature and the natural world, and a sense of its imminent demise.

Changes and Transformations

In the sources from the Second Temple period that were analyzed, a clear attribution of personality and even of will to natural phenomena was observed. Indeed, it is precisely this sort of view of the natural forces that seems to be absent from the uses of nature in the Hebrew Bible. Talk of the spirits of luminaries, or of natural forces as if they were independent beings endowed with their own will is not to be found in the latter. Since such ideas are widespread in the sources we have quoted from the period of the Second Temple, a transformation or change has obviously taken place. In the religion of the First Temple period "history is the temporal arena of action" and "this world is its spatial arena."[20] Elsewhere we have traced the movement from a radically demythologized view of time and space to their partial remythologization in post-Biblical literature.[21] Historical time was moved back towards the mythical, but without loss of the basic insights achieved by the demythologization of history. Similarly, the heavenly space returns to play a role in the world of human beings.

We suggest here that a very similar dynamic can be observed in the view of nature. The idea of deities or demi-gods connected to natural elements surely has its roots in polytheistic world views. Such attitudes were vigorously combatted in the First Temple period, precisely, it seems, because of their polytheistic connotations. They resurge again in the Second Temple period as part of the same general process that has been traced as relates to time and place. They never return, however, to a properly pagan form.

---

[20] M. E. Stone, "Three Transformations of Judaism: Scripture, History and Redemption," *Numen* 32 (1985) 227.

[21] *Ibid.*, 223-231.

The View of the Fourth Book of Ezra

In this context, therefore, the position of 4Ezra is somewhat surprising. In other literature that we have cited the animation of natural phenomena is quite striking. In 4Ezra, however, it lies only in the background of his usage. Nature serves as a paradigm of regularity precisely because of the sorts of ideas that are present in sources like the Enochic writings we have cited. Its regularity is a result of the willed action of its elements. Nonetheless, reference to natural forces as individuals or spirits, or to their angels, is strikingly absent.

This sort of position in 4Ezra coheres with the book's tendencies on other matters. 4Ezra's reservations about the possibilities of special knowledge have been stressed.[22] Its angelology is moderate, it exhibits less of the resurgent mythological elements than other similar works. It has no serious interest in speculations about the heavenly realm. So too, in its view of nature, it holds a position that assumes the process of remythologization that has taken place, and is only comprehensible in light of it. Yet in the Fourth Book of Ezra the remythologization is softened and suppressed.

---

22 Stone, "Lists," 420f. I am indebted to T. Bergren and A. Roitman, who made helpful comments on this paper, and particularly to the remarks of D. Satran.

MYTH INTO METAPHOR: THE CASE OF PROMETHEUS

Gedaliahu G. Stroumsa, Jerusalem

Do myths die? Like religions, and more than religions, myths show a rare capacity to evolve, adapt and transform themselves, even when the social and cultural context which first nurtured them is long gone. Were we to accept Claude Lévi-Strauss' famous dictum, according to which a myth is defined by the sum of all its versions, even contemporary interpretations of archaic myths would constitute an integral part of these myths.[1] Hence, the nature of a myth would include its own history; this would make it difficult to argue that myths can die at all. Yet, although myths are in a large measure resilient to the erosion of time, they are not quite immune from it. The following pages deal with some avatars of one Greek mythological figure after the emergence of Christianity, thus following the diachronical transformation of a myth by culture.

A corollary question of importance, which however will only be alluded to here, deals with the ways in which the historical consciousness of a human group is marked and modelled over time by its myths.

The myth of Prometheus, chosen here to exemplify this complex dialectic, is a very peculiar one. It appears already in two different versions in Hesiod, both in *Works and Days* and in the *Theogony*. The myth proposes nothing less than an interpretation of civilisation

---

[1] Lévi-Strauss, "La structure des mythes," in *Anthropologie structurale* (Paris, 1968), pp. 227-255.

and its origins, together with an aetiology of sacrifice and of the existence of evil in the world.[2] Through the gift of fire it is work, civilisation and culture that Prometheus offered mankind. This was indeed the main interpretation of the myth in classical Greece, as Plato's *Protagoras* makes clear. Prometheus himself, the titan who first opposed his kin then to revolt against Zeus, is a complex and peculiar figure, a *unicum* in the Greek pantheon.[3]

Throughout Western history, Prometheus has remained a major figure of reference for cultural self-consciousness and self-understanding. Indeed, the history of Western self-consciousness might be particularly well illustrated by the transformations of Prometheus.[4] Such a history, or rather meta-history, has been recently attempted by the German philosopher Hans Blumenberg.[5] Ambiguous, very learned and difficult, *Arbeit am Mythos* is an impressive achievement. Yet, it seems somehow to miss the mark. One of the reasons for the reader's frustration lies in the fact that Blumenberg does not elucidate well enough how the major chasm in Western history, that is to say the advent of Christianity, came to alter radically the conception of culture, and hence to transform, in a drastic way, the status of Prometheus and his myth in cultural self-perception. The first Christian centuries did not witness only the

---

[2] Hesiod, *Works and Days*, 42-105 and *Theogony*, 507-616, in *Hesiod*, Text with transl. by H. G. Evelyn-White (Loeb Classical Library [henceforth LCL]: London, New York, 1920), pp. 4-9 and 116-125. On the second text, see the commentary of M.L. West, *Hesiod, Theogony* (Oxford, 1966), esp. pp. 305-308.

[3] For a thorough analysis of Prometheus, according to the main Greek texts, see U. Bianchi, "Prometheus, der titanische Trickster," in his *Selected Essays on Gnosticism, Dualism and Mysteriosophy* (Suppl. *Numen* 38; Leiden, 1978), pp. 126-150. One can still consult with great profit K. Bapp's article in W. H. Roscher's *Ausführliches Lexicon der griechischen und römischen Mythologie*, III, cols. 3032-3110.

[4] For a survey of the place of Prometheus in the history of Western thought, see H. Levin, "Prometheus," *Dictionary of the History of Ideas*, III, col. 235 ff. Levin refers to various studies which I was unable to consult, such as R. Trousson, *Le thème de Prométhée dans la littérature européenne* (2 vols., Geneve, 1964); J. Duchemin, *Prométhée, histoire du mythe, de ses origines orientales à ses incarnations modernes* (Paris, 1974); or L. Sechan, *Le mythe de Prométhée* (Paris, 1951).

[5] H. Blumenberg, *Arbeit am Mythos* (Frankfurt, 1979), now also in a good English translation, *Work on Myth* (Cambridge, Ma., 1985). Cf. my review in *Revue de Métaphysique et de Morale*, forthcoming.

radical transformation of Greek culture by an alien *Weltanschauung*, but also the last full-fledged attempt in Antiquity to revive mythological patterns of thought. At the dawn of the Christian era, Gnosticism, this "acute hellenization of Christianity," as Harnack called it, offers the most radical rejection of culture and civilisation to be found in Western history. It is to a great extent as a reaction to the gnostic challenge that Christian consciousness asserted itself and crystallized. Hence, the bearing of Gnosticism upon perceptions of Prometheus.

In *Prometheus and Lucifer*, his first published book, R.J. Zwi Werblowsky noticed the "interesting ambivalence" of Prometheus, a figure "capable of developing in two directions," close sometimes to Christ, and sometimes to Satan.[6] It is on this ambivalence and on the radically new status of Prometheus in the *interpretatio christiana* that thees pages seek to reflect.

The ambiguity from which Prometheus seems never to depart is that of a trickster. Despite recent attacks, the category of the trickster remains of considerable use for analysing mythical figures who revolt by cunning against higher deities, often to the direct or indirect benefit of humans.[7] Tricksters are by definition liminal and intermediate figures, who seem to be crossing freely the borderline between good and evil. Sometimes they even appear as belonging to the "other" power. They are daring, and they are cunning.[8] Cunning intelligence, or *mētis* , belongs to Prometheus already in Hesiod, who applied to him the epithet *agkulomētēs*, "crooked of counsel."[9] *Mētis* was a major quality in early Greek thought, as Marcel Detienne and Jean-Pierre Vernant have shown.[10] Together with mythical

---

6 R.J.Z. Werblowsky, *Lucifer and Prometheus: a Study of Milton's Satan* (London, 1952), p. 63.

7 See C. Grottanelli, "Tricksters, Scapegoats, Champions, Saviors," in *History of Religions* 23 (1984), pp. 117-139, a remarkable study which could be subtitled "Apology for the Trickster;" on Prometheus, see p. 135. On tricksters see also V. Turner, in *International Encyclopedia of the Social Sciences* 10, pp. 576-581, "Myth and Symbol."

8 See, for instance, Lévi-Strauss, *Anthropologie structurale*, ch. 11, and *Myth and Meaning* (Toronto, 1978), ch. 3; cf. Grottanelli, *art. cit.*, p. 136.

9 *Theog*. 546; *Opera* 48.

10 M. Detienne and J.-P Vernant, *Les ruses de l'intelligence: la mètis des grecs* (Paris, 1974), esp. pp. 62-66 and 84-103.

patterns of thought, however, *mētis* was almost blurred by the success of philosophy - a fact which accounts for its neglect by modern scholars. Characterised by ambivalence, *mētis* is an integral part of mythological thinking, which could not be integrated in thought patterns established on the rule *tertium non datur*.

Ambivalence characterises the Greek Prometheus, as it does any mythical hero. From Hesiod to Lucian, Prometheus is described at once as positive and negative, both *in bonam* and *in malam partem*.

The most original aspect of the *Theogony* lies in Hesiod's attempt to introduce moral order in the complex world of myths which he inherits. Hence Zeus' victory, and the justification of his punishment of Prometheus. At the other end of the Greek spectrum, in Lucian's *Dialogue between Prometheus and Zeus*, Zeus summarises the chief points of accusation against the rebellious titan in the following way. He is guilty of having brought evil on three accounts: through his cunning with the parts of sacrifice, through his responsibility for the creation of man and woman, and finally by stealing fire.[11] The revolt motif is thus not always viewed quite favourably in Greek texts, although no malice is attributed to Prometheus.

The tragedians view Prometheus' stealing of fire as his main achievement. Sophocles calls him *ho pyrophoros theos titān*, while Aeschylus, in his *Prometheus Bound*, insists on his audacity, his over-daring. He also describes Prometheus giving men "blind hopes," *typhlas elpidas*, taking away their foreknowlege in order to make human life bearable.[12]

From the fourth century B.C.E. on, as a new, pessimistic attitude towards culture becomes pervading, more clearly expressed

---

[11] Lucian, *Dialogues of the Gods*, in *Works*, VII, ed., trans. M.D. Macleod, (LCL; Cambridge, Ma., London, 1961), p. 259.

[12] Sophocles, *Oedipus at Colonus*, 55; Aeschylus, *Prometheus Bound* 148-150; see 237-238, on Prometheus' daring. Cf. E. Meron, "Une lecture socratique du Prométhée d'Eschyle ou: Prométhée, fondateur de la religion," *Revue des Etudes Anciennes* 85 (1983), pp. 199-213, who describes Prometheus as a "quasi-christic mediator." For the "blind hopes" given to mankind, see C. Segal, *Tragedy and Civilization: an Interpretation of Sophocles* (Cambridge, Ma., 1981), 241, and W.C. Greene, *Moira: Fate, Good and Evil in Greek Thought* (Cambridge, Ma., 1982²), p. 120. An analysis of the dialectical relationship between bodily and inner blindness and vision (cf. Tereisias and Oedipus) in Greek texts would be worthwhile.

condemnations of Prometheus appear. For Menander, Prometheus is justly condemned since he moulded women, "an abominable cast, hated of all the gods, methinks. Is some man bent on marrying? on marrying?"[13] Even more radically, Diogenes of Sinope describes Prometheus as the author of men's corruption. From now on, the formation of human beings is more and more attributed to Prometheus.[14] Nonnos of Panopolis (fifth century C.E.) is a late witness to the dubious heritage which Prometheus left mankind:

> Nay - Prometheus himself is the cause of man's misery - Prometheus who cares for poor mortals! Instead of fire which is the beginning of all evil he ought rather to have stolen sweet nectar, which rejoices the heart of the gods, and given that to men, that he might have scattered the sorrows of the world with your own drink.[15]

One of the most revealing discussions of Prometheus in the Greek realm is found in Lucian. This sceptical and ferocious writer of Syrian origin (second century C.E.) wrote both a mock-play called *Prometheus* and the *Dialogue* already mentioned. In this *Dialogue*, Prometheus is presented as a trickster: "You'll deceive me again," fears Zeus. Prometheus is eventually released from his punishment as a reward for his advice to Zeus not to make love to the Nereid Thetis, since the child born of this union would eventually dethrone his father.[16] The *Prometheus* begins with a dialogue between Hephaestus and Hermes, who are charged wih carrying out Zeus' sentence. Hephaestus tells Hermes:

> Yes, let's look about, Hermes: we mustn't crucify (*estaurōsthai*) him low and close to the ground for fear that man, his own handiwork, may come to his aid, or yet on the summit either, for he would be out of sight from below...[17]

---

13 Menander, *The Principal Fragments*, F.G. Allinson, ed., transl. (LCL; London, New York, 1921), p. 483.

14 See Blumenberg, *Work on Myth*, pp. 325 ff.

15 Nonnos, *Dionysiaca* 7. 58-63; W.H.D. Rouse, trans. (LCL; London, Cambridge, Ma., 1962), p. 249. Cf. 2.576.

16 See n. 11 above. The whole dialogue is short: pp. 256-261.

17 Lucian, *Works*, II, ed., trans. A.M. Harmon (LCL; London, New York, 1916), p. 242.

This text is noticeable on two accounts. First, as far as I know, Lucian is the only author - the Church Fathers included - to describe the punishment inflicted upon Prometheus as a *crucifixion* (although there does not seem to be any Christian influence on him). Secondly, Prometheus appears in this text as a mediator, a *mesitēs*, of a very special kind: he should remain crucified between heaven and earth, between gods and men, at last perfect instance of his kin the titans, the intermediary race. His crucifixion is not presented as a link between the human and the divine worlds. On the contrary, it is a perpetual reminder of the boundaries that cannot be trespassed with impunity. No picture could express more poignantly Prometheus' status as a savior himself in need of salvation, a *salvator salvandus* to use the term coined by Augustine in his anti-Manichaean polemics.[18]

Lucian's play presents in a nutshell the legacy of Prometheus for classical antiquity. In his dialogue with Hermes, Prometheus attempts to justify himself: his acts have done no wrong to the gods, while they have given so much to mankind:

> the whole world is no longer barren and unbeautiful, but adorned with cities and tilled lands and cultivated plants, the sea is sailed and the islands are inhabited, and everywhere there are altars and sacrifices, temples and festivals...[19]

Despite this plea for human culture - and for his own sake - Prometheus remains the author of "that reprehensible theft" (elsewhere, Lucian calls him the god of theft, *kleptikēs ho theos*,[20] who deserved his punishment and who owes his eventual release only to his deal with Zeus.

The ambivalence of Prometheus, his cunning with the gods and his gift to mankind, is thus particularly striking in the image of the crucified titan, half Christ, half thief. This icon, as it were, illustrates the radical difference between Christianity and the classical world.

---

[18] On the mythological conception of the *erlöster Erlöser* in gnostic contexts see C. Colpe, *Die religionsgeschichtliche Schule: Darstellung und Kritik ihres Bildes vom gnostischen Erlösermythus* (FRLANT 78; Göttingen, 1961). Colpe does not refer to Prometheus in this study.

[19] Lucian, *Works*, II, p. 257.

[20] Lucian, *Works*, VI, K. Kilburn, ed., trans. (LCL; Cambridge, Ma., London, 1959), "To one who said: 'You're a Prometheus in words'", p. 426.

Yet, this is the penultimate, not the last representation of Prometheus in Greek pagan literature. In his *Oration VI to the Uneducated Cynics*, Julian the Apostate refers to Prometheus in these terms:

> The gift of the gods sent down to mankind with the glowing flame of fire from the sun through the agency of Prometheus, along with the blessings that we owe to Hermes, is no other than the bestowal of reason and mind...[21]

What is striking in this text is not so much the total spiritualisation of the civilisatory mission of Prometheus, as the fact that he is only the gods' envoy. The revolt motif has totally disappeared and with it the ambiguity which we have seen to be a constitutive quality of Prometheus throughout Greek culture. We are left with an abstract figure, quite disconnected from any mythical context. In the fourth century, indeed, the times had changed. And even Julian, the last herald of paganism, was influenced by the abhorred Galilean faith of his youth in deeper and more subtle ways than he realised: for him, myth had become metaphor.[22] This transformation through which the dying myth reappears is directly connected with the emergence of the new faith, as we shall presently see. The *myth* of Prometheus has faded out, but the *figure* of Prometheus himself survives, however univalent. Prometheus now represents a clearly defined quality, and has lost the autonomous life which was his when the myth was still alive.

In Lucian's Prometheus, men are said to have been created in the gods' shape, a fact which has fuelled some speculation about

---

[21] Julian, *Oratio VI*, C-D; Works, II, W.C. Wright, ed., trans. (LCL; London, New York, 1913), p. 89.

[22] J. Bidez was the first to unveil the deep-reaching Christian influences on Julian, in his *La vie de l'Empereur Julien* (Paris, 1930). See also G.W. Bowersock, *Julian the Apostate* (Cambridge, Ma., 1978). On the transformation of myth into metaphor with the passage from the mythology of archaic cultures into "cultural languages" of a non-mythological type, see an important paper of two Russian semiologists, J.M. Lotman and B. Uspenskij, which I could read only in Spanish translation, "Mito, nombre, cultura," in J. M. Lotman et alii, *Semiotica de la cultura* (Madrid, 1979), pp. 111-135, esp. pp. 124-125 and 133. The authors insist that metaphors cannot occur in mythological texts proper, but only as the conclusion of the "tumultuous processes which accompany the disintegration of mythical consciousness."

possible Jewish influences.[23] Lucian, however, remains poles apart from the monotheistic conception. For him, it is rather the gods who seem to be made in the image of men and to behave like them, in highly dubious ways. The advent of Christianity implanted in the Greco-Roman world the ethical dualism inherited from Judaism. God was enthroned above, beyond any ethical ambiguity, and next to him was his Son, the Savior of mankind. The strong ethical bent in early Christian thought was often, although not always, combined with cosmological, anthropological, or even theological dualism (see already Qumrān). Among pagan thinkers, this ethical earnestness was widely recognised as one of the more respectable sides of a religion seen as despicable on various other accounts.[24] It entailed a radi-cal suppression of those elements of playfulness and ambiguity ubiquitous in Greek mythology. Hence, in Christian *Weltanschauung*, the polarity between Satan and Christ as the perfect epitome of the fight between evil and good in its cosmic dimension. In Origen's words, for instance,

> Every man who has chosen evil and to live an evil life so that he does everything contrary to virtue is a Satan, that is, an adversary of the Son of God, who is righteousness, truth, and wisdom.[25]

This duality represents a radical departure from mythological thinking.[26] It creates, as it were, a *split* between the two sides of the titan who had both revolted against divine order and offered his salvific help to mankind. Moreover, early Christian soteriology was quite alien to the major trends of Greek thought. Prometheus' gift permitted mankind to build and rule the world; Jesus' sacrifice

---

23 Blumenberg, *op. cit.* p. 347.

24 See among many other instances, towards the end of the third century, the beginning of Alexander of Lycopolis, *Critique of the Doctrines of Manichaeus*, trans. P. W. van der Horst and J. Mansfeld (Leiden, 1974).

25 Origen, *Contra Celsum* VI.44, trans. H. Chadwick (Cambridge, Ma., 1980^3), p. 361.

26 The new thinking also offered an epistemology fundamentally different from that propounded by mythology: "Cet état de choses aurait pu durer mille ans; il s'est modifié parce que le champ du savoir a vu sa carte bouleversée par la formation de nouvelles puissances d'affirmation qui concurrençaient le mythe et, à la différence du mythe, posaient expressément l'alternative du vrai et du faux." P. Veyne, *Les Grecs ont-ils cru à leurs mythes*? (Paris, 1984), p. 35 and n. 44.

offered men salvation *from* "the ruler of this world." Prometheus' ambiguity could often express Greek discontent with civilisation. For the Christians, things were radically different: civilisation, that is to say a pagan construct, was perceived as negative, at least in ethical and soteriological terms - the only terms which mattered.

The drastic paradigmatic change did not wipe out all traces of mythology from the new religion. Around 170 C.E., the pagan thinker Celsus notes that Christian views of the devil are in fact transformations of various Greek myths.[27] Celsus explicitly refers here to the gigantomachy of old, the fight of titans and giants who had revolted against the gods. The persistent awareness of a deep similarity between the two systems, stemming from a common origin, was not exclusive to pagan writers. Some of the Church Fathers also refer to genetic links between Christian truth and Greek philosophy or mythology. For them, of course, divine revelation had also chronological primacy, and those elements of truth found in the pagan systems had been stolen. Thus Tertullian:

> Now whence, I ask you, do the philosophers and poets find things so similar? Whence, indeed, unless it be from our mysteries?[28]

More precisely, Clement of Alexandria elaborates his famous theory of the theft:

> Philosophy... came to us stolen or given by a thief. Some power, some angel learned a bit of truth, without staying himself faithful to truth, and revealed this knowledge to men, taught them the fruit of his theft.[29]

Structurally, this story is quite similar to the myth of Prometheus. The implicit reference, however, is not to Prometheus but to the Watchers and their fall, that is to say to the Jewish version of the ancient Near Eastern culture hero myth.[30] According to this myth,

---

27 *Ibid.*, IV. 42 ff. (pp. 218 ff. Chadwick). See J. Pépin, *Mythe et allégorie: les origines grecques et les contestations judéo-chrétiennes* (Paris, 1976²), pp. 448-452; cf. *Ibid.*, pp. 200-201 on Plotinus' interpretation of the myth.

28 Tertullian, *Apologeticus* 47.14; T.R. Glover, transl. (LCL; Cambridge, Ma., London, 1977⁴), p. 211.

29 Clement, *Strom*, I.17.81.4, in O. Stählin, ed., *Clemens Alexandrinus, Werke*, II (GCS 15; Leipzig, 1906), 53. Cf. *Strom*. V. 89-41, where Clement dwells on the Greek borrowings from Scripture.

30 See now R. Bauckham, "The Fall of the Angels as the Source of Philosophy

transmitted by Henochic literature and the *Book of Jubilees*, the secrets of civilisation were brought from heaven by the angels who revolted against God under their leaders Shemḥazzai and Assa'el. In the Jewish pseudepigrapha a clear distinction is made betwen true wisdom received by Enoch and pagan culture deriving from the fallen angels. The trends of these writings represented a manifest process of re-mythologisation inside Judaism. Paradoxically, it developed in Palestine among Hassidim and Essenes, i.e., groups who stood for the purity of Jewish culture against hellenistic influences. The myth of the fallen angels and the myth of Prometheus both represent different but parallel developments from the original Near Eastern mythical pattern.[31]

The mythical conception of the origins of culture developed in Jewish pseudepigraphic literature had a very significant *Fortleben* in early Christianity, where it formed the basis of esoteric teaching, or *doctrina arcani* as it was later called.[32] It is therefore not surprising to find it also at the root of gnostic mythology, a baroque development of these esoteric traditions. Since the Nag Hammadi discovery, moreover, research has been focusing upon remythologising trends in Second Commonwealth Judaism as the direct source of some of the core gnostic myths.[33] The leader of the fallen angels, the *Nephilim*, for instance, was transformed through a major mutation into the figure of the evil demiurge.[34] On the other hand, despite

in Hermias and Clement of Alexandria," *Vigiliae Christianae* 39 (1985), pp. 313-330.

31 On the influence of West Asian myths on the formation of Greek mythology, see for instance G.S. Kirk, *The Nature of Greek Myths* (Harmondsworth, 1974), ch. 11.

32 See my "*Paradosis*: doctrines ésotériques dans le christianisme des premiers siècles," in P. Geoltrain *et al.*, *Littérature Apocryphes* (Turnhout: Brepols), forthcoming.

33 For a bibliography, see my *Another Seed: Studies in Gnostic Mythology* (Nag Hammadi Studies 24; Leiden, 1984), p. 10, n. 40.

34 See for instance M. Scopello, "Le mythe de la 'chute' des anges dans l'*Apocryphon de Jean* (II.I) de Nag Hammadi," *Revue des Sciences Religieuses* 54 (1980), pp. 220-230, and B. Barc, ed., transl., *L'Hypostase des archontes: traité gnostique sur l'origine de l'homme, du monde et des archontes* (Bibl. Copte de Nag Hammadi, Textes 4; Quebec, Louvain, 1980), esp. pp. 32 ff. See also F.T. Fallon, *The Enthronement of Sabaoth: Jewish Elements in Gnostic Creation Myths* (Nag Hammadi Studies, 10, Leiden, 1978), pp. 28-33.

some random speculation and a few parallels, common elements between gnostic and Greek myths seem to remain very scarce. A better insight, perhaps, on similarities and dissimilarities between both mythologies might be gained by comparing structures.

Expulsed from philosophy, *mētis* returned to the fore with Gnosis, the last full-blown attempt in the ancient world to revive mythical patterns of thought. Karl Kérényi has referred to the gnostic *Anthropos*, the divine Primal Man of gnostic myth, as the only figure comparable in many ways to Prometheus (although he also alluded in the same sentence to "important differences" between the two figures).[35] What mainly seems to have struck Kérényi in this context is the strong bond with mankind of a divine trickster. In gnostic context, however, it is not primarily the *Anthropos*, but rather the demiurge, and to a certain extent the Savior, who partake in some of the trickster's qualities.

A recent study devoted to the gnostic demiurge insists on his ability to cross boundaries and on his "lack of determination" as basic features qualifying him as a particular instance of a trickster.[36] Yet the gnostic demiurge, whether he is called Yaldabaoth (i.e., creator of chaos), Saklas (the fool) or Samael (the blind one), does in no way partake in the ambivalence inherent to the trickster. He does not have any redeeming features and can only be considered as an anti-god, either threatening and dangerous or foolish and ridiculous. Actually, only a few features are common to Prometheus and Samael: both appear in myths of creation, origin of evil, and salvation. Like Prometheus, Saklas is a bringer of civilisation, but this civilisation is regarded as wholly evil. Similarly, fire is always described in strongly negative terms in gnostic texts, where work plays no role whatsoever.[37] Prometheus brought blind hopes; Samael's very name reflects his innate blindness. The son of Iapetus had saved his son, Deucalion, from the flood by advising him to

---

35 K. Kérényi, in P. Radin, *The Trickster: A Study in American Indian Mythology* (New York, 1956), pp. 180-181; cf. C. Kérényi, *Prometheus: Archetypal Image of Human Existence* (Bollingen Series 65.1; New York, 1963), pp. 3, 53-55.

36 I.S. Gilhus, "The Gnostic Demiurge - An Agnostic Trickster," *Religion* 14 (1984), pp. 301-311.

37 See my remarks in "Ascèse et Gnose: aux origines de la spiritualité monastique," *Revue Thomiste* 81 (1981), pp. 557-573.

build an arch; in the same manner, the demiurge saves Noah, his faithful servant.[38] Both Prometheus and Samael fight against the *neos theos*, the upstart who rules the world, in order to come to man's help; *boēthos*, helper, is an important epithet in some of the gnostic texts. Rather similarly to the bringer of fire, the gnostic savior is called the *phōstēr*, the illuminator. Finally even more than Prometheus, the gnostic savior is the classical instance of the *erlöster Erlöser*.[39]

In other words, although Samael and Christ can each boast of some Promethean traits, neither of them seems to fully integrate the fundamental quality thought which Prometheus was what he was. In order to help men, Prometheus used cunning against Zeus, the higher god. But it is against men that Samael's cunning is oriented, while Christ's *mētis* is oriented towards the demiurge, a false god, essentially lower than himself. Thus the functions which were filled in the Greek myth by Prometheus seem to be divided in Gnosticism between the two major protagonists. Ambiguity was an essential feature of Prometheus in the Greek myth. The change of paradigms initiated by the emergence of Christianity and of Gnosticism, through the splitting of mythical functions and the establishment of a system in which good and evil are radical polarities, has suppressed this ambiguity.

From the meeting of early Christianity and the classical world a two-tiered culture emerged. The Greek legacy, even through a radical *interpretatio christiana*, could not hope for more than an honourable second place as a culture of reference. The first rank was reserved to Christian mysteries, *historia sacra*, theology. Moreover, the Greek legacy of early Christianity was not equally composed of all fields of Greek culture. Philosophy was ranking high in the eyes of the Church Fathers, or at least of some of the more intellectually minded among them, while they could find no positive value whatsoever in pagan religion. Mythology hung somewhere in-between, closer to religion than to philosophy. It was usually referred to as

---

[38] For instance in the *Apocalypse of Adam*, 69-72, where Noah is explicitly identified with Deucalion. English text in J. Robinson, ed., *The Nag Hammadi Library*^{2} (New York, 1977), p. 258.

[39] See n. 18 *supra*.

exemplifying the errors and the nonsense of paganism. The theologians, who succeeded rather fast in integrating major chapters of Greek philosophy into Christian thought, proved much more recalcitrant with mythology.

The radical rejection of Zeus permitted at least a partial rehabilitation of Prometheus. For Tertullian, for instance, God the creator is the true Prometheus: *verus Prometheus Deus omnipotens*.[40] Lactantius offers a criticism of the myth of Prometheus in his *Divine Institutions*.[41] Both Origen and Augustine know the myth and refer to it, although in a rather perfunctory way. As expected, the Church Fathers follow the trend initiated among pagan writers: for them Prometheus was not so much the creator of man as the creator of the world.

It is an intriguing fact that Prometheus does not appear to have been described as a prototype of Christ before Shelley, whose "Prometheus Unbound" is a paean to human freedom, in which Christ revolts against Jehovah's tyranny. Giordano Bruno, on his side, was the first thinker to identify Prometheus and man, both defined for him by their *felix culpa*.[42] Even though this final *Entmythologisierung* of Prometheus was enacted only with the Renaissance, it had been prepared by the establishment of Christian dogma in the first centuries. When Augustine coined the expression *felix culpa*, he endowed Adam with the core Promethean quality, that of the trickster. Just as human culture could not have been established without the theft of fire, so only the eating of the apple rendered human salvation possible.

---

[40] Tertullian, *Adversus Marcionem* I.1; E. Evans, ed., trans. (Oxford, 1972), pp. 4-5. The phrase comes immediately after the mention of the Caucasus. See also *Apologeticus* XVIII.2 (LCL; 88-89): "... He alone is God, who made the universe, who fashioned man of mud - for He is the true Prometheus."

[41] See especially Lactantius, *Divine Institutions* II.11, *Patrologia Latina* 6, cols. 311-316, esp. 313 B: "Apparet ergo falsum esse quod de opificio Promethei narrant."

[42] Giordano Bruno, *Cabala del cavallo Pegaseo I*; *Opere italiane*, ed. P. de Lagarde (Gottingen, 1888), p. 582, cited by Blumenberg, *op. cit.*, p. 361, n. 12. On Prometheus and Christ see P. de St. Victor,*Les deux masques*, I (Paris, 1880), pp. 335-337.

According to the Augustinian pattern it is man, not a god, who is described as a basically ambiguous figure. In Christianity, and hence in western culture, it is of men, not of gods, that myths are told. With the progressive loosening of Christian grip over thought, Prometheus will regain importance. The fascinating modern history of Prometheus cannot be dealt with here. It goes from Goethe's "Prometheus," which Nietzsche called an "Hymnus der Unfrömmigkeit"[43] to the neo-gnostic Ernst Bloch, for whom Prometheus is "the god who expressed disbelief in God."[44] A figure of positive antinomianism, Prometheus remains on moral terms a one-sided metaphor rather than a mythical trickster. The post-Christian frame of cultural reference retains the dualistic ethical pattern of Christianity. As a metaphor, the former titan now stands for the civilisatory and creative urge of *man*. He is seen in opposition either to Christ, when civilisation is perceived as negative or evil, or to Satan, when this urge is deemed to be basically good and coming as a surrogate for Christian salvation. In any case, he is seen in reference and in opposition to other figures. Prometheus as a metaphoric hero has lost both the autonomy and the ambiguity inherent to the Greek myth. He is now riveted to a single sense. He is not a trickster anymore.

Prometheus' *Fortleben* in the two-tiered cultural tradition of the West expresses the same change of status that befell other important Greek myths. The cultural chasm which imposed new paradigms of civilisation and self-understanding was bound to transform in radical fashion a myth on the origins of civilisation.[45] The question remains,

---

43 Nietzsche, *Die Geburt der Tragödie*, 9, in his *Sämtliche Werke*, I (Munich-Berlin, 1980), pp. 64-71. In this paragraph, Nietzsche opposes the myth of Prometheus, as a major document of Arian (and male) mythology to the myth of the fall (of Adam), as representing the Semitic (and female) mind. He sees the "titanische Drang" as the common ground between the Promethean and the Dionysiac.

44 Reference to *Das Prinzip Hoffnung*, III, pp. 1428, 1430-32 is made by J. Bentley, "Prometheus versus Christ in the Christian-Marxist Dialogue," *Journal of Theological Studies* N.S. 29 (1978), pp. 483-494, esp. pp. 486-487. On p. 486, Bloch is referred to as claiming that "For some Gnostics (in what Bloch regards a crazy reversal of the truth) Prometheus came to signify the devil." I am unaware of such gnostic traditions.

45 Among the most important new parameters of civilization is the early Christian discovery of the self. See my "*Caro salutis cardo*: Shaping the Person in Early Christian Thought," forthcoming. On the direct bearing of this new perception on

of course, whether through a subtle dialectical process the new metaphoric figure did not, on its turn, impose its mark on Western culture. In any case, the remembrance of myths past does not quite revive them. Like the hero for Victor Hugo, Prometheus can now only be "un mythe à face humaine."

myth, see H. Jonas, "Myth and Mysticism: A Study of Objectification and Interiorization in Religious Thought," *Journal of Religion* 49 (1969), pp. 315-327.

DER EINZELNE STERN

M. Heerma van Voss, Amsterdam

Spruch 172 im ägyptischen Totenbuch (*Tb* 172) weicht in mehreren Hinsichten von den anderen Texten in dem so bezeichneten Korpus ab. Er enthält zum Beispiel einen Exkurs, der seinem regen Interesse fur astronomische, bzw. kosmologische Auseinandersetzungen[1] Mit dem fange ich diesen Aufsatz an. In der vierten Strophe[2] wird u.a. der Bauch des (verstorbenen) Menschen dem Himmel gleichgestellt und — mit einem hübschen Bild — sein Nabel dem ''einzelnen Stern.''[3] Der Passus, ein Gespräch, läutet:

(Ansprache an den Toten)
''Dein Bauch ist der ruhige[a] Himmel,
dein Nabel ist der einzelne Stern.
Er[b] öffnet (das Gewölk)[c],
nachdem er das Licht[d] in der Finsternis angekündigt hat.
Seine Opfer sind die Henna(?)-Pflanzen[e],
er verehrt die Majestät des Thot[f].''
(Antwort des Toten)
''Seine Schönheit[g] ist geliebt in meinem Grab,

[1] entspricht. Ihre Anwesenheit soll man wohl im Zusammenhang mit der Erwähnung in Zeile 40 des ''Grössten der Schauenden'' erklären. War dieser Hohepriester von Heliopolis doch auch Astronom.- Andere Stellen finden sich in den Zeilen 36/8 und 42/3.

[2] *Papyrus Nebseni*, 32/3, Z. 25/7 = Wallis Budge, *The Book of the Dead*. The Chapters of Coming Forth by Day. The Egyptian Text in Hieroglyphic Edited from Numerous Papyri, London, 1898, 447, 15-448, 4 (kollationiert mit Naville, *Das aegyptische Totenbuch* der XVIII. bis XX. Dynastie, I, Berlin, 1886). Ohne Variante.

[3] Die Lesung der verderbten Stelle ist gesichert, da die *Zaubersprüche fur Mutter und Kind* (Ed. Erman, Berlin, 1901) auch hier genau dieselbe Identifikation wie *Tb* 172 aufweisen: 4, 6-7.

mein Gott[h] wies mir den reinen Platz[i] zu."
(Schlussansprache)
"Das (?) was du liebst ist dort[j]."

[a]Vgl. *Bauer*, 244.-[b] Der Stern.-[c] So *Coffin Texts* (*CT*) V 140 b.-[d] Der Sonne.-[e] Altenmüller, *Mitteil. DAIK* 23 (1968), 7-8.-[f] Der Mond; vgl. *Pyr. Neith* 659/60.-[g] *Edfu* VI, 130: "Der einzelne Stern, bei dessen Schönheit man sehen kann." "Schönheit" bezeichnet oft auch das junge Leben -[h] Wohl der Stern.-[i] Das Grab.-[j] Im Grab.

Meinung und Zweck der Unterredung sind klar. Es gilt die endgültige Auferstehung des Verstorbenen, die vom Morgenstern vorbereitet wird. Dieser Gott, Vertreiber von Nacht und Bewölkung, kündigt ja den Aufgang der Sonne an und damit das neue Leben, auch des (mumifizierten) Toten. Für ihn ist deshalb die Anwesenheit des Sterns im Grab sehr wichtig und die ist wegen der Identifikation mit dem Nabel gesichert.

Dem "einzelnen Stern" begegnet man nicht nur im Totenbuch, sondern auch in den Sargtexten[4] und schon in den Pyramidentexten[5]. *Pyr.* 877 c wird dem Verstorbenen gesagt: *Pyr.* 877 c wird dem Verstorbenen gesagt:

"Du bist dieser einzelne Stern, der hervorgeht
auf der östlichen Seite des Himmels."
Wiederum ist also der Morgenstern gemeint.[6]

Nach den Pyr. wird unser Gott noch wiederholt erwähnt.[7] Ein Angriffspunkt zur Identifikation wie in *Pyr.* 877 und *Tb* 172 findet sich nur noch einmal, und zwar im schon zitierten (Anm. g) Passus aus Edfu. Dort wird er genannt:

"Der im Westen des Himmels am Abend erscheint."

Wie erklärt man dass der Name im Alten (Pyr.) und Neuen (Tb) Reich den Morgenstern und in der Spätzeit (Edfu) den Abendstern

---

[4] *CT* I 182 a; oben. Anm. c. Vgl. I 290 b und VI 350 q.

[5] *Pyr.* 251 b, 877 c, 1048 b; *Neith* 741, 779; oben, Anm. f; *Pepi II*, 1305.

[6] Faulkner, *Journ. NES* 25 (1966), 160/1, lehnt das ab, aber mit Unrecht; mehrere Bezeichnungen einer und derselben Gottheit sind in Ägypten üblich. So wird der Morgenstern in den *Pyr.* ebenfalls "morgendlicher Gott" (*Wörterb.* V, 423, 10/3), "morgendlicher Stern" (871 b), vielleicht auch "Morgendlicher" (Anthes, *Zeitschr. ÄS* 110, 1983, 9-12) genannt.

[7] Auch: *TT* 57, *Ritual der Einbalsam.* und *Dendera*; *Wörterb.* I, 279, 4; IV, 82, 10. Vgl. weiter Jacq, *Le voyage dans l'autre monde selon l'Egypte ancienne*, Monaco, 1986, 168, mit Anm.

bezeichnet? Da die Beobachtung dass es sich bei den beiden um ein und dasselbe Gestirn handelt den Ägyptern unbekannt war, muss es zur neuen Gleichstellung einen anderen Grund gegeben haben. Ich denke mir den Hergang wie folgt. Im Laufe ihrer immer wachsenden Klassifikation der Götterwelt stiessen die Theologen auf eine Diskrepanz. Zur Benennung des einzigen Sterns am Morgenhimmel standen drei oder vier spezifische Möglichkeiten zur Verfügung (s. Anm. 6). Für den Abendstern fehlte jedoch ein Gegenstück; Osten und Morgen waren ursprünglich interessanter als Westen und Abend. Dieses Verhältnis hat dann die Spezialisten zu einem sehr merkwürdigen Verfahren veranlasst. Sie haben Zeit und Ort diametral geändert und einen Gott in einen für sie ganz verschiedenen verwandelt.

Gerne lege ich dieses treffende Beispiel einer Transformation in der Religionsgeschichte meinem Freund Zwi Werblowsky und anderen Interessierten vor.

this section we show that the presence of high aspect ratio particles can explain both the observed frequency and salinity dependence and the high values of dielectric constants.

It is well-known that the low-frequency dielectric constant of a material made up of a layer of insulating material covered with a layer of conducting material can be extremely large when the concentration of the insulating region becomes small. This is known as the Maxwell-Wagner effect.[16,21] In this case, the material as a whole has a zero d.c. conductivity - because the layer of insulating material blocks the current path. We show that under certain circumstances $Re\epsilon^*$ can be enormously large even when the sample remains conducting. This model is more appropriate to sedimentary rocks which remain conducting to very low values of porosity. We show that the controlling factor in determining the magnitude of $Re\epsilon^*$ is the relative magnitude of the particle "aspect ratio" of the inclusion compared to the concentration of the inclusions. In order to compare our theoretical calculations with experimental values for $Re\epsilon^*$, more reliable experimental values are required together with information on particle aspect ratios. The latter information may be obtained from electron microscopy and other techniques, or through use of carefully controlled techniques of artificial sample preparation.

Consider a rock with a few platey grains distributed in it, all oriented in a given direction as shown in Fig. 2.

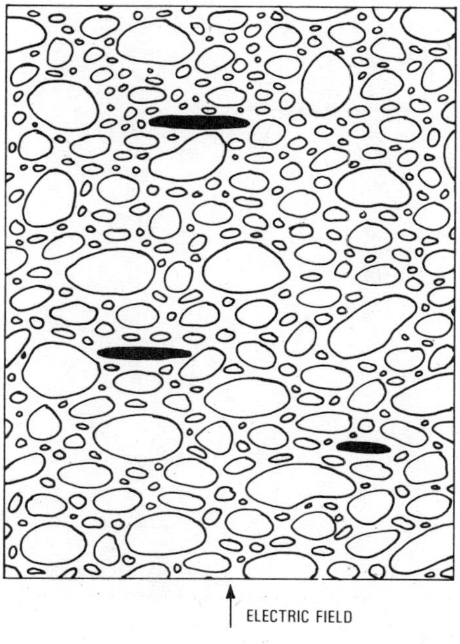

Fig. 2 - A Schematic of Rock With Platey Grains

The dielectric constant ϵ^* of a rock that contains concentration η of these plate-like particles, each of depolarization ratio L_S is given, via the self-consistent model (generalization of (11) as

$$(1-\eta)\frac{\epsilon_R^*-\epsilon^*}{L_s\epsilon_R^*+(1-L_s)\epsilon^*}+\eta\frac{\epsilon_m^*-\epsilon^*}{L_s\epsilon_m^*+(1-L_s)\epsilon^*}=0 \tag{21}$$

Here ϵ_R^* denotes the dielectric constant of the rock if there were no plate-like objects present ($\eta = 0$). Solving (21) for ϵ^* in the low frequency limit, we find for $L_S = 1 - \delta$ ($\delta = \pi\, a/2b$, a being the minor and b the major axes),

$$\sigma(0) = \lim_{\omega \to 0} \omega\epsilon_o \mathrm{Im}\,\epsilon^* = \frac{\delta - \eta}{\delta}\,\sigma_R(0) \tag{22}$$

$$\epsilon_s = \lim_{\omega \to 0} \mathrm{Re}\,\epsilon^* = \frac{\epsilon_m}{\delta - \eta} \tag{23}$$

Thus, if $\delta - \eta$ small and positive, we find $\sigma(0)$ is not zero and ϵ_s diverges. For example, if $\delta \sim 10^{-3}$, $\eta \sim 10^{-4}$, $\sigma(0)$ and $\epsilon_S \sim 10^4$, for $\epsilon_m = 10$.

In Fig. 3 we show ϵ [obtained from equation (21)] versus frequency for two values of water salinity. The relaxation frequency increases with salinity, which explains the salinity dependence of the dielectric constant observed in the MHz range. For example, if the measurements were made at 10 MHz, the dielectric would go up from 51 to 780 as the conductivity was increased from 1 mho/m to 10 mho/m.

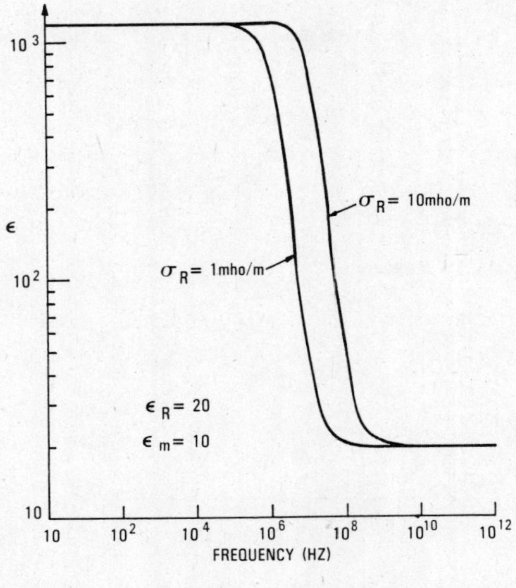

Fig. 3 - The Dielectric Constant of a Rock with Platey Grains

In actual rocks there will be a distribution of aspect ratios leading to a distribution of relaxation frequencies and a much smoother ϵ vs frequency response. An example is shown in reference 3.

The above calculation can be further improved by building up the concentration in infinitesimal steps as in the self-similar model. We incorporate, in this manner, a concentration η of plate-like grains distributed *isotropically* in a conducting rock. It can be shown that when the probability distribution is sharply peaked around $L_s = 1 - \delta$, for $\eta << 1$, $\delta << 1$,

$$\sigma(0) = \sigma_R e^{-\eta/3\delta} \tag{24}$$

$$\epsilon_S = \frac{\epsilon_m}{\delta}(1-e^{-\eta/3\delta}) \tag{25}$$

There are two cases that are of particular interest:

Case (a) $\delta < \eta$, and, Case (b) $\delta > \eta$.

For case (a) when $\delta \rightarrow 0$, ϵ_s diverges, but since $\delta < \eta$, $\sigma(0) \rightarrow 0$. This is the well-known Maxwell-Wagner effect described above. However, for case (b) $\delta > \eta$, $\mathrm{Re}\,\epsilon^*$ can be very large while the system remains conducting. When $\delta \rightarrow 0$ and $\eta \rightarrow 0$, ϵ_s diverges as long as η/δ^s remains finite and $0 < s < 2$. For $0 < s < 1$, the divergence in ϵ_s is concomittant with a conductivity threshold (Maxwell-Wagner), but for $1 < s < 2$, we obtain the new result, completely overlooked before, i.e. a divergent ϵ_s with a non-zero $\sigma(0)$.

There are geometrical shapes, other than thin plates, that can give rise to extremely high values of ϵ_s. These are discussed in reference 3. For example, for a periodic structure of conducting spheres embedded in an insulating host, ϵ_s diverges as the spheres begin to touch each other. Here, again, thin insulating regions are trapped between conducting regions. The above calculation can be given a simple physical explanation: The thin plates, at low enough frequency, can be considered to be capacitors hung parallel to the rest of the rock, and hence give a large over all capacitance, i.e. a large dielectric constant. The R-C time constant depends on the salinity, which explains Fig. 3.

We can give a simple thought experiment to show how these capacitors are charged up. When external charges are brought into the system, Maxwell's equation gives the charge density as

$$\rho_{ex} = \nabla\cdot(\epsilon \mathbf{E}) = \frac{\epsilon}{\sigma}\nabla\cdot(\sigma \mathbf{E}) + \sigma \mathbf{E}\cdot\nabla\left\{\frac{\epsilon}{\sigma}\right\}. \tag{26}$$

The first term in the right side of (26) can be replaced by $-\partial\rho_{ex}/\partial t$, using the continuity equation,

$$\nabla\cdot \mathbf{J} + \partial\rho_{ex}/\partial t = 0 \ . \tag{27}$$

Thus, the first term in (26) vanishes in the steady state. This shows a charging up effect when there is a discontinuity of ϵ/σ at a direction parallel to $\mathbf{E}$. This is maximized for thin plates perpendicular to an external field.

Since one cannot unambiguously distinguish between conduction current and displacement current (see Purcell[22]) it is preferable to have another point of view. Another way of looking at this problem is as follows: At low frequencies, the in-phase part of the total current $\mathbf{J}^{*} = (\sigma + i\omega\epsilon / 4\pi)\mathbf{E}$ domonate. Note that Maxwell's equation for ∇xB gives $\nabla\cdot(\nabla \times B) = 0$, i.e. the continuity equation for the total current $\nabla\cdot J^{*} = 0$. The scattering by an obstacle reduces the in-phase current (reducing the conductivity of the system), but gives a small out of phase component that enormously enhances $\mathrm{Re}\epsilon^{*}$ of the mixture.

It is easy to show, following Hori,[14] that the t-matrix for a thin plate-like object is given by

$$t = \epsilon_R^{*} \frac{\epsilon_m^{*} - \epsilon_R^{*}}{L\epsilon_m^{*} + (1-L)\epsilon_R^{*}} = \epsilon_R^{*}(4\pi\alpha^{*}) \tag{28}$$

where α^{*} is the polarizability of an ellipsoid subjected to an uniform field. In ATA, for example, we have,[14] when $\eta|\alpha^{*}| << 1$

$$\epsilon^{*} = \epsilon_R^{*} + \eta t = \epsilon_R^{*}[1 + 4\pi\eta\alpha^{*}] \tag{29}$$

At low frequency, $\omega \rightarrow 0$, Eq. (28)-(29) give

$$\epsilon_S = \epsilon_R(1 - \eta/\delta) + \eta\epsilon_R/\delta^2 \tag{30}$$

The in-phase term of α^{*} gives the blocking effect which reduces ϵ_R to $\epsilon_R(1-\eta/\delta)$, but the out of phase term gives $(\eta/\delta^2)\epsilon_m$ which increases enormously as $\delta \rightarrow 0$. The in-phase term of α^{*} describes the effect that a highly polarizable, i.e. conducting material has been replaced by an insulating material (plates). But the imaginary part of α^{*} when multiplied by the large $[4\pi\sigma_R/i\omega]$ term gives a large positive contribution.

Far Infra-red (FIR) Absorption by Metal Particles[23]

The FIR absorption by small metal particles ($\sim 1\ \mu$m) distributed in an insulating host is found to be much greater than that predicted for spheres. For larger particles, the eddy-current loss terms dominate the absorption. However, the eddy term is proportional to the particle size. Experimentally, it is found that the absorption is particle size independent.[24]

A picture of these ultrafine particles shows that they stick together to form needle-like structures. The electric dipole absorption by needle- like structures can explain the large absorption observed experimentally. The ω^2-frequency dependence of absorption for finite length needles is in agreement with the observed data.

The metal excludes the electric field, but the continuity of the tangential component of the electric field makes it possible for E-field to penetrate a needle parallel to it. In other words, the depolarization effects are minimum for fields parallel to the axis of needles.

Fourth Sound in ^{4}He and Biot Slow Wave [4]

The equivalence of the conduction problem and the sound propagation was known to Rayleigh[25] and Maxwell[16,25] in the last century. In a paper[25] on the conductivity of a periodic assembly of conducting spheres of a given conductivity packed in a conducting host of a different conductivity, Rayleigh mentioned this equivalence. (This semenal paper of Rayleigh[25] remains, to date, the basis of going beyond the dilute limit by taking the proximity effects in account.)

A class of the problems which are equivalent to each other have been listed byBatchelor.[26] All these problems entail solving the Laplace's equation. These problems are scale invariant, i.e. if the entire system is dialated or shrunk uniformly, the effective dielectric constant, etc. do not change. The permeability of a visicid fluid, on the other hand, depends on the actual size of the pores, and hence do not belong to the same class. However, when a sound wave is launched at a sufficiently high frequency such that the viscous skin depth is extremely small, and almost all of the fluid may be treated as an ideal fluid, the equivalence between dielectric properties and the sound velocity can be exploited. The so-called Biot slow wave,[7] at a sufficiently high frequency, can be treated in this manner. In this mode the solid frame and the fluid move out of phase with respect to each other. The problem simplifies enormously when the coupling between the solid and fluid components are minimal. This happens when there is a large mismatch of the acoustic impedance of solid and fluid parts. When the matrix is completely rigid in one extreme, or completely unconsolidated in the other, there is little coupling between solid and liquid motions. In the weak coupling case, the motion of fluid has one to one correspondence to the flow of electric current past insulating grains and the velocity of the Biot slow wave is given by

$$v = v_F/n \qquad (31)$$

Here v_F is the velocity of sound in the free fluid and n is a refractive index which is related to the ratio conductivity of the brine saturated rock $\sigma(0)$ and that of the brine $\sigma_w(0)$(exact),

$$n^2 = \phi\sigma_w(0)/\sigma(0) \qquad (32)$$

Similarly, the velocity of the fourth sound in ^{4}He saturated porous superleak below T_λ is given by (31). In this case the superfluid component has no viscosity, and the normal component is locked on to the substrate. In the fourth sound mode, the superfluid motion around the solid obstacle is exactly similar to the current flow skirting around the obstacle. Combining (1) and (30) gives

$$n^2 = \phi^{1-m} \qquad (33)$$

Eq. (31) with m given by (20) agrees well with the experiments on fourth sound. More experiments, where conductivity, Biot slow wave/fourth sound are simultaneously measured, are needed.

It is a pleasure to thank my colleagues at Schlumberger-Doll Research, with whose collaboration some of the above works were done.

References

1. P. N. Sen, C. Scala and M. H. Cohen, Geophysics 46, 781 (1981).
2. P. N. Sen, Soc. Petrol. Eng., Talk No. 9379 (Fall Meeting, 1980).
3. P. N. Sen, Geophysics (to appear in Dec. 1981 issue).
4. D. L. Johnson and P. N. Sen (to appear in Phys. Rev. B).
5. J. H. Scott, R. D. Carroll and D. R. Cunningham, J. Geo. Res. 72, 5101, (1967).
6. J. Ph. Poley., J. J. Nooteboom and P. J. DeWaal, Log Analyst, 8 (May, 1978).
7. D. L. Johnson, Appl. Phys. Lett., 37, 1065 (1980).
8. G. Schwarz, J. Phys. Chem., 66, 2636 (1962).
9. P. N. Sen, unpublished.
10. H. P. Schwan, N.Y. Acad. of Sci., 303 (1977).
11. J. Ziman, *Models of Disorder*, Cambridge U. Press (N.Y.), 1979.
12. J. A. Stratton, *Electromagnetic Theory*: McGraw Hill (N.Y.) 1941.
13. E. Schlomann, J. Appl. Phys. 33, 2825 (1962).
14. M. Hori, J. Math. Phys. 18, 487 (1977) and references therein.
15. P. P. Ewald, Ann. der Physik, 49, 1 (1916); C. W. Oseen, Ibid 48, 1 (1915).
16. J. C. Maxwell, A Treatise on Electricity and Magnetism (1873), Dover Edition (1954) N.Y.
17. H. C. Van de Hulst, Light Scattering by Small Particles, Wiley, N.Y. (1957).
18. A. K. Veinberg, Soviet Phys. Doklady 11, 593 (1967).
19. K. Mendelson and M. H. Cohen (unpublished).
20. D. A. G. Bruggeman, Ann. Phy. Lpz. 24, 636 (1935).
21. C. Kittel, Introduction to Solid State Physics, 5th Ed., John Wiley, N.Y. (1976), p. 430.
22. E. M. Purcell, Electricity and Magnetism, McGraw Hill, N.Y. (1963).
23. P. N. Sen and D. B. Tanner: Unpublished.
24. D. B. Tanner: Private communication; N. E. Russel, J. C. Garland and D. B. Tanner, Phys. Rev. B 23, 632 (1981).
25. Lord J. W. S. Rayleigh, Phil. Mag. 34, 481 (1892).
26. G. K. Batchelor, Ann. Rev. Fluid Mech. 6, 227 (1974).

EFFECTIVE DIELECTRIC FUNCTION OF COMPOSITE MEDIA

Ping Sheng

Theoretical Sciences Group
Corporate Research Science Laboratories
Exxon Research and Engineering Co.
P. O. Box 45
Linden, N.J. 07036

Abstract

This article reviews the relationship between the microstructure of a composite, i.e. geometric shapes as well as topological arrangements of the different components, and two unique characteristics of metal-insulation composites -- the percolation threshold and the optical dielectric anomaly. It is demonstrated that the effective medium approach to the calculation of effective dielectric constant $\bar{\varepsilon}$ can yield realistic results provided that the microstructural information is properly taken into account.

It is well known that the electromagnetic response of a single-component, homogeneous system can be completely characterized by a complex dielectric function[1] $\varepsilon(\omega) = \varepsilon_R(\omega) + i(4\pi\,\sigma(\omega)/\omega)$, where ε_R is the dielectric constant, σ is the conductivity, and ω is the angular frequency of the electromagnetic wave. In the case of a random inhomogeneous composite, however, the task of characterizing the electromagnetic response is generally much more involved due to the random scatterings of the probing wave by the inhomogeneities. Yet in the limit of $\lambda >> \xi$, where λ is the wavelength and ξ the typical scale of inhomogeneities, a great conceptual simplification occurs because the waves cannot resolve the individual scattering centers. Therefore, the medium would appear uniform, characterized by an effective dielectric function $\bar{\varepsilon}(\omega)$.

In the literature there are two prevalent approaches for the calculation of the effective dielectric constant $\bar{\varepsilon}$. One is Bruggeman's effective medium theory[2]. The main idea of this theory can be described as follows. Consider a random composite consisting of two components, with dielectric constants ε_1 and ε_2, as schematically illustrated in Fig. 1(a).

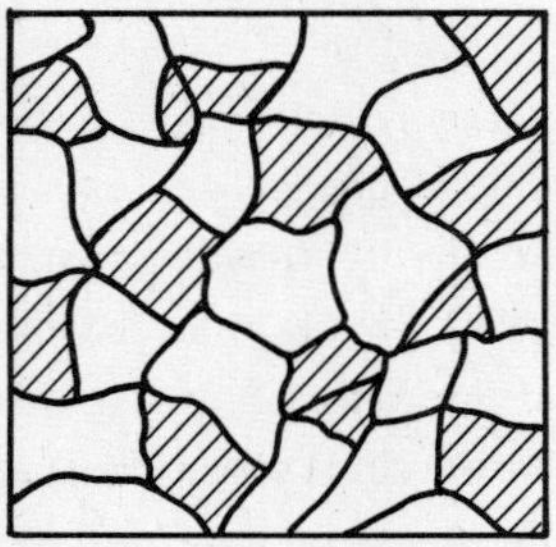

(a)

Fig. 1 (a) Schematic picture of a random composite.

Since an exact calculation of the electric field distribution for the random, infinite system is impossible, the Bruggeman approach is to focus attention on one of the grains (say a grain of component 1) and regard the rest of the composite as a homogeneous medium characterized by a yet undetermined effective dielectric constant $\bar{\varepsilon}$. This is shown in Fig. 1(b).

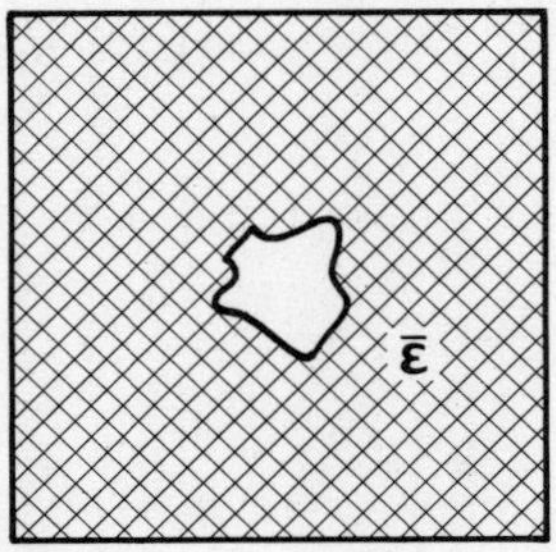

(b)

Fig. 1 (b) The rest of the medium is treated as homogeneous for the calculation of depolarization field of a single grain.

In the presence of an applied electric field, the single inclusion in the uniform medium ε will give rise to a dipole depolarization field which, in the spherical grain approximation, is proportional to $(\bar{\varepsilon} - \varepsilon_1)/(\bar{\varepsilon} + 2\varepsilon_1)$. Repeating the same problems with a grain of component 2 results in another dipole moment proportional to $(\bar{\varepsilon} - \varepsilon_2)/(\bar{\varepsilon} + 2\varepsilon_2)$. In order to be consistent with the initial assumption that the medium should appear homogeneous to the probing wave, the average depolarization field must vanish. That is,

$$p \frac{\bar{\varepsilon} - \varepsilon_1}{\varepsilon_1 + 2\bar{\varepsilon}} + (1-p) \frac{\bar{\varepsilon} - \varepsilon_2}{\varepsilon_2 + 2\bar{\varepsilon}} = 0, \quad (1)$$

where p is the volume fraction of component 1. It should be mentioned that Eq. (1) has been shown to be equivalent to the coherent potential approximation in the multiple-scattering formulism[3].

If the two components of the composite are metal and insulator, that is, $\varepsilon_1 = 1$ and $\varepsilon_2 = 0$, then it is easy to verify that the Bruggeman theory predicts an effective conductivity that vanishes at $p_c = 1/3$. This behavior, known as the percolation threshold, is physically related to the fact that below the threshold, there is no possibility for metal grains to form a connected network of infinite extent. In granular films[4-6], the percolation threshold behavior is reflected in the transmission electronmicroscope pictures of the microstructure as shown in Fig. 2.

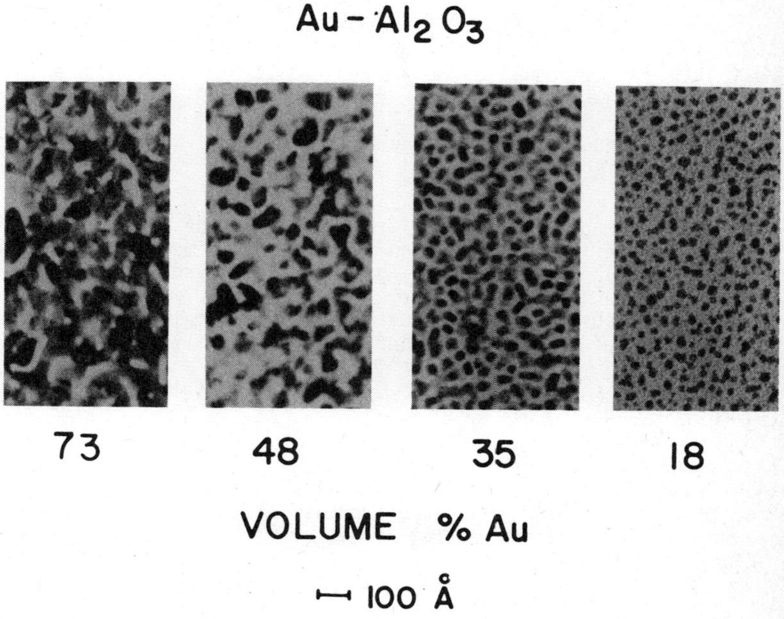

Fig. 2 Transmission electron micrographs of the granular cermets Au-Al_2O_3 for four different compositions.

It is seen that at p = 0.73, the Al_2O_3 (white) are disconnected inclusions in the metallic Au matrix (black). As p is decreased, a matrix inversion occurs until at p = 0.35 the metal particles are the inclusions in the insulator matrix. Between p = 0.48 and p = 0.35 we have a labyrinth structure, and somewhere between these two composition values it is clear that the last infinite metallic network must be broken and the dc conductivity vanishes. Therefore, Bruggeman's theory is qualitatively correct in predicting a percolation threshold. However, quantitatively the agreement is poor as shown in Fig. 3.

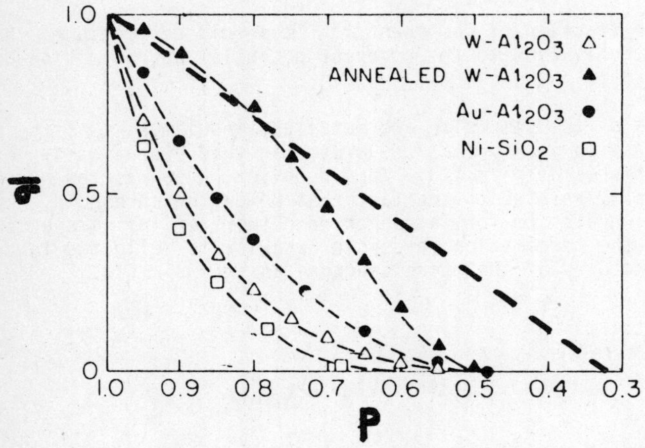

Fig. 3 Normalized dc conductivity of granular metals. The straight dashed line is the Bruggeman theory. After Abeles [1].

Another widely-used approach to the calculation of $\bar{\varepsilon}$ was the Maxwell-Garnett theory [7]. Its tranditional derivation relies on the analogy of metal-insulator composite as a polarizable medium in which the metal grains play the role of "atoms".

By using the familiar Clausius-Mosotti equation[8], one obtains a relationship between the dielectric constant of the composite and the polarizability of the metal particles:

$$\frac{\bar{\varepsilon} - \bar{\varepsilon}_2}{\varepsilon + 2\varepsilon_2} \quad \frac{4\pi n\alpha_1}{3\varepsilon_2} \ . \qquad (2)$$

Here n is the volume density of the metal particles, and α_1 is the polarizability of a metal grain. By substituting for α_1 the expression for polarizability of an isolated metal sphere immersed in a uniform medium of dielectric constant ε_2, we get the Maxwell-Garnett equation

$$\frac{\bar{\varepsilon} - \varepsilon_2}{\varepsilon_2 + 2\bar{\varepsilon}} = p\,\frac{\varepsilon_1 - \varepsilon_2}{\varepsilon_1 + 2\varepsilon_2} \ . \qquad (3)$$

Equation (3) is equivalent to the averaged T-matrix approximation in the multiple scattering formalism[3].

The Maxwell-Garnett theory can be easily shown not to yield a percolation threshold at any finite values of p. However, it does predict another peculiar property of the composite, the dielectric anomaly[9], which is absent in Bruggeman's theory.

To describe this effect, let us consider the frequency dependence for the real and imaginary parts of the metal dielectric function shown schematically in Fig. 4(a), where ω_p denotes the plasma frequency. If now we have a metal-insulator composite with insulator being the matrix component, the real and imaginary parts of the effective dielectric constant would look like Fig. 4(b) according to the Maxwell-Garnett theory.

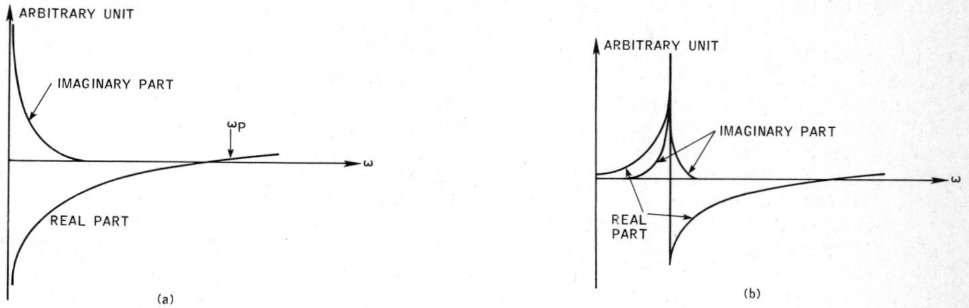

Fig. 4 Schematic illustration of the frequency dependence of the dielectric constant for (a) an ideal metal and (b) a metal-insulator composite according to the Maxwell-Garnett theory.

It is to be noted that there is a frequency ω_p above which the effective dielectric function behaves exactly like a metal. However, at $\omega << \omega_R$ the composite is more like an insulator. Therefore, ω_R is essentially a frequency threshold for the metal-insulator transition. At ω_R, there is an absorption peak arising from increased penetration of electromagnetic field into the metal grains.

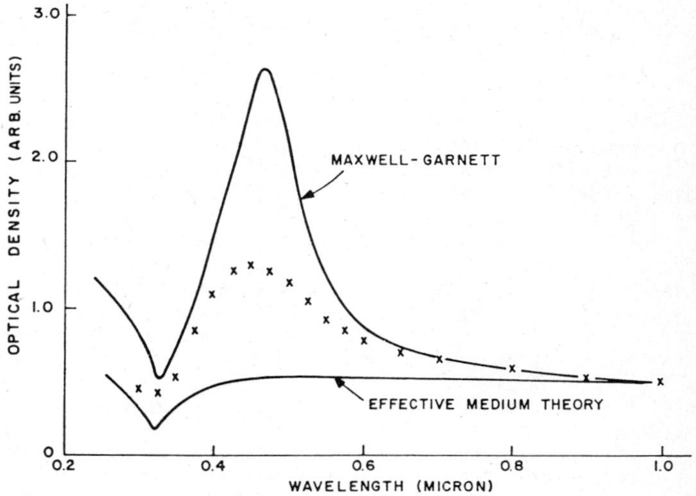

Fig. 5 Comparison of experimental results on the dielectric anomaly with both the Bruggeman and the Maxwell-Garnett theories. The sample is $Ag-SiO_2$ film containing 0.39 volume fraction Ag. After Ref. [10].

Evidence for the dielectric anomaly has been observed in granular Ag - SiO_2 and Au - SiO_2 films [9]. Figure 5 [10] compares the experimental result with both the Maxwell Garnett and the Bruggeman theories. It is seen that whereas the Maxwell-Garnett theory does produce the absorption peak at about the right frequency, the Bruggeman theory exhibits no peak at all.

Such comparisons raise the obvious question: what is the underlying physics responsible for this difference in behavior? The answer to this question is facilitated by the recognition in the last few years that the Maxwell-Garnett theory can be alternatively derived by using the effective - medium approach[11]. That is, if we consider the embedding of a coated sphere in an effective medium, then the condition of vanishing depolarization field would yield Eq. (3) provided that the sphere is of component 1 and the coating is of component 2 with a thickness determined directly by the relative volume fraction of the two components. This derivation of the Maxwell-Garnett formula immediately tells us that the difference between the two theories lies in the consideration of two types of microstructures. Whereas the Bruggeman theory treats the two components in an equivalent manner, the basic structural unit of a coated sphere in the Maxwell-Garnett case implies an asymmetrical consideration of the two components. It is clear that if we make up a composite by the random placement of coated spheres, then the coating component would always remain the matrix constituent regardless of the composition. Therefore, it is not surprising that there is no percolation threshold in the Maxwell-Garnett theory. A schematic illustration of the microstructures implicity treated by the Bruggeman and the Maxwell-Garnett theories are shown in Fig. 6.

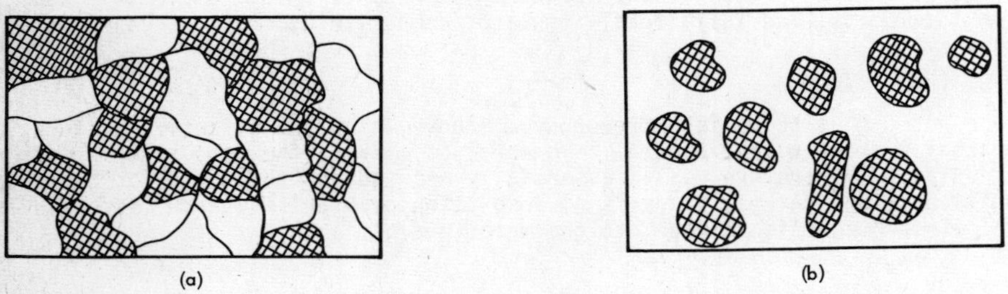

Fig. 6 Schematic illustration of the two types of microstructure treated by the Bruggeman theory (a) and the Maxwell-Garnett theory (b).

The elucidation of the difference between the two theories shows that there is only one underlying approach--the effective medium theory--to the approximate calculation of the effective dielectric constant. However, it also confronts the users of the effective medium theory with the following unresolved problems:

(1) Is the absence of the dielectric anomaly in the Bruggeman theory the physical consequence of its implicit microstructure or the result of the approximation used in its derivation?

(2) Does the fact that both theories cannot even qualitatively describe all the experimental results of granular metals signify (a) the need for carrying the effective medium approach to higher orders of approximation, or (b) the need for better modelling of the granular metal microstructure?

Consideration of the two problems shows that in both cases the question revolves around the role of microstructure in the calculation of effective dielectric constant. In this article, we wish to use the concept of "structural units" as a means for incorporating the microstructural information, i.e. geometric shapes as well as topological arrangement of the grains, in a statistical manner. For example, the structural unit in the Maxwell-Garnett case is a coated sphere, but the basic unit in the Bruggeman theory is a grain of either component. An alternative choice of structural unit for (the microstructure of) the Bruggeman case is a two-grain combination[12] in which each grain can be either component 1 or component 2, denoted here as a pair-cluster. The possible advantages of using a two-grain pair-cluster unit rather than the usual one-grain unit lies in the explicit presence of the two-component interface in the basic structural units. As we may recall, in the derivation of the Bruggeman theory the only interfaces explicitly considered are those between the individual grain and the effective medium. Therefore, any phenomenon intrinsically associated with the interfaces between the two components, such as the dielectric anomaly, are not expected to be adequately accounted for. The use of the pair-cluster units thus holds promise to answer the first problem posed above.

To calculate the effective dielectric constant in the pair-cluster theory, we will approximate the geometry of the two-grain pair by a sphere in which each half can be either one of the two components. By embedding this sphere in an effective medium and calculating the resulting depolarization field, we obtain an equation for the effective dielectric constant $\bar{\varepsilon}$ after averaging over all two-hemisphere combinations and all orientations of the applied field relative to the plane separating the two hemispheres:

$$p^2 \frac{\bar{\varepsilon} - \varepsilon_1}{2\bar{\varepsilon} + \varepsilon_1} + (1-p)^2 \frac{\bar{\varepsilon} - \varepsilon_1}{2\bar{\varepsilon} + \varepsilon_2} \frac{4}{9} p(1-p) \frac{2\bar{\varepsilon} - \varepsilon_1 - \varepsilon_2}{K \bar{\varepsilon} (\varepsilon_1 - \varepsilon_2)^2 + (\varepsilon_1 + \varepsilon_2 + 4\bar{\varepsilon})/3}$$

$$+ \frac{2}{9} p(1-p) \frac{\bar{\varepsilon} (\varepsilon_1 + \varepsilon_2) - 2\varepsilon_1\varepsilon_2}{H\bar{\varepsilon}(\varepsilon_1 - \varepsilon_2)^2 + 2(\varepsilon_1\varepsilon_2 + \varepsilon_1\bar{\varepsilon} + \varepsilon_2\bar{\varepsilon})/3} = 0, \qquad (4)$$

where

$$H = \frac{1}{4} \sum_{m=1}^{\infty} \frac{I_m}{[\, m(\varepsilon_1 + \varepsilon_2) + (2m + 1)\, \bar{\varepsilon}]}, \qquad (5)$$

$$K = \frac{1}{4} \sum_{m=1}^{\infty} \frac{I_m}{[\, 2m\, \varepsilon_1\varepsilon_2 + (n + 1/2)\, (\varepsilon_1 + \varepsilon_2)\bar{\varepsilon}]}, \qquad (6)$$

$$I_m = \frac{m(4m + 1)\, [(2m + 1)!]^2}{4^{2m}\, (m!)^4 (2m - 1)^2 (m + 1)^2\, (2m + 1)} \qquad (7)$$

Details of the derivation can be found in Ref. (12). To compare the results of the pair-cluster theory with the Bruggeman theory, we show in Fig. 7 the calculated optical transmission spectrum for a series of 500-A-thick Ag-SiO_2 films using realistic Ag and SiO_2 dielectric constant values. The optical dielectric constant of the composite is then evaluated by using both the pair-cluster theory (solid line) and the Bruggeman theory (dashed line). It is easily seen that the pair-cluster theory displays an extra absorption peak (or transmission dip) near $\lambda \simeq 0.37$ µm, the dielectric anomaly, which the Bruggeman theory does not have. The peak disappears, however, in the composition regime of $0.4 < p < 0.7$ where a matrix inversion occurs. Since in this particular composition range the two components is expected to exhibit a labyrinth structure, the disappearance of the absorption peak indicates that the dielectric anomaly may be associated with the particular microstructure of isolated inclusions embedded in a continuous matrix.

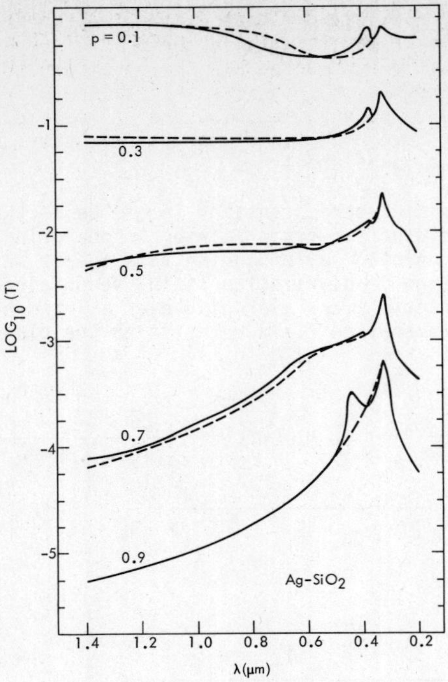

Fig. 7 Calculated optical transmission as a function of wavelength for a series of 500-A $Ag-SiO_2$ films. (-) pair-cluster theory, (---) Bruggeman theory. For clarity, the curves are displaced vertically with respect to each other.

To further accentuate the effect of microstructure, we show in Fig. 8 the transmission spectrum for the same $Ag-SiO_2$ films calculated in the Maxwell-Garnett theory. By comparing Figs. 7 and 8, it becomes clear that the position and the magnitude of the dielectric anomaly are drastically different. Therefore, although the complete absence of the dielectric anomaly in the Bruggeman theory can be ascribed to the neglect of two-component interfaces in its derivation, the microstructure, nevertheless, does govern the manifestation of the phenonemon.

Let us now consider the problem of constructing a realistic theory for the effective dielectric function of granular metals[6]. We will hypothesize at this stage that the discrepancies between the experimental results and the predictions of both the Bruggeman and the Maxwell-Garnett theories stem from the inadequacy of their structural units in modelling the cermet microstructure. To search for new structural units appropriate for these granular composites, we observe that the cermet is formed by the two-step process of surface diffusion and coalescence. That is, the molecules that land on the substrate (of the film) usually have excess energy and, therefore, tend to move about before they stick with other molecules of the same component and form the grain. The average distance of this surface motion is usually denoted as the surface diffusion length, which is the basic scale of inhomogeneity. Suppose now let us consider a spherical region with the dimension of a diffusion length. Inside such a region there can be a large number of molecules of either component. Therefore, statistically the relative volume fraction occupied by the two components should be close to the macroscopic average value. If a grain is formed inside this region through surface diffusion and coalescence, there are two possible outcomes as shown in Fig. 9. That is, component 1 may form the grain and component 2 the coating, which we denote as a type 1 structural unit, or component 2 may form the grain and component 1 the coating, which we denote as a type 2 structural unit. At a given composition p, the relative probability of occurrence for the two types of structural unit can be estimated by counting the number of equally probable final configurations corresponding to different positions of the grain inside the region.

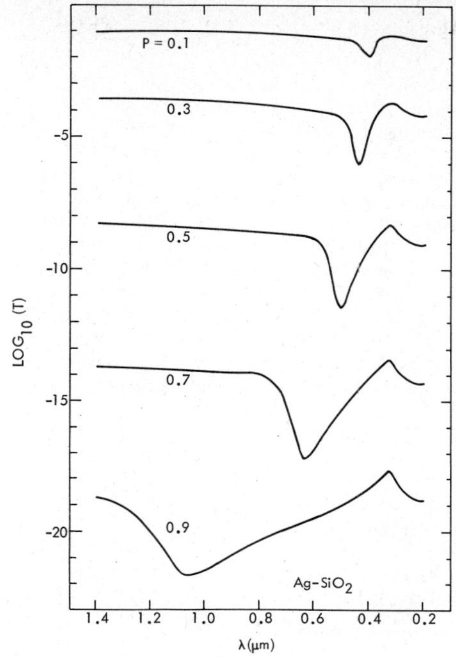

Fig. 8 Optical transmission as a function of wavelength for a series of 500-Å $Ag-SiO_2$ films, calculated by the Maxwell-Garnett theory. For clarity, the curves are vertically displaced with respect to each other.

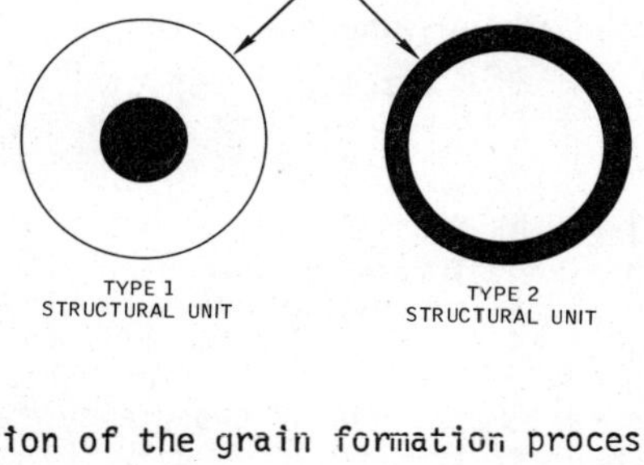

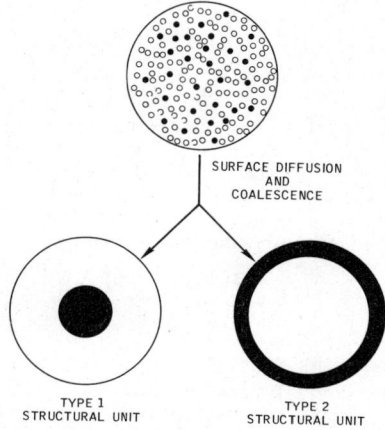

Fig. 9 Schematic illustration of the grain formation process in granular metal films.

By assuming the grain to be spherical, it is clear, that, in case of type 1, the number of configurations is proportional to $u_1 = (1-p^{1/3})^3$. By the same reasoning, the number of configurations for the type 2 unit is proportioned to $u_2 = [1 - (1-p)^{1/3}]^3$. It follows that the relative probability of occurrence for the type 1 unit is $f = u_1/(u_1 + u_2)$, and that for the type 2 unit is 1-f.

If we now build up a random composite from these two structural units according to their assigned statistical weights, the system will be dominated by type 1 structural units in the range $0.35 > p > 0$, since f only varies between 1 and 0.92. That is, the structural would essentially look like isolated grains of component 1 embedded in the continuous matrix of component 2. On the other hand, in the range of $1 > p > 0.65$ we expect the reverse structure in which component 2 becomes isolated and component 1 constitutes the continuous phase. Therefore, there is a matrix inversion occuring in the range $0.65 > p > 0.35$, where we can expect a labyrinth structure. Comparing the above structural description with Fig. 2, we see that the model composite is in reasonable accord with the reality. Now the construction of a theory for the effective dielectric function proceeds along the following three steps: (1) embedding the structural units in a uniform effective medium, (2) calculating the dipole moments of the structural units when they are polarized by a uniform applied field, and (3) requiring the average dipole moments to vanish. By approximating the dipole moment of a structural unit (in arbitrary configuration) by the dipole moment of the concentric configuration, $D_{1,2}$, we get the effective medium condition as

$$fD_1 + (1 - f)\, D_2 = 0 \qquad (8)$$

Since the arguments leading to the value of f remains unchanged if one relaxes the condition of spherical geometry and considers a speroidal particle enclosed in a similar-shaped region, Eq. (8) remains valid for spheroidal structural units. In that case $D_{1,2}$ stands for the orientationally averaged dipole moment of confocal spheroidal particles embedded in an effective medium $\bar{\varepsilon}$:

$$D_1 = \frac{2}{3} D[\bar{\varepsilon}, \varepsilon_1, \varepsilon_2, p, A(\alpha, u), B(\alpha)] + \frac{1}{3} D[\bar{\varepsilon}, \varepsilon_1, \varepsilon_2, p, 3\text{-}2A(\alpha,u), 3\text{-}2B(\alpha)] \qquad 9(a)$$

$$D_2 = \frac{2}{3} D[\bar{\varepsilon}, \varepsilon_2, \varepsilon_1, 1\text{-}p, A(\beta, v), B(\beta)] + \frac{1}{3} D[\bar{\varepsilon}, \varepsilon_2, \varepsilon_1, 1\text{-}p, B\text{-}2A(\beta,v), 3\text{-}2B(\beta)] \qquad 9(b)$$

Where α is the ratio between the minor (major) and major (minor) axes of the elliptic cross section for the type - 1 oblated (prolate) spheroidal unit, β is the similar quantity for the type - 2 unit, $u = (p/\alpha)^{1/2}$ and $v = ((1-p)/\beta)^{1/2}$. The functions D, A, and B have the following forms:

$$D(\bar{\varepsilon},x,y,\mu,A,B) = \frac{[A\bar{\varepsilon} + (3-A)y]\,[y-x]\mu + [Bx+(3-B)y]\,[\bar{\varepsilon}-y]}{A\,(3-A)\,(\bar{\varepsilon}-y)\,(y-x)\mu + [Bx + (3-B)y]\,[Ay + (3-A)\,\bar{\varepsilon}]} \qquad (10)$$

$$A(\gamma, w) = \frac{3}{2}\,\frac{1}{w^3(1-\gamma^2)}\,\left[\frac{1}{\sqrt{1-\gamma^2}}\,\tan^{-1}\frac{w\sqrt{1-\gamma^2}}{\sqrt{s^2+\gamma^2w^2}} - w(s^2+\gamma^2w^2)\right], \qquad (11)$$

$B(\gamma) = A(\gamma, 1/\gamma^{1/3})$ evaluated at s=0, where s is the solution of the equation $(s^2 + w^2)^2\,(s^2 + \gamma^2w^2) = 1$. A and B assumes the special value of 1 for spherical geometry. It is noted that if f is set equal to 1, Eq. (8) becomes the generalized Maxwell-Garnett equation which specializes to Eq. (3) in the spherical case.

A comparison of the calculated optical transmissions spectrum for a series of thin Au-SiO_2 films with the experimental results are shown in Fig. 10. The theoretical inputs are the realistic dielectric constants of Au and SiO_2, $\alpha = 1$, $\beta = 2$, the p values marked to the right of each curve, and the film thickness marked above each curve. It is seen that the new theory reproduces all the characteristics features of the data. In particular, the position and magnitude of the dielectric anomaly, and its eventual disappearance for $p \geq 0.8$ are all in good agreement. For effective dc conductivity

$\bar{\sigma}$ and its variation with p, we show in Fig. 11 two sets of experimental data corresponding to the same sample before and after the annealing treatment and their best theoretical fits. The theory curves are obtained by using $\varepsilon_1 = 1$, $\varepsilon_2 = 0$, $\alpha = 1$, and the β values marked in the figure. The strikingly good agreement, especially the reproduction of the opposite curvatures in the two sets of experimental data, shows that the insulator inclusions before annealing are mostly in the form of oblate platelets, which becomes rounded upon annealing. The increase in the effective conductivity can be intuitively understood by recognizing that the platelets are more effective than spheres in impeding the current flow.

The success of the new theory in explaining both the optical and dc response of granular films brings us to the essential point of this article. Namely, the effective medium approach to the calculation of effective material parameters can indeed yield realistic results provided that the microstructure of the random composite is properly taken into account. This conclusion, which may seem natural in hindsight, nevertheless does emphasize the need for future research in quantifying the different types of microstructure in random inhomogeneous systems.

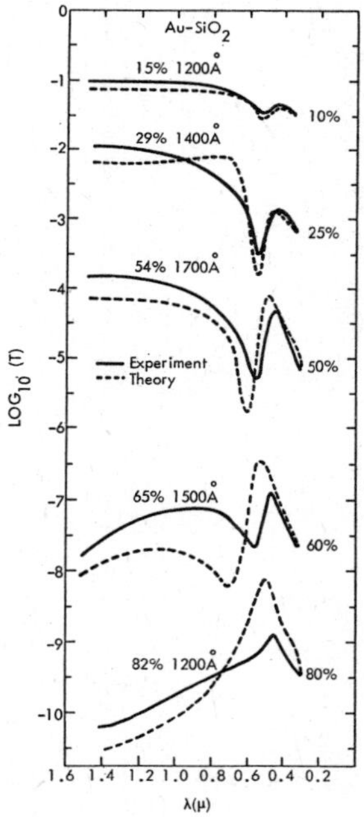

Fig. 10 Optical transmission as a function of light wavelength for a series of Au-SiO_2 samples. The metal volume fraction and the film thickness are labeled above each curve. Theoretical curves are normalized to the experimental values at 0.3 μm. For clarity, the curves are displaced with respect to one another.

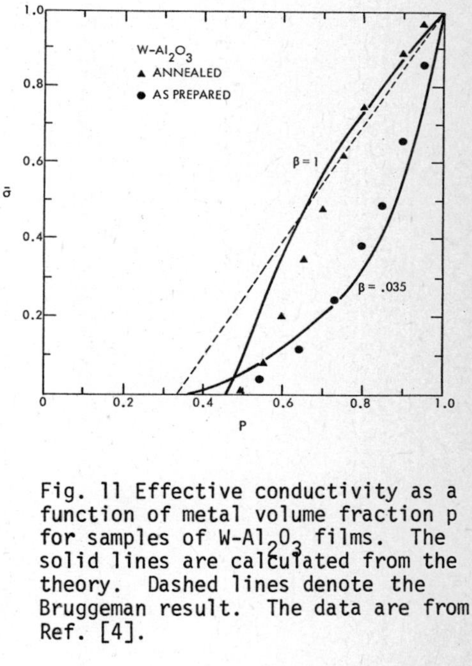

Fig. 11 Effective conductivity as a function of metal volume fraction p for samples of W-Al_2O_3 films. The solid lines are calculated from the theory. Dashed lines denote the Bruggeman result. The data are from Ref. [4].

References

[1] See, for example, Born and Wolf, Principles of Optics (Pergamon Press, New York, 1964).

[2] D. A. G. Bruggeman, Ann. Phys. (Leipzig) 24, 636 (1935).

[3] J. E. Gubernatis, AIP Conference Proc. No. 40, 84 (1978).

[4] B. Abeles, P. Sheng, M.D. Coutts, and Y. Arie, Adv. Phys. 24 407 (1975).

[5] P. Sheng, B. Abeles, and Y. Arie, Phys. Rev. Lett. 31, 44 (1973).

[6] P. Sheng, Phys. Rev. Lett. 45, 60 (1980).

[7] J. C. Maxwell-Garnett, Philos. Trans. Roy. Soc. London 203, 385 (1904).

[8] See, for example, J. D. Jackson, Classical Electrodynamics (John Wiley & Sons, New York, 1967).

[9] R. W. Cohen, G. D. Cody, M. D. Coutts, and B. Abeles, Phys. Rev. B8, 3689 (1973).

[10] J. I. Gittleman and B. Abeles, Phys. Rev. B15, 3273 (1977).

[11] D. Stroud, Phys. Rev. B12, 3368 (1975); see also W. Lamb, D. M. Wood, and N. W. Ashcroft, AIP Conf. Proc. No. 40, 240 (1978).

[12] P. Sheng, Phys. Rev. B22, 6364 (1980).

MACROSCOPIC AND MICROSCOPIC FIELDS IN ELECTRON AND ATOM TRANSPORT

R. S. Sorbello
Department of Physics
University of Wisconsin-Milwaukee
Milwaukee, WI 53201/USA

Introduction

Application of an electric field to a metal gives rise to transport of electrons and atoms. If the metal is homogeneous, one usually regards the electric field and the particle currents to be macroscopic quantities satisfying some generalized Ohm's law, where the conductivities are spatially constant parameters in the theory. On the microscopic- or atomic-scale, however, the fields and currents are not homogeneous. The nature of these microscopic inhomogeneities was first described by Landauer[1] in an important paper in 1957. Here we base our discussion on some recent work which delves more deeply into the structure of these microscopic inhomogeneities from a quantum-mechanical viewpoint.[2]

The important quantity which connects the microscopic and macroscopic levels is the residual resistivity dipole (RRD). According to Landauer,[1,3] the RRD is set-up around each scattering center in the presence of current flow. The RRD charge is analogous to the dipolar surface-polarization charge which is set-up on the surface of poorly conducting inclusions in an otherwise homogeneous conductor. When these individual RRD fields are added, their space-average gives the macroscopic electric field that is needed to drive the current past these scatterers. The picture is thus self-consistent.

Before studying the RRD, we present the phenomenological equations (generalized Ohm's Law) for homogeneous media. This allows us to define a useful parameter Z^* which is a measure of the driving field in electromigration.[4] Various questions and controversies are discussed, and the structure of the RRD is examined. We then show how the RRD can be used to calculate Z^*. Finally, we apply the RRD to Landauer's method of calculating the conductivity of one-dimensional disordered media.[5]

Phenomenological Equations

The linear phenomenological equations of transport theory relate fluxes and forces. The fluxes in our problem are the electronic particle current $\vec{J}_e$ and the ionic particle current $\vec{J}_i$. (For simplicity we assume only one ionic species). The forces are the gradients of the electrochemical potentials. The equations for a system at constant temperature are

$$\vec{J}_i = -L_{ii}\nabla(\mu_i+q_i\phi) - L_{ie}\nabla(\mu_e+q_e\phi) \tag{1}$$

$$\vec{J}_e = -L_{ei}\nabla(\mu_i+q_i\phi) - L_{ee}\nabla(\mu_e+q_e\phi) \tag{2}$$

where the L's are the generalized conductivities, μ_i and μ_e are the chemical potentials of ions and electrons, respectively, and ϕ is the macroscopic electrical potential. The charge of the ion and of the electron are q_i and q_e, respectively. The macroscopic electric field is given by $\vec{E} = -\nabla\phi$.

In the usual conductivity experiment, there are no concentration gradients ($\nabla\mu_i = \nabla\mu_e = 0$), and the electrons and ions undergo simple drift. One can write

$$\vec{J}_i = L_{ii}\, q_i^* \,\vec{E} \tag{3}$$

where we have defined the effective charge

$$q_i^* = q_i + \frac{L_{ie}}{L_{ii}} q_e \tag{4}$$

One can interpret $\vec{J}_i$ to be the current which would arise from an effective local field $\vec{E}_L = (q_i^*/q_i)\vec{E}$ which acts directly on the ions without any additional cross-contribution due to electron-ion coupling.

In a diffusion experiment for which $\vec{E} = 0$ and $\nabla\mu_e = 0$, we have $\vec{J}_i = -L_{ii}\nabla\mu_i$ and $\vec{J}_e = -L_{ei}\nabla\mu_i$. The charge transported per ion is

$$\frac{q_i\vec{J}_i + q_e\vec{J}_e}{J_i} = q_i^* \tag{5}$$

where the equality follows upon use of the Onsager relation[4] $L_{ie} = L_{ei}$.

Experimental results for q_i^* are traditionally expressed in terms of the parameter $Z^* = -q_i^*/q_e$. Determination of this "effective valence" is the prime concern of workers in electromigration.[4]

Questions and Controversies

There has been considerable effort in electromigration theory to try to determine Z^*, or equivalently, the local field $\vec{E}_L$ seen by an ion. It was suggested by Landauer and Woo[6] that the RRD may be the dominant contribution. This would lead to an intensification of the local field at the ion, and hence we would expect $Z^* > 0$. Yet for simple metals where band structure can be ignored, measurements reveal that $Z^* < 0$ and moreover $|Z^*|$ is typically larger than unity.[4] What has happened to the RRD? Where are the negative electrical charges which would accompany a moving ion according to Eq. (5)?

Other questions and controversies include the role of external vs. internal charges in setting up the macroscopic field.[7] What kind of charge is set up at the boundaries or electrodes? When one performs a quantum calculation and introduces into the hamiltonian the perturbation due to the electric field, is this a microscopic, macroscopic, or external field?

Questions such as these are often ignored in traditional treatments of transport theory. Landauer's viewpoint puts these questions in a deservedly central position in the theory.

Calculation of the Local Field

We consider the local field $\vec{E}_L(\vec{r})$ at some position $\vec{r}$ measured from an origin taken to be the nucleus of the ion in question. The ion is visualized as the only scatterer within some small region of an electron gas. Since we ignore explicit scattering by other agents in this region, we should restrict our attention to $r < \ell$, where ℓ is the electron mean-free-path. The relaxation time τ and the Fermi velocity v_F are related to ℓ according to $\ell = v_F\tau$.

In general, we can write $\vec{E}_L(\vec{r}) = -\nabla\Phi(\vec{r})$, where we introduce the local electrical potential Φ. The quantum mechanical expression for Φ is of the same form as the classical one, namely,[2]

$$\Phi(\vec{r}) = \int n(\vec{r}')v_b(\vec{r}'-\vec{r})d^3r' \tag{6}$$

where $n(\vec{r}')$ is the electron density at position $\vec{r}'$ and where $v_b(\vec{r}'-\vec{r}) = -e/|\vec{r}'-\vec{r}|$ is the bare potential for point charges. $e = |q_e|$ is the magnitude of the electron charge. The integration is over all space. Here and in what follows we are only concerned with that part of the density which is linear in $\vec{E}$.

Quantum-mechanical calculation of the electron density in the presence of $\vec{E}$ is difficult. Schaich[8] has derived from first principles an expression which had been used[9] or suggested[10] by others. His result for the non-interacting electron gas is

$$n_o(\vec{r}) = \sum_k g_{\vec{k}} \, |\psi_{\vec{k}}(\vec{r})|^2 \tag{7}$$

where $g_{\vec{k}}$ is the standard solution of the Boltzmann equation for the electron distribution in an electric field and $\psi_{\vec{k}}(\vec{r})$ is the electron scattering state which gives the wavefunction of an incoming electron $\exp(i\vec{k}\cdot\vec{r})$ being scattered by the ion. The sum is over all states, and the system is assumed to have unit volume.

To convert the non-interacting density $n_o(\vec{r})$ to the correct self-consistent density $n(\vec{r})$ one needs to include the screening response. Using Fourier-transformed quantities, this implies $n(\vec{q}) = n_o(\vec{q})/\varepsilon(q)$ where $\varepsilon(q)$ is the dielectric function. Assuming small screening length, these results can be used in Eq. (6) to yield[2]

$$\Phi(\vec{r}) = -(4\pi e/q_{TF}^2)n_o(\vec{r}) \tag{8}$$

where q_{TF} is the Thomas-Fermi wavevector. Explicitly, $q_{TF}^2 = 4\pi e^2/(\partial\varepsilon_F/\partial\bar{n})$ where ε_F

is the Fermi energy and $\bar{n}$ is the average density of electrons in equilibrium. For the 3-d electron gas $q_{TF}^2 = 4mk_F e^2/\pi\hbar^2$ where k_F is the Fermi wavevector and m is the electron mass. Expression (8) is valid beyond the small screening length assumption ($q_{TF} >> k_F$) if one resorts to averaging fields and densities over distances of several electron wavelengths, as in Landauer's work.[1]

In the asymptotic limit $n_o(\vec{r})$ and $\Phi(\vec{r})$ are easily evaluated.[2,8] Using the asymptotic form $\psi_k(\vec{r}) \to \exp(i\vec{k}\cdot\vec{r}) + [f(\theta')/r]\exp(ikr)\cos\theta'$, where θ' is the angle between $\vec{k}$ and $\vec{r}$, and f is the scattering amplitude one finds

$$\Phi(\vec{r}) = -\frac{p_o\cos\theta}{r^2} + (\text{osc. terms}) \tag{9}$$

where

$$p_o = S\ell\ E/4\pi \tag{10}$$

and S is the (momentum-weighted) cross-section for scattering of electrons by the ion. θ is the angle between $\vec{r}$ and $\vec{E}$. The value of p_o is precisely the value of the RRD dipole moment calculated by Landauer. The leading oscillatory terms in (9) are of the form $r^{-2}\sin(2k_F r+\gamma)$ where γ is a phase angle.

We have obtained Landauer's form of the potential due to the RRD provided that we ignore the oscillatory terms in Eq. (9). The latter terms will wash away if one averages $\Phi(\vec{r})$ over regions whose dimensions are several wavelengths long. This coarse graining is just what one must do to calculate the macroscopic field. Landauer's conclusions thus apply to the macroscopic field. In particular, the macroscopic field generated by a density N of ions (in a slab-geometry) is given by $\Delta E = 4\pi Np_o$, and this is precisely the field needed to overcome the scattering by the ions, i.e., $\Delta E = eJ_e\Delta\rho$ where $\Delta\rho$ is the extra resistance introduced by the ions.

While the oscillatory terms in $\Phi(\vec{r})$ are not important for the macroscopic field, they are important for the microscopic field. We have verified this in a calculation of $n_o(r)$ and $\Phi(\vec{r})$ close to the ion for the model of s-wave scattering.[2] We found that the dipole-moment p_o cannot really be said to arise from a well defined localized charge distribution near the ion. This lack of a pure dipole near the ion explains why the local field is not strongly intensified by the RRD as one would have expected were there pure dipole behavior close-in to the ion. Thus $Z^* > 0$ does not follow.

An implication of the existence of RRD's is that boundary effects might not be adequately considered in quantum treatments of transport. The "external" field one inserts into the hamiltonian finds its origins in the RRD's, and not in external charges. There are complicated distributions of surface charges which are not strictly external, but rather are vestiges of RRD's and the response to RRD's. Traditional treatments ignore RRD's except as they might implicitly set up a macroscopic "external" field. This leaves uncertain whether interactions between RRD's are correctly accounted for in the traditional treatments. It remains to be seen whether these quantum mechanical analyses correctly treat such effects as the Lorentz corrections obtained by Landauer and Woo.[11]

Relationship Between Z^* and RRD

We have seen that the local field is not entirely governed by the RRD. There are other contributions to $\vec{E}_L$ or Z^*. It is possible, however, to derive an expression for Z^* solely from RRD considerations. To this end, consider the diffusion of ions through a slab under open circuit conditions for electrons. Let the ions be diffusing at average velocity $\vec{v}_o$ through the slab. The macroscopic field which is set up is the average field of the RRD's in the equivalent problem where the ions are fixed but the electrons move at a drift velocity of $-\vec{v}_o$. The equivalence follows by Galilean transformation. Now the RRD field set-up from a density of N ions per unit volume is $E = 4\pi N p_o$, where p_o is the RRD moment appropriate to an electron drift velocity $-\vec{v}_o$. Thus p_o is given by Eq. (10) with E in that equation replaced by $mv_o/\tau e$ which is the usual expression for the electric field in terms of a drift velocity v_o. The sample is thus acting as an open circuit battery which generates a field $4\pi N p_o$ internally. If we now short-out the battery to force $E = 0$, we will induce an electron current $J_e = 4\pi N p_o/\rho e$, where $\rho = m/\bar{n}e^2\tau$ is the resistivity. If we now use this value of J_e in Eq. (4) for q_i^*, we find

$$q_i^* = q_i - e\bar{n}\ell S \tag{11}$$

which is precisely the Huntington-Fiks result[4] for q_i^*. This result has also been derived quantum mechanically by others.[12,13] Our line of reasoning shows how the result follows from RRD considerations.

Landauer's 1-d Conductivity Formula

The RRD is also relevant to a very powerful 1-d conductivity formula which was derived by Landauer[5] and which is currently being debated in the literature.[14] To obtain the conductivity for a sample of length L one calculates $\sigma = J/E$ where J is now the electronic charge current and E is the average field across the sample. An electron of velocity v incident on the sample from the left of the sample is described by the plane wave exp(ikx), where $v = \hbar k/m$. There is a reflected wave r exp(-ikx) to the left and a transmitted wave t exp(ikx) coming out of the sample on the right, where $|r|^2 + |t|^2 = 1$. The current is thus $J = -ev|t|^2$. Landauer derived his formula by calculating the diffusion coefficient appropriate to this current and relating it to σ via the Einstein equation. Here we follow the more direct route[3] and evaluate E from our expression (8) for $\Phi(x)$.

The density to the left of the sample is $n_o(x) = |\exp(ikx) + r\exp(-ikx)|^2$. To the right, $n_o(x) = |t\exp(ikx)|^2$. Since the density, and thus the potential, are constant on the right we conveniently choose $\Phi(x) = 0$ there. Then everywhere to the left we find from Eq. (8) and our $n_o(x)$ expressions the result

$$\Phi(x) = -\left(\frac{4\pi e}{q_{TF}^2}\right)[2|r|^2 + r\,e^{-2ikx} + r^*\,e^{2ikx}] .$$

Upon averaging over a few wavelengths, we can ignore the oscillatory terms. The average potential drop across the sample is thus $8\pi e|r|^2/q_{TF}^2$. Equating this to $-EL$, we determine E. The conductivity $\sigma = J/E$ then becomes $\sigma = q_{TF}^2 v|t|^2 L/8\pi|r|^2$, which is precisely Landauer's formula when one makes use of the fact that $q_{TF}^2 = 4\pi e^2/(\partial\varepsilon_F/\partial\bar{n})$.

We see that the RRD is playing a central role in setting up the self-consistent potential $\Phi(x)$ in the sample. If one ignores the self-consistency aspects of the problem one obtains an incorrect expression for σ.[14,15]

Conclusion

We have seen that macroscopic and microscopic fields are naturally related via the RRD. Although the calculations based on expression (7) for $n_o(\vec{r})$ are only appropriate for distances within a distance ℓ from the ion, the results for the electric field coarse-grained over several wavelengths is the same as Landauer's. To extend the results for $n_o(\vec{r})$ and hence $\Phi(\vec{r})$ to distances $r > \ell$ is difficult within a strict quantum mechanical framework which treats background scattering as incoherent. One possible approach is to add the $\Phi(\vec{r})$ from each scatterer (ions and background) independently and to disregard incoherent scattering in damping the electron propagation and consequently $n_o(\vec{r})$ and $\Phi(\vec{r})$. The incoherence would instead enter as a result of the random placement of RRD's. This would effectively wash-out the oscillatory terms in Eq. (9) and restore Landauer's result for the macroscopic field automatically. Such an approach is quite different from the traditional one employed in quantum mechanical analyses of electron transport. A correct quantum calculation in the $r \geq \ell$ region requires careful consideration of RRD-RRD interactions. As we pointed out earlier it is not clear that the traditional quantum approach can handle these interactions correctly. In terms of conductivity corrections, or deviations from Matthiessen's rule, we are here dealing with the notoriously difficult corrections of order $1/k_F\ell$ or of second-order in impurity ion density.

Although we have not obtained new answers here by appealing to a picture based on microscopic inhomogeneities, we have gained better insight into the response of electrons and atoms to electric fields. More important, these considerations have led us to identify some possible inconsistencies in traditional quantum mechanical approaches to transport theory.

Acknowledgments

I am grateful to Rolf Landauer for valuable discussions and correspondence. This work was supported by the Graduate School of the University of Wisconsin-Milwaukee.

References

1. R. Landauer, IBM J. Res. Dev. 1, 223 (1957).
2. R. S. Sorbello, Phys. Rev. B23, 5119 (1981). Note the following corrections: The right-hand side of Eqs. (12) and (16) should be divided by $\hbar$. The right-hand side of Eq. (26) should be multiplied by $e/\hbar$. In Eq. (20), p_0 should read $2p_0$. In Eq. (21), 2m should read $\hbar/m$. The values of p/p_0 on the vertical axis of Fig. 3 should be doubled.
3. R. Landauer, Z. Physik B21, 247 (1975).
4. See, for example, H. B. Huntington in Diffusion in Solids: Recent Developments, edited by A. S. Nowick and J. J. Burton (Academic, New York, 1974).
5. R. Landauer, Philos. Mag. 21, 863 (1970).
6. R. Landauer and J.W.F. Woo, Phys. Rev. B10, 1266 (1974).
7. R. Landauer, Phys. Rev. B16, 4698 (1977).
8. W. L. Schaich, Phys. Rev. B13, 3350 (1976).
9. C. Bosvieux and J. Friedel, J. Phys. Chem. Solids 23, 123 (1962).
10. R. S. Sorbello, Comments Solid State Phys. 6, 117 (1975).
11. R. Landauer and J.W.F. Woo, Phys. Rev. B5, 1189 (1972).
12. L. Sham, Phys. Rev. B12, 3142 (1975).
13. See P. R. Rimbey and R. S. Sorbello, Phys. Rev. B21, 2150 (1980) and references cited therein.
14. See D. S. Fisher and P. A. Lee, Phys. Rev. B23, 6851 (1981) and references cited therein.
15. R. Landauer, pre-print.

Propagation and Attenuation in Composite Media[*]

Victor Twersky[**]

Mathematics Department
University of Illinois
Chicago, Illinois 60680

1. INTRODUCTION

In recent papers[1,2] we analyzed coherent scattering of waves by randomly distributed pair-correlated particles. We worked with the ensemble average of the functional equation for the field of a scatterer within the distribution in terms of its field when isolated, and derived representations and deterministic approximations for the coherent wave (the ensemble average of the solution over the realizable configurations of particles). The associated bulk parameters and corresponding indices of refraction specify a composite medium whose physical properties depend on the particles' properties and their distribution, as well as on the properties of the embedding medium. In the present paper we summarize some of the earlier results and consider later developments.

We start with results for the long wavelength (λ) limit which include refraction and absorption effects but no scattering losses. Then we introduce the leading term of the scattering losses to obtain results for absorbing particles that suffice if the net attenuation is small, and also consider generalizations. To facilitate applications, we first emphasize the different bases for anisotropy of the bulk parameters and indices of refraction of general composites and the physical import of key approximations, and then consider the analytical aspects on which the development is based.

For an ensemble of configurations of identical aligned scatterers, we specify the one-particle statistics by the average number (ρ) of scatterers in unit volume, and the two-particle statistics by $\rho f(\mathbf{R})$ with $f(\mathbf{R})$ as the distribution function for the separation $(\mathbf{R})$ of pairs. The minimum separation of centers as a function of $\hat{R}$ specifies the exclusion surface $\mathbf{R} = \mathbf{b}(\hat{R})$; we require $f(\mathbf{R}) = 0$ for $R < |\mathbf{b}(\hat{R})|$, and $f(\mathbf{R}) \sim 1$ for $R \sim \infty$. If $\mathbf{b} = b\hat{R}$ is a sphere with radius $b \geq 2a$, then $f(R)$ is the usual radial distribution function. We use $f(R)$ not only for spherical obstacles of radius a but also for more general shapes $\mathbf{R} = \mathbf{a}(\hat{R})$ (identical and aligned, or averaged over shape, alignment, etc.) regarded as if enclosed in transparent coatings whose outer surfaces are spheres of diameter b. The transparent shell has no direct influence on an isolated obstacle's scattering properties but preserves the radial symmetry of the distribution, and specifies a minimum separation between centers as an additional parameter. For cases where we average over alignment we assume the distribution of alignments to be uniform and uncorrelated with position or separation; similarly for averages over particle shapes, sizes, or parameters. The general case we consider corresponds to differently aligned nonsimilar scatterer $(\underset{\sim}{a})$ and exclusion $(\underset{\sim}{b})$ surfaces, such that $\underset{\sim}{R} = \underset{\sim}{b}/2$ (the outer surface of the transparent coating) represents impenetrable statistical-mechanics particles whose shape and volume fraction govern the configurational aspects. Exclusive of the properties of the embedding space, the shape and parameters (tensors, in general) of aligned particles and the shape of the exclusion surface provide three distinct bases for anisotropy.

For ellipsoidal particles specified by major semidiameters $a_j (j = 1,2,3)$ along the directions $\hat{\xi}_j$ with associated depolarization integrals $q_j = q_j(a_j)$ normalized to satisfy $\Sigma q_j = 1$, we write the particle's shape parameter as a dyadic $\tilde{q} = \Sigma q_j \hat{x}_j \hat{x}_j$. Similarly we specify the particle's material properties by a dyadic parameter $\tilde{p} = \Sigma p_j \hat{\xi}_j \hat{\xi}_j$, or by two such dyadics (for the general electromagnetic case), or by one dyadic and one scalar parameter (for general small-amplitude acoustics). The exclusion-correlation surface b_i with depolarization factors $Q_j = q_j(b_j) = q_j(b_j/2)$ is specified by the dyadic $\tilde{Q} = \Sigma Q_j \hat{X}_j \hat{X}_j$. In general, the orthogonal sets of unit vectors $\hat{x}_j$, $\hat{\xi}_j$, and $\hat{X}_j$ do not coincide, and the cocentered ellipsoids q and Q (the surfaces of the particle and of its transparent coating) are not necessarily similar or conformal.

2. LOW-FREQUENCY LIMITS

For monopole particles each of volume v specified by a scalar parameter c in an embedding medium c_0, the bulk parameter C is given by

$$C = c_0 + w(c-c_0) = wc + (1-w)c_0, \quad w = \rho v \tag{1}$$

where w is the volume fraction occupied by particles (parameter c), and 1-w is the void (c_0) fraction of the composite (C). The second equality in (1), the representation of the bulk parameter C as the volume-weighted mean of the parameters of the components goes back to Archimedes. In terms of shifted normalized values, we rewrite (1) as

$$\Gamma = w\gamma; \quad \gamma = (c/c_0)-1, \quad \Gamma = (C/c_0)-1 \tag{2}$$

In general the parameters are complex, $c = c_r + ic_i$ such that c_r and $c_i = |c_i|$ are real; c_i accounts for absorption. In small amplitude acoustics, in the simplest case, c is the compressibility.

For aligned dipole particles with parameter $\tilde{p}$ in an embedding medium $\tilde{p}_0$, for particle and exclusion surfaces $\tilde{q}$ and $\tilde{Q}$, the analog of (2) is

$$\tilde{\Delta} = w\tilde{\delta}\cdot(\tilde{I}+\tilde{D}\cdot\tilde{\delta})^{-1}; \; \tilde{\delta} = \tilde{p}\cdot\tilde{p}_0^{-1} - \tilde{I}, \; \tilde{\Delta} = \tilde{P}\cdot\tilde{p}_0^{-1} - \tilde{I}, \; \tilde{D} = \tilde{q} - w\tilde{Q}. \tag{3}$$

Here $\tilde{I}$ is the identity, and $\tilde{D}$ is the compound depolarization factor. In small amplitude acoustics, in the simplest case p^{-1} is the particle's mass density; more generally, $p = p_r - ip_i$ with p_r and $p_i = |p_i|$ real. In electromagnetics, $\tilde{p}$ represents either the particle's dielectric parameter $\tilde{\epsilon}'$ or its magnetic parameter $\tilde{\mu}'$, $\tilde{p}_0$ represents $\tilde{\epsilon}_0$ or $\tilde{\mu}_0$, and $\tilde{P}$ the corresponding bulk value $\tilde{\epsilon}$ or $\tilde{\mu}$; we emphasize the dielectric case $p = \epsilon' = \epsilon'_r + i\epsilon'_i$, $\epsilon'_i = |\epsilon'_i|$.

To first order in $\tilde{\delta}$, (3) reduces to $\tilde{\Delta} \approx w\tilde{\delta}$, i.e., the tensor version of (2). The factor $(\tilde{I}+\tilde{D}\cdot\tilde{\delta})^{-1}$ in (3) arises from the dipole character of the particle. To make the physical content more accessible we decompose $\tilde{D}$ and rewrite (3) as

$$\tilde{\Delta}\cdot(\tilde{I}+\tilde{Q}\cdot\tilde{\Delta})^{-1} = w\tilde{\delta}\cdot(\tilde{I}+\tilde{q}\cdot\tilde{\delta})^{-1}. \tag{4}$$

If the principal axes of all dyadics coincide, then for each component,

$$\frac{\Delta_j}{1 + Q_j\Delta_j} = w\,\frac{\delta_j}{1 + q_j\Delta_j} \tag{5}$$

In particular for spherical particles $(q_j = 1/3)$ and spherical coats $(Q_j = 1/3)$ and isotropic parameters $(\delta_j = p/p_0-1)$, we have

$$\frac{P - p_0}{P + 2p_0} = w\,\frac{p - p_0}{p + 2p_0} \tag{6}$$

i.e., the classical form obtained originally by Maxwell[3] (and attributed to Clausius, Mossotti, Lorenz, and Lorentz). Maxwell constructed (6) by equating the potential of a sphere of volume V and equivalent parameter P to the uncoupled sum of the potentials of N spheres of volume v and parameter p within V. Writing $w = \rho v = Nv/V$ in

(6) and multiplying through by V gives Maxwell's initial form; although useful as a mnemonic device, we stress that the left side of (6) corresponds to the radially symmetric shape of the region excluding the centers of all neighbors of one particle $(Q_j = 1/3)$, and not to the volume of the distribution, and that there is no equivalent sphere. The same construction suffices for (5) and (4); these serve to relate the sum of the distant potentials of N ellipsoids $(v,\tilde{p},\tilde{q})$ to an equivalent ellipsoid $(V,\tilde{P},\tilde{Q})$, but actually $\tilde{Q}$ corresponds to the shape of the exclusion region and not to that of the distribution as a whole, and there is no equivalent ellipsoid.

For scalar waves and composites specified by bulk parameters C and $\tilde{P}$ the index of refraction (η) corresponding to a direction of propagation $\hat{K}$ is determined by

$$\eta^2 = C/\hat{K}\cdot\tilde{P}\cdot\hat{K} \tag{7}$$

See References 1 and 4 for illustrations and applications to a plane wave incident at an arbitrary angle on a slab region of composite corresponding to (7). For electromagnetic waves and composites with bulk parameters $\tilde{\epsilon}$ and $\tilde{\mu}$, the index is specified by the determinantal equation

$$|(\tilde{I}-\hat{K}\hat{K})\eta^{-2} + (\hat{K}\times\tilde{\mu}^{-1}\times\hat{K})\cdot\tilde{\epsilon}^{-1}| = 0. \tag{8}$$

If $\tilde{\mu}' = \tilde{\mu}_0$, then $\tilde{\mu} = \tilde{I}$, and (8) simplifies to

$$\hat{K}\cdot(\tilde{I}\eta^{-2} - \tilde{\epsilon}^{-1})^{-1}\cdot\hat{K} = 0. \tag{9}$$

See References 2 and 5-7 for illustrations and applications.

3. SCATTERING LOSSES

To include the leading term in $k = 2\pi/\lambda$ corresponding to scattering losses we replace (2) by

$$\Gamma = w\gamma + i\alpha\gamma^2 w\mathfrak{w} \tag{10}$$

where α depends on k, and $\mathfrak{w}$ depends on the volume fraction W of the coated particles. For scatterers in the form of slabs, cylinders, or ellipsoids $(n = 1,2,3)$ we have

$$\alpha = k^n v_n/d_n,\ v_n = \{2a_1, \pi a_1 a_2, 4\pi a_1 a_2 a_3/3\},\ d_n = \{2,4,4\pi\} \tag{11}$$

corresponding to incidence perpendicular to a generator for $n = 1,2$. The function

$$\mathfrak{w} = 1 + \rho \int [f(\underset{\sim}{R})-1] d\underset{\sim}{R} \qquad (12)$$

is a statistical mechanics packing factor proportional to the variance (fluctuations) in the number (N_c) of particles in a central region (V_c), i.e., $\mathfrak{w} = [\langle N_c^2\rangle - \langle N_c\rangle^2]/\langle N_c\rangle$ such that $\langle N_c\rangle/V_c = N/V = \rho$. The dependence of $\mathfrak{w}$ on W is illustrated by results based on the scaled-particle equations[8] of state $(\mathcal{E})$ for impenetrable particles of volume fraction W governed by radially symmetric pair statistics, or by lattice gas statistics. From $\mathfrak{w} = (\partial\mathcal{E}/\partial\rho)^{-1}$ we construct

$$\mathfrak{w}_n = (1-W)^{n+1}/[1+(n-1)W]^{n-1}, \quad \mathfrak{w}_0 = 1-W \qquad (13)$$

The cases $n = 3,2,1$ correspond to correlated spheres, cylinders, slabs, and 0 to uncorrelated space-occupying particles (random lattice gas). More generally, we could determine $\mathfrak{w}$ were $f(\underset{\sim}{R})$ known, e.g., by numerical computations based on the Percus-Yevick equation.

The corresponding form for the dyadic parameter (3) is

$$\tilde{\Delta} = w\underline{\tilde{\delta}} + i\beta\underline{\tilde{\delta}}\cdot\underline{\tilde{\delta}}w\mathfrak{w}, \quad \underline{\tilde{\delta}} = \tilde{\delta}\cdot(\tilde{I}+\tilde{D}\cdot\tilde{\delta})^{-1} = (\tilde{I}+\tilde{\delta}\cdot\tilde{D})^{-1}\cdot\tilde{\delta} \qquad (14)$$

For acoustic dipoles with index as in (7), we have

$$\beta = -\alpha/n = -k^n v_n/d_n^a, \quad d_n^a = \{2,8,12\pi\} \qquad (15)$$

with α as in (11). For dielectric poles $\underset{\sim}{P} = \tilde{\epsilon}$ with index as in (9),

$$\beta = k^n v_n/d_n^e, \quad d_n^e = \{2,4 \text{ or } 8,6\pi\}. \qquad (16)$$

The two values of $n = 2$ correspond to incident polarization $(\underset{\sim}{E})$ parallel or perpendicular to a generator; for $\underset{\sim}{E}$ parallel, the cylinder is a monopole (as is the slab for normal incidence), i.e., $\tilde{D} = 0$.

4. COMPLEX DIELECTRICS

Initially we apply (3) and (4) for the components of $\tilde{P} = \tilde{\epsilon}$ for complex $\tilde{p} = \tilde{\epsilon}'$, and then we include the scattering loss terms (14). For coincident dielectric and geometric axes, and polarization parallel to a principal axis, we write

$$\Delta = \frac{w\delta}{1 + \delta D}, \quad D = q - wQ, \quad \delta = \delta_r + i\delta_i, \quad \delta_i \geq 0 \qquad (17)$$

where the common subscript j has been suppressed. For uncoated infinite slabs or circular cylinders and longitudinal polarization, $q = Q = 0$, and (17) reduces to $\Delta = w\delta$, the form in (2); for transverse polarization, $q = Q = 1$ for the slab, and $1/2$ for the cylinder. The results for the slab are due to Maxwell[3], and those for the cylinder to Rayleigh.[9] Wiener[10] applied the results for the corresponding indices to investigate form effects in birefringence and dichroism studies.

From (17) we have

$$\Delta = \Delta_r + i\Delta_i, \quad \Delta_r = w\,\frac{(\delta_r + |\delta|^2 D)}{|1+\delta D|^2}, \quad \Delta_i = \frac{w\delta_i}{|1+\delta D|^2}. \tag{18}$$

For the cases at hand the indices of refraction are equal to the square roots of the parameters, i.e., $\eta^2 = P$, $\eta'^2 = p$, $\eta_0^2 = p_0$. We take η_0 as real and construct the corresponding bulk indices:

$$\eta = \eta_r + i\eta_i = \eta_0(1+\Delta)^{1/2}, \quad \begin{Bmatrix}\eta_r\\ \eta_i\end{Bmatrix} = \eta_0\left[\frac{|1+\Delta| \pm (1+\Delta_r)|}{2}\right]^{1/2}. \tag{19}$$

To express (19) in terms of η', we introduce

$$\nu = \frac{\eta'}{\eta_0} - 1 = \left(\frac{\eta_r'}{\eta_0} - 1\right) + i\,\frac{\eta_i'}{\eta_0} = \nu_r + i\nu_i \tag{20}$$

such that $\delta = (\eta'/\eta_0)^2 - 1 = \nu(2+\nu)$, and work with

$$\delta_r = 2\nu_r + \nu_r^2 - \nu_i^2, \quad \delta_i = 2\nu_i(1+\nu_r). \tag{21}$$

To include the scattering terms of (14), we replace (17) by

$$\Delta \approx w(\underline{\delta} + i\underline{\delta}^2 S), \quad \underline{\delta} = \delta/(1+\delta D), \quad S = \beta\mathfrak{w} \tag{22}$$

with $\mathfrak{w}$ as in (12) and $\beta = \beta(k^m)$ as in (16). Because δ of (22) does not include terms of order k^2 (higher order terms of the dipole at hand, contributions of other multipoles, and from k-dependent distribution integrals), we retain at most only the first order term of $S = S(k^m)$ in the corresponding η. To delineate conditions on the retention of S, we first consider non-absorbing particles, $\delta_i = 0$. For such cases

$$\Delta_r = w\delta_r/(1+\delta_r D), \quad \Delta_i = wS\delta_r^2/(1+\delta_r D)^2 \tag{23}$$

where the next terms in k of Δ_r and Δ_i are of order k^2 and k^{m+2} respectively. If $|\Delta_i| \ll |1+\Delta_r|$, then from (19),

$$\frac{\eta_r}{\eta_0} \approx (1+\Delta_r)^{1/2} = \left[1 + \frac{w\delta_r}{1+\delta_r D}\right]^{1/2}, \quad \frac{\eta_i}{\eta_0} = \frac{\Delta_i\eta_0}{2\eta_r} = \frac{\Delta_i}{2(1+\Delta_r)^{1/2}} \tag{24}$$

where the corrections in k to η_r, η_i are of order k^2, k^{m+2} respectively.

To third order in δ_r, we construct

$$\eta_r/\eta_0 = 1 + \frac{1}{2} w\delta_r - \frac{1}{8} w\delta_r^2 (w+4D) + \frac{1}{16} w\delta_r^2 (w^2+4wD+8D^2) \qquad (25)$$

and

$$\eta_i/\eta_0 = \frac{1}{2} wS\delta_r^2 \left[1 - \frac{1}{2}\delta_r(w+4D)\right] . \qquad (26)$$

Substituting for δ_r from (21), we see that $\delta_i = 0$ implies either $\nu_i = 0$ or $1 + \nu_r = 0$; for the first, $\delta_r = 2\nu_r + \nu_r^2$ as before[6], but for the second, $\delta_r = -\nu_i^2 - 1$.

If the particles are absorbing, then from (22) for $\delta = \delta_r + i\delta_i$,

$$\Delta_r = w\underline{\delta}_r(1-2\underline{\delta}_i S), \quad \Delta_i = w[\underline{\delta}_i + (\underline{\delta}_r^2 - \underline{\delta}_i^2)S]$$

$$\underline{\delta}_r = (\delta_r + |\delta|^2 D)/\mathcal{D}, \ \underline{\delta}_i = \delta_i/\mathcal{D}, \ \mathcal{D} = |1+\delta D| = (1+\delta_r D)^2 + (\delta_i D)^2 . \qquad (27)$$

Although we may use these heuristically in (19), they are inconsistent in k except for $S = 0$ or $\delta_i = 0$. For small δ_i, we use (27) to generalize (24). Thus, if $\delta_i \ll \delta_r$, then to first order in δ_i and S,

$$\Delta_r = w\delta_r/(1+\delta_r D), \quad \Delta_i = w(\delta_i + \delta_r^2 S)/(1+\delta D)^2 . \qquad (28)$$

Substituting into (19), we obtain (24) in terms of the present Δ_i. Explicitely, we have

$$\frac{\eta_r}{\eta_0} = \left[\frac{1 + \delta_r(w+D)}{1 + \delta_r D}\right]^{1/2}, \quad \frac{\eta_i}{\eta_0} = \frac{w(\delta_i + \delta_r^2 S)}{2(1+\delta_r D)^{3/2}[1+\delta_r(w+D)]^{1/2}} \qquad (29)$$

which suffice for situations where the net attenuation is small. The real index η_r is the same as in (24)-(25). For η_i, to order $\delta_i\delta_r^2$ we have

$$\frac{2\eta_i}{w\eta_0} = S\delta_r^2[1 - \frac{1}{2}\delta_r(w+4D)] + \delta_i[1 - \frac{1}{2}\delta_r(w+4D) + \frac{3}{8}\delta_r^2(w^2+4wD+8D^2)]. \qquad (30)$$

The net attenuation coefficient $2k\eta_i$ consists of two sets of terms, one corresponding to scattering losses and one to absorption losses.

To display the different bases of the anistropic effects explicitly, and to obtain simple forms for practical applications, we work with the leading terms of the power series expansions of P and η. To avoid repetition we keep terms to third order in δ_i and first order in S with the understanding that if $S = 0$ we work with terms through δ_i^3, but if $S \neq 0$ we keep only the leading terms in δ_i and drop the coupling terms in $\delta_i S$ because of the neglected k^2 terms. The coupling terms are not significant for numerical computations but we display them for physical import. Thus, from (22) to third order in δ we have

$$(P-p_0)/p_0w = \Delta/w = \delta - \delta^2(D-iS) + \delta^3 D(D-2iS) \tag{31}$$

Introducing $\delta = \delta_r + i\delta_i$, the real part of (31) is the real dielectric contrast

$$\Delta_r/w = \delta_r(1-\delta_r D+\delta_r^2 D^2) + \delta_i^2 D(1-3\delta_r D) - 2S\delta_r\delta_i + 2S\delta_i(3\delta_r^2-\delta_i^2)D \tag{32}$$

and the imaginary part is the normalized net loss

$$\Delta_i/w = \delta_i[1-2\delta_r D+(3\delta_r^2-\delta_i^2)D^2] + S(\delta_r^2-\delta_i^2) - 2S\delta_r(\delta_r^2-3\delta_i^2)D. \tag{33}$$

In Δ_r, the terms that involve δ_i^2 and not S arise from absorption and those that involve $\delta_i S$ arise from the interplay of absorption and scattering losses. To order S, there are no pure scattering loss corrections in Δ_r; if $\delta_i = 0$, all loss corrections vanish to third order in δ and first order in S. In Δ_i, there are essentially three kinds of attenuation processes: pure absorption, pure scattering, and the interaction terms that depend on $\delta_i^2 S$.

From (31), we construct the corresponding representations of η in terms of $\nu = (\eta'-\eta_0)/\eta_0$ by using $\delta = \nu(2+\nu)$ and expanding $\eta/\eta_0 = (1+\Delta)^{1/2}$ to third order in ν and first order in S. Thus,

$$\frac{\eta-\eta_0}{\eta_0 w} = \frac{h}{w} = \nu + \frac{1}{2}\nu^2(A+i4S) + \frac{1}{2}\nu^3(B+i4AS). \tag{34}$$

$$A = 1 - (w+4D), \qquad B = -(1-w)(w+4D) + 8D^2.$$

Writing $\nu = \nu_r + i\nu_i$, we separate real and imaginary parts to obtain the refractive contrast $h_r = (\eta_r-\eta_0)/\eta_0$,

$$h_r/w = \nu_r\left(1+\frac{1}{2}\nu_r A+\frac{1}{2}\nu_r^2 B\right) - \frac{1}{2}\nu_i^2(A+3\nu_r B) - 4S\nu_i\nu_r - 2S\nu_i(3\nu_r^2-\nu_i^2)A \tag{35}$$

and the normalized attenuation $h_i = \eta_i/\eta_0$,

$$h_i/w = \nu_i\left[1 + \nu_r A + \frac{1}{2}(3\nu_r^2-\nu_i^2)B\right] + 2S(\nu_r^2-\nu_i^2) + 2S\nu_r(\nu_r^2-3\nu_i^2)A. \tag{36}$$

The grouping of terms in (35) and (36) is the same as in (32) and (33), and similar considerations apply. As before for Δ, if $S = 0$ we work with terms through ν_i^3, but if $S \neq 0$ we keep only the leading terms in ν_i and drop the coupling terms in $\nu_i S$ because of the neglected k^2 **terms.**

To stress physical import, we write (32) to second order terms as

$$\Delta_r = w\delta_r - w|\delta|^2 D + 2w\delta_i(\delta_i D - \delta_r S). \tag{37}$$

The leading term is a volumetric (intrinsic) contribution, and the second term $-w|\delta|^2 D = -w|\delta|^2 q + w^2|\delta|^2 Q$ consists of a decrease determined by particle shape (q) and an increase arising from pair (w^2) interactions governed by the correlation-congifurational exclusion surface (Q). The third term shows the effects of absorption and the interaction of absorption and scattering: the pure absorption term shows an increase arising from shape and a decrease arising from correlations; the mixed term for positive δ_r represents a decrease, with S determined by fluctuations. Similarly for

$$\Delta_i = w\delta_i + wS|\delta|^2 - 2w\delta_i(\delta_r D + \delta_i S), \tag{38}$$

the leading term is the volumetric (intrinsic) absorption, and the second term is the scattering loss arising from fluctuations. The term in $\delta_i \delta_r D$ for $\delta_r > 0$ involves a decrease due to particle shape and an increase because of correlations, and the mixed term is a decrease arising from interaction of the two loss mechanisms.

For the corresponding bulk refractive index contrast, we have

$$\hbar_r = w\nu_r + w|\nu|^2 A/2 - w\nu_i(\nu_i A + 4S\nu_r) \tag{39}$$
$$A = 1-w - 4D = (1-4q) - w(1-4Q)$$

where if $Q = q$, then $A = (1-w)(1-4Q)$ is positive for $Q < 1/4$, negative for $Q > 1/4$. Splitting A into $1-w$ and $-4D$, we see that the D and S contributions show the same trends as in (37), but now there are two additional effects symmetrical in volume and void fractions, i.e., in $w(1-w)\left(\frac{1}{2}|\nu|^2 - \nu_i^2\right)$. Similarly for

$$\hbar_i = w\nu_i + 2wS|\nu|^2 + w\nu_i(\nu_r A - 4\nu_i S) \tag{40}$$

where we decompose wA in $w(1-w)$ and $-w4D$ for comparison with (38).

We apply the above results elsewhere in terms of η_0 as the variable to analyze birerfingence $(\eta_{r1}-\eta_{r2})$ and dichroism $(\eta_{i1}-\eta_{i2})$ measurements in which the index of the embedding medium is varied to help determine the properties and shapes of the particles.

5. ANALYTICAL ASPECTS

In previous sections we considered the key forms (10) and (14) for the bulk parameters and (7)-(9) for the associated indices of refraction with emphasis on their physical content and implications for propagation and attenuation of the coherent field. Now we indicate essential steps of their analytical derivation. For brevity we restrict initial considerations to the three-dimensional case of bounded obstacles.

For the scalar problem of Helmholtz's equation, we take the field incident on an arbitrary obstacle as the plane wave

$$\phi = e^{i\underset{\sim}{k}\cdot\underset{\sim}{r}}, \quad \underset{\sim}{r} = r\hat{r}(\theta,\varphi), \quad \underset{\sim}{k} = k\hat{k} \tag{41}$$

We write the corresponding scattered wave as a radiative function in the form of an integral over the obstacle's surface $\mathfrak{S}(\underset{\sim}{r}')$,

$$u(\underset{\sim}{r}) = \{h(k|\underset{\sim}{r}-\underset{\sim}{r}'|), u(\underset{\sim}{r}')\},$$
$$h(x) = h_0^{(1)}(x) = \frac{e^{ix}}{ix}, \quad \{h,u\} = \frac{k}{i4\pi}\int(h\nabla u - u\nabla h)\cdot d\underset{\sim}{\mathfrak{S}}. \tag{42}$$

We take the origin of $\underset{\sim}{r}$ as the center of the smallest sphere circumscribing the obstacle. For $r \sim \infty$,

$$u \sim h(kr)g(\hat{r},\hat{k}), \quad g(\hat{r},\hat{k}) = \{e^{-i\underset{\sim}{k}_r\cdot\underset{\sim}{r}'}, u\} \quad \underset{\sim}{k}_r = k\hat{r} \tag{43}$$

with g as the normalized scattering amplitude. An inverse to $g[u]$ of (43), at least for r greater than the scatterer's projection on $\hat{r}$, is the complex spectral representation, say $u[g]$:

$$u(\underset{\sim}{r}) = \int_c e^{i\underset{\sim}{k}_c\cdot\underset{\sim}{r}} g(\hat{r}_c,\hat{k}), \quad \underset{\sim}{k}_c = k\hat{r}_c, \quad \int_c = \frac{1}{2\pi}\int d\Omega(\theta_c,\varphi_c) \tag{44}$$

with contours as for $h_0^{(1)}$.

We use analogous forms for the corresponding multiple scattered wave of one element (say s) of a configuration of N obstacles, i.e., $U_s[G_s]$ and $G_s[U_s]$. Applying Green's operator $\{u,v\}$ as in (42) to the solution of Helmholtz's equation for one obstacle and N-obstacles we obtain the key representation

$$G_t(\hat{r}) = g_t(\hat{r},\hat{k})e^{i\underset{\sim}{k}\cdot\underset{\sim}{r}_t} = \sum_{s\neq t}\int g_t(\hat{r},\hat{r}_c)G_s(\hat{r}_c)e^{i\underset{\sim}{k}_c\cdot\underset{\sim}{R}_{ts}}, \quad \underset{\sim}{R}_{ts} = \underset{\sim}{r}_t - \underset{\sim}{r}_s \tag{45}$$

where g_t and G_t are the isolated and multiple scattering amplitudes of obstacle t. Equation (45) determines G in terms of g (the direct problem), or g in terms of G (the inverse), at least if the scatterer's projections on $\hat{R}_{ts}$ do not overlap.

The ensemble average of $\Psi = \phi + \Sigma U_s$ yields a system of hierarchy integrals. The first expresses the ensemble average $\langle\Psi\rangle$, the coherent wave (a set of plane waves with propagation coefficients $\underset{\sim}{K}_1 = k\eta_1\hat{K}_1$), in terms of an integral over $\langle G_t\rangle_t$, the ensemble average of G_t with obstacle-t fixed. The second relates $\langle G_t\rangle_t$ to an integral over

$\langle G_s\rangle_{st}$, the ensemble average of G_s with obstacles s and t fixed, etc. For a distribution with one-particle and two-particle statistics specified by $\rho = N/V$ and $f(\underset{\sim}{R}_{ts}) = f(\underset{\sim}{R})$, we truncate the hierarchy system by $\langle G_s\rangle_{st} \approx \langle G_s\rangle_s$ to obtain a deterministic approximation; see References 11-13. In terms of the radiative function

$$\mathfrak{u} = \int_c g(\hat{r},\hat{r}_c)\mathfrak{G}(\underset{\sim}{k}_c|\underset{\sim}{K})e^{i\underset{\sim}{k}_c\cdot\underset{\sim}{R}}, \quad \underset{\sim}{K} = k\eta\hat{K} \tag{46}$$

we determine η by

$$\mathfrak{G}(\underset{\sim}{k}_r|\underset{\sim}{K}) = -\frac{i4\pi\rho}{k^3(\eta^2-1)}\left\{e^{-i\underset{\sim}{K}\cdot\underset{\sim}{R}},\mathfrak{u}\right\}_s + \rho\int_{V-\bar{v}}[f(\underset{\sim}{R})-1]e^{-i\underset{\sim}{K}\cdot\underset{\sim}{R}}\mathfrak{u}d\underset{\sim}{R} \tag{47}$$

where $s(k)$ and $\bar{v}(k)$ are the exclusion surface and volume, and V is taken as the volume of all space.

See Reference 1 for detailed derivation of (47), and for volume integral representations of the bulk parameters C and $\tilde{P}$. These representations show that if the obstacles are specified solely by the parameter c, then $\tilde{P} = \tilde{I}$ and $\eta^2 = C$; similarly, if $c = 1$, then $C = 1$ and $\eta^2 = \hat{K}\cdot\tilde{P}\cdot\hat{K}$. Here and in the following we have set c_0, p_0 and η_0 equal to unity so that all quantities C, $\tilde{P}$, and η are normalized values relative to those of the embedding medium. See also Reference 1 for reduction of (47) to obtain the results for η^2 derived originally by Rayleigh, Reiche, Foldy, and by Lax, and for the relations to the procedures of Lax[11] and of Keller.[12]

To derive (10) and (14), we start with

$$g(\hat{r},\hat{k}) \approx a_0 + \hat{r}\cdot\tilde{a}_1\cdot\hat{k} \tag{48}$$

$$a_0 \approx a_0'(1+a_0') \qquad a_0' = i\alpha\gamma$$

$$\tilde{a}_1 \approx \tilde{a}_1'\cdot(\tilde{I}+\tilde{a}_1'/n), \; \tilde{a}_1' = -i\alpha(\tilde{I}+\tilde{\delta}\cdot\tilde{q})^{-1}\cdot\tilde{\delta}$$

where γ, $\tilde{\delta}$, and $\alpha = \alpha(k^n)$ are given in (2), (3) and (11). [Note for $c_0 = 1$ and $\tilde{p}_0 = \tilde{I}$, we have $\gamma = c-1$ and $\tilde{\delta} = (\tilde{p}-\tilde{I})$ in terms of relative particle parameters.] This approximation is correct to lowest order in k for the real and imaginary parts of g. The imaginary part of g, i.e., the k^n terms for the isotropic case $\tilde{\delta} = \delta\tilde{I} = (p-1)\tilde{I}$ were obtained by Rayleigh[14] from the corresponding potential theory problems.[3]

If $\tilde{p} = \tilde{I}$, then $g = a_0$, and similarly for the multiple scattering amplitude $\mathfrak{G} = A_0$. For this case of pure monopoles, $\mathfrak{u} = a_0 h_0(kR)A_0$, and from (47) to lowest order in k for the real and imaginary parts,

$$\eta_m^2 = C \approx 1 + w\gamma + i\alpha\gamma^2 w\mathfrak{w}, \; w = \rho v, \; \mathfrak{w} = 1 + \rho\int_V [f(\underset{\sim}{R})-1]d\underset{\sim}{R} \tag{49}$$

where $\eta_m^2 = C$ follows from (7) because $\tilde{p} = \tilde{I}$ yields $\tilde{P} = \tilde{I}$. Here $\mathfrak{w}$ involves $f(\underset{\sim}{R})$ for elliptically symmetric statistics determined by the shape dyadic $\tilde{Q}$ of the exclusion surface; the integration over all space (V) corresponds to the volume integral over $V - \bar{v}$ in (47) minus $\rho \int_{\bar{v}} d\underset{\sim}{R}$ as generated by evaluating the surface integral form.

If $c = 1$, then from $g(\hat{r},\hat{R}) = \hat{r}\cdot\tilde{a}_1\cdot\hat{R}$ and $\mathfrak{G}(k\hat{R}|\underset{\sim}{K}) = \hat{R}\cdot\tilde{A}\cdot\hat{K} = \hat{R}\cdot\underset{\sim}{A}$, we have $u = \hat{r}\cdot\tilde{a}_1\cdot\tilde{h}_a(kR)\cdot\underset{\sim}{A}$ with $\tilde{h}_a = [\tilde{I}h_0 + (\tilde{I}-n\hat{R}\hat{R})h_2]/n$ as the acoustic dipole propagator. From (47), and using $c = 1$ implies $C = 1$, we obtain

$$\eta_d^{-2} = \hat{K}\cdot\tilde{P}\cdot\hat{K},\ \tilde{P} \approx \tilde{I} + w\tilde{\underline{\delta}} - i\alpha\tilde{\underline{\delta}}\cdot\tilde{\delta}w\mathfrak{w}/n,\ \tilde{\underline{\delta}} = [\tilde{I} + \tilde{\delta}\cdot(q-w\tilde{Q})]^{-1}\cdot\tilde{\delta}\ . \quad (50)$$

To the present order in k, the index of refraction for distributions of scatterers specified by two-parameters c and $\tilde{p}$ is the product of the indices for pure monopoles and pure dipoles. Writing the results in (49) and (50) in terms of real quantities as $C = C_1 + iC_2$, $\hat{K}\cdot\tilde{P}\cdot\hat{K} = P_1 - iP_2$ with $C_2 > 0$ and $P_2 > 0$, we have

$$\eta^2 = \frac{C}{\hat{K}\cdot\tilde{P}\cdot\hat{K}} \approx \eta_m^2\eta_d^2 \approx \frac{C_1}{P_1}\left[1 + i\left(\frac{C_2}{C_1} + \frac{P_2}{P_1}\right)\right]. \quad (51)$$

See Reference 1, Equations (126)-(128) for values of η corresponding to an arbitrary direction of incidence on a slab distribution of finite thickness.

For the corresponding electromagnetic problems, we use the vector and dyadic analogs of (41)-(47) developed in Reference 2. In particular, we work with the present (47) in terms of vector functions $\underset{\sim}{\mathfrak{G}}$ and $\underset{\sim}{u}$. The resulting equation, say (47)′, determines η via

$$\underset{\sim}{u} = \int_c \tilde{g}(\hat{r},\hat{r}_c)\cdot\underset{\sim}{\mathfrak{G}}(\underset{\sim}{k}_c|\underset{\sim}{K})e^{i\underset{\sim}{k}_c\cdot\underset{\sim}{R}} \quad (52)$$

as in Reference 2, Equation (62) [henceforth (2:62) for brevity] in terms of the isolated dyadic scattering amplitude $\tilde{g}$. The representations for the bulk dyadics $\tilde{\epsilon}$ and $\tilde{\mu}$ and their connections with η^2, as developed in (2:36)-(2:52), show that if the particle is specified by one parameter either $\underset{\sim}{\epsilon}'$ or $\underset{\sim}{\mu}'$, then so is the distribution (i.e., the composite).

To derive (14) for $\tilde{\epsilon}$ or $\tilde{\mu}$, we consider the isolated scattering amplitude as a sum of an electric and a magnetic dipole. Correct to lowest order in k for the real and imaginary parts, we use[15]

$$\tilde{g}(\hat{r},\hat{k}) = \tilde{g}_e + \tilde{g}_m,\ \tilde{g}_e(\hat{r},\hat{k}) = (\tilde{I}-\hat{r}\hat{r})\cdot\tilde{a}_e\cdot(\tilde{I}-\hat{k}\hat{k}) \equiv \tilde{T}_r\cdot\tilde{a}_e\cdot\tilde{T}_k$$

$$\tilde{g}_m(\hat{r},\hat{k}) = -(\tilde{I}x\hat{r})\cdot\tilde{a}_m\cdot(\tilde{I}x\hat{k}) \equiv -\tilde{J}_r\cdot\tilde{a}_m\cdot\tilde{J}_k$$

$$\tilde{a} \approx -\tilde{a}_1'\cdot[\tilde{I}-\tilde{a}_1'(n-1)/n)] \qquad (53)$$

where $\tilde{a}_1'$ is the form in (48) with $\tilde{\delta} = \tilde{\epsilon}' - \tilde{I}$ for $\tilde{a}_e'$ and $\tilde{\mu}' - I$ for $\tilde{a}_m'$. Both operators $\tilde{T}_r = (I-\hat{r}\hat{r})$ and $\tilde{J}_r = \tilde{I}x\hat{r} = \hat{r}x\tilde{I}$ are planar dyadics transverse to $\hat{r}$. If $\tilde{\mu}' = \tilde{I}$, then from $\tilde{g} = \tilde{g}_e(\hat{r},\hat{R}) = \tilde{T}_r\cdot\tilde{a}_e\cdot\tilde{T}_R$ and $\underset{\sim}{g}(k\hat{R}) = \tilde{T}_R\cdot\underset{\sim}{A}$ we have $\underset{\sim}{u}_e = \tilde{T}_r\cdot\tilde{a}_e\cdot\tilde{h}_e\cdot\underset{\sim}{A}$ with $\tilde{h}_e = \tilde{I}h_0-\tilde{h}_a$ as the electric dipole propagator. Substituting into (47)′, we obtain the form $\tilde{M}\cdot A = 0$ with $|\tilde{M}| = |\tilde{T}_K[\eta^{-2}\tilde{I} - (\tilde{I}+\tilde{\Delta})^{-1}]| = 0$ with $\tilde{\Delta}$ as in (14) for two cases of β of (16) corresponding to $d_3^e = 6\pi$ and $d_2^e = 8$ (the dipole cases). Comparing with (8) for $\tilde{\mu} = \tilde{I}$, and using $\hat{K}x\tilde{I}x\hat{K} = \tilde{J}_K\cdot\tilde{J}_K = -\tilde{I}_K$ we identify $\tilde{\epsilon}$ as $\tilde{I} + \tilde{\Delta}(\tilde{\epsilon}')$. Similarly if $\tilde{\epsilon}' = \tilde{I}$, then from $\tilde{g} = \tilde{g}_m(\hat{r},\hat{R}) = -\tilde{J}_r\cdot\tilde{a}_m\cdot\tilde{J}_R$ and $\underset{\sim}{g}(k\hat{R}) = -\tilde{J}_R\cdot\underset{\sim}{A}'$, we have $\underset{\sim}{u}_m = -\tilde{J}_R\cdot\tilde{a}_m\cdot\tilde{h}_e\cdot\underset{\sim}{A}'$. Substituting into (47)′ we obtain $|\tilde{J}_K\cdot[-\tilde{I}\eta^{-2} + (\tilde{I}+\tilde{\Delta})^{-1}]\cdot\tilde{J}_K| = 0$, or equivalently $|\tilde{T}_K\eta^{-2} + \hat{K}x(\tilde{I}+\tilde{\Delta})^{-1}x\hat{K}| = 0$ by using $(\tilde{I}x\hat{K})\cdot\underset{\sim}{V} = \hat{K}x\underset{\sim}{V}$. Comparing with (8) for $\tilde{\epsilon} = \tilde{I}$ we identify $\tilde{\mu}$ as $\tilde{I} + \tilde{\Delta}(\tilde{\mu}')$. To the present order in k, we use (8) in terms of $\tilde{\mu} = I + \tilde{\Delta}(\tilde{\mu}')$ and $\tilde{\epsilon} = I + \tilde{\Delta}(\tilde{\epsilon}')$ to determine η^2. See Reference 2 for detailed applications and special cases.

ACKNOWLEDGEMENTS

Part of this work was done in the Mathematics Departments of The Weizmann Institute of Science in Israel and of Stanford University during sabbatical leave from the University of Illinois. I am grateful to the Departments for their hospitality, and to the John Simon Guggenheim Foundation and to the National Science Foundation for their support.

FOOTNOTES.

* Work supported in part by National Science Foundation Grant MCS-79-01718.

** Fellow of the John Simon Guggenheim Foundation, 1979-1980.

REFERENCES.

[1] V. Twersky, "Coherent Scalar Field in Pair-Correlated Random Distributions of Aligned Scatterers", J. Math. Phys. 18, 2468-2486 (1977).

[2] V. Twersky, "Coherent Electromagnetic Waves in Pair-Correlated Random Distributions of Aligned Scatterers", J. Math. Phys. 19, 215-230 (1978).

[3] J.C. Maxwell, A Treatise on Electricity and Magnetism, (Cambridge, 1873; Dover, N.Y., 1954); spheres are considered in Section 314, and slabs in Section 321.

[4] V. Twersky, "Acoustic Bulk Parameters in Distributions of Pair-Correlated Scatterers", J. Acoust. Soc. Am. 64, 1710-1719 (1978).

[5] V. Twersky, "Form and Intrinsic Birefringence", J. Opt. Soc. Am. 65, 239-245 (1975).

[6] V. Twersky, "Intrinsic, Shape, and Configurational Birefringence", J. Opt. Soc. Am. 69, 1199-1205 (1979).

[7] V. Twersky, "Propagation in Pair-Correlated Distributions of Small-Spaces Lossy Scatterers", J. Opt. Soc. Am. 69, 1567-1572, (1979).

[8] H. Reiss, H.L. Frisch, and J.L. Lebowitz, "Statistical mechanics of rigid spheres", J. Chem. Phys. 31, 379-380 (1959); E. Helfand, H.L. Frisch, and J.L. Lebowitz, "Theory of the two- and one-dimensional rigid sphere fluids", J. Chem Phys. 34, 1037-1042 (1961).

[9] Lord Rayleigh, "On the Influence of Obstacles Arranged in Rectangular Order upon the Properties of a Medium", Philos. Mag. 34, 481-501 (1892).

[10] O. Wiener, "Formdoppelbrechung bei Absorption", Kolloidchemische Beihefte 23, 189-198 (1926); "Die Theorie des Mischkorpers fur das Feld der stationaren Stromung", Sachische Akad. Wiss. 32, 507-604 (1912).

[11] M. Lax, "Multiple Scattering of Waves", Rev. Mod. Phys. 23, 287-310 (1951); "The Effective Field in Dense Systems", Phys. Rev. (2) 88, 621-629 (1952).

[12] J.B. Keller, "Wave Propagation in Random Media", Proc. Sympos. Appl. Math. Vol. 13, 227-246, Amer. Math. Soc., Providence, R.I. (1962); "Stochastic Equations and Wave Propagation in Random Media", Vol. 16, 145-170 (1964).

[13] V. Twersky, "On Propagation in Random Media of Discrete Scatterers", Proc. Sympos. Appl. Math. Vol. 16, 84-116, Amer. Math, Soc., Providence, R.I. (1964).

[14] Lord Rayleigh, "On the Incidence of Aerial and Electric Waves upon small Obstacles", Phil. Mag. 44, 28-52 (1897).

[15] V. Twersky, "Multiple Scattering of Electromagnetic Waves by Arbitrary Configurations", J. Math. Phys. 8, 589-610 (1967).

FREQUENCY DEPENDENT DIELECTRIC CONSTANTS OF DISCRETE RANDOM MEDIA

V.V. Varadan†, V.N. Bringi* and V.K. Varadan†
Wave Propagation Group
Boyd Laboratory
The Ohio State University, Columbus, Ohio 43210

Abstract

Numerical computations of the effective dielectric constant of discrete random media are presented as a function of frequency. Such media have a complex dielectric constant giving rise to absorption of a propagating wave both due to geometric dispersion or multiple scattering as well as absorption, if any, due to the viscosity of the particles and the matrix medium. We are concerned with the absorption due to multiple scattering. The scattering characteristics of the individual particles are described by a transition or T-matrix. The effects of two models of the pair correlation function which arises in the multiple scattering analysis are considered. We conclude that the well stirred approximation (WSA) is good for sparse concentrations and/or high frequencies whereas the Percus-Yevick approximation (P-YA) is preferred for higher concentrations.

Introduction

The study of the frequency dependence of the effective dielectric constant of statistically inhomogeneous media is important for practical applications such as geophysical exploration, artificial dielectrics etc. In such dielectrics a propagating electromagnetic wave undergoes dispersion and absorption. Some materials are naturally absorptive due to viscosity whereas inhomogeneous media exhibit absorption due to geometric dispersion or multiple scattering.

In this paper the effective, complex frequency dependent dielectric constant of a discrete random medium containing a distribution of aligned spheroidal dielectric scatterers in free space is calculated for different concentrations of the scatterers as well as for different material properties of the scatterers. We use a multiple scattering formalism analogous to that used by Twersky[1] but use the concept of a transition matrix or T-matrix to characterize the scattering from a single obstacle. All details of the geometry and material properties of the scatterer are contained in the T-matrix leaving the general formalism independent of the type of scatterer. Spherical statistics are used even though the scatterers may be non-spherical. Lax's[2] quasi-crystalline approximation (QCA) is used to truncate the heirarchy of equations that result when an ensemble average is performed on the multiply scattered field.

The resulting equations for the average field require a knowledge of the pair correlation function of the dielectric scatterers. In previous work[3,4,5], we assumed that the particles did not penetrate each other but were otherwise uncorrelated. Willis[6] has called this the well stirred approximation (WSA). However, the WSA lead to unphysical results for the absorption coefficient of the average medium for scatterer concentrations $c > 0.125$. In many artificial dielectrics, the scatterer concentration is often greater than 0.125. In this paper, we have also considered the Percus-Yevick[7] approximation (P-YA) to the pair correlation function. Wertheim[8] has provided a semi-analytical solution of the resulting integral equation for a system of hard spheres. Throop and Bearman[9] have provided tabulated values of the pair correlation function for different values of the concentration as a function of the inter particle distance. We have used these tabulated values in the numerical computations.

Calculations are presented for a system of polyethylene spheres and spheroids as well as ice particles for $0 < c < 0.26$ for several values of the non-dimensional wavenumber $ka = \frac{\omega a}{c}$ ranging from 0 to 5.0. ('a' is a characteristic dimension of the scatterer). Two types of results are presented. In the first instance the validity of the WSA and P-YA and their effect on the absorption coefficient is studied as a function of concentration and frequency. Secondly, the complex plane locus of the effective dielectric constant is plotted for the systems considered. For artificial dielectrics the locus deviates dramatically from the circular arc locus commonly noticed for ordinary solids and liquids that exhibit absorption due to viscosity.

Wave propagation in a discrete random medium

Consider N identical rotationally symmetric dielectric scatterers that are aligned but distributed randomly in free space (see Fig. 1). Let 0 be the origin of a coordinate system located outside the scatterers whose centers are denoted by $0_1, 0_2, 0_3 \ldots 0_N$. Monochromatic plane electromagnetic waves of frequency ω propagate along the symmetry axis of the scatterers which is taken to be the z-axis. Since the medium is isotropic about the z-axis there are no depolarization effects. The time dependence of the incident and hence the fields scattered by the individual scatterers is all of the form $\exp(-i\omega t)$ and this is suppressed in the equations that follow.

Let $\vec{E}_o(\vec{r})$ be the electric field arising from the incident plane wave and $\vec{E}_i^s(\vec{r})$ the field scattered by the i-th scatterer. The total field at a point $\vec{r}$ outside all the N scatterers, denoted by $\vec{E}(\vec{r})$ is given by

$$\vec{E}(\vec{r}) = \vec{E}^o(\vec{r}) + \sum_{i=1}^{N} \vec{E}_i^s(\vec{r}) \tag{1}$$

The field incident on or exciting the i-th scatterer is given by

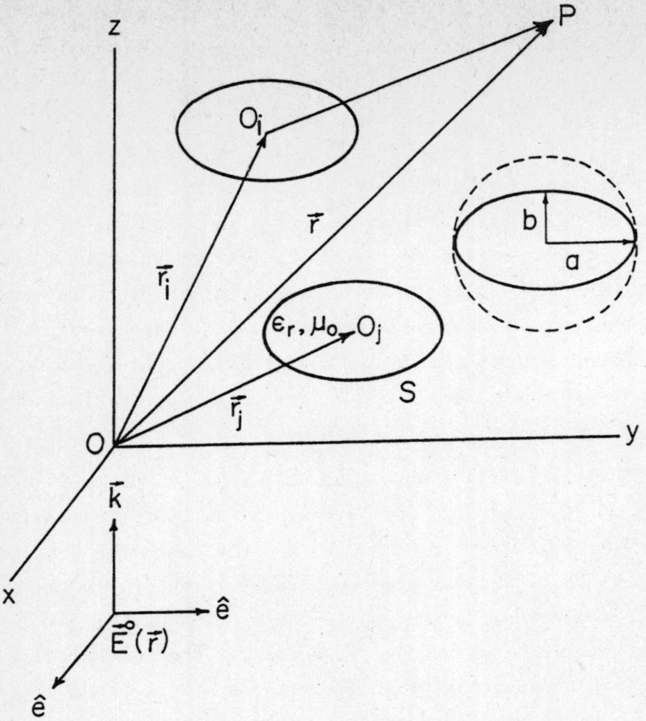

Figure 1. Scattering geometry

$$\vec{E}_i^e(\vec{r}) = \vec{E}^o(\vec{r}) + \sum_{j\neq i}^{N} \vec{E}_j^s(\vec{r}) \; ; \; a \leq |\vec{r}-\vec{r}_i| < 2a \tag{2}$$

where 'a' is a typical dimension of the scatterer. From Eqs. (1) and (2) we note that

$$\vec{E}(\vec{r}) = \vec{E}_i^e(\vec{r}) + \vec{E}_i^s(\vec{r}) \tag{3}$$

We need an additional equation relating $\vec{E}_i^e$ and $\vec{E}_i^s$ in order to make the fields microscopically self-consistent.

Vector spherical functions are used to expand the exciting and scattered fields associated with each scatterer with respect to an origin at the center of that scatterer. Thus

$$\vec{E}_i^e(\vec{r}) = \sum_{\tau=1}^{2} \sum_{\ell=1}^{\infty} \sum_{m=0}^{\ell} \sum_{\sigma=1}^{2} A^i_{\tau\ell m\sigma} \mathrm{Re}\, \vec{\psi}_{\tau\ell m\sigma}(\vec{\rho}_i) \; ; \; a \leq |\vec{\rho}_i| < 2a \tag{4}$$

and

$$\vec{E}_i^s(\vec{r}) = \sum_{\tau=1}^{2} \sum_{\ell=1}^{m} \sum_{m=0}^{\ell} \sum_{\sigma=1}^{2} F^i_{\tau\ell m\sigma} \mathrm{Ou}\, \vec{\psi}_{\tau\ell m\sigma}(\vec{\rho}_i) \; ; \; |\vec{\rho}_i| \geq 2a \tag{5}$$

where

$$\vec{\rho}_i = \vec{r}-\vec{r}_i \tag{6}$$

and the vector spherical functions are defined as

$$\left\{\begin{matrix} Ou \\ Re \end{matrix}\right\} \vec{\psi}_{1\ell m\sigma}(\vec{r}) = \nabla x \left\{\vec{r} \begin{matrix} h_\ell(kr) \\ j_\ell(kr) \end{matrix}\right\} Y_{\ell m\sigma}(\theta\phi) \; ; \tag{7}$$

$$\left\{\begin{matrix} Ou \\ Re \end{matrix}\right\} \vec{\psi}_{2\ell m\sigma}(\vec{r}) = \frac{1}{k} \nabla x \left\{\begin{matrix} Ou \\ Re \end{matrix} \vec{\psi}_{1\ell m\sigma}(\vec{r})\right\} \tag{8}$$

In Eqs. (7) and (8) j_ℓ and h_ℓ are the spherical Bessel and Hankel functions and the $Y_{\ell m\sigma}(\theta,\phi)$ are the normalized spherical harmonics defined with real angular functions. To make the notation more compact we introduce a super index 'n' to represent $\{\tau\ell m\sigma\}$ as follows

$$\begin{matrix} Ou \\ Re \end{matrix} \vec{\psi}_{\tau\ell m\sigma} = \begin{matrix} Ou \\ Re \end{matrix} \vec{\psi}_n$$

We observe that the coefficients of expansion A_n^i and F_n^i associated with the exciting and scattered fields depend on the position of all N scatterers. Further, since Eq. (3) is satisfied, we can relate the two sets of coefficients by means of the T-matrix as defined by Waterman[10]. We have

$$F_n^i = \sum_m T_{nm}^i A_n^i \tag{9}$$

The T-matrix depends on the frequency of the wave exciting the scatterer as well as its geometry and material properties.

If Eqs. (4), (5) and (9) are substituted in Eq. (2), we would need the translation addition theorems for the vector spherical functions in order that we may refer all expansions in Eq. (2) to a common origin. In compact form

$$Ou\,\vec{\psi}_n(\vec{\rho}_j) = \begin{cases} \sum_{n'} \sigma_{nn'}(\vec{r}_{ij})\, Re\,\vec{\psi}_{n'}(\vec{\rho}_i) \; ; & |\vec{r}_{ij}| > |\vec{\rho}_i| \\ \sum_{n} R_{nn'}(\vec{r}_{ij})\, Ou\,\vec{\psi}_{n'}(\vec{\rho}_i) \; ; & |\vec{\rho}_i| > |\vec{r}_{ij}| \end{cases} \tag{10}$$

where $\vec{r}_{ij} = \vec{r}_i - \vec{r}_j$ is the vector connecting 0_j to 0_i and $\sigma_{nn'}$ is the translation matrix for the vector functions and $R_{nn'}$ is the same as $\sigma_{nn'}$ with the spherical Hankel functions in $\sigma_{nn'}$ replaced by spherical Bessel functions. Detailed expressions for the matrices are given by Boström[11].

The incident electric field $\vec{E}^o$ can be expanded with respect to an origin at 0_i as

$$\vec{E}^o(\vec{r}) = e^{ikz} = e^{i\hat{kz}\cdot\vec{r}_i} \sum_n a_n \, Re\,\vec{\psi}_n(\rho_i) \tag{11}$$

where the coefficients a_n are known (see for example Morse and Feshbach[12]). We observe that for a plane wave propagating in the z-direction the only non-zero values of $a_n = a_{\tau\ell m\sigma}$ are $a_{1\ell 12}$ and $a_{2\ell 11}$; $\ell\varepsilon[1,\infty]$, all other coefficients being zero.

Using Eqs. (4),(5),(9)-(11) in Eq. (2), using the orthogonality of the vector spherical functions we obtain

$$A_n^i = e^{ik\hat{z}\cdot\vec{r}_i}\, a_n + \sum_{j\neq i}^{N} \sum_{n'} \sum_{n''} \sigma_{n'n}(\vec{r}_{ij})\, T^j_{n'n}\, A^j_{n''} \tag{12}$$

Equation (12) is a set of coupled algebraic equations for the exciting field coefficients associated with each scatterer. If the number of scatterers N is finite and the position of all the scatterers is known, then Eq. (12) can be solved in principle. But we wish to consider the case $N\to\infty$, $V\to\infty$ such that $N/V = n_o$ is a finite number density. Since N is large, we are only interested in the configurational average of Eq. (12) over the positions of all particles

The coherent field

The average of Eq. (12) over the position of all scatterers (the average exciting field) is the same as the ensemble average, where the ensemble is composed of different possible configurations of the scatterers. Equation (12) is averaged over the position of all particles except the i-th. But the right hand side of Eq. (12) explicitly depends on the position of the j-th particle. Hence we must specify the two particle joint probability density $P(\vec{r}_j|\vec{r}_i)$ Further, we assume that all scatterers are identical, so that

$$\left\langle A_n^i \right\rangle_i = e^{ik\hat{z}\cdot\vec{r}_i} a_n + (N-1) \sum_{n'} \sum_{n''} T_{n'n''} \int_V P(\vec{r}_j|\vec{r}_i)\, \sigma_{n'n}(r_{ij}) \left\langle A_n^j \right\rangle_{ij} d\vec{r}_j \tag{13}$$

We note that the average exciting field with one scatterer held fixed is given in terms of the average with two scatterers held fixed, leading to a heirarchy that requires knowledge of higher order probability densities. It has been customary to truncate the heirarchy by invoking the 'quasi crystalline approximation' (QCA) first introduced by Lax[2]. According to this approximation

$$\left\langle A^j_{n''} \right\rangle_{ij} \simeq \left\langle A^j_{n''} \right\rangle_j \tag{14}$$

Specifically the QCA neglects multiple scattering between pairs of scatterers. Improvements to the QCA have been suggested by Twersky[1] and in previous work by us[5].

The joint probability density is defined as

$$P(\vec{r}_j|\vec{r}_i) = \begin{cases} \frac{1}{V}\, g(|\vec{r}_j-\vec{r}_i|) \;; & |\vec{r}_j-\vec{r}_i| \geq 2a \\ 0 \;; & |\vec{r}_j-\vec{r}_i| < 2a \end{cases} \tag{15}$$

Equation (15) implies that the particles are hard (no-interpenetration) and the excluded volume is a sphere of radius 'a' although the particles themselves may be non-spherical. The function $g(|\vec{r}_i-\vec{r}_j|)$ is called the pair correlation function and depends only on $|\vec{r}_j-\vec{r}_i|$ due to translational invariance of the system under consideration.

We assume that the coherent field propagates in the same direction as the incident field with a new, effective wavenumber K that is complex and frequency dependent. Hence

$$\left\langle \vec{E}_i^e(\vec{r}) \right\rangle_i = A\, e^{iK\hat{z}\cdot\vec{r}} \tag{16}$$

where A is the amplitude of the coherent wave. Thus the average exciting field coefficient

$$\left\langle A_n^i \right\rangle_i = \left\langle A_{\tau\ell m\sigma}^i \right\rangle_i = e^{iK\hat{z}\cdot\vec{r}_i}\, X_{\tau\ell m\sigma}\, \delta_{m1}\, [\delta_{\tau1}\delta_{\sigma2} + \delta_{\tau2}\delta_{\sigma1}] \tag{17}$$

The Kronecker deltas in Eq. (17) indicate that only the azimuthal index m=1 contributes, since the coherent wave propagates in the z-direction and those in the square bracket indicate that there is no depolarization.

Equations (14)-(17) are substituted in Eq. (13). Since the T-matrix of a rotational symmetric scatterer is block diagonal in the azimuthal index (see Waterman[10]) and the coherent field propagates in the z-direction, the sums associated with the azimuthal indices of the super indices n' and n'' in Eq. (13) are removed. Further, as shown in previous work by us[5] as well as Twersky[1], the extinction theorem can be used to cancel the incident wave term in Eq. (13) with the contribution of the integral at infinity. Finally Eq. (13) can be written in the form

$$X_{\tau\ell m\sigma}\, \delta_{m1}\, [\delta_{\tau1}\delta_{\sigma2} + \delta_{\tau2}\delta_{\sigma1}] = \frac{N-1}{V} \sum_{\tau'\ell'\sigma'} \sum_{\tau''\ell''\sigma''} T_{\tau'\ell'1\sigma',\tau''\ell''1\sigma''} \cdot$$

$$\sum_{\lambda=|\ell-\ell'|}^{\ell+\ell'} I(K,k,c,\lambda)\, X_{\tau''\ell''1\sigma''}\, D^{(\lambda)}_{\tau'\ell'1\sigma',\tau\ell1\sigma} \tag{18}$$

where

$$I(K,k,c,\lambda) = \frac{6c}{(Ka)^2-(ka)^2}\, [2kaj_\lambda(2Ka)h'_\lambda(2ha) - 2Kah_\lambda(2ka)j'_\lambda(2Ka)] +$$

$$24c \int_1^\infty x^2[g(x)-1]\, h_\lambda(kx)j_\lambda(Kx)dx \tag{19}$$

and

$$D^{(\lambda)}_{\tau'\ell'1\sigma',\tau\ell1\sigma} = i^{\ell-\ell'+\lambda} \left[\frac{(2\lambda+1)(2\ell+1)}{2\ell(\ell+1)}\right] \left[\frac{\ell'(\ell'+1)}{\ell(\ell+1)}\right]^{1/2} \begin{bmatrix} \ell & \ell' & \lambda \\ 1 & -1 & 0 \end{bmatrix} \cdot$$

$$\left\{ \begin{bmatrix} \ell & \ell' & \lambda \\ 0 & 0 & 0 \end{bmatrix} [\ell'(\ell'+1) + \ell(\ell+1) - \lambda(\lambda+1)]\, \delta_{\tau\tau'}\, \delta_{\sigma\sigma'} + i \begin{bmatrix} \ell' & \ell & \lambda-1 \\ 0 & 0 & 0 \end{bmatrix} \cdot \right.$$

$$\left. (\lambda^2-(\ell'-\ell)^2) \quad (\ell'+\ell+1)^2-\lambda^2) \quad ^{1/2} \quad (1-\delta_{\tau\tau'})\, (\delta_{\sigma'1}\delta_{\sigma2} - \delta_{\sigma'2}\delta_{\sigma1}) \right\} \quad (20)$$

In Eq. (19) $c = \frac{4\pi}{3} n_o a^3$ is the effective spherical concentration of the particles and in Eq. (20) $\begin{bmatrix} j_1 & j_2 & j_3 \\ m_1 & m_2 & m_3 \end{bmatrix}$ is the Wigner 3-j symbol.

If the integral in Eq. (19) can be evaluated for suitable models of the pair correlation function, then Eq. (18) is a set of coupled, homogeneous, algebraic equations for the coherent field expansion coefficients. For a non-trivial solution, the determinant of the coefficient matrix must vanish. This yields the required dispersion equation for the effective or average medium. In general the system of equations can be solved only numerically to yield the effective wave number K as a function of frequency ($k=\omega/c$) which is complex ($K = K_1+iK_2$). The real part K_1 yields the phase velocity in the medium and the imaginary part K_2 leads to damping of a propagating wave due to geometric dispersion as well as real losses if any, associated with the discrete particles. We now proceed to consider the evaluation of the integral in Eq. (19).

The Percus-Yevick pair correlation function

The pair correlation function for an ensemble of particles depends on the nature and range of the interparticle forces. The average of several measurements of a statistical variable that characterizes an ensemble will depend on the pair correlation function. As we have seen, the coherent or average electric field in an ensemble of dielectric scatterers depends on the pair correlation function (Eqs. (18)-(19)). To obtain expressions for the pair correlation function, one needs a description of the interparticle forces. In our case we assume that the dielectric scatterers behave like effective hard spheres (where the radius 'a' is that of the sphere circumscribing the scatterer). Percus and Yevick[7] have obtained an approximate integral equation for the pair correlation function of a classical fluid in equilibrium. Wertheim[8] has obtained a series solution of the integral equation for an ensemble of hard spheres. The statistics of the fluid are then same as those of the ensemble of discrete hard particles that we are considering.

Although integral expressions for the correlation functions also result in a heirarchy, Percus and Yevick have truncated the heirarchy by making certain approximations that result in a self-consistent relation between the pair correlation function $g(x)$ and the direct correlation function $C(x)$. The direct correlation function may be interpreted as the correlation function resulting from an 'external potential' that produces a simultaneous density fluctuation at a point and the external potential is taken to be the potential seen by a particle given that there is a particle fixed at another site. Fisher[13] comments that the Percus-Yevick approximation is a strong statement of the extremely short range nature of the direct correlation function. The integral equation has the form

$$\tau(x) = 1 + n_o \int_{x<2a} \tau(x')dx' - n_o \int_{\substack{x'<2a \\ |x-x'|>2a}} \tau(x')\tau(x-x')dx' \tag{21}$$

where

$$\begin{aligned} \tau(x) &= g(x) \ ; \ x > 2a \\ g(x) &= \ \ 0 \ \ ; \ x < 2a \\ \tau(x) &= -C(x) \ ; \ x < 2a \\ C(x) &= \ \ 0 \ \ ; \ x > 2a \end{aligned} \tag{22}$$

Wertheim[8] has solved the integral equation by Laplace transformation that results in an analytic expression for C(n) in the form

$$C(x) = -(1-\eta)^{-4} \ [(1+2\eta)^2 - 6\eta(1+\frac{1}{2}\eta)^2 x + \eta(1+2\eta)^2 \ x^3/2] \ ; \ \eta = c/8 \tag{23}$$

where 'c' is the effective spherical concentration of the particles. The Percus-Yevick approximation fails as the concentration approaches the close packing factor for spheres and is expected to be good for $c < 0.3$ or 0.4.

Equation (23) can be substituted back into Eq. (21) to yield a series solution for g(x) in the form[8]

$$g(x) = \sum_{n=1}^{\infty} g_n(x) \tag{24}$$

where

$$g_n(x) = \frac{1}{24\eta x i} \int e^{t(x-n)} \ [L(t) \mid S(t)]^n \ tdt \tag{25}$$

where

$$S(t) = (1-\eta^2)t^3 + 6\eta(1-\eta)t^2 + 18\eta^2 t-12\eta(1+2\eta) \tag{26}$$

and

$$L(t) = 12\eta \ [(1+\eta 2)t + (1+2\eta)]. \tag{27}$$

Throop and Bearman[9] have tabulated g(x) as a function of x for values of $\eta = c/8$. A few representative plots of the pair correlation function are shown in Fig. 2. These tabulated values were used in evaluating the integral in Eq. (19).

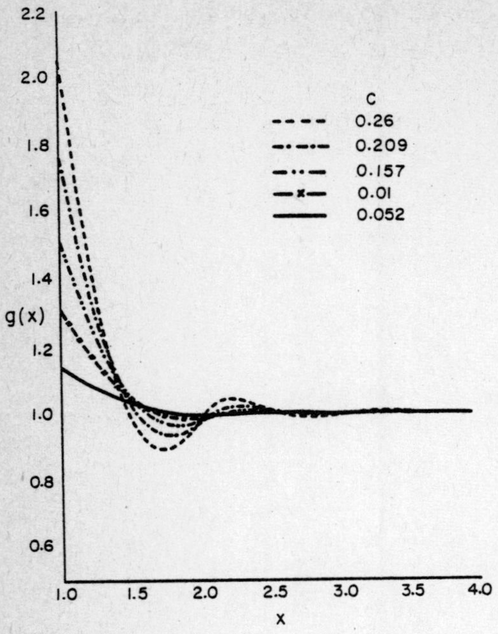

Figure 2. The Percus-Yevick pair correlation function g(x)

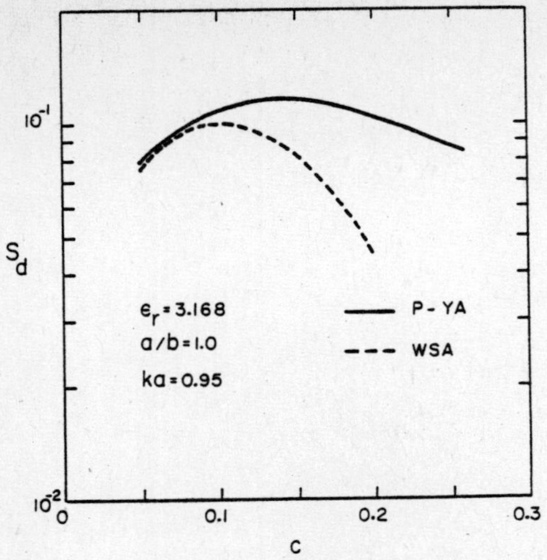

Figure 3. Coherent attenuation vs. concentration for spherical ice particles

Comparison of WSA and P-YA

The homogeneous system of algebraic equations for the effective exciting field were solved numerically for two different models of the correlation integral I appearing in Eq. (18). In eq. (19) if the second term is set equal to zero, we just have a system of uncorrelated hard particles. This is what we have referred to as the well stirred approximation (WSA)[6] earlier. Computations were also performed by numerically evaluating the integral in eq. (19) by using the tabulated values of the Percus-Yevick approximation to the pair correlation functions provided by Throop and Beerman[9].

In Fig. 3, the specific damping $S_d = 4\Pi\ K_2/K_1$ is plotted as a function of concentration for a random distribution of numerical ice particles (ε_r = 3.168) in free space at ka = 0.55. The WSA agrees with the P-YA solution only up to concentrations C $\backsim$ 0.075 and then there is a marked difference and the WSA fails completely at C > 0.125 leading to unphysical results. In Fig. 4, the calculations are repeated

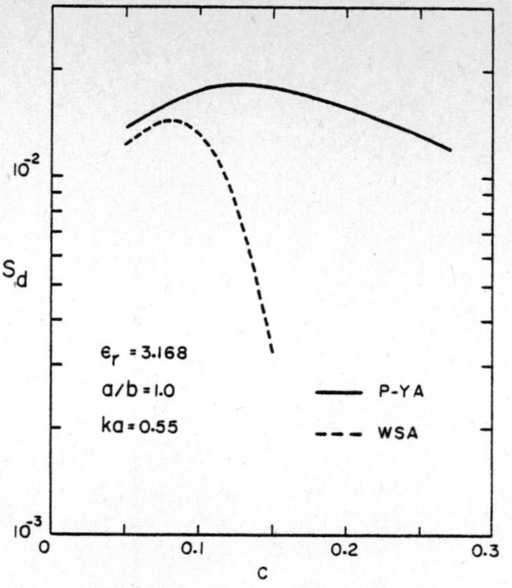

Figure 4. Coherent attenuation vs. concentration for spherical ice particles

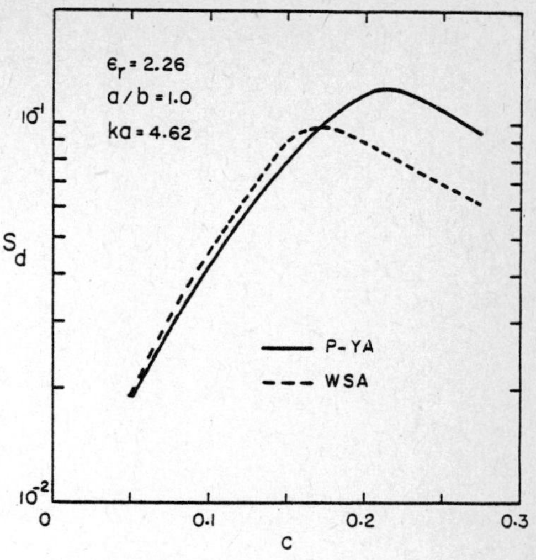

Figure 5. Coherent attenuation vs. concentration for polyethylene spheres

for the same system at a higher value of ka = 0.95. Here the WSA agrees with P-YA up to C = 0.1 and in Fig. 5 similar calculations were performed for polyethylene spheres (ε_r = 2.26) at ka = 4.62. For this case WSA and P-YA results agree up to C = 0.15.

From these results it would appear that although the WSA is very poor at higher scatterer concentrations, the results improve dramatically at higher values of ka, yielding reasonably good results for higher concentrations. The natural explanation is that at higher values of ka, multiple scattering effects between pairs of particles become smaller and thus pair correlation effects are not significant and the QCA also becomes more exact. But for arbitrary concentration and frequency it is safer to use the Percus-Yevick approximation.

The effective dielectric constant

Once the effective complex wavenumber K has been computed by solving Eq. (18) numerically, we can proceed further and evaluate the effective dielectric constant of the medium which is also complex and frequency dependent. In the usual way, the dielectric constant $\varepsilon_r^*(\omega)$ of the random medium is defined as

$$\varepsilon_r^*(\omega) = \frac{K^2}{k^2} = \varepsilon_1(\omega) + i\varepsilon_2(\omega)$$

where ε_1 and ε_2 are the real and imaginary parts of the dielectric constant and the

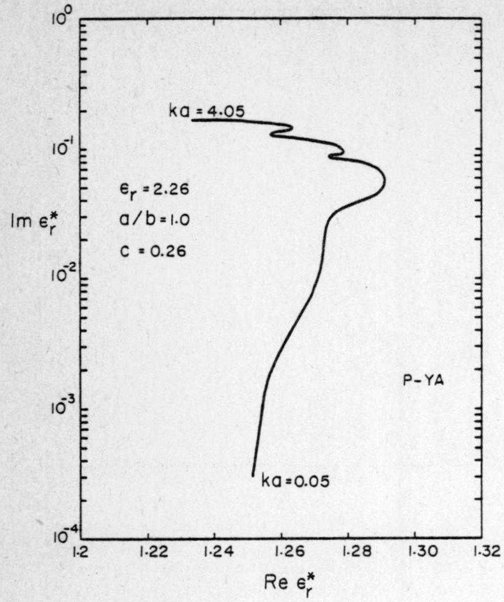

Figure 6. Complex plane locus of the effective dielectric constant for a system of polyethylene spheres

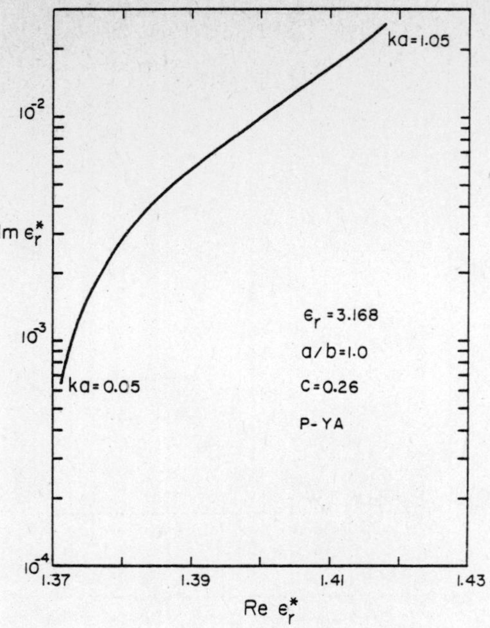

Figure 7. Complex plane locus of the effective dielectric constant for a system of spherical ice particles

subscript on ε_r^* denotes 'relative to the matrix medium'. The real part ε_1 is related to the refractive index and phase velocity in the artifical medium and the imaginary part ε_2 accounts for the damping in the medium. In real materials, the damping is intrinsic to the system and is due to macroscopic viscosity of the dielectric. For the artificial or effective medium under consideration, in addition to natural losses there is damping due to geometric dispersion or scattering.

Cole and Cole[14] have given a convenient representation of the dispersion and absorption in a dielectric by means of an Argand diagram or a plot in the complex ε-plane of ε_1 versus ε_2, each point of the plot being characteristic of a particular frequency. For many types of loss mechanisms, the locus of the points is a semi circle with its center on the real axis or a circular arc. In Ref. 14, the complex dielectric constant of several liquids and solids is plotted conforming to the circular arc.

In the present case the complex dielectric constant $\varepsilon(\omega)$ corresponding to the effective wavenumber K of the effective medium is studied for several values of the frequency. Overall results show a dramatic deviation from the circular arc locus. This is to be expected since the medium is artificial.

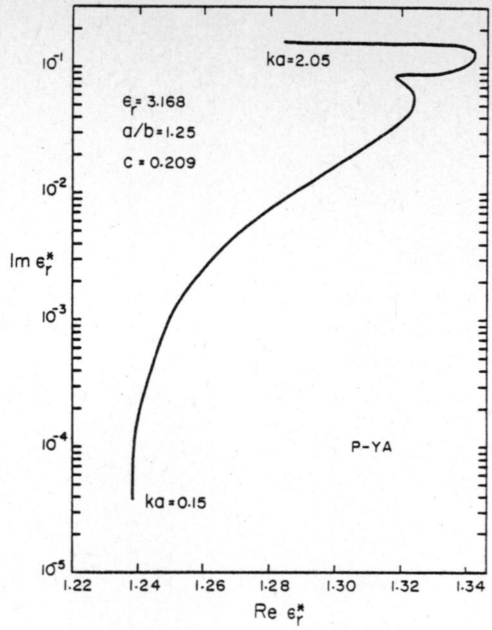

Figure 8. Complex plane locus of the effective dielectric constant for a system of oblate spheroidal ice particles

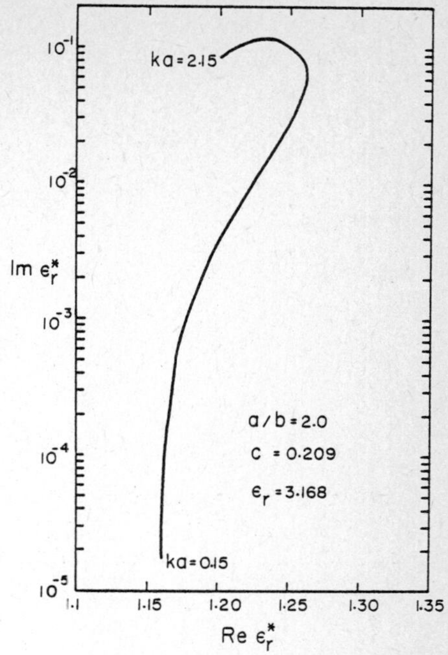

Figure 9. Complex plane locus of the effective dielectric constant for a system of oblate spheroidal ice particles

In Fig. 6 the complex plane locus of the relative dielectric constant of a random distribution of polyethylene spheres in free space is presented at a concentration of 26%. The calculations were done using the Percus-Yevick approximation (P-YA) for the pair correlation function from ka = 0.05 to 4.05. As can be seen, the figure bears no resemblance to a circular arc locus. By extrapolating the locus at the low value of ka, one can find the intercept on the Re ε_r^* axis which is equal to the static dielectric constant of the effective medium. Since the dielectric constant of the spherical particles is assumed to be real, the effective medium shows no absorption at low frequencies. The static dielectric constant thus obtained will correspond to the one that can be obtained from mixture theory. In real media displaying a circular arc locus the high frequency value of ε^* also intercepts the real axis and this yields the optical limit or ε_∞ for the material. In our case, it is not at all clear at what value of ka, if at all, the locus will intercept the real axes.

In Figs. 7,8 and 9 the complex plane locus of the effective dielectric constant of spherical and oblate spheroidal ice particles is presented where 'a' and 'b' are the semi major and semi minor axes respectively. They all show marked deviation from the circular arc locus and it is unclear what ε_∞ will be for these effective media.

At the present time there are no experimental results available to verify these calculations. The practical applications of these computations are many. Such calculations will provide reasonable estimates of the frequency dependence dielectric constant as a function of particle concentration, size and shape for inhomogeneous media.

Acknowledgements

This work was supported in part by NOAA under grant No.: 04-78-Bol-21, NRL(USRD) contract No: N00014-80-C-0483, and NRL (Washington) contract No: N00014-80-C-0835. The use of the Instructional and Research Computer Center at the Ohio State University is gratefully acknowledged.

† Department of Engineering Mechanics

* Department of Electrical Engineering and now at Colorado State University, Fort Collins, Colorado.

References

1. V. Twersky, J. Math Phys. 18, 2468 (1977), and 19, 215 (1978).

2. M. Lax, Phys. Rev. 85, 621 (1952).

3. V.K. Varadan, V.N. Bringi, and V.V. Varadan, Phys. Rev. D 19, 2480 (1979).

4. V.V. Varadan and V.K. Varadan, Phys. Rev. D 21, 388 (1980).

5. V.N. Bringi, T.A. Seliga, V.K. Varadan and V.V. Varadan, 'Bulk propagation characteristics of discrete random media' in Multiple Scattering of Waves in Random Media (Edited by P.L. Chow, W.E. Kohler and G. Papanicolaou), North-Holland Publishing Company, Amsterdam (1981).

6. D.R.S. Talbot and J.R.Willis, Proc. Roy. Soc. Lond. A 370, 351 (1980).

7. J.K. Percus and G.J. Yevick, Phys. Rev. 110, 1 (1958).

8. M.S. Wertheim, Phys. Rev. Letters 10, 321 (1963).

9. G.J. Throop and R.J. Bearman, J.Chem. Phys. 42, 2408 (1965).

10. P.C. Waterman, Phys. Rev. D. 3, 825 (1971).

11. A. Bostrom, J. Acoust. Soc. Am. 67, 399 (1980).

12. P.M. Morse and H. Reshbach, Methods of Theoretical Physics, Vol II., McGraw Hill Book Company Inc., New York (1953).

13. I.Z. Fisher, Statistical Theory of Liquids, The University of Chicago Press, Chicago, 309 (1965).

14. K.S. Cole and R.H. Cole, J. Chem. Phys. 9, 341 (1941).

A VARIATIONAL METHOD TO FIND EFFECTIVE COEFFICIENTS FOR PERIODIC MEDIA. A COMPARISON WITH STANDARD HOMOGENIZATION

Michael Vogelius*
Courant Institute of Mathematical Sciences
New York University
New York, N. Y. 10012

1. Introduction

Elliptic boundary value problems with rapidly varying coefficients (i.e. coefficients varying significantly on a small scale) naturally occur in dealing with problems involving composite materials. A problem of utmost practical importance is then to find an effective constant coefficient operator (or generally one with slowly varying coefficients) to replace the rapid variations. In the literature this process is often denoted homogenization and is traditionally performed by means of some sort of multiple scale asymptotic expansion.

As we shall point out later techniques of asymptotic expansion have certain deficiencies in connection with the determination of boundary layers and solutions containing singularities.

Accurate knowledge of the boundary layers or singularities is important for many practical applications, such as predicting whether a composite will delaminate or cracks occur.

In this paper we shall review an alternate method for homogenization which is much better suited to determine the boundary layers or the solution near a singularity. This method is based on a combination of an asymptotic expansion and a variational principle. We compare this method to the more standard both theoretically and computationally.

As our model problem we consider the following of diffusion in a periodic structure.

$$(1) \qquad -\nabla_x \cdot (\underline{\underline{A}}(x/\varepsilon)\ \nabla_x u^{\varepsilon})(x) + b(x/\varepsilon)u^{\varepsilon}(x) = f(x) \text{ in } \Omega$$

$$u^{\varepsilon}(x) = 0 \quad \text{on } \partial\Omega.$$

Ω is a bounded domain in $\mathbb{R}^n$ with a Lipschitz boundary. The components of $\underline{\underline{A}}$ and the single function b are periodic elements of $L^{\infty}(\mathbb{R}^n)$ with a period = 1. $\underline{\underline{A}}$ is uniformly positive definite and b is nonnegative.

*
This work was supported by the Army Research Office under Contract No. DAAG29-78-G-0177.

Since both $\underline{\underline{A}}$ and b for convenience are taken to be functions only of the "fast" variable x/ε and not explicitly of the slow variable x the result of homogenization shall be a constant coefficient operator.

2. The "standard" approach.

Introduce the new independent variable $y = x/\varepsilon$. The problem (1) then "transforms" into

(2) $-(\nabla_x + 1/\varepsilon\ \nabla_y)\cdot(\underline{\underline{A}}(y)(\nabla_x + 1/\varepsilon\nabla_y)U^\varepsilon(x,y)) + b(y)U^\varepsilon(x,y) = f(x)$

in $\Omega \times [0,1]^n$

U^ε is periodic in y with period $= 1$, and

$U^\varepsilon(x,y) = 0 \quad \forall(x,y) \in \partial\Omega \times [0,1]^n$.

To be more exact, if $U^\varepsilon(x,y)$ is a solution to (2) then $u^\varepsilon(x) = U^\varepsilon(x,x/\varepsilon)$ solves (1).

Formally one can now expand $U^\varepsilon(x,y)$ in powers of ε. By matching terms of same order of ε in the equation (2) one obtains

(3) $$u^\varepsilon(x) = U^\varepsilon(x,x/\varepsilon) = u(x) + \varepsilon\underline{\chi}(x/\varepsilon)\cdot\nabla_x u(x) + \ldots ,$$

where $\underline{\chi}(y) = (\chi_1(y),\ldots,\chi_n(y))$ is a periodic solution to

$$-\nabla_y\cdot(\underline{\underline{A}}(y)\ \nabla_y\underline{\chi}) = \nabla_y\cdot\underline{\underline{A}}(y) ,$$

and the function u solves

(4) $$-\nabla_x\cdot(\underline{\underline{\mathcal{a}}}\nabla_x u(x)) + \bar{b}u(x) = f(x) \text{ in } \Omega$$
$$u(x) = 0 \quad \text{on } \partial\Omega ,$$

with $\underline{\underline{\mathcal{a}}} = \overline{\underline{\underline{A}}(y) + \underline{\underline{A}}(y)\nabla_y\underline{\chi}(y)}$.

Here we have adopted the notation $\overline{\quad}$ for averages.

The reference [3] contains a very rigorous analysis of this approach particularly concerning convergence properties as $\varepsilon \to 0$.

Let $W^{s,p}(\Omega)$ denote the Sobolev space of order $s > 0$ based on $L^p(\Omega)$ (cf. [1]). For the particular case $p = 2$ we shall use the more standard notation $H^s(\Omega)$ instead of $W^{s,2}(\Omega)$. The norm on $H^s(\Omega)$ is denoted $\|\cdot\|_s$. By $\overset{o}{H}{}^1(\Omega)$ we understand the set of functions $u \in H^1(\Omega)$ such that $u = 0$ on $\partial\Omega$.

One can show that $u^\varepsilon(x) - u(x) \to 0$ (weakly) in $H^1(\Omega)$ and therefore strongly in $H^s(\Omega)$ for any $s < 1$. It is however easy to see that $u^\varepsilon(x) - u(x)$ does not in general converge strongly in $H^1(\Omega)$.

In order to obtain strong H^1-convergence (which is the equivalent of L^2-convergence of stresses or strains for problems of elasticity) we have to include the next term in the asymptotic expansion. For specific information concerning the boundary layers it is important to satisfy the boundary conditions exactly. This can within the present framework most naturally be accomplished by introducing a cut-off function $m^{\varepsilon}(x) = m(d(x)/\varepsilon)$, where $m \in W^{1,\infty}([0,\infty[)$ satisfies $m(0) = 0$ and $m(t) = 1$ for $t \geq 1$ and $d(x) = \text{dist}(x,\partial\Omega)$. The exact formulation of a convergence result is as follows.

Theorem 2.1. Assume that $\chi_j \in W^{1,\infty}([0,1]^n)$, $1 \leq j \leq n$. If $u \in H^2(\Omega) \cap W^{1,p}(\Omega)$ then there exists C such that

(5) $$\| u^{\varepsilon}(x) - (u(x) + \varepsilon \sum_{j=1}^{n} \chi_j(x/\varepsilon) m^{\varepsilon}(x) \frac{\partial}{\partial x_j} u(x)) \|_1 \leq C\varepsilon^{\nu}$$

for any ε in $]0,1]$, where $\nu = \max\{(1-1/p)/2,\ 1/4\}$.

Some clear disadvantages of this approach and the result in this theorem are

(a) The cut-off function m^{ε} can be chosen rather arbitrarily. This leaves totally open the very difficult question of how to select it optimally in order to obtain a smallest possible error.

(b) If the right hand side f is not in $L^2(\Omega)$ so that $u \notin H^2(\Omega)$, then in general the expression

(6) $$u(x) + \varepsilon \sum_{j=1}^{n} \chi_j(x/\varepsilon)\ m^{\varepsilon}(x) \frac{\partial}{\partial x_j} u(x)$$

does not make sense in $H^1(\Omega)$, and standard homogenization thus fails to produce a family s^{ε} such that $\| u^{\varepsilon} - s^{\varepsilon} \|_1 \to 0$.

(c) If the boundary $\partial\Omega$ is not sufficiently smooth that $u \in H^2(\Omega)$ then this result does not apply. The expression (6) still makes sense in $H^1(\Omega)$ provided f is at least in $L^2(\Omega)$ (and for an appropriately chosen cut-off function m^{ε}), but a separate analysis is needed to see if we recover the convergence in $H^1(\Omega)$ and at what rate. An analysis of this sort is to the author's best knowledge not found in the literature.

(d) The estimate (5) is asymptotic in ε. As shall be clear from numerical evidence later on this reflects a deficiency in the very approach. The formula (6) does not in general perform well for large to moderate size ε .

(e) From a computational point of view (6) is not very natural either. If u is approximated by a Finite Element Method as u^{Δ} , then for the above expression to be in $H^1(\Omega)$ requires that $\frac{\partial}{\partial x_j} u^{\Delta} \in H^1(\Omega)$, $1 \leq j \leq n$.
This means we have to use C^1-elements or alternatively treat (4) by a so called mixed method.

In the following section we shall introduce the variationally based method and review some of its basic properties. In short: this alternate method has the same approximation properties as (6) for smooth data and small ε, and at the same time all the problems we mentioned above do no longer occur. The review will be very brief, for more details see [5].

3. The variationally based approach.

As before we introduce the new independent variable $\mathbf{y} = x/\varepsilon$. The corresponding equation (2) has the following natural variational formulation.

(7) $$B_\varepsilon(U^\varepsilon, V) = \iint_{\Omega \times [0,1]^n} f(x)V(x,y)\, dx\, dy$$

$\forall\ V \in H^1(\Omega \times [0,1]^n)$, with the properties that

V is periodic (period = 1) in $\mathbf{y}$

$V = 0$ on $\partial\Omega \times [0,1]^n$.

$B_\varepsilon(U,V)$ here denotes the bilinear form

$$\iint_{\Omega \times [0,1]^n} (\underline{\underline{A}}(y)(\nabla_x + 1/\varepsilon\, \nabla_y)U(x,y)(\nabla_x + 1/\varepsilon\, \nabla_y)V(x,y) + b(y)U(x,y)V(x,y))\, dx\, dy .$$

We intend to utilize part (but not all) of the information contained in the asymptotic expansion (3), namely the fact that

$$U^\varepsilon(x,y) = u_0^\varepsilon(x) + \varepsilon \sum_{j=1}^n \chi_j(y)\, u_j^\varepsilon(x) + \ldots$$

We do this by restricting the U^ε and V appearing in (7) to elements of the space

(8) $$\{v_0(x) + \varepsilon \sum_{j=1}^n \chi_j(y) v_j(x) \mid v_0, \{v_j\}_1^n \subseteq \overset{\circ}{H}{}^1(\Omega)\}$$

As a result we obtain the following system

(9) $$-\nabla_x \begin{Bmatrix} \overline{\underline{\underline{A}}} & \varepsilon\overline{\underline{\underline{A}}\chi_j} \\ \varepsilon\overline{\underline{\underline{A}}\chi_k} & \varepsilon^2\overline{\underline{\underline{A}}\chi_k\chi_j} \end{Bmatrix} \nabla_x \begin{Bmatrix} u_0^\varepsilon \\ \{u_j^\varepsilon\} \end{Bmatrix} + \begin{Bmatrix} 0 & -\nabla_x \cdot \overline{\underline{\underline{A}}\nabla_y\chi_j} \\ \overline{\underline{\underline{A}}\nabla_y\chi_k} \cdot \nabla_x & \overline{\underline{\underline{A}}\nabla_y\chi_k\nabla_y\chi_j} \end{Bmatrix} \begin{Bmatrix} u_0^\varepsilon \\ \{u_j^\varepsilon\} \end{Bmatrix}$$

$$+ \begin{Bmatrix} \overline{b} & \varepsilon\overline{b\chi_j} \\ \varepsilon\overline{b\chi_k} & \varepsilon^2\overline{b\chi_k\chi_j} + \varepsilon\overline{\underline{\underline{A}}(\nabla_y\chi_k\chi_j - \chi_k\nabla_y\chi_j)} \end{Bmatrix} \begin{Bmatrix} u_0^\varepsilon \\ \{u_j^\varepsilon\} \end{Bmatrix} = \begin{Bmatrix} f \\ \{\varepsilon\overline{\chi}_k f\} \end{Bmatrix}$$

with the boundary conditions that

$$u_0^\varepsilon \ , \ \{u_j^\varepsilon\} = 0 \text{ on } \partial\Omega \ .$$

Note. In order for the system (9) to be a positive definite elliptic system it is necessary and sufficient that the functions $1 \cup \{\chi_j\}_{j=1}^n$ are linearly independent.

In case they are not linearly independent the problem actually simplifies:

"Pick $1 \cup \{\chi_{j_k}\}_{k=1}^m (m \leq n)$ to be a maximally linearly independent subset of $1 \cup \{\chi_j\}_{j=1}^n$ and instead of (8) use the space

$$\{v_0(x) + \varepsilon \sum_{k=1}^m \chi_{j_k}(y) v_k(x) \ | \ v_0, \{v_k\} \subseteq \overset{o}{H}{}^1(\Omega)\}$$

as test and trial functions for the variational procedure."

Whether the set $1 \cup \{\chi_j\}_{j=1}^n$ consists of linearly independent functions can easily be checked once the χ_j's are computed. For the case of an isotropic material it can directly be seen already in the original equation (1). The matrix $\underline{\underline{A}}(y)$ is here given by $a(y)\underline{\underline{I}}$ ($\underline{\underline{I}}$ denoting the identity), and linear dependency in the set $1 \cup \{\chi_j\}_{j=1}^n$ is equivalent to the fact that there exists $\underline{\beta} \in \mathbb{R}^n \setminus \{0\}$ with $\underline{\beta} \cdot \nabla_y a(y) = 0$.

One can prove the following convergence result for the alternate method given by the system (9).

Theorem 3.1 Assume that $\partial\Omega$ is sufficiently smooth and that the functions $\{\chi_j\}_{j=1}^n$ are elements of $W^{1,\infty}([0,1]^n)$ and satisfy a certain nondegeneracy condition. If $f \in H^s(\Omega)$, $-1 < s$, then for any $t < s$ there exists C_t such that

$$\|u^\varepsilon(x) - (u_0^\varepsilon(x) + \varepsilon \sum_{j=1}^n \chi_j(x/\varepsilon)\, u_j^\varepsilon(x))\|_1 \leq C_t \varepsilon^\nu \tag{10}$$

for any ε in $]0,1]$, where $\nu = \min\{(1+t)/N, 1/2\}$ and $N = \max\{n,2\}$.

Note. The nondegeneracy required is essentially that the set $1 \cup \{\chi_j\}_{j=1}^n$ be linearly independent, for more details see [5]. The existence of linear dependent exceptional cases to the theorem is quite unimportant, especially in the light of the previous note, which showed how linear dependency among $1 \cup \{\chi_j\}_{j=1}^n$ actually represented a simplification (for which the theorem is now valid). A question of much more interest is how the estimate, i.e., the constant C_t, depends on the distance to an exceptional set of χ_j's. This is also analyzed in [5], although only for the case $n = 1$, and it is shown that the constant C_t is totally independent of how close the $\underline{\underline{A}}$ gets to an element for which the χ degenerates. (In this case that happens if $\underline{\underline{A}}$ is a constant.) We conjecture that the same is true in more dimensions.

If f and $\partial\Omega$ are sufficiently smooth both Theorem 2.1 and Theorem 3.1 give a convergence rate of $\varepsilon^{1/2}$ (which incidentally in both cases is the optimal rate). This is the basis for our claim that the two procedures perform equally well for smooth data and small ε.

We shall now individually address the points (a)-(e) which were brought up in the previous section and see how these are resolved for the variationally based procedure.

(a) Let u be sufficiently regular and assume that none of the derivatives $(\partial/\partial x_j)u$ vanish identically on $\partial\Omega$. Let $\{m_j^\varepsilon\}_{j=0}^n$ be an "optimal cut-off" for $u(x) + \varepsilon \sum_{j=0}^n \chi_j(x/\varepsilon)(\partial/\partial x_j)u(x)$. By this we mean that $m_j^\varepsilon(x) = m_j(d(x)/\varepsilon)$ where $d(x) = \mathrm{dist}(x,\partial\Omega)$, and where $m_j \varepsilon W^{1,\infty}([0,\infty[)$, satisfying $m_j(0) = 0$, $1 \leq j \leq n$, $m_j = 1$ on $[1,\infty[$, $0 \leq j \leq n$, have been selected such as to minimize the energy norm of

$$u^\varepsilon(x) - (m_0^\varepsilon(x)u(x) + \varepsilon \sum_{j=1}^n \chi_j(x/\varepsilon)\ m_j^\varepsilon(x)\frac{\partial}{\partial x_j}\ u(x))$$

asymptotically for small ε. We can show that the boundary layer behavior of

$$u_0^\varepsilon(x) + \varepsilon \sum_{j=1}^n \chi_j(x/\varepsilon)u_j^\varepsilon(x)$$

near $\partial\Omega$ is the same as that of

$$m_0^\varepsilon(x)u(x) + \varepsilon \sum_{j=1}^n \chi_j(x/\varepsilon)m_j^\varepsilon(x)\frac{\partial}{\partial x_j}\ u(x)\ .$$

(b) As is clear from Theorem 3.1 the variational approach has no problem if f is not in $L^2(\Omega)$. As long as $f \varepsilon H^s(\Omega)$, $-1 < s$, it will always produce a sequence $s^\varepsilon\ \varepsilon\ \overset{o}{H}{}^1(\Omega)$ such that $\|u^\varepsilon - s^\varepsilon\|_1 \to 0$. Note that $f \varepsilon H^{-1}(\Omega)$ is necessary in order for our original problem (1) to have a solution in $\overset{o}{H}{}^1(\Omega)$.

(c) Theorem 3.1 only covers the case that $\partial\Omega$ has a certain degree of smoothness. For the practically very important case of a <u>piece-wise</u> smooth domain with a finite number of corners of arbitrarily large angles (here the dimension n = 2) we have been able to show that

$$\|u^\varepsilon(x) - (u_0^\varepsilon(x) + \varepsilon \sum_{j=1}^n \chi_j(x/\varepsilon)u_j^\varepsilon(x))\|_1$$

still converges to 0 as $\varepsilon \to 0$. (The actual convergence rate of course depends on the maximal angle as well as the regularity of f). The proof of this fact is based on (i) the stability of the variationally based approach even for very rough boundaries (ii) a nontrivial interpolation result for a scale of Sobolev spaces on a domain with corners, and finally (iii) regularity properties of solutions to constant coefficient elliptic boundary value problems on nonsmooth domains.

(d) The numerical experiments that are reported in the next section clearly show that the expression

$$u_0^\varepsilon(x) + \varepsilon \sum_{j=1}^{n} \chi_j(x/\varepsilon) u_j^\varepsilon(x)$$

generally performs much better than

$$u(x) + \varepsilon \sum_{j=1}^{n} \chi_j(x/\varepsilon) m^\varepsilon(x) \frac{\partial}{\partial x_j} u(x)$$

for large to moderate size ε. This is not quite unexpected, since the first expression is almost a projection.

(e) From a computational point of view

$$u_0^\varepsilon(x) + \varepsilon \sum_{j=1}^{n} \chi_j(x/\varepsilon) u_j^\varepsilon(x)$$

is also very desirable. By a Finite Element approximation we can use C^0-elements for all the fields u_0^ε, $\{u_j^\varepsilon\}$. The variationally based approach has many similarities to so called mixed methods for the Finite Element Method (cf.[4]), which commonly treat a function and its derivatives as independent variables. We also refer to [2] for a discussion of a conceptually very related procedure used by some engineers.

4. <u>Numerical experimentation</u>

Let $E^\varepsilon(\cdot)$ denote the energy functional associated with our original problem (1), i.e.,

$$E^\varepsilon(\cdot) = 1/2 \iint_\Omega [\underline{\underline{A}}(x/\varepsilon)\nabla_x \cdot \nabla_x \cdot + b(x/\varepsilon)(\cdot)^2]\, dx - \iint_\Omega f \cdot dx$$

For any $v \in \overset{o}{H}{}^1(\Omega)$ it is clear that

$$\begin{aligned} &\| u^\varepsilon - v \|_E^2 \\ (11) \quad &= \iint_\Omega [\underline{\underline{A}}(x/\varepsilon)\nabla_x(u^\varepsilon - v)\nabla_x(u^\varepsilon - v) + b(x/\varepsilon)(u^\varepsilon - v)^2]dx \\ &= 2[E^\varepsilon(v) - E^\varepsilon(u^\varepsilon)] . \end{aligned}$$

(This illustrates the close connection between reliable upper bounds for the energy and good approximation of the fluxes.)

The relative error in (energy-norm)^2:

$$\|u^\varepsilon - v\|_E^2 \,/\, \|u^\varepsilon\|_E^2$$

and the relative error in energy

$$(E^\varepsilon(u^\varepsilon) - E^\varepsilon(v))/E^\varepsilon(u^\varepsilon)$$

are as consequence of (11) the same.

The computations performed here are for the simplest case n = 1. As our domain Ω we picked the interval [0,1]. $\underline{\underline{A}}(\underset{\sim}{y}) = a(\underset{\sim}{y})$ and $b(\underset{\sim}{y})$ are two-phased, i.e., both are periodic with period 1,

$$a(y) = \begin{cases} a_0, & 0 \le y < D \\ a_1, & D < y \le 1 \end{cases}$$

and the same for b, with constants b_0 and b_1 respectively. Here D (the "volume" fraction of a_0 and b_0) is a given number in [0,1].

The cut-off function m that enters in the sum

$$u(x) + \varepsilon\chi(x/\varepsilon)\; m^\varepsilon(x)\frac{d}{dx}u(x)$$

is defined as

$$m^\varepsilon(x) = m(d(x)/\varepsilon)$$

where

$$d(x) = \min\{1-x, x\}$$

and

$$m(t) = \begin{cases} t & \text{for } 0 \le t \le 1 \\ 1 & \text{for } 1 \le t \end{cases}$$

Without performing any analysis to find the optimal m this seems a most natural and simple choice.

The function χ, being the periodic solution to

$$-\frac{d}{dy}a(y)\frac{d}{dy}\chi(y) = \frac{d}{dy}a(y)$$

with $\overline{a\chi} = 0$, is expressed explicitly as a function of y parametrized by a_0, a_1 and D.

Based on this we can compute values for the coefficients of the system (9) and the effective diffusivity entering the equation (4).

Actually the effective diffusivity can be derived directly from a by means of the formula $(a_0^{-1}D + a_1^{-1}(1-D))^{-1}$ (the harmonic average), but it should be noted that this is a strictly one-dimensional phenomenon.

The equations (4) and (9) respectively are now solved by a Finite Element Method. In the first case we use piecewise cubic C^1-elements as test and trial functions (since we have to compute a derivative), in the second case we only use piecewise linear C^0-elements as test and trial functions for the two fields. In both cases we take more than 1000 degrees of freedom. We now form the two expressions

$$\text{I:} \quad u(x) + \varepsilon\chi(x/\varepsilon)m^{\varepsilon}(x)\,\frac{d}{dx}\,u(x)$$

$$\text{II:} \quad u_0^{\varepsilon}(x) + \varepsilon\chi(x/\varepsilon)u_1^{\varepsilon}(x) \quad ,$$

where u denotes the solution to (4) and $(u_0^{\varepsilon}, u_1^{\varepsilon})$ the solution to (9).

In order to compare the performance of these two expressions we also compute the true solution u^{ε} to (1). This is done also by a Finite Element Method with piecewise linear C^0 test and trial functions and more than 1000 degrees of freedom. The solutions of all the involved algebraic equations are performed by Gauss elimination.

The numbers in the following tables are the obtained values for the relative error in energy

$$(E^{\varepsilon}(u^{\varepsilon}) - E^{\varepsilon}(v))/E^{\varepsilon}(u^{\varepsilon})$$

in the case that v is given by I and II, respectively. The very refined meshes of the Finite Element Methods were taken to ensure that these numbers only reflect the relative error introduced by the homogenization and not any numerical errors.

For Table 1, the various constants are given by the following values: $a_0 = 2$, $a_1 = 1$, $D = 0.5$, $b_0 = b_1 = 1$ and the right hand side f is the constant function = 1. The table clearly shows that for as smooth data as this there is only little to gain from the expression II.

TABLE 1

ε	Relative Energy Error with I in %	Relative Energy Error with II in %
0.5	6.77	7.84
* 0.45	9.26	5.09
* 0.4	11.92	10.02
* 0.35	6.51	5.04
* 0.3	7.70	4.48
0.25	5.01	4.97
0.2	4.31	4.15
* 0.15	4.04	2.12
0.1	2.48	2.25
0.05	1.34	1.19
0.04	1.07	0.93
* 0.03	0.89	0.45
0.02	0.55	0.45
0.01	0.28	0.20

Special attention should be called to the entries marked by an asterisk; these are the ones where ε does not divide 1, i.e., there is a chopped-off cell at the end of the interval [0,1]. In more than one dimension chopped-off cells will always occur near $\partial\Omega$ (unless the domain Ω is an interval and ε divides the respective lengths). As is clear from the table the decrease in error from I to II is most significant among the marked entries. This gives high hopes for the performance of our variational method in more than one dimension.

Table 2 contains the relative errors in energy for the case $a_0=100$, $a_1 = 1$, $D = 0.3$, $b_0 = b_1 = 0$ and $f \equiv 1$.

TABLE 2

	Relative Energy Error with I in %	Relative Energy Error with II in %
0.5	2119.9	92.4
* 0.45	4691.1	98.2
* 0.4	2925.9	88.4
* 0.35	1612.5	75.7
* 0.3	3162.5	95.6
0.25	1102.5	60.7
0.2	905.9	54.3
* 0.15	892.0	39.5
0.1	484.9	36.6
0.05	282.1	47.1
0.04	193.9	12.0
* 0.03	273.0	11.6
0.02	98.0	6.3
0.01	49.0	3.2

It is evident from the last four entries in Table 1 and Table 2 that all the energy errors converge like ε , exactly as predicted for this kind of smooth right hand side by Theorems 2.1 and 3.1, respectively.

It is quite strikingly clear however that the large jumps in the coefficient a make the expression II a much better approximation to u^ε than I. This is particularly clear for $\varepsilon \geq 0.03$, where I according to Table 2 consistently produces an error larger than 100%, meaning that even the constant = 0 is a better approximation. In terms of upper bounds for the energies this is reflected in the fact that I for $\varepsilon \geq 0.03$, in the example of Table 2, always gives a positive upper bound, which is not very informative as we well know that the exact energy is negative. II on the other hand consistently produces upper bounds that are strictly negative.

Let us for a moment imagine that one is only interested in finding a good approximate value for the energy, but is not particularly interested in good approximations to fluxes of u^ε or one-sided bounds. If u denotes the solution to (4) then one can form

(12) $\frac{1}{2} \iint_{\Omega} [\underline{\underline{a}} \nabla_x u \, \nabla_x u + \bar{b} u^2] \, dx - \iint_{\Omega} f u \, dx$.

According to [3] the difference between this and the exact energy behaves like $O(\varepsilon)$.

Table 3 lists the values of the exact energy of u^{ε} for the same case as before, namely $a_0 = 100$, $a_1 = 1$, $D = 0.3$, $b_0 = b_1 = 0$ and $f \equiv 1$.

TABLE 3

ε	Exact Energy
0.5	-0.02560
0.45	-0.01878
0.4	-0.02196
0.35	-0.02656
0.3	-0.02131
0.25	-0.02835
0.2	-0.02855
0.15	-0.02741
0.1	-0.02899
0.05	-0.02871
0.04	-0.02927
0.03	-0.02842
0.02	-0.02929
0.01	-0.02929

The energy computed directly according to (12) is -0.02929. From the table it is clear that -0.02929 is a very good approximation to the exact energy for most values of ε . (Here it appears as lower bound, but that is insignificant, there are examples where it is always above the energy and examples where it is neither.)

As a final example Table 4 contains the results for a singular load $f(x) = (1-x)^{-3/4}$ and $a_0 = 2$, $a_1 = 1$, $D = 0.5$, $b_0 = b_1 = 1$. Note that the expression I is well defined in $H^1([0,1])$ only because of the cut-off.

TABLE 4

	Relative Energy Error with I in %	Relative Energy Error with II in %
0.3	13.03	6.94
0.15	4.46	1.71
0.075	6.26	3.22
0.0375	1.66	0.55
0.01875	3.71	1.74

(The major contribution to the error in this example comes from near $x = 1$. This is the reason only to display entries with ε that do not divide 1. If ε divides 1 the two methods perform almost identical, even more so than in Table 1 , but this is misleading).

Many more computations have been carried out with different coefficients a and b and other loads f, but the pattern that has emerged is exactly as illustrated by the previous numbers.

5. Conclusions

If either all the data is smooth or one is only interested in approximate values for integrated quantities, such as the energy, and convergence in norms not measuring derivatives, then "standard" homogenization seems to provide the kind of accuracy one would need for most practical applications. If however the data is unsmooth and it is essential to get good approximations also to the fluxes of the exact solution (in elasticity e.g. the stresses, in order to predict cracking), then "standard" homogenization leaves much to be desired. The same is true if one wants consistent upper (or lower) bounds for the energy. For these purposes our variationally based procedure (9) seems to be the right answer. (To obtain lower bounds for the energy one should of course develop a variationally based procedure from the dual variational formulation of (1).)

References

[1] Adams, R.A., Sobolev Spaces, Academic Press, 1975.

[2] Babuska, I., Homogenization approach in engineering. pp. 137-153, in Computing Methods in Applied Sciences and Engineering. Lecture Notes in Economics and Mathematical Systems, 134. Springer, 1976.

[3] Bensoussan, A., Lions, J.L., and Papanicolaou, G., Asymptotic Analysis for Periodic Structures. North-Holland, 1978.

[4] Ciarlet, P.G., The Finite Element Method for Elliptic Problems. North-Holland, 1978.

[5] Vogelius, M. and Papanicolaou, G., A projection method applied to diffusion in a periodic structure. To appear in SIAM Journal on Applied Mathematics.

EFFECTIVE MEDIUM APPROXIMATION FOR DIFFUSION ON RANDOM NETWORKS*

Itzhak Webman
Departments of Mathematics and Physics
Rutgers University
New Brunswick, N. J. 08903
and
Courant Institute of Mathematical Sciences
New York University
New York, N. Y. 10012

There is a rapidly growing interest in the problem of classical diffusion in random systems.[1-3] It is relevant to a number of physical processes in disordered media such as dispersive hopping transport in amorphous semiconductors[1,2,4] and the migrations of localized electronic excitations among guest molecules in a host.[5,6] The main current theoretical approach to these phenomena is based on the continuous time random walk theory.[1,2,4,7] Alternative methods were recently used to study the problem of one-dimensional systems where some aspects of it can be treated more rigorously.[3,8,9]

In this paper a new self consistent effective medium approximation is proposed for the related problem of a diffusion on a lattice characterized by random values of transfer rate $W_{n'n} = W_{nn'}$ between pairs of nearest neighbor sites. These values are assigned to the lattice bonds according to a given p.d.f. $\pi(W)$ in a random manner. The approach presented here is closely related to the effective medium theory for the macroscopic conductivity and dielectric properties of random inhomogeneous media (EMT),[10] and to the coherent potential approximation for the electronic properties of alloys (CPA).[11]

For a given realization of the random lattice the diffusion process is described by the following master equation for $P_n(t)$, the probability to be at site n at time t. Given that the diffusing quantity is at $n = 0$ at time $t = 0$.

$$(1) \qquad \frac{\partial P_n(t)}{\partial t} = \sum_{\substack{n' \\ \text{nearest neighbors} \\ \text{of } n}} (W_{nn'} P_{n'}(t) - W_{n'n} P_n(t))$$

*Supported by AFOSR Grant No. 78-3522, and U.S. DOE Contract No. DE-AC02-79ER10353 and U.S. DOE Contract EY-76-C-02-3077.

with the boundary conditions $P_n(t = 0) = \delta_{n,0}$.

Consider the Laplace transform of Eq. (1),

$$\sum_{\substack{n' \\ \text{nearest neighbors} \\ \text{of } n}} \left[W_{nn'} \tilde{P}_{n'}(\omega) - W_{n'n} \tilde{P}_{n'}(\omega) \right] = \omega \tilde{P}_n(\omega) + \delta_{n,0} \tilde{P}_n(0) \tag{2}$$

Here

$$\tilde{P}_n(\omega) = \int e^{-\omega t} P_n(t)\, dt \,. \tag{3}$$

Eq. (2) can be recast as the following matrix equation,

$$A(\omega)\, \hat{P}(\omega) = S \tag{4}$$

where, using "bra-ket" notation

$$\hat{P}(\omega) \equiv \sum \tilde{P}_n(\omega)\ |n> \tag{5a}$$

$$S = \sum_n \delta_{n,0}\ |n> \tag{5b}$$

and

$$A(\omega) \equiv \sum_{k\ell} k> [(\omega + \sum_i W_{ik})\delta_{k\ell} - W_{k\ell}] <\ell| \tag{6}$$

where the summation is over all pairs of nearest neighbor sites.

All the information concerning the diffusion process can be derived from $\{<P_n(\omega)>\}$, where < > denotes an average over the ensemble of random lattices. For example, the mean square displacement of the diffusing quantity from the origin at time t is given by

$$<\vec{R}^2(t)> = \mathcal{L}^{-1} \left[\sum_n <\tilde{P}_n(\omega)> \vec{R}_n^2 \right] \tag{7}$$

where R_n is the location of site n and $\mathcal{L}^{-1}$ denotes inverse Laplace transform. Accordingly what is needed is an approximation to $<A(\omega)^{-1}>$.

$A(\omega)$ can be represented as a sum of a homogeneous term and a term which contains the random fluctuations:

$$A(\omega) = A_M(\omega) + \delta A(\omega) \tag{8a}$$

where

$$A_M(\omega) = \sum_{k\ell} |k> [(\omega + zW_M)\delta_{k\ell} - W_M \Delta_{k\ell}] <\ell| \tag{8b}$$

$$\delta A(\omega) = \sum_{k,\ell} 2(W_{k\ell} - W_M)\hat{Q}_{k\ell} \tag{8c}$$

$$\hat{Q}_{k\ell} = \frac{1}{2} [|k> - |\ell>][<k| - <\ell|] \tag{8d}$$

and

$$(9) \qquad \Delta_{k\ell} = \begin{cases} 1 & \text{if } k, \text{ are nearest-neighbors} \\ 0 & \text{otherwise.} \end{cases}$$

A^{-1} can now be expressed as a t matrix expansion:[12,13]

$$(10) \qquad A^{-1} = A_M^{-1} + A_M^{-1}\, T\, A_M^{-1}$$

where

$$(11) \qquad T = \sum_{k\ell} t_{k\ell} + \sum_{k\ell \neq mn} t_{k\ell}\, A_M^{-1}\, t_{mn} + \sum_{\substack{k \neq mn \\ mn \neq pq}} t_k\, A_M^{-1}\, t_{mn}\, A_M^{-1} t_{pq}$$

and the t matrix for the bond $k\ell$ is:

$$(12) \qquad t_{k\ell} = Q_{k\ell} \frac{W_M - W_{k\ell}}{1 - \frac{1}{2}\,(\langle k| - \langle \ell|)\, A_M^{-1}\, (|k\rangle - |\ell\rangle)(W_M - W_{k\ell})}$$

An effective homogeneous lattice which represents the ensemble of random lattices will be characterized by a ω-dependent transfer rate $W_M(\omega)$ which solves

$$(13) \qquad \langle T(W_M(\omega))\rangle = 0$$

such that

$$(14) \qquad \langle A^{-1}\rangle = A_M^{-1}(W_M(\omega)) \; .$$

Eq. (14) implies that the ensemble averages $\langle \tilde{P}_n(\omega)\rangle$ obey the following equation,[14]

$$\sum_{\substack{n' \\ \text{nearest neighbors} \\ \text{of } n}} W_M(\omega)\,(\langle \tilde{P}_{n'}(\omega)\rangle - \langle \tilde{P}_n(\omega)\rangle) = \omega \langle \tilde{P}_n(\omega)\rangle \; .$$

The effective medium approximation for $W_M(\omega)$ is obtained by setting

$$(15) \qquad T \cong \sum_{k\ell} t_{k\ell}$$

and solving

$$(16) \qquad \langle t\rangle = \int t(W', W_M(\omega))\; \pi(W')\, dW' = 0 \; .$$

Using Eq. (12) one is led to the following equation for $W_M(\omega)$:

$$(17a)\quad \left\langle \frac{W_M(\omega) - W'}{W'(1-\varepsilon G_0(\varepsilon)) + [(\frac{z}{2}-1) + \varepsilon G_0(\varepsilon)]\, W_M(\omega)} \right\rangle = 0$$

where $G_0(\varepsilon) \equiv \langle 0| \; A_M^{-1}(W_M(\omega)) \; |0\rangle$ is the diagonal element of the lattice Green function at $\varepsilon = \omega/W_M(\omega)$, and z is the coordination number of the lattice. For a cubic lattice in d dimensions $G(\varepsilon)$ is given by:

$$(17b)\quad G_0(\varepsilon) = \int^{\infty} e^{-(\frac{z}{2}+\varepsilon)t} \; [I_0(t)]^d \, dt$$

where $I_0(t)$ is the modified Bessel function of order 0.

The mean square displacement $\langle R^2(t)\rangle$, and the frequency dependent conductivity $\sigma(\omega)$ for the hopping transport on the lattice are related to $W_M(\omega)$ by the following relations.[2]

$$(18)\quad \begin{aligned} \langle R^2(t)\rangle &= \mathcal{L}^{-1}\left(\frac{z}{\omega^2} W_M(\omega)\right) \\ \sigma(\omega) &= \frac{z}{2} W_M(i\omega) \end{aligned}$$

The approximation presented here has the following features in common with the CPA and EMT.

(a) The condition $\langle t\rangle = 0$ leads to the vanishing of the averages of the next two terms in the expansion of T given by Eq. (11). This result is due to the absence of correlation between values of W' assigned to different bonds, together with the restrictions on the summations in Eq. (11). The first nonvanishing term in $\langle T\rangle_{EMA}$ is thus $O(t^n)$.

(b) Since this scheme is based on expansion in t matrices (rather than expansion in δA) it is not perturbative and thus not limited to weak disorder.

(c) The corrections to the effective inclusion approximation can be estimated by studying the nonvanishing term in $\langle T\rangle_{EMA}$.[16]

(d) It is amenable in principle to systematic improvement by including terms of higher order than t^3 in T and solving $\langle T(W_A(\varepsilon)\rangle = 0$.

For $\omega = 0$, Eq. (17) reduces to an equation equivalent to the EMT for the D.C. conductivity, and it yields a result for the diffusion coefficient $D = \frac{z}{2} W_M(0)$. The limits of validity of the EMT for the disordered resistor network have been studied by comparison with numerical results.[13,17] It was found to be a good approximation even for rather broad distributions of local transfer rates $\pi(W')$.

An interesting example for which one can obtain some analytical results from Eq. (17) is the case of a disordered lattice with the following distribution $\pi(W')$,

(19) $$\pi(W') = p\delta(W' - W_0) + (1-p)\delta(W')$$

i.e. the case where a fraction (1-p) of the bonds are characterized by a zero transfer rate.

Using the asymptotic expression for $G_0(\varepsilon)$ for $\varepsilon << 1$ for a S.C. lattice in Eq. (17) one obtains the following results for $W_M(\omega)$,

(20) $$W_M(p,\omega) = \frac{3}{2} W_0(p-p_c) \; [1 + \frac{2}{9} \frac{a\omega}{W_0(p-p_c)^2}], \qquad p > p_c$$

$$\frac{a\omega}{3|p-p_c|} \; [1 - \frac{1}{18} \frac{a\omega}{W_0(p-p_c)^2}], \qquad p < p_c$$

in the small ω limit, $\omega << W_0(p-p_c)^2$. Here $p_c = \frac{1}{3}$ and $a = G_0(0)$.

An analysis of the long time diffusive behavior based on Eq. (20) leads to the following results:

(a) In the limit of large t,

(21) $$\langle R^2(t)\rangle = D\,t, \quad D \propto W_0(p-p_c) \qquad \text{for } p > p_c$$

$$\lim_{t\to\infty} \langle R^2(t)\rangle \propto \frac{a}{p_c-p} \qquad \text{for } p < p_c$$

(b) For both $p > p_c$ and $p < p_c$ the above asymptotic behavior is obtained for $t >> \tau$ where τ diverges as $p \to p_c$.

(22) $$\tau \sim W_0^{-1}(p - p_c)^{-2}$$

These results reflect in a qualitative manner the properties of the clusters of bonds of one type on a lattice with a percolation threshold at $p = p_c$. The absence of infinite clusters of conducting bonds for $p < p_c$ leads to the vanishing of D at $p = p_c$ and to the absence of diffusion at $p < p_c$. The increasing tortuosity of the large clusters as $p \to p_c$ results in the divergence of the time of approach to asymptotic behavior at both $p > p_c$ and $p < p_c$.

At the percolation threshold $p = p_c$

(23) $$W_M(\omega) = (\frac{a\omega}{W_0})^{1/2}$$

At long times one obtains anomalous diffusive behavior of the type

(24) $$\langle R^2(t)\rangle \propto (W_0 t)^{1/2} .$$

The expressions for $W_M(\omega)$ in Eq. (20) and Eq. (23) can be recast in the following scaling form:

$$W_M(p-p_c,\omega) = W_0(p-p_c)^{t_c} f(y) \tag{25}$$

$$y = a\omega W_0^{-1}|p-p_c|^{-\gamma} \quad .$$

A similar scaling form near p for an analogous problem has been suggested by Stephen.[18]

Eq. (25) leads to the following general time dependent diffusive behavior near the percolation threshold:

$$\langle R^2(t)\rangle = Dt \qquad p > p_c \tag{26}$$

$$D \propto W_0(p-p_c)^{t_c} \qquad t \gg \tau$$

$$\lim_{t\to\infty} \langle R^2(t)\rangle \propto a|p-p_c|^{-(\gamma-t_c)} \qquad p < p_c$$

$$\tau \sim W_0^{-1}|p-p_c|^{-\gamma} \qquad t \gg \tau$$

and at $p = p_c$

$$\langle R^2(t)\rangle \propto (W_0 t)^{(\gamma-t_c)/\gamma} \quad . \tag{27}$$

The EMA value for the percolation conductivity exponent is $t_c = 1$ while $\gamma_{EMA} = 2$. The numerical values for t_c are ~ 1.6 in $d = 3$ and $1.1 - 1.3$ in $d = 2$ [13,17]. A scaling law $\gamma = t_c + 2\nu - \beta$ where β is the percolation probability exponent has been proposed.[18] Accordingly $\gamma \cong 2.8$ in $d = 3$. Thus, the EMA results follow the correct scaling behavior but yields incorrect values for the exponents. One can expect the EMA to be more accurate away from the critical region or for random systems with distributions $\pi(w')$ which do not lead to critical behavior.

Work is presently in progress on obtaining results for various distributions $\pi(W')$. Numerical studies intended to assess the range of validity of the effective medium approximation in various cases will also be carried out.

The author is grateful for stimulating discussions with M. H. Cohen, J. Klafter, J. L. Lebowitz and J. K. Percus.

NOTE: The author's present address is Exxon Research and Engineering, P.O. Box 45, Linden, N.J. 07306.

REFERENCES

1. H. Scher and M. Lax, Phys. Rev. B7 4491, 4502 (1973).

2. E.W. Montroll and B.J. West in "Fluctuation Phenomena," E.W. Montroll and J.L. Lebowitz, eds., North Holland, 1979; and references therein.

3. S. Alexander, J. Bernasconi, W.P. Schneider and R. Orbach, Rev. Mod. Phys. 53, 175 (1981); and references therein.

4. H. Scher and E.W. Montroll, Phys. Rev. B12, 2455 (1975).

5. S.W. Haan and R. Zwanzig, J. Chem. Phys. 68, 1877 (1977).

6. J. Klafter and R. Silbey, J. Chem. Phys. 72, 843 (1980).

7. E.W. Montroll and G.H. Weiss, J. Math. Phys. 6, 167 (1965).

8. J. Bernasconi, S. Alexander and R. Orbach, Phys. Rev. Lett. 41, 185 (1978).

9. T. Odagaki and M. Lax, Phys. Rev. Lett. 45, 847 (1980).

10. R. Landauer, Phys. Rev. 94, 1386 (1954).

11. R.J. Elliot, J.A. Krumhansl and P.L. Leath, Rev. Mod. Phys. 46, 465 (1974).

12. K.M. Watson, Phys. Rev. 103, 489 (1956); Phys. Rev. 105, 1388 (1957).

13. S. Kirkpatrick, Rev. Mod. Phys. 45, 574 (1973).

14. The time dependent averages $\{\langle P_n(t)\rangle\}$ will now be the solution of a Generalized Master Equation:

$$\frac{\partial\langle P_n(t)\rangle}{\partial t} = \sum_{n'} \int W_M(t-t')(\langle P_{n'}(t')\rangle)dt \quad .$$

This result agrees with the observation made by J. Klafter and R. Silbey, Phys. Rev. Lett. 64, 55, 1980.

15. G.F. Koster and J.L. Slater, Phys. Rev. 96, 1208 (1954).

16. I. Webman and M.H. Cohen (unpublished); J. Koplik (unpublished); D.J. Bergman and Y. Kantor (unpublished).

17. I. Webman, J. Jortner and M.H. Cohen, Phys. Rev. B11, 2885 (1975).

18. M.J. Stephen, Phys. Rev. B17, 4444 (1978).

LIST OF PARTICIPANTS*

G. Leigh Anderson
Exxon Production Research Co.
PO Box 2189
Houston, TX 77001

D. K. Babu
Dept. of Civil Engineering
Princeton University
Princeton, NJ 08544

Neil Berger
Dept. of Mathematics
Univ. of Illinois at
Chicago Circle
Box 4348
Chicago, Ill. 60680

Gregory Beylkin
Courant Institute

Richard Bourret
Dept. of Physics
University of Miami
Coral Gables, Fla.

Russel Caflisch
Dept. of Mathematics
Stanford University
Stanford, CA 94305

A. Callegari
Exxon Res. & Eng. Co.
Corporate Research Laboratories
PO Box 45
Linden, NJ 07036

I-Chung Chang
Courant Institute

Gary Chirlin
Dept. of Civil Engineering
Princeton University
Princeton, NJ 08544

Doina Cioranescu
Lab. Analyse Numérique
Paris VI France

Virginia A. Clark
Exxon Production Research Co.
PO Box 2189
Houston, TX 77001

Benoit Cushman-Roisin
Dept. of Oceanography, WB-10
University of Washington
Seattle, WA 98195

Robert Dautray
C.E.L. B.P. 27
94190 Villeneuve Saint-Georges
France
(French Atomic Energy Commission)

David Dellwo
U.S. Merchant Marine Academy

A. K. Didwania
Exxon Res. & Eng. Co.
Corporate Research Laboratories
PO Box 45
Linden, NJ 07036

Nat Fisch
Plasma Physics Lab.
Princeton University
Princeton, NJ 08544

Kenneth M. Golden
Courant Institute

Malcolm Goldman
Courant Institute

Lynne Ipiña
Courant Institute

Joel Koplik
Schlumberger-Doll Research Ctr.
PO Box 307
Ridgefield, Conn. 06877

Rolf Landauer
IBM Research Ctr.
PO Box 218
Yorktown Hts., NY 10598

Florian Lehner
Div. of Engineering
Brown University
Providence, R.I. 02912

G. Marshall
The Rockefeller University
1230 York Avenue
New York, NY 10021

---

*Excluding those participants who presented papers at the conference as their names and affiliations are included therein.

PARTICIPANTS continued

Jeff McFadden
Courant Institute

R. E. Meyer
Mathematics Research Center
University of Wisconsin
Madison, WI 53706

Satoshi Mochizuki
Exxon Production Research Co.
PO Box 2189
Houston, TX 77001

George Morikawa
Courant Institute

C. Morshedi
Courant Institute

C. Nicholson
New York University
Medical Center
Dept. of Physiology
New York, NY 10016

Mark Orman
Riverside Research Institute
80 West End Ave.
New York, NY 10023

Lowell Palecek
University of Minnesota

Bradley Plohr
Rockefeller University
1230 York Avenue
New York, NY 10021

Raghu Raghavan
Riverside Research Institute
80 West End Ave.
New York, NY 10023

Marty Reiman
Bell Laboratories
600 Mountain Ave.
Murray Hill, NJ 07974

Ed Rinehart
Exxon Production Research Co.
PO Box 2189
Houston, TX 77001

Joel C.W. Rogers
Applied Physics Laboratory
Johns Hopkins University
Laurel, Md. 20810

Vladimir Rokhlin
Exxon Production Research Co.
PO Box 2189
Houston, TX 77001

Rodolfo Rosales
Massachusetts Institute of Tech.
872 Massachusetts Ave. 507
Cambridge, Mass. 02139

P. Sarnak
Courant Institute

Len Schwartz
Exxon Res. & Eng. Co.
Corporate Research Laboratories
PO Box 45
Linden, NJ 07036

Tim Secomb
Bioengineering Institute
Columbia University
638 Mudd Bldg.
New York, NY 10027

Renato Spigler
Courant Institute
(Univ. of Padua (Italy))

George Stell
SUNY at Stony Brook
Dept. of Mech. Eng. & Chemistry
Stony Brook, NY 11794

D. Sulsky
Courant Institute

Charles Tier
Dept. of Mathematics
Univ. of Illinois at
Chicago Circle
Box 4348
Chicago, IL 60680

Aydin Tozeren
Dept. of Civil Engineering
Columbia University
New York, NY 10027
(Visiting Professor)

Eugene Trubowitz
Courant Institute

Hung-Sheng Tsao
Rockefeller University
500 E. 63 Street
New York, NY 10021

PARTICIPANTS continued

J. Watson
Dept. of Mathematics
Stanford University
Stanford, CA 94305

Abel Weinrib
Harvard University
Physics Dept.
Cambridge, MA 02138

J. Willemsen
Schlumberger-Doll Research Ctr.
PO Box 307
Ridgefield, CT 06877

Dennis Willen
Exxon Production Research Co.
PO Box 2189
Houston, TX 77001

Michael Williams
Dept. of Mathematics
Virginia Polytechnic Institute
and State University
Blacksburg, Va. 24061

Shao-Ping Wu
Courant Institute
(Hangchow University)

Erich Zauderer
Polytechnic Institute of N.Y.
333 Jay Street
Brooklyn, NY 11201

Xi-Chang Zhong
Courant Institute

Springer Series in

Synergetics

Series Editor: H. Haken

Volume 1: **H. Haken**
Synergetics
An Introduction. Nonequilibrium Phase Transitions and Self-Organization in Physics, Chemistry and Biology. 2nd enlarged edition. 1978.
152 figures, 4 tables. XII, 355 pages.
ISBN 3-540-08866-0

Volume 2:
Synergetics
A Workshop. Proceedings of the International Workshop on Synergetics at Schloß Elmau, Bavaria, May 2–7, 1977
Editor: **H. Haken**
1977. 136 figures. VIII, 274 pages.
ISBN 3-540-08483-5

Volume 3:
Synergetics
Far from Equilibrium
Proceedings of the Conference Far from Equilibrium: Instabilities and Structures, Bordeaux, France, September 27–29, 1978
Editors: **A. Pacault, C. Vidal**
1979. 109 figures, 3 tables. IX, 175 pages.
ISBN 3-540-09304-4

Volume 4:
Structural Stability in Physics
Proceedings of Two International Symposia on Applications of Catastrophe Theory and Topological Concepts in Physics, Tübingen, Federal Republic of Germany, May 2–6 and December 11–14, 1978
Editors: **W. Güttinger, H. Eikemeier**
1979. 108 figures, 8 tables. VIII, 311 pages.
ISBN 3-540-09463-6

Volume 5:
Pattern Formation by Dynamic Systems and Pattern Recognition
Proceedings of the International Symposium on Synergetics at Schloß Elmau, Bavaria, April 30–May 5, 1979
Editor: **H. Haken**
1979. 156 figures, 16 tables. VIII, 305 pages.
ISBN 3-540-09770-8

Volume 6:
Dynamics of Synergetic Systems
Proceedings of the International Symposium on Synergetics, Bielefeld, Federal Republic of Germany, September 24–29, 1979
Editor: **H. Haken**
1980. 146 figures, some in color, 5 tables.
VIII, 271 pages. ISBN 3-540-09918-2

Volume 7: **L. A. Blumenfeld**
Problems of Biological Physics
1981. 38 figures. IX, 224 pages. ISBN 3-540-10401-1

Volume 8:
Stochastic Nonlinear Systems
in Physics, Chemistry, and Biology
Proceedings of the Workshop, Bielefeld, Federal Republic of Germany, October 5–11, 1980
Editors: **L. Arnold, R. Lefever**
1981. 48 figures. VIII, 237 pages.
ISBN 3-540-10713-4

Volume 9:
Numerical Methods in the Study of Critical Phenomena
Proceedings of a Colloquium, Carry-le-Rouet, France, June 2–4, 1980
Editors: **J. Della Dora, J. Demongeot, B. Lacolle**
1981. 83 figures. IX, 269 pages. ISBN 3-540-11009-7

Volume 10: **Yu. L. Klimontovich**
The Kinetic Theory of Electromagnetic Processes
ISBN 3-540-11458-0. In preparation

Volume 11:
Chaos and Order in Nature
Proceedings of the International Symposium on Synergetics at Schloß Elmau, Bavaria, April 27–May 2, 1981
Editor: **H. Haken**
1981. 134 figures. VIII, 275 pages.
ISBN 3-540-11101-8

Volume 12:
Nonlinear Phenomena in Chemical Dynamics
Proceedings of an International Conference, Bordeaux, France, September 7–11, 1981
Editors: **C. Vidal, A. Pacault**
1981. 124 figures. X, 280 pages. ISBN 3-540-11294-4

Volume 13: **C. W. Gardiner**
Handbook of Stochastic Methods
for Physics, Chemistry and the Natural Sciences
1982. Approx. 29 figures. Approx. 480 pages.
ISBN 3-540-11357-6. In preparation

Volume 14: **W. Weidlich, G. Haag**
Quantitative Sociology
Concepts and Models for the Dynamics of Interacting Populations
ISBN 3-540-11358-4. In preparation

Volume 15: **W. Horsthemke, R. Lefever**
Nonequilibrium Transitions Induced by External Noise
ISBN 3-540-11359-2. In preparation

Volume 16: **L. A. Blumenfeld**
Physics of Bioenergetic Processes
ISBN 3-540-11417-3. In preparation

Springer-Verlag
Berlin
Heidelberg
New York

Lecture Notes in Physics

Vol. 114: Stellar Turbulence. Proceedings, 1979. Edited by D. F. Gray and J. L. Linsky. IX, 308 pages. 1980.

Vol. 115: Modern Trends in the Theory of Condensed Matter. Proceedings, 1979. Edited by A. Pekalski and J. A. Przystawa. IX, 597 pages. 1980.

Vol. 116: Mathematical Problems in Theoretical Physics. Proceedings, 1979. Edited by K. Osterwalder. VIII, 412 pages. 1980.

Vol. 117: Deep-Inelastic and Fusion Reactions with Heavy Ions. Proceedings, 1979. Edited by W. von Oertzen. XIII, 394 pages. 1980.

Vol. 118: Quantum Chromodynamics. Proceedings, 1979. Edited by J. L. Alonso and R. Tarrach. IX, 424 pages. 1980.

Vol. 119: Nuclear Spectroscopy. Proceedings, 1979. Edited by G. F. Bertsch and D. Kurath. VII, 250 pages. 1980.

Vol. 120: Nonlinear Evolution Equations and Dynamical Systems. Proceedings, 1979. Edited by M. Boiti, F. Pempinelli and G. Soliani. VI, 368 pages. 1980.

Vol. 121: F. W. Wiegel, Fluid Flow Through Porous Macromolecular Systems. V, 102 pages. 1980.

Vol. 122: New Developments in Semiconductor Physics. Proceedings, 1979. Edited by F. Beleznay et al. V, 276 pages. 1980.

Vol. 123: D. H. Mayer, The Ruelle-Araki Transfer Operator in Classical Statistical Mechanics. VIII, 154 pages. 1980.

Vol. 124: Gravitational Radiation, Collapsed Objects and Exact Solutions. Proceedings, 1979. Edited by C. Edwards. VI, 487 pages. 1980.

Vol. 125: Nonradial and Nonlinear Stellar Pulsation. Proceedings, 1980. Edited by H. A. Hill and W. A. Dziembowski. VIII, 497 pages. 1980.

Vol. 126: Complex Analysis, Microlocal Calculus and Relativistic Quantum Theory. Proceedings, 1979. Edited by D. Iagolnitzer. VIII, 502 pages. 1980.

Vol. 127: E. Sanchez-Palencia, Non-Homogeneous Media and Vibration Theory. IX, 398 pages. 1980.

Vol. 128: Neutron Spin Echo. Proceedings, 1979. Edited by F. Mezei. VI, 253 pages. 1980.

Vol. 129: Geometrical and Topological Methods in Gauge Theories. Proceedings, 1979. Edited by J. Harnad and S. Shnider. VIII, 155 pages. 1980.

Vol. 130: Mathematical Methods and Applications of Scattering Theory. Proceedings, 1979. Edited by J. A. DeSanto, A. W. Sáenz and W. W. Zachary. XIII, 331 pages. 1980.

Vol. 131: H. C. Fogedby, Theoretical Aspects of Mainly Low Dimensional Magnetic Systems. XI, 163 pages. 1980.

Vol. 132: Systems Far from Equilibrium. Proceedings, 1980. Edited by L. Garrido. XV, 403 pages. 1980.

Vol. 133: Narrow Gap Semiconductors Physics and Applications. Proceedings, 1979. Edited by W. Zawadzki. X, 572 pages. 1980.

Vol. 134: γγ Collisions. Proceedings, 1980. Edited by G. Cochard and P. Kessler. XIII, 400 pages. 1980.

Vol. 135: Group Theoretical Methods in Physics. Proceedings, 1980. Edited by K. B. Wolf. XXVI, 629 pages. 1980.

Vol. 136: The Role of Coherent Structures in Modelling Turbulence and Mixing. Proceedings 1980. Edited by J. Jimenez. XIII, 393 pages. 1981.

Vol. 137: From Collective States to Quarks in Nuclei. Edited by H. Arenhövel and A. M. Saruis. VII, 414 pages. 1981.

Vol. 138: The Many-Body Problem. Proceedings 1980. Edited by R. Guardiola and J. Ros. V, 374 pages. 1981.

Vol. 139: H. D. Doebner, Differential Geometric Methods in Mathematical Physics. Proceedings 1981. VII, 329 pages. 1981.

Vol. 140: P. Kramer, M. Saraceno, Geometry of the Time-Dependent Variational Principle in Quantum Mechanics. IV, 98 pages. 1981.

Vol. 141: Seventh International Conference on Numerical Methods in Fluid Dynamics. Proceedings. Edited by W. C. Reynolds and R. W. MacCormack. VIII, 485 pages. 1981.

Vol. 142: Recent Progress in Many-Body Theories. Proceedings. Edited by J. G. Zabolitzky, M. de Llano, M. Fortes and J. W. Clark. VIII, 479 pages. 1981.

Vol. 143: Present Status and Aims of Quantum Electrodynamics. Proceedings, 1980. Edited by G. Gräff, E. Klempt and G. Werth. VI, 302 pages. 1981.

Vol. 144: Topics in Nuclear Physics I. A Comprehensive Review of Recent Developments. Edited by T.T.S. Kuo and S.S.M. Wong. XX, 567 pages. 1981.

Vol. 145: Topics in Nuclear Physics II. A Comprehensive Review of Recent Developments. Proceedings 1980/81. Edited by T. T. S. Kuo and S. S. M. Wong. VIII, 571-1.082 pages. 1981.

Vol. 146: B. J. West, On the Simpler Aspects of Nonlinear Fluctuating. Deep Gravity Waves. VI, 341 pages. 1981.

Vol. 147: J. Messer, Temperature Dependent Thomas-Fermi Theory. IX, 131 pages. 1981.

Vol. 148: Advances in Fluid Mechanics. Proceedings, 1980. Edited by E. Krause. VII, 361 pages. 1981.

Vol. 149: Disordered Systems and Localization. Proceedings, 1981. Edited by C. Castellani, C. Castro, and L. Peliti. XII, 308 pages. 1981.

Vol. 150: N. Straumann, Allgemeine Relativitätstheorie und relativistische Astrophysik. VII, 418 Seiten. 1981.

Vol. 151: Integrable Quantum Field Theory. Proceedings, 1981. Edited by J. Hietarinta and C. Montonen. V, 251 pages. 1982.

Vol. 152: Physics of Narrow Gap Semiconductors. Proceedings, 1981. Edited by E. Gornik, H. Heinrich and L. Palmetshofer. XIII, 485 pages. 1982.

Vol. 153: Mathematical Problems in Theoretical Physics. Proceedings, 1981. Edited by R. Schrader, R. Seiler, and D.A. Uhlenbrock. XII, 429 pages. 1982.

Vol. 154: Macroscopic Properties of Disordered Media. Proceedings, 1981. Edited by R. Burridge, S. Childress, and G. Papanicolaou. VII, 307 pages. 1982.